Springer Proceedings in Business and Economics

Springer Proceedings in Business and Economics brings the most current research presented at conferences and workshops to a global readership. The series features volumes (in electronic and print formats) of selected contributions from conferences in all areas of economics, business, management, and finance. In addition to an overall evaluation by the publisher of the topical interest, scientific quality, and timeliness of each volume, each contribution is refereed to standards comparable to those of leading journals, resulting in authoritative contributions to the respective fields. Springer's production and distribution infrastructure ensures rapid publication and wide circulation of the latest developments in the most compelling and promising areas of research today.

The editorial development of volumes may be managed using Springer Nature's innovative EquinOCS, a proven online conference proceedings submission, management and review system. This system is designed to ensure an efficient timeline for your publication, making Springer Proceedings in Business and Economics the premier series to publish your workshop or conference volume.

This book series is indexed in SCOPUS.

Alina Mihaela Dima · Elena Rodica Danescu
Editors

Fostering Recovery Through Metaverse Business Modelling

Interdisciplinary Perspectives on an Emerging Paradigm Shift

Springer

Editors
Alina Mihaela Dima
Faculty of Business Administration
in Foreign Languages
The Bucharest University of Economic
Studies
Bucharest, Romania

Elena Rodica Danescu
Belval Campus
University of Luxembourg
Esch-sur-Alzette, Luxembourg

ISSN 2198-7246 ISSN 2198-7254 (electronic)
Springer Proceedings in Business and Economics
ISBN 978-3-031-28254-6 ISBN 978-3-031-28255-3 (eBook)
https://doi.org/10.1007/978-3-031-28255-3

This Springer imprint is published by the registered company Springer Nature Switzerland AG
The registered company address is: Gewerbestrasse 11, 6330 Cham, Switzerland

Organizers

Proceedings of the 5th edition of the International Conference on Economics and Social Sciences (ICESS), organized by the Bucharest University of Economic Studies (BUES) and its partners: the Higher Education and Research in Management of European Universities (HERMES) Network, the Romanian Academy, Sapienza University of Rome, EM Strasbourg Business School, the Luxembourg Ministry of Finance, Europe Direct at the University of Luxembourg, the University of Luxembourg and the interdisciplinary Luxembourg Centre for Contemporary and Digital History (C2DH) (Bucharest, 15–17 June 2022).

Main Organizer

icESS

Partners

Foreword

5th International Conference on Economics and Social Sciences (16–17.6.2022), Bucharest

Dear Reader,
The 5th International Conference on Economics and Social Sciences in Bucharest on 16–18 June 2022 was a success from an academic, intellectual and cultural perspective. The cultural component of this academic conference was dedicated to Pierre Werner to mark the commemoration of the 20th anniversary of the euro.

It was a great pleasure and an honour for me to act as patron for the exhibition "Pierre Werner (1913–2002)—a life dedicated to Luxembourg and Europe", especially since the photos and documents on display came from the Pierre Werner family archives and were made available for this publication by Mr Henri Werner, the son of Pierre Werner.

The 20th anniversary of the euro is a fitting moment to explore some of the core economic and social issues facing our world and to acknowledge the main achievements of European integration, as the conference authors demonstrated with a series of innovative research topics that touched on both historical and current subjects. In these difficult times, as war is once again raging in Europe, it is especially important to reflect and remind ourselves of the path Europe and the EU have taken, and the lessons we can draw for today. After the ravages of World War II, we have enjoyed more than 70 years of peace thanks to the European project. The European Union is not a finished project; it is a continuous work in progress. Today, in the face of daunting challenges ahead of us, we need a united Europe more than ever.

One person who has become an iconic figure in the launch of post-war European integration is without doubt one of my predecessors, Pierre Werner, a European who deeply marked post-war Europe. He was formerly Minister of Finance and then became Prime Minister of Luxembourg. The plan he proposed in 1970, the so-called Werner Plan, was the blueprint for European Monetary Union and the euro.

For Luxembourg, Werner contributed greatly to our nation and our international financial centre; he was a visionary who led the country into new economic sectors. As a Luxembourgish national and as Minister of Finance, I am proud of his achievements and his role in the European integration process.

The war in Ukraine is certainly a wake-up call for those who take peace, freedom, rule of law and fundamental rights for granted. At the same time, it shows clearly how Europe can stand united in the face of a crisis, coming together to tackle problems such as inflation, energy and commodity prices while imposing sanctions and welcoming refugees.

Today's risks should encourage us to further promote the study of European history, in order to ensure that our future stays European and united. I believe that academic research is one of the most fundamental ways to lead the world towards more just, equitable and sustainable economic models. Alongside passion, intellectual curiosity and an openness to new ideas, these core characteristics will drive our world forward.

I am convinced that one has to understand the past in order to navigate present and future challenges successfully. And I am confident that the answer to the challenges we face is inevitably European, whether in terms of providing humanitarian aid and financial and emergency assistance; working together for energy security; or driving the energy transition. We can only tackle the biggest challenges of our times, including climate change, if we work in concert and stick to our common European commitments.

The conference held in Bucharest was an important reminder of this spirit, and giving Pierre Werner such a prominent place was an excellent idea. Let us be inspired by this outstanding Luxembourg statesman and by the views and ideas of the authors who presented their findings at the conference as we reflect on how we can drive our economy forward. In this book, you will find a selection of more than 20 of the key scholarly contributions presented at the conference in Bucharest. Enjoy the inspiring read.

Esch-sur-Alzette, Luxembourg

Yuriko Backes
Minister of Finance of the Grand
Duchy of Luxembourg

Acknowledgements

The editors would like to acknowledge all the individuals and institutions that gave their time and energy to organize the 5th edition of the International Conference on Economics and Social Sciences (ICESS), held in a hybrid mode from 15 to17 June 2022 at the Bucharest University of Economic Studies (BUES) and online, on which these proceedings are based.

We are particularly grateful to the partners that joined forces with us for the event including the Higher Education and Research in Management of European Universities (HERMES) Network, the Romanian Academy, Sapienza University of Rome, EM Strasbourg Business School, the Luxembourg Ministry of Finance, Europe Direct at the University of Luxembourg, the University of Luxembourg and the interdisciplinary Luxembourg Centre for Contemporary and Digital History (C2DH).

Our heartfelt gratitude especially goes to Mrs. Yuriko Backes, Minister of Finance of the Grand Duchy of Luxembourg, who kindly accepted to preface this volume and generously share her thoughts and insights about the role of Luxembourg in the contemporary history of Europe, and, in the context of the multidimensional crisis gripping our continent, she invited academics and researchers to draw on interdisciplinary lessons of the past in order to improve the critical understanding of the present situation and to help shape the future of the European Union, inspired by Pierre Werner's contribution to European integration.

We would like to express our sincere thanks to Mr. Henri Werner for opening Pierre Werner's private collections and his family archives for research purposes and for his efforts in sharing various historical sources, some previously unpublished, through the exhibition he has created and designed in order to paint a picture of his father from various angles—his personality, his social ties and intellectual interests—while also outlining the theoretical approach, political action, and achievements of Pierre Werner as a Luxembourg statesman and committed European.

Many thanks to the authors, whose expert analysis and research, based on an extraordinary wealth of sources, perceptions, and understandings, have made a valuable contribution to the field and ensured the quality of these proceedings. We would like to highlight that the ICESS started with the plenary session entitled "Economic

Ideas and Political Action in Shaping Economic and Monetary Union: Pierre Werner and Luxembourg"—including a presentation and the vernissage of a documentary exhibition—organized by the University of Luxembourg under the high patronage of the Minister of Finance of the Grand Duchy and opened by a video message from Minister Yuriko Backes. The programme of the conference encompassed 13 parallel sessions focused on specific topics—such as: digital leadership and resilient entrepreneurship in the metaverse era; the role of digital transformation in fostering recovery of public and private organizations; building business in times of crisis through entrepreneurship; financial perspectives in turbulent times; digitalization impact on economic recovery in the context of the COVID-19 pandemic; global world after crisis: towards a new economic model; innovative strategies and models in higher education; experimental economics; applied economics and statistics and data science; resilient agri-food and environmental systems for sustainable development and agile entrepreneurship; marketing and sustainability; the role of accounting frameworks and digitalization in fostering recovery; challenges within demographic data: measurement, collection, retrieval, analysis and reporting, and a round-table debate about digital disruption in financial markets (official website: https://icess.ase.ro/).

We have benefited greatly from the efforts of the scientific committee of the conference and the peer review committee of this volume which brought together experts from Chile, Croatia, France, Germany, Greece, Italy, Japan, Luxembourg, Netherlands, Poland, Portugal, Romania, Russia, Serbia, Slovakia, Spain, Switzerland, the UK, the USA, whose informed advice and critical review of the entire manuscript were invaluable.

Finally, a special mention should go to Mrs. Sarah Cooper (University of Luxembourg), Mrs. Cordelia Chaton (the Luxembourg Ministry of Finance), and the Scientific Committee of the Bucharest University of Economic Studies (BUES) particularly to Mr. Nicolae Istudor, the Rector of the Bucharest University of Economic Studies.

Contents

Introduction

Elena Rodica Danescu and Alina Mihaela Dima

Over the past decade, the global economy as a whole has found itself at the conjunction of an unprecedented series of phenomena, creating far-reaching challenges for the very workings of society and the daily lives of individuals—including in the European Union (EU). These challenges can be analysed from a threefold perspective.

Firstly, with innovation proving to be a crucial factor in economic growth (OECD 2016; UNCTAD 2019), we are witnessing an expansion of the knowledge economy, driven by intellectual capabilities rather than physical inputs and natural resources. This is determining the acceleration (and obsolescence) of technical and scientific progress and changing the mechanisms underpinning value creation and competitiveness, signifying a paradigm shift in the long line of industrial revolutions (Powell and Kaisa 2004; Stiglitz and Greenwald 2014). The globalization of digitalization is indicative of a changing multidimensional model shaped by multiple aspects: the dominance of intangible assets in value creation; the increasingly transnational nature of production and consumption, for both goods and services; a move away from human workforces and towards artificial intelligence; the growing power of networks as opposed to individuals; the development of innovative new methods for collaboration, content creation and sharing; and the importance of harmonizing standards and practices within a multilateral framework (Danescu 2020).

Secondly, the implementation of the knowledge economy is taking place in an unstable environment, characterized by an ever more complex mix of overlapping,

E. R. Danescu
University of Luxembourg, Belval Campus, 11 Porte des Sciences, 4366 Esch-sur-Alzette, Luxembourg
e-mail: elena.danescu@uni.lu

A. M. Dima (✉)
Bucharest University of Economic Studies, Bucharest, Romania
e-mail: alina.dima@ase.ro

A. M. Dima and E. R. Danescu (eds.), *Fostering Recovery Through Metaverse Business Modelling*, Springer Proceedings in Business and Economics,
https://doi.org/10.1007/978-3-031-28255-3_1

interwoven global crises and risks, each with a different timeframe and intensity but all converging to create high levels of volatility. These include the ongoing COVID pandemic, the military invasion of Ukraine, the migration crisis, climate change, banking and financial scandals, as well as social upheavals related to racial inequality, the need for reskilling, the trend towards remote working, the wealth gap, etc. In these conditions, the whole is more dangerous than the sum of its parts. We are in a situation dominated by multiple rifts, a "global polycrisis". The latter concept has been defined by American economic and crisis historian Adam Tooze as "any combination of three or more interacting systemic risks with the potential to cause a cascading, runaway failure of Earth's natural and social systems that irreversibly and catastrophically degrades humanity's prospects. [...] A global polycrisis, should it occur, will inherit the four core properties of systemic risks—extreme complexity, high nonlinearity, transboundary causality and deep uncertainty—while also exhibiting causal synchronization among risks" (Tooze 2022). A brief incursion into history reveals that the political concept of polycrisis was coined in 2011 by Jean-Claude Juncker, former Prime Minister of Luxembourg (1995–2013), first President of the Eurogroup (2005–2013) and former President of the European Commission (2014–2019), in his description of the internal and external crisis situation that the European Union then faced—and is still facing (Juncker 2011; European Commission 2016). The term was subsequently used in the scientific literature to refer specifically to the Eurozone crisis and global governance matters, and in 2020, it entered the institutional vocabulary of the World Trade Organization. It is interesting to note that the equivalent notion of "permacrisis"—defined as the feeling of living through "an extended period of instability and insecurity, esp[ecially] one resulting from a series of catastrophic events"—was chosen by the Collins English Dictionary as its word of the year for 2022, and given its extensive use in the media, it has now become part of everyday language (Collins 2022).

Tackling the problems generated by these new unavoidable global processes requires a long-term vision that reconciles future goals with present imperatives. Academia has a central role to play in developing this vision, especially higher education institutions with their missions of teaching, research, innovation and knowledge sharing and their integrated research–education–business strategies. "The academic profession has a responsibility to determine how to educate knowledge workers, how to shape the research agenda and promote the public value of knowledge, and how to connect the national and global economy with the responsibility to social demand [...] with the ultimate goal of advancing the human condition" (Bain and Cummings 2021). As a key determinant of the competitiveness of the knowledge economy, academia can generate synergies with various stakeholders and both public and private networks (authorities, local communities, entrepreneurs, the general public, etc.), while promoting collaborative behaviour and contributing to improvements in legislation, in social, economic, cultural and spatial development, and in welfare (De Jong et al. 2014; Compagnucci and Spigarelli 2020; Dieppe 2021). At the same time, an inter-, multi- and transdisciplinary approach is required to find appropriate responses to such heterogeneous, complex, large-scale transformations. This will involve the integration of concepts, ideas, scholarly approaches and methodologies from various disciplines, with the aim of obtaining new scientific knowledge at the intersection of different fields (Neves 2017; Tobi and Campen 2018; Guimarães et al. 2019). To fully gauge the economic situation in such a way as to facilitate anticipation and reaction, the analytical perspective must be pluralistic, incorporating social sciences (history, sociology, anthropology and psychology), politics and law, mathematics, information and communication technology, natural sciences and linguistics. The knowledge society paradigm and the principles of inter-, multi- and transdisciplinarity are having a major impact on higher education and university research on every continent. Since the early 2000s, the EU has set forth its ambition to build "the most competitive and dynamic knowledge-based economy in the world, capable of sustainable economic growth with more and better jobs and greater social cohesion" (European Council 2000). This aspiration still holds, although competition with the USA, China and Japan (among other competitive nations) and disparities among the 27 Member States are constantly putting it to the test.

The fifth edition of the International Conference on Economics and Social Sciences (ICESS 2022) set out to explore these questions. More than 200 paper presentations by scholars (economists, political scientists, historians and legal experts) from around 30 different countries worldwide discussed the results of their research, compared contrasting and complementary viewpoints emanating from several disciplines and schools of thought, and came up with some valuable ideas on the theme "Fostering recovery through metaverse business modelling: interdisciplinary perspectives on an emerging paradigm shift". An analysis of the metaverse through the lens of interdisciplinarity provides a key to understanding the new paradigm that is currently taking shape across the world, dominated by the power of technology and its critical impact on geopolitics, on globalized, dematerialized and deterritorialized socioeconomic and monetary processes and flows, on the essence of work and value creation, and on multilateral institutional developments and transnational regulation.

This issue of the proceedings includes a series of selected papers dealing with relevant topics from a multi- and interdisciplinary perspective, offering new insights into the challenges of the knowledge-based society from the viewpoint of international experts and providing tools for a novel critical understanding of the future. In this regard, the following considerations are of relevance:

The Grand Duchy of Luxembourg—a founding member of the EU and permanent capital of the European institutions—is currently one of the most politically stable, consensus-oriented, innovative and prosperous countries in the world, characterized by an advanced social market economy based on services and cutting-edge fields (finance, digitalization, satellites) and a level of material wellbeing above the EU average. The research paper *Regional Heterogeneity and Individual Characteristics in the Development of a European Tax Policy: Historical Insights from Luxembourg* aims to investigate the specific features of the tax system in Luxembourg from a multidisciplinary perspective by analyzing historical sources and exploring the development of these particularities over time, their impact on the socioeconomic context and their repercussions for the European integration process, especially in the design and completion of Economic and Monetary Union and in the governance of new transnational networks. Luxembourg is home to the European Investment Bank (EIB), the EU's financing institution, owned by the 27 EU Member States, which has been operating since 1958. The paper *The EIB: Fostering Recovery in an Uncertain World* explains the origins, objectives and missions of an institution that is unique, with a lending capacity superior to that of the World Bank, but that paradoxically remains relatively unknown to the public; its progressive consolidation (organizational, institutional and in terms of governance) through the EIB Group (the EIB and the European Investment Fund); and how it is addressing challenges in the face of crises (Brexit, COVID-19, the war in Ukraine, the energy transition) by adapting, upscaling and diversifying its instruments while cooperating with its many partners worldwide.

- The exhibition *Pierre Werner (1913–2002)—A life dedicated to Luxembourg and Europe,* which is also highlighted in this volume, offers further insights into Luxembourg history and the European integration process. As a long-standing senior civil servant, minister and prime minister from the end of the Second World War until the mid-1980s, Pierre Werner was closely involved in integration and policy-making efforts at the national, regional and European levels, and he is unanimously recognized as one of the main architects of Economic and Monetary Union: the 1970 Werner Report provided a detailed blueprint for EMU and sketched out the fundamental features of what would later become the euro. The exhibition presents a wide range of photos and documents, some previously unpublished, based essentially on Pierre Werner's private collections—which have been opened for research purposes by members of the Werner family—and other relevant Luxembourg and European archives. It is significant to note that Pierre Werner was the first Luxembourger to be elected as an honorary member of the Romanian Academy (in 1993), to be awarded an honorary doctorate from the Lucian Blaga University of Sibiu and to be named as an honorary citizen of the city of Sibiu (in 1998).
- Important research results present the implications of the digital transformation process for the Asian economy in the near future. The paper *Factors Affecting Firm Innovation: An Evidence from Vietnam* shows that factors such as the manager's work experience, competition, access to finance, corruption, employee numbers and professional training are affecting business innovation in Vietnam. The research paper *The Moderating Role of Trust in Managers between Strategic Innovation and Firm Performance* emphasizes the importance of trust in managers in moderating the relationship between strategic innovation and company performance in Turkish service firms. Strategic innovation and trust in managers are crucial to improving company performance, and high levels of strategic innovation may improve performance, since service companies' trust in managers is often directly related to corporate success. The study *Transformation for Supporting Business Resilience in the COVID-19 Pandemic Period: Role of Digitalization* aims to clarify the role of digitalization in improving business resilience in Vietnam, an emerging Asian economy. The main results show that digital transformation brought initial positive outcomes for enterprises during the pandemic,

and this process is expected to continue to play an important role in accelerating the recovery of business in the post-COVID-19 pandemic period.

- Higher education institutions have faced several challenges which have strengthened their cooperation to share and learn from other institutions' practices. The results presented in the paper *Open Lab—an Innovative Model to Increase Students' Civic Engagement* show that although students are relatively unaware of the opportunities offered by the Open Lab, their willingness to get involved is high and their engagement level is correlated with communication about opportunities and effective motivation strategies. The findings demonstrate that communication and motivation mechanisms are a way of increasing the effectiveness of the Open Lab. Offering a comprehensive overview of research on the impact of COVID-19 on higher education, the study *Effects of COVID-19 Pandemic on Higher Education. A Bibliometric Perspective* analyzed publications from 2020 to 2022, revealing an initial focus mainly on the negative effects of the pandemic. But the diversity of topics subsequently increased, shifting to technological acceptance, quality of education and its outcomes, satisfaction with teaching and learning, and quality of life of all actors.
- Women experienced higher job losses and declining incomes both during and after the pandemic. The main objective of the paper *Female Labour Precariousness during the Pandemic Lessons for a Future Better Normal* was to study how the precariousness of female employment changed under COVID conditions. The results of the study showed that in 2020, there was a significant increase in the share of women whose jobs were characterized by precariousness, compared to 2019. The paper also identified the behaviour patterns of European countries in terms of the gender gap in employment quality under COVID-19 pandemic conditions.
- The organizational environment is very complex and constantly changing, and resilience is of great importance. The results of the paper *Developing Organizational Resilience through Decreasing Artificial Intelligence Anxiety in VUCA World* concluded that managers see organizational resilience as having an important role in decreasing anxiety about artificial intelligence. Moreover, technological development has a major impact on economic systems, transforming all their components. The study *Skills in Demand for Blockchain Related Jobs* presents a snapshot of the current situation in Romania, revealing two main subsets of characteristics required for blockchain-related jobs. These define two broad categories of vacancies: software engineers, who are expected to have a computer science background and programming skills; and product designers, for whom marketing, communication and design skills are essential.
- Over the years, Benford's Law has been used to spot possible irregularities not only in financial data but also in other data sets. The paper *Applying Benford's Law to detect fraud in the insurance industry—a case-study from the Romanian market* used extracts from financial statements of companies in the Romanian insurance market and showed compliance with Benford's Law. Understanding Benford's Law is essential because it allows forensic investigators to design tests that can effectively detect fraud.

- In the past couple of decades, the level of healthcare expenditure has grown significantly in many countries worldwide. The paper *European Union's Portrayal of Health Expenditure Funding Challenges in Pandemic Crises* examines the economic repercussions of COVID-19 in terms of healthcare funding in European Union Member States over the period 2000–2019. It presents considerable discrepancies among Member States regarding health expenditure, between developed and developing countries, which brings the European Union to a relatively low percentage for health expenditure: 7.14% of GDP. The study *A Dynamic Heterogeneous Panel Model for Predicting Healthcare Expenditure in the Middle East Countries* presents evidence concerning the long-run income elasticity of public and private health expenditure and its key determinants in fifteen countries of the Middle East, for the period 2005–2016. The elasticity estimates suggest that public healthcare is a luxury, while private healthcare is a necessity in this context.
- The issue of sustainability in Africa remains linked to governance factors. The field of African development is subject to inter-African disparities. In this regard, the paper *Impact of Governance Indicators on Inclusive Growth and the Achievement of the Sustainable Development Goals in Africa* examines the impact of good governance in ensuring inclusive and sustainable growth in Africa. The results show that countries with the lowest economic growth have a higher growth rate than the most developed countries because they have improved their governance over time. The most concrete example is Rwanda, which has attempted to improve its state of governance by decreasing the subnational poverty rate for more inclusive growth. The correlation between economic growth and progress in governance sheds light on how to improve inclusive growth in Africa.
- In the field of sustainable development, specifically the reduction of the use of passenger cars as a mechanism for environmental preservation and fulfilment of the Sustainable Development Goals, the paper *Individual Attitudes and Social Norms as Determinants of the Electric Vehicle Purchase* analyzes purchase intentions for electric vehicles according to the postulates of the theory of reasoned action and the advances of other previous research. Its results indicate that personal reasons outweigh social norms and can therefore overcome cultural and value differences in different societies so that individual environmental awareness can prevail even in countries that are less committed to ecological sustainability.
- Bioeconomy is a field that can contribute to Romania's economic development in the context of the European Union's environmental protection policies. The paper *Bioeconomy Sectors in Romania: An Analytical Cluster Approach* analyzes the cluster hierarchy of economic sectors included in the bioeconomy field in Romania. The research results show that the most important sectors of the Romanian bioeconomy are agriculture, bio-based electricity, fishing and aquaculture, and biofuels.

This volume aims to provide readers with new interdisciplinary reflections forged by academia in response to a novel research question that can only be addressed with knowledge, creativity and a collaborative forward-looking approach.

References

Bain, O., Cummings, W.: Higher education in the era of knowledge economy. In: Aarrevaara, T., Finkelstein, M., Jones, G.A., Jung, J. (eds). Universities in the Knowledge Society. The Changing Academy—The Changing Academic Profession in International Comparative Perspective, vol. 22, pp. 33–47. Springer, Cham. Here p. 33 (2021)

Collins Online Unabridged English Dictionary: https://www.collinsdictionary.com/dictionary/english/permacrisis (consulted 22 November 2022) (2022)

Compagnuci, L., Spigarelli, F.: The Third Mission of the university: a systematic literature review on potentials and constraints. In Technological Forecasting and Social Change, vol. 161, https://doi.org/10.1016/j.techfore.2020.120284 (consulted 22 November 2022) (2020).

Danescu, E.: Taxing intangible assets: issues and challenges for a digital Europe, Internet Histories, DOI: https://doi.org/10.1080/24701475.2020.1749806. In Internet Histories—Digital Technology, Culture and Society. ISSN: 2470–1475 (Print) 2470–1483 (Online) (2020)

De Jong, S., Barker, K., Cox, D., Sveinsdottir, T., Van Den Besselaar, P.: Understanding societal impact through productive interactions: ICT research as a case. Res. Eval. **23**(2), 89–102 (2014)

Dieppe, A. (ed.): Global Productivity: Trends, Drivers, and Policies. World Bank: Washington, DC, USA (2021)

European Commission: Speech by President Jean-Claude Juncker at the Annual General Meeting of the Hellenic Federation of Enterprises, 21 June 2016. https://ec.europa.eu/commission/presscorner/detail/en/SPEECH_16_2293 (consulted 22 November 2022)

European Council: Presidency conclusions. Lisbon European Council, 23 and 24 March 2000. https://www.consilium.europa.eu/ueDocs/cms_Data/docs/pressData/en/ec/00100-r1.en0.htm (consulted 22 November 2022)

Guimarães, M.H., Pohl, C., Bina, O., Varanda, M.: Who is doing inter- and transdisciplinary research, and why? An empirical study of motivations, attitudes, skills, and behaviours. In Futures **112**, 1–15 (2019). https://doi.org/10.1016/j.futures.2019.102441(consulted22November2022)

Juncker, J.-C.: Conférence "Du plan Werner à l'euro: 40 ans de succès et de crises" par Monsieur Jean-Claude Juncker, Premier ministre, président de l'Eurogroupe. In Danescu, E. (ed.). Pierre Werner and Europe—Proceedings of the conference (Luxembourg, 27 January 2011), CVCE: Luxembourg, pp. 48–59. https://www.cvce.eu/en/obj/pierre_werner_and_europe_proceedings_of_the_conference_luxembourg_27_january_2011-en-093e3d72-f456-430c-b933-0fe2afecb937.html (consulted 22 November 2022) (2011)

Neves, V.: Economics and interdisciplinarity: an open-systems approach. In Revista De Economia Política **37**, 343–362 (2017). https://doi.org/10.1590/0101-31572017v37n02a05

OECD: Frascati Manual: Proposed standard practice for surveys on research and experimental development (6th ed.). Technological Innovation. https://stats.oecd.org/glossary/detail.asp?ID=2688 (2016)

Powell, W.W., Snellman, K.: The knowledge economy. Ann. Rev. Sociol. **30**(1), 199–220 (2004). https://www.annualreviews.org/doi/https://doi.org/10.1146/annurev.soc.29.010202.100037 (consulted 22 November 2022) (2004)

Stiglitz, J.E., Greenwald, B.C.: Creating a Learning Society: A New Approach to Growth, Development, and Social Progress. Columbia University Press, New York, NY, USA (2014)

Tobi, H., Kampen, J.K.: Research design: the methodology for interdisciplinary research framework. Quality & Quantity **52**(3), 1209–1225 (2018). https://doi.org/10.1007/s11135-017-0513-8 (consulted 22 November 2022)

Tooze, A.: "Defining polycrisis—from crisis pictures to the crisis matrix" (24 June 2022). https://adamtooze.com/2022/06/24/chartbook-130-defining-polycrisis-from-crisis-pictures-to-the-crisis-matrix/ (consulted 22 November 2022)

United Nations Conference on Trade and Development (UNCTAD): Digital Economy Report 2019. Value Creation and Capture: Implications for Developing Countries, UNCTAD/DER/2019 (2019)

Regional Heterogeneity and Individual Characteristics in the Development of a European Tax Policy: Historical Insights from Luxembourg

Elena Rodica Danescu

Abstract Luxembourg is currently one of the most politically stable, consensus-oriented, innovative, and prosperous countries in the world, characterised by an advanced social market economy, and a level of material well-being above the EU average. Its strong fiscal position is well illustrated by a long-standing AAA credit rating, a significant accumulation of government financial assets, and a distinct fiscal approach. In this light, this paper aims to investigate the specific features of the tax system in Luxembourg from a multidisciplinary perspective by analysing historical sources and exploring the development of these particularities over time, their impact on the socioeconomic context, and their repercussions for the European integration process, especially in the design and completion of Economic and Monetary Union (EMU). It will look at the development of Luxembourg's domestic fiscal and social policies, driven by national interests and by membership of European and international organisations (which imposes requirements in terms of harmonisation and taxation) and also by constant contact with the multilateral international environment and involvement in the governance of new transnational networks. This research is based on a broad spectrum of multilingual and multimedia archival sources, relevant data, and clarifications of terminology as needed.

Keywords Luxembourg · Tax policy · European integration

1 Introduction

One of the achievements of the European integration process, of which Luxembourg (alongside Germany, Belgium, France, Italy, and the Netherlands) is a founder member, has been the creation of the Single Market—a borderless area within which people, services, goods, and capital can move freely. The European Union (EU) has a certain degree of harmonising power aimed at approximating national

E. R. Danescu (✉)
University of Luxembourg, Belval Campus, 11 Porte des Sciences, 4366 Esch-sur-Alzette, Luxembourg
e-mail: elena.danescu@uni.lu

A. M. Dima and E. R. Danescu (eds.), *Fostering Recovery Through Metaverse Business Modelling*, Springer Proceedings in Business and Economics,
https://doi.org/10.1007/978-3-031-28255-3_2

legislation to compensate for the disadvantages of liberalisation and guarantee-free competition. But this harmonisation is only partial, with some vital fields—such as taxation, employment law, and social protection—remaining largely outside its scope. The subsidiarity principle introduced by the 1992 Maastricht Treaty gave budgetary authorities in the Member States sovereignty over decisions in the area of taxation, thereby furthering the heterogeneous nature of national tax systems. The free movement of factors of production (labour and capital), coupled with the specific features of the various national systems (Zucman 2014), have given rise to "fiscal competition", whose adverse effects include weakening sincere competition among the Member States and influencing public policy (Schmidt 2015). Taxation is becoming an increasingly important factor in international relations, reflecting competing national interests in a system dominated by horizontal competition, multi-dimensional regulation (with varying levels of restriction), and multilevel governance (national, bilateral, and multilateral). This has led to calls for a degree of harmonisation. It should be noted that direct taxation is the sole responsibility of the Member States, whereas indirect taxation (VAT) is subject to EU and international regulation in the framework of the OECD, the G20, and the ITO (Hanusch et al. 2017).

The 2008 economic and financial crisis, which began with the subprimes phenomenon in the USA and resulted in global contagion and severe recession—with huge job losses, the collapse of the global financial system, fundamental changes in monetary policy, and an unprecedented rise in sovereign debt—highlighted the globalisation and financialisation of the economy and the inequalities among countries in terms of vulnerability and resilience. These tendencies are being further exacerbated by the current polycrisis (the COVID-19 pandemic in 2020, the outbreak of war in Ukraine in February 2022, the energy and food crises, etc.) (Tooze 2022).

As Luxembourg gets to grips with new trends arising from globalisation—including dematerialisation, deterritorialisation, cyberspace, and e-governance (Fickers and Griset 2019)—it is faced with multiple questions about the nature of work, national sovereignty and territoriality (Degryse 2016), and the interplay of power and democracy (Patel 2018). This new environment raises a host of social, economic, fiscal, environmental, and democratic challenges that are liable to have a profound impact on society (Peña-Casas et al. 2018). Public authorities, European organisations (the EU and the Council of Europe), and transnational and international bodies (the UN, OECD, G20, WTO, IMF, and ILO) have a clear role to play in regulating multidimensional global growth and anticipating and preventing the problems that it may cause.

The 2008 crisis highlighted the fundamental weakness of the Economic and Monetary Union: although the EMU has a single monetary policy, each Member State still pursues its own economic policy—including the fundamental issue of tax policy—and significant discrepancies can be observed (Alesina et al. 2010). When dealing with the crisis, in the absence of an EU-wide solution, countries initially had to take action in areas where they had the scope to do so at the national level, by imposing fiscal discipline and austerity policies combining tax increases with reductions in public spending. They then turned their focus to areas of "pooled sovereignty" and sought multilateral solutions within the EU and the Organisation for Economic

Cooperation and Development (OECD). Progress remained difficult because of a lack of suitable mechanisms (federalism in terms of budgetary and fiscal policy, etc.) and concerted political will, owing to divergent national interests. The advances made—the European Stability Mechanism, the Fiscal Compact, the Macroeconomic Imbalance Procedure, the banking union—seem to have been insufficient. It is also worth pointing out that the European Commission's power to legislate in the area of taxation does not apply and that all decisions on taxation require the unanimous agreement of the Council, which has led to several years of deadlock. Harmonisation of taxation is therefore a major challenge for the completion of the EMU, both for the Member States and for the Commission (European Commission 2019).

The free movement of people and capital at global level, the absence of (adequate) international regulation regarding taxation, and the disparities in national legislation—with shortcomings for some proving to be opportunities for others—have paved the way for transfers of wealth and further inequalities between countries, geographical areas, and continents. In this context, the issue of tax competition has become an interdisciplinary field of study for researchers from a variety of backgrounds (historians, economists, sociologists, legal and political experts, etc.) and a source of scoops for the media.

Luxembourg has become a subject in the debate, along with Switzerland, Belgium, Ireland, the Netherlands, the UK, and certain other countries around the world; it is referred to as the "tax haven of the eurozone", an "offshore country", and a "champion of tax competition" (Cobham et al. 2015). This is due to its tax system, which for example is characterised by non-taxation of dividends, non-taxation of capital gains on corporate securities, and tax withholding at very low rates. But these mechanisms are now common place in many European countries, and the comparative advantages that Luxembourg enjoyed in the past because of the historical particularities of its tax system are disappearing in the current environment of harmonisation and regulatory convergence.

1.1 Terminology

Fiscality can be defined as the result of bringing together under the same authority both "fiscal responsibility" and "fiscal power over a tax or a series of taxes", but the notion essentially reflects the relations between the state and society from the specific angle of taxation (Maîtrot de la Motte 2012b). In a broader sense, fiscality reveals interactions not only between the state and citizens ("taxpayers"), but also between the government and the "social partners", and between political authorities and business leaders. The notion of fiscality is also related to state interests and to the competitive relationships between countries, which are fuelled by clashes between these interests. Concepts including utilitarianism, responsibility, sovereignty, legitimacy, justice, and democracy are therefore inherent in the idea of fiscality and may give rise to multiple contradictions and tensions.

The way in which a given country manages taxation is inevitably influenced by its history, traditions, and particularities and its integration at regional and international level. Unlike political sovereignty, which implies supremacy, fiscal sovereignty requires both powers to introduce taxation in a given area and the power to apply it. Although fiscal sovereignty primarily belongs to the state, it may share this sovereignty—especially in terms of indirect taxation—with other entities, whether at supranational level (European and international organisations) or subnational level (regions, local authorities). However, a state cannot irrevocably waive its power over taxation. Federal states generally have two levels of fiscal sovereignty that reflect the two levels of political sovereignty: the federal state and the federated entities.

Despite the internationalisation and subsequent globalisation of production, taxation continues to be dominated by national state-based economies, resulting in a juxtaposition of fiscal sovereignties. One consequence of this is double or even multiple taxation, which requires regulation by means of bilateral or multilateral arrangements. It can also lead to embezzlement and related issues such as tax fraud and tax evasion. Tensions can arise as countries move towards an open, international order (in which the state no longer controls the main economic levers), but taxation remains a strictly national realm (essentially introduced and controlled by the state).

Therefore, the main source of taxation is the state. Another source is international arrangements, both bilateral and multilateral, which lay down standard rules for signatory states. Alongside the UN and the OECD, there is the World Trade Organization (WTO, formerly GATT); the Treaty of Rome (1957) and subsequent treaties—the Treaty of Maastricht (Treaty on European Union, 1992) and the Treaty of Lisbon (Treaty on the Functioning of the European Union, 2007); and the Vienna Conventions on Diplomatic Relations (1961) and Consular Relations (1963). The Convention for the Protection of Human Rights and Fundamental Freedoms (Council of Europe 1950) also contains provisions on criminal tax law (Article 6).

2 Luxembourg, Belgium, and the Netherlands—A Shared History

Luxembourg has always had historical links with its neighbours Belgium, Germany, and France, as well as with the Netherlands, owing to its geographical position, changing statehood, and political and national development.

By the late thirteenth century, the County of Luxembourg—subsequently, the Duchy of Luxembourg—occupied a vast territory stretching between the Meuse and Moselle rivers, but in the fifteenth century, it became a province of the Netherlands. Its fate would be conditioned by the political destiny of this territorial complex over the next four centuries (Pauly 2014). In 1795, following the victory of the French revolutionary troops, Luxembourg was annexed to France and became the "Département des Forêts", until the collapse of the Napoleonic Empire, which led to a reorganisation of Europe. In 1815, the major powers met at the Congress of Vienna and decided to create a large Kingdom of the Netherlands—including Holland, Liège, and the former Austrian Netherlands—to counter any new French ambitions. Luxembourg became an independent political entity, which was raised to the status of a Grand Duchy and was ceded in personal union to the King of the Netherlands, William I of Orange-Nassau (1772–1843), who became Grand Duke of Luxembourg. At the same time, Luxembourg joined the German Confederation with the capital becoming a federal fortress stationed with Prussian troops. Although Luxembourg was theoretically independent, the King of the Netherlands ruled it in the same way as the 18 provinces of his kingdom. Consequently, the Dutch constitution was extended to Luxembourg and Dutch economic and fiscal policies were applied.

Following the Belgian Revolution and the proclamation of independence of Belgium (4 October 1830)—which convened a National Congress including some representatives from Luxembourg—the major powers decided to separate Belgium and the Netherlands. The Kingdom of Belgium was created, and the Grand Duchy of Luxembourg was shared between the two adversaries (Treaty of 14 October 1831): the Dutch oversaw the city fortress, and the rest of the country was under Belgian rule.

Finally, the Treaty of London (19 April 1839), which laid down the terms for the division of the Grand Duchy between the two countries, marked the creation of an independent Luxembourgish state. There were now two Luxembourgs: the Grand Duchy (which remained under the sovereignty of the House of Orange-Nassau) and Belgian Luxembourg (which became a province of Belgium). Luxembourg's borders were redrawn and have remained unchanged ever since. The absence of a territorial link with the Netherlands forced the Dutch King-Grand Duke to grant Luxembourg its own administrative system. A constitutional charter (1841) and three successive constitutions (1848, 1856, and 1868) gave the young state an institutional basis and guaranteed rights and fundamental freedoms for its citizens. Luxembourg, which was also still associated with Germany through its membership of the German Confederation, further strengthened these ties by entering into a customs union with Germany (the *Zollverein*) in 1842. The second Treaty of London on 11 May 1967 consolidated Luxembourg's international status. The country remained under the rule of the House of Orange-Nassau, but it was now a perpetually neutral state under the guarantee of the signatory powers. The former fortress was dismantled and Luxembourg City was opened up. The personal union with the Netherlands came to an end in 1890, and Luxembourg now had its own dynasty, the House of Nassau-Weilburg, with Grand Duke Adolphe (1817–1905) as the country's monarch.

During the First World War, Luxembourg was occupied by German troops (1914–1918). The country's authorities protested against the invasion, but remained strictly neutral towards the belligerents. Grand Duchess Marie-Adélaïde (1894–1924) and the government remained in power, and this gave rise to political consequences after the war: in January 1919, the sovereign abdicated and was replaced by her sister Charlotte, who became Grand Duchess of Luxembourg (1896–1985). In September 1919, the Grand Duchy's government held a double referendum on the form of government (monarchy or republic) and the economic direction of the country now that it had left the Zollverein. The population, which was voting for the first time by universal suffrage, expressed its preference for a monarchy and an economic union with France. But France rejected this idea, and the Luxembourg government instead concluded an economic union with Belgium in 1921 (which provided for a monetary association), forming the Belgium-Luxembourg Economic Union (BLEU). Luxembourg adopted the Belgian franc as the currency for the BLEU, while retaining the Luxembourg franc in limited issue. In the 1930s, the country consolidated its position on the international stage and actively participated in the work of the League of Nations, while maintaining its neutrality.

On 10 May 1940, German troops once again invaded Luxembourg. Grand Duchess Charlotte and the Luxembourg government went into exile and joined the Allied camp. The establishment of a German civil administration demonstrated the Nazis' determination to destroy the existing government structures in the country and to "Germanise" the population. After the Liberation (10 September 1944), the Grand Duchy began a process of reconstruction with the help of the European Recovery Program (known as the Marshall Plan) (Kreins 2009a).

At the end of the Second World War, the country abandoned its neutral status and embarked on a new policy of international cooperation in the economic and military fields, contributing to the development of all the international bodies for multilateral cooperation that took shape during this time. Luxembourg was a founder member of the UN (1945), the Benelux Customs Union (1948), followed by the Benelux Economic Union (1958) (with Belgium and the Netherlands), the Organisation for European Economic Cooperation (OEEC) (1948), which subsequently became the Organisation for Economic Cooperation and Development (OECD), the Brussels Treaty Organisation which led to Western European Union (WEU) (1948), the Council of Europe (1949), and the North Atlantic Treaty Organisation (NATO) (1949).

In the post-war period, Luxembourg also played an active part in the European integration process. It was a founding member of the European Coal and Steel Community (ECSC) (1951), the European Economic Community (EEC), and the European Atomic Energy Community (Euratom) (1957). The country initially became a provisional "workplace" (1952) and then a "permanent capital" of the European institutions (1992), along with Brussels and Strasbourg (Majerus 2007). It should be noted that the influential nature of the Grand Duchy's leadership has given Luxembourg a role in the building of a united Europe that far outweighs the country's socio-economic size. For example, three Luxembourgers have been appointed as head of the European Commission: Gaston Thorn (1928–2007) (Prime Minister in 1974–79 and President of the European Commission in 1981–85), Jacques Santer (born in 1937) (Prime Minister in 1984–95 and President of the European Commission in 1995–99), and Jean-Claude Juncker (born in 1954) (Prime Minister in 1995–2013 and President of the European Commission in 2014–99). Also, in 1970, Pierre Werner (1913–2022) (Prime Minister in 1959–74 and in 1979–84) chaired the committee of experts that drafted the plan by stages for economic and monetary union in the European Economic Community (the Werner Report), which laid the foundations of the European single currency.

3 Regional Economic Integration, Regulatory Convergence, and Common Roots of Taxation

In order to shed light on the sources and structure of taxation in Luxembourg, the country is considered at the centre of a historical analysis that will be divided into two broad periods: before and after the German invasion of 10 May 1940—a crucial turning point that had a profound impact on existing legislation and has strongly influenced all regulations developed since. At the same time, a distinction will be made between direct and indirect taxation, reflecting the dividing line between the two types of contribution to the country's tax system.

3.1 Indirect Taxation

The lengthy period under the sway of the Netherlands left Luxembourg deeply influenced by Dutch legislation. The primary manifestation of this is indirect taxation, which is the older and more stable part of the country's taxation system, even if many of these taxes have been progressively abolished over time. Falling within this category are excise duties on salt, the miller's toll and tree felling duties (none of which exists today), and also excise duties on spirits and inheritance tax, which have resisted the test of time (Trausch 2017).

The lasting impact of French sovereignty in the seventeenth and eighteenth centuries can be seen in the continued existence in Luxembourg, even today, of some taxes on the legal circulation of goods, including registration duties, stamp duties, and mortgage duties (Dujardin 2007).

Belgium's influence is more recent and can be traced back to 1921, when the Belgium-Luxembourg Economic Union (BLEU) was founded, following the bilateral treaty concluded on 25 July 1921 (for a 50-year period). The treaty's provisions positioned BLEU as a genuine economic union and a monetary association between Belgium and Luxembourg: the currency of BLEU was the Belgian franc, which was legal tender in Luxembourg, but the Grand Duchy retained the right to issue its own currency. The Grand Duchy had its own customs administration, but adopted its partner's legislation on customs and excise duties. This would pave the way for the broader economic integration of Luxembourg, Belgium, and the Netherlands, initially within a customs union (the trilateral Customs Convention was signed on 5 September 1944 by the three governments-in-exile in London) and then in a Benelux economic union (on the basis of the treaty signed on 3 February 1958 in The Hague). Thus, the partners committed to achieving the free movement of people, goods, capital, and services and to pursuing a coordinated policy in economic, financial, and social matters. With the latter agreement, the three countries strengthened their position as small states under threat on the international stage, especially at a time when negotiations were being held for the multilateral Bretton Woods monetary agreements (1944). The Benelux was considered as a single entity within the OEEC.

The three governments managed to overcome their divergent views (on European cooperation, their attitude to Germany, and the use of Marshall Plan aid) and would gradually come to adopt a joint position on international policy issues. The European integration process, of which the Benelux countries were among the founders, was largely inspired by the lessons drawn from this cooperation, especially in terms of the free movement of people and the definition of the single market.

Belgium was a pioneer in the area of tax cooperation: from 1843 to 1845, the country concluded agreements with France, the Netherlands, and Luxembourg providing for tax cooperation between government bodies to enable the automatic exchange of information required for the establishment of a taxable base for inheritance tax (Jogarajan 2011).

Inspired by Germany (which introduced a general tax on turnover in 1916) and France (with its proportional tax on payments introduced in 1917), Luxembourg also introduced a tax on turnover in 1922, which was replaced in 1940 by the occupying Germans with a similar tax (the *Umsatzsteuer*). All these taxes were cumulative, in that they affected all industrial and business transactions at all their successive stages. This caused multiple problems: long production chains were penalised and exportations were hampered. It was only European Community legislation, namely the VAT Directive adopted in 1967 by the EEC, that addressed these concerns. Similarly, legislation was introduced at the Community level for the harmonisation of customs and excise duties.

3.2 Direct Taxation

After the Treaty of London (1839), Luxembourg was governed by Dutch legislation, which stipulated three main categories of direct taxation: (1) the personal contribution (which was calculated on the basis of six criteria including the value of one's home, the number of doors, windows and fireplaces, furniture, servants, and horses); (2) patent duty (representing an annual duty calculated as a fixed flat rate and payable by business and factory owners); and (3) property tax (which was a tax distributed proportionally on all land ownership, with a rate of 10%).

Following the 1849 tax reform, the personal contribution and patent duty were replaced by a movable property tax (the *contribution mobilière*), which was a schedular income tax. It was based on the distribution of taxable income into schedules for two categories of revenue, with specific tax rates, namely salaries and assimilated income (1%) and revenue from capital and assimilated benefits (2%). In 1913 the *contribution mobilière* was reformed and the schedular system was abandoned. All categories of revenue were subject to the same rate, which became progressive, ranging from 0.2% to 6%. A "minimum subsistence exemption" was adopted (Susini 1922). In 1919, a general income tax was introduced, grouping together all previous forms of direct taxation.

The occupation of Luxembourg by the Nazi army in May 1940 resulted in traditional Luxembourg laws being replaced by corresponding German provisions by means of various *Verordnungen* (decrees). This was also the case for tax legislation: following the decree adopted by the *Chef der Zivilverwaltung* (Chief of Civil Administration) on 18 July 1941, a German system of taxes, duties, contributions, and levies covering all categories of taxpayers was introduced and continued to operate even after the re-establishment of Luxembourg sovereignty.

The Grand Ducal decree of 26 October 1944 confirmed that the German system of direct taxation would be maintained (although various discriminatory clauses were removed) and indirect taxes would be replaced by those in place in Luxembourg before the occupation (this was the Tax Adjustment Act or *Steueranpassungsgesetz*). Historians believe that "the intrinsic quality of German legislation is the real reason why it was maintained even after the withdrawal of the occupying power" (Delvaux 1956). Taxes and social security contributions subsequently became an important means of redistribution for the welfare state.

These provisions were overhauled in the major tax reform introduced by the Act on income tax of 4 December 1967. In terms of income tax (for both individuals and companies), the new Act enshrined the basic principles of German taxation (Olinger 1970).

The early 1990s was a period of ongoing reform for Luxembourg: in terms of direct taxation, the system needed to be adapted to the country's economic performance and public finances needed to be balanced, and in terms of indirect taxation, the country needed to comply with the harmonisation requirements stipulated by the OECD and the EU. The main changes introduced in 1990, 1997, and 2001 were one-off adaptations intended to bring national taxation into line with EU law.

4 The Early Origins of European Tax Policy (1951–1970)—Overview and Criticism

To synchronise the combined action of national and supranational sovereignties on the coal and steel industry, the 1951 ECSC Treaty aimed to regulate the coexistence of six national systems and one supranational authority within a single geographical area. Nevertheless, the Member States were able to intervene in promoting their national companies in the coal and steel sectors, thereby distorting fair competition between businesses at the European level. Taxation was one of the main tools used to this end: although the production and sales activities of coal and steel companies came under the remit of the supranational authority, they continued to be subject to national taxes and duties, which impacted the competitiveness of the respective industries.

The High Authority—which had no direct power over taxation; this remained the prerogative of individual countries—was responsible for protecting competing industries in the Member States. In line with Art. 67 of the ECSC Treaty, Member States were obliged to notify the High Authority of any legislative or regulatory measures that might have noticeable repercussions on the conditions of competition in the coal and steel industries (European Steel and Coal Community 1951). According to its prerogatives, the High Authority could "address a recommendation" to a given state, "but this was not binding and gave the state the choice of appropriate methods to achieve the desired result. These were the roots of the "original sin" of European fiscality" (Danescu 2020b).

The original source of European law is the Treaty of Rome (25 March 1957). Because taxation was considered a sovereign right for states, the treaty confers no fiscal powers on the Community that enable it to introduce taxes in the same way as a state would. However, it encourages the harmonisation of national tax legislation, or at the very least a "minimal approximation". The treaty set out a framework for a federal tax system with own revenue and a Community tax administration.

European taxation particularly affects indirect taxes. With a view to ensuring the creation of a customs union and, as an ultimate goal, a unified economic area (common market–single market–internal market) within which people, goods, services, and capital could circulate freely, without distortion of competition, the treaty introduced the principle of tax neutrality in the area of trade and the abolition of fiscal frontiers. It also provided for the harmonisation of state legislation on turnover taxes, excise duties, and other indirect taxes (European Economic Community 1957). EU harmonisation in the area of indirect taxation currently applies to value-added tax (VAT) and excise duties (tobacco and alcohol), and there is direct taxation on capital gains (capital duty).

It should be noted that voting on taxation is subject to the unanimity rule. Article 100 of the treaty provides for the application of this principle to "issue directives for the approximation of such provisions laid down by law, regulation or administrative action in Member States as directly affect the establishment or functioning of the common market" (EEC 1957).

Direct taxation is not within the scope of Community decision-making and remains the prerogative of the Member States, "which retain absolute sovereignty in this respect". Pursuant to the principle of fiscal subsidiarity introduced by the Treaty of Maastricht (1992), the overall harmonisation of tax systems is not seen as necessary, since Member States are free to opt for tax systems that are best adapted to their economic and social choices, as long as they comply with Community legislation (European Communities 1992). Harmonisation in this area is being developed via provisions on the approximation of legislation and various fiscal strategies (European Commission 2001).

According to the institutional framework recommended by the treaty, "the Commission has the sole right of initiative, Parliament is only consulted on fiscal matters, while the Council of Ministers must adopt decisions on taxation by unanimity. The Court of Justice is responsible for compliance with EU law. This structure, as well as questions of interests and the need for political will in the Member States, explains why there have been deadlocks in European policy on taxation. [...] As soon as the Treaty of Rome came into force, it became clear that European taxation was a subject that needed to be addressed urgently—and that it was also likely to be a source of tension, because several Member States considered this matter as a threat to their supreme political interests" (Danescu 2020a). For example, in 1958 France exercised its refusal to harmonise corporate taxation in the EEC. The abolition of fiscal frontiers would ultimately involve the creation of a supranational tax authority responsible for enforcing and collecting VAT. Due to the fact that, in these circumstances, France would lose a significant part of its tax revenues, the country categorically refused the abolition of fiscal frontiers in Europe, and its position remained inflexible between 1959 and 1970.

In view of the goal of achieving the Common Market—in which tariff barriers were gradually dismantled from 1 July 1962 onward and were completely eliminated by 1 July 1968—and given the continued existence of different tax systems, Community-wide harmonisation of turnover tax seemed to be crucial. The Member States therefore agreed to set up three working groups to "review the feasibility of harmonising indirect levy legislation". In June 1960, the EEC Commission set up a committee of independent experts chaired by German academic Fritz Neumark (1900–1991) to assess the impact of tax issues on the establishment of the Common Market. The Neumark Report (published in 1962) adopted a federative outlook, recommending the abolition of fiscal frontiers and the introduction of a value-added tax (VAT) and the harmonisation of corporate tax (Commission of the European Economic Community 1962). On this basis, in November 1962, the Commission adopted its first draft directive in the field, followed by another step forward in October 1963: a "convergence clause" for tax legislation between EEC Member States to ensure that the common market would function in a way that was comparable to an internal market.

In 1964, the EEC Commission launched "Initiative 1964", an official timetable for the abolition of customs barriers, and one year later, Germany and the Netherlands submitted a working document to the Council of Ministers on tax harmonisation in the EEC, advocating the abolition of fiscal frontiers by 1 January 1972. Thereafter, the Commission increasingly called on experts to identify avenues for progress in the area of European taxation, including Claudio Segré (born in 1932), who drafted the Segré Report on the development of a European capital market (Segré 1966), and Professor Arnold Jan van den Tempel (1910–2000), who prepared the Van den Tempel Report, which paved the way for the introduction of a traditional corporate tax system in the Community (Commission of the European Communities 1970a).

It is worth noting that the first EEC budgets were affected by the "empty chair crisis", triggered by General de Gaulle's France to ensure the continued funding of the common agricultural policy (CAP). The solution to the crisis (the "Luxembourg Compromise" of January 1966) introduced the unanimity rule for all European budget decisions, which is still applicable today. The first directive on indirect taxation (VAT) was finally adopted in 1967 and subsequently extended and generalised over the next decade (The first two VAT Directives 1967). From 1975 onward, VAT became the third own resource in the Community budget (alongside agricultural levies and customs duties on extra-Community imports).

At the Hague Summit (1 and 2 December 1969), the Heads of State agreed that a plan by stages should be drawn up by the Council in 1970 for the establishment of an economic and monetary union in the Community over a period of a decade. An ad hoc committee of experts was set up for this purpose, and Pierre Werner (1913–2022)—at that time Finance Minister and Prime Minister of Luxembourg—was appointed as chairman of the group (Danescu 2019a). During the work of the Werner Committee (March–October 1970), which resulted in the Werner Report (Commission of the European Economic Community 1970), taxation policy was intrinsically linked to discussions on the development of an economic and monetary union and the future single European currency. Fiscal matters remained highly controversial, because of the divergent—and competing—views of the Member States. There are several explanations for this, including: (1) the constitutive fiscal dimension of the concept of currency (Keynes 1930/1971); (2) progressing towards common taxation at the European level was considered not only an instrument for the convergence of Member States' economies, but also among the Commission's main political priorities; (3) in adopting the single currency, the Member States would be deprived of any control over monetary and exchange rate policy, which are two major instruments for economic adjustment. Taxation thus appeared to be the only instrument in the hands of Member States with a direct impact on competitiveness within their national economic territory.

Before the committee of experts started its work, several governments put forward proposals for the implementation of economic and monetary union, and memoranda were published by Belgium (on 27 January 1970), Germany (on 17 February 1970), and Luxembourg (on 23 February 1970) (Danescu 2016). All of these plans addressed the fiscal dimension, but it was particularly prioritised in the Schiller Plan, which identified the first two stages (1970–1975) as the most important; their objective was the harmonisation of economic, monetary, and fiscal policy and the establishment of a system of medium-term assistance in the event of a serious imbalance in the balance of payments (Bundesministeriums für Wirtschaft 1970). The four plans all viewed the issue from a different standpoint, but the Commission identified two landmark positions: first, the Luxembourg Plan, which took the most purely monetary approach, and second, the Schiller Plan, which put most emphasis on the role of the measures to be undertaken in the various spheres of economic (and fiscal) policy (Commission of European Communities 1970d). However, when the EC Commission published a paper comparing the proposals set out in the three monetary plans mentioned above and the second Barre memorandum, it produced a comparative table showing four "strategic" areas for the future EMU: the coordination of economic policies, the money market, the fiscal domain, and the monetary domain. The issue of taxation was subsequently included on the agenda of seven (out of 14) of the plenary meetings of the Werner Committee. Of particular interest in the outcomes of discussions among the committee's experts is the document "The state of economic and monetary union in 1978 following completion of the plan by stages" (debated on 7 April 1970), which dealt with monetary solidarity between EEC currencies, general use of a European unit of account, a European Reserve Fund, taxation matters (harmonisation of indirect taxation and limits on VAT rate variation between countries to around 2–3%, substantial rapprochement in the area of excise duties and the advisability of extending forms of direct taxation) and taxation related to capital markets (Danescu 2019b); reflections on the implications of British accession for the coordination of economic policies, the capital market and taxation in the EEC and the role of the pound sterling in the mechanisms of monetary cooperation and the European

Reserve Fund; and the analysis "The method for the achievement of an economic and monetary union from the perspective of conjunctural policy" (delivered in May 1970 by the EEC's Anti-Cyclical Policy Committee), which aimed to identify priorities for the establishment of a homogeneous common market in which short-term economic policy, taxation, and fiscal harmonisation would serve as an instrument for optimum growth.

The presentation of the interim Werner Report (29 May 1970) gave rise to discussions on "relaunching fiscal harmonisation"—especially in the areas of turnover tax (the gradual adoption of VAT in the six Community countries was under way), excise duties, and corporate taxation—with the aim of implementing a unified, non-discriminatory capital market and a high degree of harmonisation of corporate taxation by 1978 (Commission of European Communities 1970b). Pierre Werner therefore asked the Budgetary Policy Committee to draw up a comprehensive picture of the fiscal aspects of the plan by stages for the EMU. This document (discussed on 3 July 1970) analysed taxation from the perspective of coordinating budgetary policies and emphasised "the degree of fiscal harmonisation which should be planned for at the various stages in the establishment of EMU and in drawing up the calendar for work on budgetary issues" (Commission of the European Communities 1970c)

While the idea of committing to real progress in the area of European fiscality resulted in clashes between the "economists" (Germany and the Netherlands) and the "monetarists" (mainly France), following the consensus reached by Pierre Werner and the agreement of 7 October 1970, the question of taxation was one of the main objectives of the Werner Report, and it contained a number of specific measures to be introduced from the first stage (Commission of the European Communities 1970e). The first concern was to improve budgetary consultation between Member States in line with Community objectives, in order to achieve some degree of harmonisation in the fiscal field, to closely coordinate currency and credit policy, and to step up the integration of the financial markets. Regarding common fiscal policy (indirect taxes were a matter of the highest priority), VAT would become general practice, and a programme of action to bring taxation rates closer together would be adopted. At the same time, some direct taxes which could influence capital movements at the European level (e.g. the system for taxing interest on fixed-interest securities and dividends and, in some respects, corporation tax) would have to be harmonised.

The Werner Report, officially presented by Pierre Werner on 8 October 1970 in Luxembourg, confirmed that the ultimate goal of EMU was the creation of a zone in which goods, services, people, and capital would be able to move freely and without distorting competition, yet without causing any structural or regional imbalances. To this end, tax frontiers could be abolished, but it should also remain flexible enough to allow fiscal policy to perform its functions at the various levels.

Despite its "intrinsic weaknesses" (Baer, Padoa-Schioppa 1989) and its postponement in 1974 against the backdrop of the first oil crisis and international monetary disturbances, the Werner Report has the merit not only of outlining the architecture of a full, symmetrical EMU, but also of laying the groundwork for a fiscal union—which remains a priority for today's EU—by recommending "strong macroeconomic governance" through the coordination of budgetary and monetary policies (even if the introduction of a single currency was not expressly stated). The report provided for full financial integration involving tax harmonisation, including taxation of capital (Danescu 2019c).

5 Taxation, Social Protection, and Consultation as Cornerstones of the Luxembourg Model

Given its geostrategic position between the major European powers (France and Germany), its small territory (with a total area of just 2,586 sq km) and a restricted national market, a lack of natural resources and a workforce that is inevitably limited because of the country's small population but is nevertheless multilingual and multicultural (645,397 inhabitants in January 2022, of whom 47.1% were foreigners of about 170 different nationalities), Luxembourg has had no choice but to open to the outside world.

Until the nineteenth century, the Luxembourg economy was dominated by agriculture, but the discovery of iron ore deposits ("minette") in 1842 heralded the country's entry into the industrial era—and at the same time into an era of prosperity—with the iron and steel industry as the primary driver of innovation and growth. The country's first steel plant was opened in Dudelange in 1886, and by 1913, Luxembourg was already an industrial power at the European and international level (STATEC 2012). The process of industrialisation, facilitated by Luxembourg's membership of the Zollverein—which gave it access to German experts and capital and the German banking system—resulted in the modernisation and urbanisation of the country (rail and road networks, communications, etc.) and ushered in an era of social emancipation. The Luxembourg steel industry developed in regional synergy with Lorraine and the Saar, both of which also belonged to the customs union with Germany. On the eve of the First World War, the three entities together formed the second leading industrial powerhouse in the Reich after the steel region in North Rhine-Westphalia (Kieffer 1997).

The industrial transition led to the progressive development of salaried employment and the emergence of a system of social protection for labourers—enshrined in the Act of 31 July 1901 on health insurance, the Act of 5 April 1902 on accident insurance, and the Act of 6 May 1911 on pension insurance, adopted under the impetus of Prime Minister Paul Eyschen (1841–1915)—prompted by drivers at three levels: the workings of social policy, social expectations, and the government (Braun 1982). A new field of law emerged—employment law—bringing about major changes in the labour market. Under the impetus and control of the government, the new movement towards social protection resulted in progressive and lasting improvements to material living conditions for the general population, boosting social cohesion and building a sense of community. But until the interwar period, there remained a significant imbalance between management and workers in legislative, economic, and social terms. This imbalance was subsequently mitigated to a large extent with the establishment of the Special Committee on Employment (1919), the various professional chambers (1924), the industrial tribunal (1938), etc. At the same time, the welfare regime for workers was considerably improved, with apprenticeship contracts (1929), the system of collective agreements—which also guaranteed freedom of association (1936)—regulations on the working day and annual leave (1937), etc. (Scuto 1989). Luxembourg approved the 25 Conventions adopted by the International Labour Conference from 1919 to 1927, many of which concerned the employment of young people and women (night work, working time limited to 8 hours a day and 48 hours a week in industrial undertakings, maternity protection for women's employment before and after childbirth) and transposed them into national legislation (Service Central de Législation 1928).

The state authorities sought to establish permanent consultation mechanisms at a very early stage as a means of ensuring social stability. "Factory councils" were set up from 1919, subsequently becoming "workers' delegations" (1925), with the aim of "encouraging agreement between management and workers by creating a legal framework for matters of common interest" (Service Central de Législation 1919). In 1936, the National Employment Council (Conseil National du Travail—CNT), "composed equally of management and employee representatives", was set up to settle labour disputes (Service Central de Législation 1936). The principle of equal representation subsequently became a central factor in maintaining peaceful labour relations in Luxembourg. All these mechanisms contained provisions, both for the government and for companies, which had consequences in financial and fiscal terms. This was the case, for example, with the "sliding scale system" for wages introduced in 1921 (following the fall in spending power caused by inflation associated with the war)—which is still in force today—and the various solidarity taxes introduced during periods of crisis.

While Luxembourgers cultivated an affinity with France on a cultural level, they turned to Germany for economic matters: the technology and capital underpinning the Luxembourg steel industry were German. In 1919, after leaving the Zollverein, Luxembourg found itself in a position of economic isolation. Since another economic partnership was vital for its economic survival, the country sought to establish closer links with France, but the latter did not wish to pursue a union with Luxembourg, so it instead approached Belgium and forged the BLEU. However, the Grand Duchy experienced difficulties caused by the disparity in competitiveness with regard to Belgium. Since the German market had been lost, the French market (including Lorraine) was blocked by customs duties, and the Belgian market was saturated, the Luxembourg steel industry shifted its focus to products with a higher quality finish and sought to attract a global customer base. The creation of Columeta SA (a contraction of Comptoir luxembourgeois de métallurgie) in 1920 by ARBED/Terres Rouges reflected this new approach. The paradigm shift was a revolution in "vertical integration" (Barthel 2008). In 1926, under the leadership of the eminent Luxembourgish industrialist Emile Mayrisch (1862–1928), the Entente internationale de l'acier, an international steel cartel that served as a forum for consultation and mediation between France and Germany, was founded. The new economic realities also brought about a shift in the financial landscape: the previously omnipresent German capital was progressively replaced by French, Belgian, and Luxembourgish capital.

Although the state played a minimal role in the Luxembourg economy before the First World War (the share of government revenue/expenditure as a proportion of national revenue was approximately 8%), in the post-war years, the economic situation became increasingly closely linked with the government budget, with economic and social issues progressively coming within the scope of government spending (STATEC 1949). The question of how to fund social policy while achieving a balanced budget and sound government finances was a constant source of concern for successive Luxembourg governments, especially in the latter part of the twentieth century.

During the second half of the nineteenth century, as industrialisation continued apace, Luxembourg also saw the early stages of the emergence of its financial sector. In 1856, two "systemic banks"—the Banque Internationale (BIL) and the Caisse d'Épargne (Spuerkeess)—were founded and went on to develop a network of branches in the country. At that time, Luxembourg had an extensive network of notary firms, which developed banking activities, and a web of small specialist companies. The first foreign bank, the Société générale alsacienne de banque, arrived in Luxembourg in 1893. Given that the country was lacking in national capital, the funding for Luxembourg's large steel companies mainly came from Germany via the Zollverein. In the absence of a stock exchange, the Luxembourg securities market was based on bonds issued by the government and by various Luxembourg companies, which were traded by banks in the country. In 1863, the government launched its first major bond issue (8.5 million francs), with the help of a consortium created by the BIL and composed of three banks based in Amsterdam, Frankfurt, and Hamburg (Trausch et al. 1995). To meet the economy's need for capital, the internationally oriented Luxembourg Stock Exchange (LuxSE) was founded in 1927 (Service Central de Législation 1927), with the country's two systemic banks among its stakeholders. Before the Luxembourg Stock Exchange was created, the country's securities market was composed of two parts: bonds issued by the government and bonds issued by Luxembourg companies (the national railway company (CFL), ARBED, the Diekirch brewery, the BIL, etc.), with securities traded by the banks in Luxembourg. Another way of attracting capital was the special regime for joint ventures, introduced by the 1929 Act on holding companies (Chambre des Députés 1929; Service Central de Législation 1929). A similar system had already been set up in the early 1920s, first in Switzerland (1920) and then in Liechtenstein (1923), with the aim of attracting foreign capital and obtaining additional tax revenue (Farquet 2006). Luxembourg law offered both flexibility and a special tax regime, which provided for the payment of a subscription tax but exempted companies from paying income tax, business tax, and wealth tax. The Luxembourg system, seen as more advantageous than those in Switzerland and Liechtenstein, made the country more attractive in tax terms (Delvaux 1938). This was an early example of tax competition. The holding company regime was finally abandoned at the end of 2010 on the initiative of the European Commission.

Luxembourg's financial sector experienced major growth after the war, when the country, a Marshall Plan beneficiary, had to decide how to channel the grants and loans (in US dollars) received via the initiative. The number of banks (and their respective capital) increased, transactions (and the currencies traded) diversified, the local network grew, and the banking sector professionalised. It is worth noting that participation in the Marshall Plan not only gave Luxembourg access to financial resources (dollars) and material goods, equipment, and services to modernise its economy; it also enabled it to embark on major infrastructure projects (like the hydroelectric development of the Upper Sûre and the canalisation of the Moselle). Moreover, "while the Marshall Plan aid enabled Belgium and Luxembourg to import goods from the dollar zone, it also facilitated exports from Belgium and Luxembourg to the other participating countries" (Kreins 2009b). In 1952, when Luxembourg, fully committed to the fledgling European integration process, became the first workplace of the ECSC, the country's banking sector was boosted by its management of the contributions paid by the ECSC Member States in Luxembourg.

The real turning point in the transformation of Luxembourg's banking centre into a financial centre began in 1963 and can be attributed to events that took place largely outside the country. First, the interest equalisation tax—the so-called "Kennedy tax", amounting to 15% of interest received from bonds issued by non-residents—introduced in 1963 in the USA to curb the balance of payments deficit led to a massive influx of US capital to Europe. Many American companies also located on the continent. The second factor was the specific regulatory measures introduced by Germany—a withholding tax on interest (1965) and an increase in unremunerated required reserves (stipulated by the Bundesbank in 1968)—that resulted in pressure for German banks to relocate elsewhere. The flexibility of the Luxembourg legislative and regulatory system in financial terms and the proactive policy of successive governments—especially under the impetus of Prime Minister and Finance Minister Pierre Werner—made Luxembourg the ideal home for both US capital and new banks (initially German and Scandinavian, then from other countries) (Moyse et al. 2014). In 1963, the Luxembourg Stock Exchange listed the first Eurobond issuance (for the Italian motorway network Autostrade), following the launch by another Luxembourg-based bank—Kredietbank Luxembourg (KBL)—of a bond issue in European units of account (EUAs) for the Portuguese company Sacor (although this was not recognised as the first Eurobond). From that point on, Luxembourg specialised in Euromarket activities. Alongside the stock exchange, the European Investment Bank, which moved to Luxembourg in 1968, played an active role in this. After the publication of the Werner Report (1970), which laid the foundations for the euro, the Luxembourg financial centre became a laboratory for the single European currency.

The growth in the financial centre enabled Luxembourg to move away from its industrial homogeneity and embark on a process of diversification. It is worth pointing out that the emergence and subsequent development of the financial sector were inversely proportional to the decline of the steel industry and provided the country with a second economic pillar. After the post-war boom period, although finance remained central for Luxembourg, the country turned more to state-of-the-art industries, knowledge-intensive services in a broader sense characterised by high-performing human capital, audiovisual technologies, and the space sector (Trausch 2017; Trausch 2005)—as reflected in companies such as the Compagnie Luxembourgeoise de Télédiffusion and the Société Européenne des Satellites (SES), which today is the world's leading satellite operator (reaching 99% of the global population)—as well as to digitalisation, in particular during the past decade.

To reconcile economic interests and social stability, the consecutive governments therefore pursued the country's traditional proactive social policy, with key measures including an automatic wage indexation mechanism based on increases in the cost of living (1965), the 40-hour working week (1975), a guaranteed minimum income (1986), and the expansion of the healthcare system. Labour relations were strengthened. In 1977, during the steel crisis, a Consultative Tripartite Committee (comprising the government, employers, and the unions) was established, acting as a shock absorber for both sides of industry, thereby creating an environment conducive to social solidarity where any potential disagreements can be identified and resolved in advance. The Committee formed the basis of the Luxembourg social model, which relies on democracy, social solidarity, and consensus to underpin social and economic development.

From the mid-1980s, the country's economic growth accelerated, driven by its financial centre, whose contribution to GDP increased from 20% in 1998 to 26.8% in 2020 (followed by distributive trades, transport, and communication, with 22.3%). From 1985 to 2018, the average annual GDP growth in Luxembourg was about twice as much as that of neighbouring countries and of the EC/EU Member States. At the same time, between 1970 and 2019, the share of industry contracted sharply, from 47% to 6.9% of GDP, and from 33 to 12% in total employment. The weight of agriculture in the economy has also decreased considerably, representing just 0.2% of GDP and 0.8% of total employment in 2020. The country has the highest ratio of capital tax to GDP (12.3%), which reflects the systemic importance of the financial sector in the economy (Danescu 2021).

6 Asymmetric Competition Versus Fiscal Harmonisation in Completing EMU

Since the 1970s, as European integration has continued and the European Communities have undergone successive enlargements, the bloc has been particularly slow to take action in the area of taxation, largely because of limited competence in the field and major discrepancies among Member States in terms of economic, financial, and tax infrastructures and policies. The Treaty of Maastricht (1992), which launched the EMU (European Communities 1992), also promoted the subsidiarity principle, and sovereignty over decisions on taxation was left to Member States' budgetary authorities, which were free to set taxes in accordance with their national interests, needs, and political choices.

Given the considerable inertia on direct taxation, the first steps towards a European fiscal policy came in the area of indirect taxation. The main European rules in this area have three broad aims: (a) to avoid double taxation for companies (based in several Member States); (b) to harmonise taxation on savings (giving European citizens the option of opening a savings account in any EU country); and (c) to establish European cooperation to tackle tax evasion and fraud. The EMU therefore did not provide for tax harmonisation, but set common criteria for goals on budgetary policy, inflation, and public debt. As a result, there has been a continuing need for common rules to promote healthy tax competition, since the diverse nature of tax systems and national legislation combined with the free movement of people, goods, services, and capital within the Single Market encourages economic players to minimise their tax burden through tax planning, further fuelling inequalities and injustice. At the same time, in a globalised economy that is becoming increasingly borderless and cloud-based, in which value and income creation are based to a growing extent on knowledge, innovation, and intangible assets, Europe is in direct competition with the USA, Japan, China, etc., and taxation has a decisive impact (whether positive or negative) on the comparative advantages of competitors. There is often a discrepancy between where value is created and where tax is payable on the corresponding income—as can be seen with the example of web giants Google, Amazon, Facebook, Apple, and Microsoft, and more recently Netflix, Airbnb, Tesla, and Uber. Since the criterion of physical presence clearly no longer applies to the digital economy, the rules for distributing global profits between different territorial entities need to be reviewed.

Because decisions on taxation require unanimity, it took three decades of discussions and political wrangling before the first European directives on corporate taxation emerged—the Parent Subsidiary and Merger Directives (European Communities 1990). Other subsequent breakthroughs included the tax package (1997), the Electronic Commerce Directive (2000), and the Savings Directive (2005). In 2004, the European Commission set up a working group representing the 25 Member States to establish the Common Consolidated Corporate Tax Base (CCCTB) in line with international standards (IAS/IFRS). Tangible results were therefore achieved by combining a consensus-based, non-binding approach ("soft law") with legislation in key fields (e.g. taxation on savings). But it was also becoming clear that the way decisions on taxation were taken in the EU needed to change (a shift to qualified majority voting rather than unanimity was required in certain areas) and that only further global cooperation (OECD, G20, UN, IMF, World Bank) on a long-term basis would pave the way for wide-ranging solutions that would be fairer and more transparent (Dumoulin et al. 2007). One unexpected issue has been the emergence of virtual currencies, which have experienced enormous growth in the past decade, driving trade and maximising opportunities for value creation. However, the issuance of these currencies is not regulated by a central bank, a sovereign state, or a supranational organisation (such as the European Central Bank—ECB), but by private operators with no guarantees. In terms of taxation, virtual currencies make it easier to reduce the scope of monetary transactions and optimise their territorial allocation so as to optimise the distribution of related profits (European Central Bank 2019; Lastra, Allen 2018; Mersch 2018).

To ensure it has a say in the regulation of international tax systems, the EU is developing synergies with multilateral institutions and networks. In 2013, following on from the report "Addressing Base Erosion and Profit Shifting" (BEPS) (OECD 2013), the OECD and G20 countries, with the participation of the European Commission, adopted an Action Plan that identifies a series of measures to achieve three priority objectives: (1) introducing coherence in the domestic rules that affect cross-border activities; (2) reinforcing existing international standards; and (3) improving transparency (OECD 2013). The OECD manages a multilateral framework of around two thousand international tax treaties designed to avoid double taxation among signatory states. Several developed countries, including Luxembourg, have been involved in this process by participating in the OECD Committee on Fiscal Affairs.

Luxembourg has initiated a process of reform to improve transparency in accordance with internationally agreed regulations. Measures include the automatic exchange of tax information for individuals, pursuant to the Foreign Account Tax Compliance Act (adopted in July 2015), the end of banking secrecy as required under the OECD Common Reporting Standard, and the forthcoming law transposing the EU Anti-Tax Avoidance Directive. Luxembourg is also bound by the OECD Multilateral Convention to implement tax treaty-related measures to prevent BEPS and is involved in international working groups tackling harmful tax competition. The EU has adopted a series of Directives on Administrative Cooperation: DAC 5 on access to anti-money-laundering information collected by tax authorities; DAC 6 on transparency rules for intermediaries (implemented in 2020); and DAC 7, which introduces a reporting obligation for digital platforms, whether located inside or outside the EU, and requires automatic exchange of information between Member States' tax administrations on revenues generated by sellers on these platforms from 1 January 2023. It is also worth noting that in 2019, in accordance with EU directives, Luxembourg improved its legislation on the prevention of money laundering and terrorist financing by implementing the Register of Beneficial Owners for Luxembourg-registered entities. Finally, the General Data Protection Regulation has been in force since 2018.

"The attractiveness of Luxembourg as a financial centre is liable to be affected by the process of tax and financial harmonization at the EU and OECD level and the new regulatory environment: namely, the three pillars of Banking Union (the Single Supervisory Mechanism, the Single Resolution Mechanism and the European deposit guarantee scheme) and the liquidity regulation provided under the Basel III agreement. To offset this risk, the country is pursuing the diversification and specialization of its financial industry. Luxembourg's investment fund industry benefits from EU passports under the regulatory framework provided by the Undertakings for Collective Investment in Transferable Securities Directive and the Alternative Investment Fund Managers Directive. These enable Luxembourg to offer investment funds to other EU countries which remain under the supervision of the ECB/the Commission de Surveillance du Secteur Financier (CSSF)" (Danescu 2021).

7 Conclusion

Luxembourg's history has been shaped by its geographical position, its political and institutional stability, its political choices and strategies—focussed on growth niches, high value-added economic diversification and integration into larger economic areas, and the development of sustainable links with its neighbours and partners. Stable political leadership has given the country long-term continuity, and a proactive approach among the political class has turned seeming challenges into opportunities as part of a creative economic policy. From a long-term strategic perspective, the economy can be seen as a point of political convergence, with action in this area characterised by a balanced approach and a culture based on consensus and peaceful labour relations. This has given rise to a high degree of social stability and is reflected in the "Luxembourg consultation model", in which agreement is reached between the "social partners" (within the Consultative Tripartite Committee and the Economic and Social Council) before any legislation is passed through parliament, meaning that any potential obstacles can be resolved in advance. For Luxembourg, opening up to the international community has always been an imperative and has actually served to consolidate its national identity. The country's economy bears the hallmarks of German ordoliberalism and the social market economy model, which Luxembourg has maintained even as it has embraced regional integration (BLEU, Benelux) and European integration.

Since the twentieth century, Luxembourg has undergone several major transitions. The first was from a primarily agriculture-based economy to an industrial economy, driven by an influential steel industry, which dominated the economic landscape from the post-Second World War years to the mid-1970s. The second major transition—triggered by the steel crisis in 1974 and characterised by considerable structural changes—was from an industrial economy to a service economy with a strong emphasis on the financial sector, which became the main source of the country's added value. In the early 2000s, Luxembourg underwent its third major transition, from an economy based on financial services to a knowledge-driven economy in which innovation and digitalisation are prompting smart, sustainable, and inclusive growth. But the financial sector, which is diversifying as it embraces new technologies, continues to be a key source of economic growth in the country. Luxembourg is one of only a handful of countries worldwide (and one of just two in the eurozone, alongside Germany) to be constantly awarded the top rating by all the leading credit rating agencies. These ratings also recognise the Government's sustained effort to improve fiscal transparency. It is worth pointing out that in OECD peer reviews of tax transparency in recent years, Luxembourg now enjoys the same ranking as Germany, the UK, and the USA.

Luxembourg, a founding country in the processes of European integration and Economic and Monetary Union, has become one of the main financial centres in Europe (characterised by the international dimension of its financial products and services) and has contributed to the development of a European tax policy, in which indirect taxation (VAT and customs and excise duties) has undergone a degree of standardisation, while direct taxation (taxation on income and capital) remains the prerogative of Member States. Luxembourg is involved in the development of international regulations on taxation within the multilateral framework of the OECD, governed by the principle of consensus. If it is to safeguard its welfare state and boost its long-term competitiveness, particularly given the ongoing climate of geopolitical uncertainty, the country will have to address three issues: an ageing population; unemployment (particularly among young people and from a long-term perspective); and the sustainability of the social security system, which is highly dependent on taxation (mainly direct taxation)—especially as it seems likely that future developments to restrict Luxembourg's particularities could considerably weaken its position.

It is clear that moving towards the convergence (or even harmonisation) of European taxation is a condition for the achievement of the EMU and that it will not impinge on the sovereignty of Member States, since, in the analysis of Pierre Werner, which still holds true today, "the history of confederations and federations amply demonstrates that the last bastion of national sovereignty is not currency but taxation, as the distributor of national revenue" (Werner 1969).

References

Alesina, A., Ardagna, S., Galasso, V.: The Euro and Structural Reforms. In: Alesina, A., Giavazzi, F. (eds.) Europe and the euro, pp. 57–93. University of Chicago Press, Chicago (2010)

Baer, G., Padoa-Schioppa, T.: The Werner report revisited. In: Committee for the Study of Economic and Monetary Union. Report on economic and monetary union in the European Community, April 1989, pp. 53–60. Office for Official Publications of the European Community, Luxembourg (1989). Here p. 57

Barthel, C.: Emile Mayrisch (1862–1928). In: Bertoncini, Y., Chopin, T., Dulphy, A., Kahn, S. and Manigand, C. (eds), Dictionnaire critique de l'Union européenne, pp. 274–276. Armand Colin, Paris (2008). Here p. 275

Braun, M.: Die luxemburgischen Sozialversicherungen bis zum Zweiten Weltkrieg. Entwicklung, Probleme und Bedeutung. Beiträge zur Wirtschaftsgeschichte, pp. 578. Verlag Klett-Cotta, Stuttgart (1982)

Cobham, A., Jansky, P., Meinzer, M.: The financial secrecy index: shedding new light on the geography of secrecy. Econ. Geogr. **91**(3), 281–303 (2015)

Commission of the European Communities: Communication from the Commission to the Council on the development of a plan by stages for an economic and monetary union" in Bulletin of the European Communities, Supplement, 3 (1970a). Office for Official Publications of the European Communities, Luxembourg (1970)

Commission of the European Communities: Corporation Tax and Individual Income Tax in the European Communities, by Prof. Dr. A.J. van den Tempel, Brussels (1970b). http://aei.pitt.edu/40293/1/A4688.pdf, Accessed 15 August 2022

Commission of the European Communities: Draft minutes of the 35th conference of the Finance Ministers of the Commission of the European Communities, held in Venice on 29 and 30 May 1970, confidential. Directorate-General for Economic and Financial Affairs, ref. ORII/57/70-F, Brussels, 5 June 1970. Historical Archives of the European Union (1970c)

Commission of the European Communities: Draft minutes of the fifth meeting of the ad hoc "plan by stages" group, 7 July 1970. European Communities, Secretariat of the "plan by stages" group, Brussels (14 July 1970d), OR II/67–70-F. Pierre Werner family archives, ref. PW 047 (1970)

Commission of the European Communities: Jeu de tableaux synoptiques concernant les quatre plans par étapes vers une union économique et monétaire: plan Werner, plan Schiller, plan belge et plan C.C.E [Comparative tables concerning the four plans for the achievement by stages of an economic and monetary union: the Werner Plan, the Schiller Plan, the plan drawn up by Belgium and the plan drawn up by the EEC], 18 March 1970. Commission of the European Communities/Directorate-General for Economic and Financial Affairs/Working Party on Economic and Monetary Union), Brussels (1970). Pierre Werner family archive. Reproduced in Dierikx, M. (ed.) Common Fate. Common Future. A Documentary History of Monetary and Financial Cooperation, 1947–1974, pp. 123–136. CVCE-Huygens ING, The Hague (2012)

Commission of the European Economic Communities: Communication et propositions de la Commission au Conseil relatives à l'institution par étapes d'une union économique et monétaire de la Communauté [Communication and proposals from the Commission to the Council on the establishment by stages of economic and monetary union]. Document COM (70)1250 (29 October 1970e). In Official Journal of the European Communities, annex C 140 of 26 November 1970, supplement to bulletin 11/1970, Luxembourg (11 November 1970). https://www.cvce.eu/content/publication/2012/2/15/533fad26-83a6-4f8a-9ece-aeea932b74e8/publishable_fr.pdf. Accessed 15 August 2022

Commission of the European Economic Community: Rapport du Comité fiscal et financier (Rapport Neumark). Brussels 1962. Source: http://aei.pitt.edu/33686/1/A220.pdf. Accessed 15 August 2022

Danescu, E.: Luxembourg economy facing challenges: A historical overview. In: Hatley, C. (ed.) Western Europe 2022, 24th edn., pp. 464–481. Routledge, Abington (2021)

Danescu, E.: Pierre Werner and Europe: The Family Archives Behind the Werner Report. Foreword by Jean-Claude Juncker, President of the European Commission, and Foreword by Professor Harold James (Princeton University). Palgrave Macmillan, Oxford (2019a)

Danescu, E., Pierre Werner and Europe: The Family Archives Behind the Werner Report. Foreword by Jean-Claude Juncker, President of the European Commission, and Foreword by Professor Harold James (Princeton University). Palgrave Macmillan, Oxford, p. 104 (2019b)

Danescu, E., Pierre Werner and Europe: The Family Archives Behind the Werner Report. Foreword by Jean-Claude Juncker, President of the European Commission, and Foreword by Professor Harold James (Princeton University). Palgrave Macmillan, Oxford, p. 336 (2019c)

Danescu, E.: Pierre Werner, a visionary European and consensus builder. In: Dyson, K., Maes, I. (eds), Architects of the Euro. Intellectuals in the making of European Monetary Union, pp. 93–116. Oxford University Press, Oxford (2016)

Danescu, E.: Taxing intangible assets: issues and challenges for a digital Europe. Internet Histories **4**(2), 196–216, p. 205 (2020a)

Danescu, E.: Taxing intangible assets: issues and challenges for a digital Europe. Internet Histories **4**(2), 196–216, p. 204 (2020b)

Degryse, C.: Les impacts sociaux de la digitalisation de l'économie. WP 2016.02, ISE, Brussels (2016)

Delvaux, B.: Les sociétés "holding" au Grand-Duché de Luxembourg. Étude théorique et pratique de la loi du 31 juillet 1929, Recueil Sirey & Victor Buck, Paris, Luxembourg (1938)

Delvaux, F.: Considérations générales sur la situation fiscale créée par l'arrêté grand-ducal du 20 oct.1944. Luxembourg, p. 145 (1956)

Dujardin, F.-X.: Le contentieux fiscal dans le département des forêts (1795–1799). In: Droit administratif et fiscal: 10 années de juridictions administratives, pp. 267–291. Portalis, Luxembourg (2007)

Dumoulin, M., et al.: La Commission européenne, 1958–1972: Histoire et mémoires d'une institution. Office des Publications Officielles des Communautés européennes, Luxembourg (2007)

European Central Bank: Crypto-assets: Implications for financial stability, monetary policy, and payments and market infrastructures. Occasional Paper Series, 223 (May 2019), ECB, Frankfurt (2019); Lastra, R., Allen, J. G.: Virtual currencies in the Eurosystem: challenges ahead. Study for the Committee on Economic and Monetary Affairs. Policy Department for Economic, Scientific and Quality of Life Policies. European Parliament, Luxembourg (2018); Mersch, Y.: Virtual or virtueless? The evolution of money in the digital age. Lecture given by Yves Mersch, Member of the Executive Board of the ECB, at the Official Monetary and Financial Institutions Forum, London, 8 February 2018

European Commission: Deepening Europe's Economic and Monetary Union. Taking stock four years after the Five Presidents' Report. Communication from the Commission to the European Parliament, the European Council, the Council and the European Central Bank. European Commission's contribution to the Euro Summit on 21 June 2019. https://ec.europa.eu/info/sites/default/files/economy-finance/emu_communication_en.pdf. Accessed 15 August 2022

European Commission: Tax Policy in the European Union: Priorities for the Years Ahead. COM (2001) 260. Final. Brussels (2001)

European Communities: Directive of 23 July 1990 on the common system of taxation applicable to mergers, divisions, transfers of assets and exchanges of shares concerning companies of different Member States, 90/434/EEC (1990). https://eur-lex.europa.eu/legal-content/EN/ALL/?uri=celex%3A31990L0434. Accessed 15 August 2022

European Communities: Treaty on European Union including the Protocols and Final Act. Maastricht, 7 February 1992 (the Treaty entered into force on 1 November 1993). In Official Journal of the European Communities (OJEC). 29.07.1992, No C 191. [s.l.]. ISSN 0378–6986. https://eur-lex.europa.eu/legal-content/EN/TXT/PDF/?uri=CELEX:11992M/TXT&from=EN, last accessed 15 August 2022.

Farquet, C.: Lutte contre l'évasion fiscale: l'échec de la SDN dans l'entre-deux-guerres. In L'économie Politique **44**, 93–112 (2006)

Fickers, A., Griset, P. (eds): Communicating Europe. Technologies, Information, Events. Palgrave Macmillan, London (2019)

Hanusch, H., Chakraborty, L., Khurana, S.: Fiscal Policy, Economic Growth and Innovation: An Empirical Analysis of G20 Countries. Working Paper No. 883. Levy Institute of Bard College, Annandale-on-Hudson, NY (2017)

Jogarajan, S.: Prelude to the international tax treaty network: 1815–1914. Early tax treaties and the conditions for action. Oxford J. Legal Studies **31**(4), 679–707 (2011)

Keynes, J.M.: A Treatise on Money. The Pure Theory of Money. The Collected Writings of John Maynard Keynes, vol. 5, p. 3. Ed. D. E. Moggridge, Macmillan, London (1930/1971). "Money [...], namely that in which debts and prices and general purchasing power are expressed, is the primary concept of a theory of money"

Kieffer, M.: Le Grand-Duché de Luxembourg: le pays du fer et de l'acier. In Fréchet, H., Attal, F. (eds), Questions d'histoire—Industrialisation et sociétés en Europe occidentale de 1880 à 1970), pp. 176–190. Éditions Du Temps, Paris. Here p. 178 (1997)

Kreins, J.-M.: La réception du plan Marshall au Grand-Duché de Luxembourg. Hémecht **61**(3), 309–343, and **61**(4), 437–465. Here. p. 438. The European Recovery Program (known as the Marshall Plan), launched on 5 June 1947 by George C. Marshall, was implemented by the United States, via the OEEC, to help the countries of Western Europe rebuild after the war (2009a)

Kreins, J.-M.: La réception du plan Marshall au Grand-Duché de Luxembourg. Hémecht **61**(3), 309–343, and 61(4), 437–465. Here. p. 438 (2009b)

Maîtrot de la Motte, A.: Droit fiscal de l'Union européenne, p. 2. Bruylant, Brussels (2012)

Majerus, B.: Le petit Européen parfait. L'Europe, le Luxembourg et la construction nationale. In Beaupré, N., Moine, C. (eds). L'Europe de Versailles à Maastricht, pp. 225–235. Seli Arslan, Paris (2007)

Moyse, L., Meiers, C., Maquil, M.: The architects of Luxembourg's financial industry: personal accounts on the origins and growth of the international financial centers, Editions Saint-Paul, Luxembourg (2014)

OECD: Action plan on base erosion and profit shifting. OECD Publishing, Paris (2013). https://www.oecd.org/ctp/BEPSActionPlan.pdf. Accessed 15 August 2022

OECD: Addressing base erosion and profit shifting. OECD Publishing, Paris (2013). https://www.oecd-ilibrary.org/taxation/addressing-base-erosion-and-profit-shifting_9789264192744-en. Accessed 15 August 2022

Olinger, J.: Les problèmes de l'intégration de la loi sur l'impôt sur le revenu du 4 décembre 1967 dans le système légal existant. In Études fiscales, no. 31. ALOSS, Luxembourg (1970)

Patel, K.K.: Projekt Europa: Eine kritische Geschichte. C.H. Beck Verlag, Munich (2018)

Pauly, M.: Geschichte Luxemburgs. C.H.Beck Verlag, Munich (2014). Pauly explains that the Duchy of Luxembourg belonged successively to the Dukes of Burgundy (15th century), the Spanish Habsburgs (16th and 17th centuries) and the Austrian Habsburgs (18th century), with a short period of French rule between 1684 and 1697. All along, Luxembourg occupied a strategically important position in Europe. Luxembourg City was gradually turned into a fortress, known as the "Gibraltar of the North", and was fought over by Europe's powers.

Peña-Casas, R., Ghailani, D., Coster, S.: Transition digitale dans l'Union européenne: quels impacts sur la qualité de l'emploi? In: Vanhercke, B., Ghailani, D., Sabato, S. (eds). Bilan social de l'Union européenne 2018. Observatoire social européeen/European Social Observatory, ETUI, Brussels (2018)

Schmidt, V.: Changing the policies, politics, abd processes of the Eurozone in crisis: will this time be different? In: Natali, B., Vanhercke, B. (eds.) Social policy in the European Union: state of play 2015, pp. 1–19. ETUI, Brussels (2015)

Scuto, D.: La naissance de la protection sociale au Luxembourg (Le contexte économique et social, les acteurs et les enjeux politiques). In: Bulletin luxembourgeois des questions sociales, vol. 10, pp. 39–59. ALOSS, Luxembourg (2001). Thill, A.: La protection sociale. In Mémorial 1989, La société luxembourgeoise de 1839 à 1989, pp. 619–664. Les Publications Mosellanes, Schengen (1989)

Segré, C.: The development of a European capital market. Report of a Group of Experts appointed by the EEC Commission. November 1966. [EEC Commission—Working Document]. http://aei.pitt.edu/31823/. Accessed 15 August 2022

Service Central de Législation: Grand Ducal decree of 23 January 1936 establishing a National Employment Council to settle labour disputes. Mémorial **1936**, 69–71 (1936)

Service Central de Législation: Grand Ducal decree of 26 April 1919 on the establishment of factory councils in industrial undertakings. Mémorial **1919**, 397–400 (1919)

Service Central de Législation: The Act of 30 December 1927 on the establishment of a commodities exchange. http://legilux.public.lu/eli/etat/leg/loi/1927/12/30/n4/jo. Accessed 15 August 2022

Service Central de Législation: The Act of 31 July 1929 on the tax regime of holding companies. http://legilux.public.lu/eli/etat/leg/loi/1929/07/31/n1/jo, last accessed 15 August 2022. See also Chambre des Députés: Loi sur les holding companies. Travaux préparatoires et Discussions parlementaires, séances des 16 et 17 juillet 1929. Victor Buck, Luxembourg (1929)

Service Central de Législation: The Act of 5 March 1928 approving the Conventions adopted by the International Labour Conference at its first ten sessions (1919 to 1927). Mémorial **1928**, 293–295 (1928)

STATEC: Cahier économique du Statec, no. 113, p. 97. Service d'Etudes et de Documentation Economique, Luxembourg (2012)

STATEC: Statistiques économiques luxembourgeoises—Résumé rétrospectif, pp. 239–240. Service d'Etudes et de Documentation Economiques, Luxembourg (1949)

Susini, J. de: L'effort fiscal du Grand-Duché de Luxembourg au lendemain de la guerre 1914–1918. A. Rousseau (ed.), Paris (1922)

The first two VAT Directives of 11 April 1967, 67/227/EEC and 67/228/EEC, in Official Journal of the European Communities, 14 April 1967, pp. 1301–1312

Tooze, A.: Defining polycrisis—from crisis pictures to the crisis matrix. Chartbook #130. https://adamtooze.substack.com/p/chartbook-130-defining-polycrisis (24 June 2022). Accessed 15 August 2022

Trausch, Gé.: Histoire économique du Grand-Duché de Luxembourg. 1815–2015. STATEC, Luxembourg (2017); Trausch, Gi.: Le rôle et la place des petits pays en Europe au XXe siècle/Small countries in Europe: their role and place in the XXth century. Nomos Verlag, Baden-Baden (2005)

Trausch, Gé.: Histoire économique du Grand-Duché de Luxembourg. 1815–2015. STATEC, Luxembourg (2017)

Trausch, Gi., de Vreese, M.: Luxembourg et les banques: de la révolution industrielle au 7e centre financier mondial. Banque Indosuez, Luxembourg (1995)

Treaty of Rome: Treaty establishing the European Economic Community, 25.03.1957, Part Three, Title I, Section 3, Chapter 2, "Tax Provisions", Art. 95–99. https://eur-lex.europa.eu/legal-content/EN/TXT/PDF/?uri=CELEX:11992E/TXT&from=EN. Accessed 15 August 2022 (1957)

Treaty on European Union signed at Maastricht on 7 February 1992, Official Journal of European Communities C 191, Volume 35, 29.07.1992, pp. 0001–0110, https://eur-lex.europa.eu/legal-content/EN/TXT/PDF/?uri=OJ:C:1992:191:FULL&from=NL. Accessed 15 August 2022

Werner, P.: Déclaration de Monsieur Pierre Werner, ministre d'État, président du gouvernement luxembourgeois, faite à la Conférence des chefs d'État ou de gouvernement. The Hague: 1 December 1969. In: Bulletin de documentation, no. 14 of 10 December 1969. Luxembourg: Service Information et Presse, Ministry of State of the Grand Duchy of Luxembourg, December 1969, pp. 3–7

Zucman, G.: Taxing across borders: Tracking personal wealth and corporate profits. J. Econ. Perspect. **28**(4), 121–148 (2014)

The EIB: Fostering Recovery in an Uncertain World

Bruno Rossignol

Abstract The European Investment Bank is Europe's best kept secret. Although it is both the Bank of the European Union, owned by the 27 EU Member States, and has been operating since 1958, few EU citizens know it exists, and even fewer know that in almost 65 years the EIB has invested over €1.5 trillion for more than 14.400 investment projects, generating an overall investment of €4.8 trillion. The Oresund bridge between Denmark and Sweden, the Milhau viaduct in France, high-speed trains in Spain, solar farms in Italy and offshore windfarms in Germany… there is virtually not one large infrastructure project in the EU that has not benefited from EIB financing. The EIB is a unique institution with a lending capacity superior to that of the World Bank. It is a crowding-in bank that generally does not invest more than 30% of a given project and finances projects according to four main priorities: innovation, digital, and human capital; sustainable energy and natural resources; sustainable cities and regions; and SMEs. These projects are overwhelmingly in the EU: 90% of the projects the EIB supports are in EU countries. The EIB Group—made of the European Investment Bank and the European Investment Fund—is used to responding rapidly and efficiently to crises. This is what it did in 2008 during the subprime financial crisis, which was quickly followed by the European sovereign debt crisis, or when Europe was confronted to the migrant crisis, when the United Kingdom left the EU and the Bank lost one of its four major shareholders (with Germany, France, and Italy) and had to restructure its capital. Each time, the EIB Group took up the challenge by adapting, upscaling, and diversifying its instruments while cooperating with its many partners. It is no different today when the EIB Group is faced with the aftermath of the COVID-19 pandemic and the war in Ukraine, while

"The findings interpretations and conclusions are those of the author and do not necessarily reflect the views of the European Investment Bank" and "This paper includes frequent verbatim quotes from the EIB website of which the EIB is aware and other public sources. The author has done his best to identify them in each single instance".

B. Rossignol (✉)
Head of Climate and Heritage Programme, European Investment Bank Institute, 98-100, Boulevard Konrad Adenauer, 2950 Luxembourg, Luxembourg
e-mail: bruno.rossignol@eib.org

A. M. Dima and E. R. Danescu (eds.), *Fostering Recovery Through Metaverse Business Modelling*, Springer Proceedings in Business and Economics,
https://doi.org/10.1007/978-3-031-28255-3_3

having to finance Europe's transition to the ineluctable, indispensable, and urgent adaptation to a decarbonised society.

Keywords Luxembourg · EIB · European Integration

1 Introduction

Ask any citizen in any of the 27 EU Member States whether he or she has heard of the European Investment Bank, and the answer will probably be a negative one. Nevertheless, the EIB is the Bank of the European Union, and its history is closely linked to that of the European project itself. First imagined between the two world wars, the idea of an institution for the financing of major infrastructure in Europe resurfaced in 1949 at the time of reconstruction and the Marshall Plan, when the French Minister for Finance Maurice Petsche (1895–1951) presented it to the Organisation for European Economic Cooperation.

The EIB was created by the Treaty of Rome establishing the European Economic Community (EEC) signed in Rome on 25 March 1957 and entered into force on 1st January 1958 (articles 129 and 120). Every Member State was to become a shareholder of the newly founded bank (article 129) whose statutes were established in a protocol annexed to the Treaty. And its role was so defined: "The task of the EIB shall be to contribute, by having recourse to the capital market and utilising its own resources, to the balanced and steady development of the common market in the interest of the community. For this purpose, the Bank shall, operating on a non-profit-making basis, grant loans and give guarantees which facilitate the financing of the following projects in all sectors of the economy:

(A) Projects for developing less-developed regions;
(B) Projects for modernising and converting undertakings or for developing fresh activities called for by the progressive establishment of the common market, where these projects are of such a size or nature that they cannot be entirely financed by the various means available in the individual Member States;
(C) Projects of common interest to several Member States which are of such a size or nature that they cannot be entirely financed by the various means available in the individual Member States (European Investment Bank 2020).

As well as contributing to the financing of projects of common interest, it also met the concerns of those who feared that the common market would accentuate imbalances in regional development or hasten the decline of certain industries. The EIB would thus mobilise capital to promote the cohesion of the European area and modernise the economy (European Investment Bank 2020).

Strengthening its shareholder base with every new enlargement of the European Union—the last shareholder, Croatia, joined in 2013, the EIB's capital base grew to €243 billion, rated AAA by the rating agencies (European Investment Bank 2021a). This capital base has allowed the Bank to raise money on the financial market allowing it to finance projects mostly in the EU (90% of the EIB financing is for investment projects in EU countries). This is done through lending (for the public and private sectors or via intermediated loans for SMEs), equity participation or guarantees, blending (combining EIB loans and EC grants, for instance), and advising (making technical and financial expertise available to our clients to develop and implement investment projects and programmes, and to improve institutional and regulatory frameworks).

In almost 65 years of existence, the EIB has invested over €1.5 trillion for more than 14.400 investment projects, generating overall investment of €4.8 trillion. These are huge amounts which have greatly contributed to the EU's economic development, as per the Bank's statutes and as exemplified by the Bank's early focus on Italy.

In fact, the first two EIB Presidents, Pietro Campilli (1958–1959), a former Minister for the "Mezzogiorno" and Paride Formentini (1959–1970) were Italian, and the EIB contributed to the building of the Southern heavy and basic industry and supported public and private capital investments in the iron and steel and chemical and engineering sectors. Between 1958 and 1972, more than 60% of the Bank's loans went to projects in Italy from heavy industry (iron, steel, and chemistry (Italy's biggest steel factory in Taranto…)) to dams and irrigation schemes (Metaponto…) (Bonatesta 2019a).

Since then, the Europe of Six has become the Europe of 28 then 27. National economies are now part of the single market, a single currency and a Eurozone have been created, and the EIB has become a feature in the economic life of every region of Europe and, often, beyond. The Oresund bridge between Denmark and Sweden, the Milhau viaduct in France, high-speed trains in Spain, solar farms in Italy and wind farms in Germany, there is not one large infrastructure project in the EU that has not benefited from EIB financing. Interconnectedness has been at the heart of its work throughout its history, and it continues to be so today. Across Europe, the Bank's investment draws the many countries of the European Union closer together. Outside the EU, its support for North Africa, the Middle East, and Europe's eastern neighbours creates growth and opportunity in these regions that, in turn, makes the Union's countries stronger.

The EIB is a unique institution, as it is both an EU body and a bank. It is governed by both public and corporate governance principles with four statutory bodies (those referred to in the EIB Statute):

Three decision-making bodies: the Board of Governors—comprising Ministers designated by each of the 27 Member States, usually Finance Ministers and responsible for determining the general directives of the EIB—the Board of Directors responsible for the strategic management of the Bank (European Investment Bank 2021b) and the Management Committee, its permanent collegiate executive body (European Investment Bank 2021c). In addition, there is one control body: the Audit Committee, which verifies that the Bank's operations have been conducted properly.

With a lending capacity superior to that of the World Bank, it is a crowding-in bank that does not invest more than 30% of a given project and finances projects according to four main priorities: innovation, digital, and human capital; sustainable energy and natural resources; sustainable cities and regions; and SMEs. Most of all, the Bank improves lives all over the world. At a time when the value of multilateralism is being challenged, the EIB's work serves as a constant reminder of the power of integrated European efforts.

In a world where disease and war are shaping our economy, the EIB Group, made of the European Investment Bank, and the European Investment Fund, which is used to responding rapidly and efficiently to crises. This is what it did in 2008 during the subprime financial crisis which was quickly followed by the European sovereign debt crisis, or when Europe was confronted to the migrant crisis, when the United Kingdom left the EU and the Bank lost one of its four major shareholders (with Germany, France, and Italy) and had to restructure its capital. Each time the EIB Group took up the challenge by adapting, upscaling, and diversifying its instruments while cooperating with its many partners. It is no different today when the EIB Group is facing the aftermath of the COVID-19 pandemic and the war in Ukraine, while having to finance Europe's transition to the ineluctable, indispensable, and urgent adaptation to a decarbonised society. This is what this paper will describe.

2 The EIB—A Brief History

The Bank was founded in Brussels in 1958 as the Treaty of Rome establishing the European Economic Community (EEC) came into force. The members of the first management committee were appointed in February 1958, with Pietro Campilli, a member of several post-war Italian governments and a former Minister for the "Mezzogiorno" as President. On 21 April 1959, the first EIB loan was signed. The final beneficiaries of this transaction, carried out jointly with the International Bank for Reconstruction and Development—better known today as the World Bank—were three Italian companies: Sincat and Celene (to build a large petrochemical complex in Sicily), and Mercure (to exploit a seam of lignite in Lucania to produce electricity).

At that time, the EIB was endowed with a subscribed capital of 1.000 m units of account, of which 250 m was to be paid in. Units of account were expressed in gold and, as long as the US dollar was pegged to the gold standard, the value of a unit of account was equal to one US dollar. On 1 June 1959, Paride Formentini became the second President of the EIB. The charismatic Italian, former Head of the Banca d'Italia, would lead the Bank for 11 years, until September 1970. Both Campilli and Formentini thought that Europe could only exist if each of its regions enjoyed economic growth and that the new institution was not a fund, but a proper bank that could "only grant its loans or its guarantee to economically profitable projects while at the same time being an instrument of economic policy and, to that extent, having to make sure it coordinated its actions with the economic policies of the Member States of the common market" (Formentini 2008).

From 1959 to 1972, over 60% of EIB lending to Member States was granted to Italy contributing to the building of the Southern heavy and basic industry (iron, steel, and chemistry (Taranto…)) and supported public and private capital investments in the iron and steel and chemical and engineering sectors. Of this, 43% went to infrastructure projects such as the Autostrada del Sole, connecting Milan with Naples, via Rome and Florence, and to dams and irrigation schemes (Metaponto…) (Bonatesta 2019b).

In 1962, following the launch of its first borrowing operation, the EIB was authorised to finance projects outside the European Community. This marked the beginning of the extension of EIB's activities around the globe to support emerging and developing economies, also in Africa, Asia, and Latin America (as of 1993 for these two continents). As an example, in 1965, the Bank financed the construction of a new packaging facility for bananas in Abidjan, Côte d'Ivoire, and in 1991, it was authorised to operate in South Africa.

In 1968, the EIB moved its headquarters from Brussels to Luxembourg. The first external offices were also inaugurated, starting with Brussels and Rome. Under its third President, Frenchman Yves Le Portz, the Bank focused mainly on financing strategic infrastructure, as well as on supporting the European industry in response to the energy crisis, such as financing of the original manufacturing facilities of the Airbus A300 in Toulouse and St. Nazaire, France, in December 1971. This was the beginning of a long partnership, as the EIB has been on board every new Airbus developed since the A300. Three new Member States, Denmark, Ireland, and the UK became shareholders.

In 1980, as the EIB relocated to its current site in a building typical of the "brutalist" style designed in 1974 by the prestigious British architect, Sir Denys Lasdun, it launched its first borrowing operation in European currency unit (ECUs), created to sail on the stormy seas of the international monetary system, following the end of fixed exchange rates of the post-war period. Under the chairmanship of its first German President, Ernst-Gunther Bröder, the Bank financed innovative European companies as well as strategic infrastructure that can connect the common European market has been a goal since the EIB's inception. Three new countries, Greece, Spain, and Portugal joined the EU.

The 1990s saw the fall of the Berlin Wall and the collapse of the Soviet Union, with the EIB starting to provide financing to Eastern European countries. The EIB was a founding member of a new institution, the European Bank for Reconstruction and Development, extended its activities to the Czech and Slovak Federal Republic, Bulgaria and Romania (1991) and two years later to the Baltic countries (Estonia, Latvia and Lithuania), and launched a pre-accession facility in 1998. Under the leadership of its first British President, Sir Brian Unwin, it created a subsidiary, the European Investment Fund the subsidiary of the EIB (1994) as a specialist provider of risk finance for small and medium-sized enterprises (SME) across Europe of which it became a majority shareholder in 2000, creating the EIB Group. Other shareholders are the European Commission, and a wide range of public and private banks and financial institutions. The number of shareholders expanded in 1995 with three new countries Austria, Finland, and Sweden joining the EU, and the Bank launched its first borrowing operation in euros, over a year before the new European currency was born on 1 January 1999. The lead managers of the issuing syndicate were the Caisse des Dépôts et Consignations, Paribas, and Warburg. This was a decade of firsts: first operations in euros, first investments in Gaza/West Bank, first activities in South Africa.

In 1997, the Bank financed one of its many flagship projects, the construction of the Öresund bridge, connecting Copenhagen (Denmark) and Malmö (Sweden), a vital transport link in the Trans European Transport Network (TEN-T). Every day 75 000 people use the bridge, 45% of them taking the 35-min train ride.

During the 2000s, under the presidency of former Belgian finance minister Philippe Maystadt (2000–2012), the EIB became more involved in climate change. The Green European Council of Gothenburg (15–16 June 2001) asked the Bank to promote the sustainable development strategy. Coordinating its efforts with the European Commission, the EIB began supporting investments aimed at protecting the planet from the negative effects of climate change. What was true for lending was also true for funding, as the Bank issued the first Climate Awareness Bonds on the capital markets, the world's first Green Bonds in 2007. The funds raised are earmarked to match the disbursements to EIB lending projects in the field of renewable energy and energy efficiency.

On 2 June 2008, as the EIB inaugurated its new building, known as the East building, created by German architects Ingenhoven Architekten in association with Werner Sobek Ingenieure, the number of its shareholders had increased considerably, with Cyprus, Estonia, Hungary, Latvia, Lithuania, Malta, Poland, Czech Republic, Slovakia, and Slovenia joining the EU in 2004 followed by Bulgaria and Romania in 2007. Little did it know that it was about to transform into a Bank for all crises, an institution able to support to the economic recovery with additional € 60 billion thanks to a special EIB capital increase in response to the financial crisis of 2008 and to kick start investment in the EU with the European Fund for Strategic Investment with the Commission; to help the EU face the refugee crisis of 2016 with the creation of a new Economic Resilience Initiative; to play a crucial role in Europe's response to the economic consequences of the COVID-19 pandemic in 2020 and to be part of the answer of the EU to the brutal invasion of Ukraine by Russia on 24 February 2022.

In its sixty-five-year history, the EIB has grown exponentially. Its lending went from ECU 10bn in 1988 to annual lending near €45bn in the mid-2000s before jumping to €79bn in 2009 as a temporary response to the financial and economic crisis. It was €94.89 bn in 2021. This amount was split between the European Investment Bank (€65.36 billion) and the European Investment Fund (€30.50 billion). Of the total financing, €86.74 billion went to projects inside the EU, while €8.14 billion went to projects around the world. Around €360 billion of investment was supported, while 43% of total EIB financing was dedicated to green financing (climate action and environmental sustainability).

This surge in activity is based on a strong capital base, from less than ECU 30bn in the early 1990s, to €243bn on 1st February 2020 and an increase of the number of partner countries: the first agreements with non-Member States and non-European countries were made in the early 1960s. Today, the EIB works with more than 135 non-EU states which receive around 10% of our funding. Last but not least, though the EIB still has fewer staff than corresponding institutions like the World Bank, its staff went from a workforce of 66 in 1958, to 1000 staff members in 1999 and close to 4000 today. All this has allowed the Bank to have considerable impact on the lives of citizens.

3 A Bank for all Crises

When the COVID-19 pandemic turned the world upside down at the beginning of 2020, the world learned to cope with a new normal. For firms and workers, this new normal meant more digitalisation, more remote working, more innovation.

According to EIB research (EIB 2022), the COVID-19 crisis accelerated the digital transformation of Europe's economy. Before the pandemic, cutting-edge digital technologies were primarily used by the most innovative and modern firms. The COVID-19 crisis, however, brought the digital transformation to the larger society—and made digitalisation integral to firms' survival.

Digital firms were better able to cope with the disruption unleashed by the pandemic, and they were less likely than non-digital firms to see sales decline significantly from 2020 onwards. Many of them used the crisis as an opportunity to accelerate their digitalisation.

But, while we were still working through the socioeconomic consequences of the pandemic, Europe and the world were confronted with the most dramatic uncertainty: war. Russia's invasion of Ukraine has led to significant humanitarian crises. Lives are being lost and livelihoods disrupted; cities are being destroyed, and all the countries neighbouring Ukraine are facing an unprecedented, massive inflow of refugees.

The economic impact of the war is severe: energy prices are soaring; inflation is growing, and shortages coming. Growth is slowing down, and business activity is facing considerable challenges in Ukraine, in neighbouring countries, in the entire EU, and beyond.

At the same time, we need to address our planet's climate and environment emergency. Like violent conflicts with authoritarian states, climate change is causing human suffering and costing lives. The war has made clear Europe's reliance on Russian fossil fuels, making it vulnerable to the whims of autocrats. It is forcing us to accelerate the transition towards a decarbonised economy. While it is too late to avoid all climate change, we must nevertheless stop it spiralling out of control, and we have to adapt to its unavoidable consequences.

Within this critical decade 2021–2030, we must:

- limit global warming to 1.5 °C above pre-industrial levels by the end of this century;
- adapt to the unavoidable impacts of climate change such as extreme weather events;
- combat environmental degradation;
- halt biodiversity loss;
- stop widening inequalities.

To achieve this, trillions of investment are required. According to McKinsey's research, the transformation of the global economy needed to achieve net-zero emissions by 2050 would require $9.2 trillion in annual average spending on physical assets.

Being one of the world's main financiers of climate action and environmental sustainability, the EIB, the EU's climate bank, will play its part. Coming out of a pandemic which left it reeling, confronted with war in Europe and climate emergencies, floods in Pakistan, famine in Madagascar, heatwaves and drought in Europe and the US, it is fair to say that the world has probably never been faced with such radical uncertainty. What does this mean for the EIB Group?

The EIB Group—made of the European Investment Bank and the European Investment Fund—is used to responding rapidly and efficiently to crises. It did so during the 2008 Financial Crisis and the subsequent European Sovereign Debt Crisis. As the EIB was put under negative watch by rating agencies worried of the potential insolvency of some Member States and forced to reduce its activity, its shareholders agreed a special EIB paid-in capital increase in response to the financial crisis. In return, the EU Member States asked the Bank to lend an additional EUR 60 billion over three years. This has allowed us to increase our support for the economic recovery and has a considerable impact on the lives of citizens. In November 2014, the European Commission launched the Investment Plan for Europe, also known as the Juncker Plan, as a response to the crisis which had severely hindered the investment capacity of EU Member States. The European Fund for Strategic Investment (EFSI) was one of its key elements, providing loan guarantees that enable the European Investment Bank to support higher risk projects. EFSI is essentially an agreement between the European Commission and the Bank under which losses incurred from operations included in the EFSI portfolio are covered up to €33.54 billion, €26 billion of which is provided by the European Commission and €7.54 billion of which comes from the EIB's own funds. It initially aimed to mobilise €315 billion and was then extended to €500 billion by 2020. Over the years, thousands of projects benefitted from its financing, making Europe more modern, social, and green.

The fund has been operating since 2015. According to an independent evaluation (European Investment Bank 2021d), the EFSI guarantees had done a good job mobilising investment to address structural gaps, but the fund arrived too late to effectively help the European economy attract investment after the financial crisis. The guarantee provided by the fund helped the EIB Group mobilise more than €540 billion from 2015 to 2020, plugging investment gaps created by the 2008 financial crisis and, more recently, the COVID-19 crisis.

More specifically, the evaluation found that EFSI effectively harnessed public money and the EIB Group's financing and expertise to unlock private investment throughout the European Union; fostered cooperation between national promotional banks and the EIB Group, although this cooperation could be improved to take into account the needs and diversity of the different national banks; and transparently embedded the EIB Group's activities into overarching the EU policy.

3.1 The Migrant Crisis

In 2015, Europe was confronted to one of its greatest challenges ever faced by the European Union when following the war in Syria 1.3 million people came to the continent to request asylum. Political instability and conflict in the EU's neighbouring countries and beyond were and still are driving this mass movement of people. At the request of the European Council, the Bank developed a specific initiative, the EIB's Economic Resilience Initiative (ERI) to support economic resilience in the EU's southern neighbourhood and the Western Balkans regions, both of which have been significantly impacted by the refugee crisis on the EU's doorstep. The EIB tries to combine short-term humanitarian interventions with medium- and long-term efforts to ease the burden on community services and social infrastructure, whilst addressing the root causes of forced displacement and creating economic resilience in both host and origin countries.

The Bank focused on the socioeconomic aspects of the crises, helping communities to facilitate the acceptance and inclusion of the forcibly displaced, and supporting economic resilience, through initiatives such as investing in the private sector to create jobs and real economic opportunities.

ERI creates jobs and economic growth in the region by investing in key infrastructure and in private sector development. It may also help migration flows. ERI offers a package of loans and innovative financial products, while blending funds from the donor community with EIB financing. The initiative is implemented in close cooperation with EU countries, the European Commission, and other partners. The first countries to contribute to ERI were Bulgaria, Croatia, Italy, Lithuania, Luxembourg, Poland, Slovakia, Slovenia, and the United Kingdom, and 61 projects have been signed for a total of €5.2 billion in investment. The initiative is expected to provide a total of more than €15 billion in additional financing. Well over half of that went into private sector development. Lending through partner banks alone is set to benefit more than 11.800 smaller businesses and mid-caps, helping to sustain almost 221 000 jobs. Public sector investments amount to €1.4 billion.

The refugee crisis is a reminder of the interconnectedness of development issues, not only with geopolitics, but also with growth and investment policies in every country. As the EU's bank and the largest IFI lender for projects in the pre-accession and Middle East North Africa regions, the EIB will continue to assist EU Member States in addressing the refugee crisis in host countries, transit countries and countries of origin.

3.2 The Migrant Crisis

When the UK left the EU, the Bank lost one of its four major shareholders (with Germany, France, and Italy) and had to restructure its capital. Following the referendum on 23 June 2016, the UK government formally notified its intention to leave the European Union on 29 March 2017 starting the withdrawal process under Article 50 of the Treaty. On 31st January 2020, the United Kingdom stopped becoming a member of the European Investment Bank, as part of its withdrawal from the European Union. A year ago, the Governors of the European Investment Bank, Europe's finance ministers had unanimously agreed last that the departure of the United Kingdom from the European Union would not affect the financing activity or have any impact on the EIB's business model.

The UK's share of the EIB's paid-in capital prior to Brexit represented EUR 3.5 billion, alongside EUR 35.7 billion of callable capital. The UK's callable capital disappeared on Brexit day and was replaced by the UK's liability on callable capital. On 1 March 2020, two member states, Romania and Poland, contributed additional capital, providing the EIB with a higher capital base than before Brexit. The EIB will reimburse the UK's EUR 3.5 billion paid-in share over 12 annual instalments following Brexit.

The UK will remain liable for the EIB's pre-Brexit operations. This liability will be reduced as the EIB's pre-Brexit (some €50 billion) exposure declines. Brexit had no impact on EIB's and EIF's AAA rating.

As EIB President Werner Hoyer (European Investment Bank 2019) then stated, "the EIB Group is an important benefit of European Union membership. In the UK, we have supported transformational investments, enhanced economic opportunities, helped small businesses, and improved social infrastructure since 1973. I look forward to a new kind of relationship, which should reflect our unique commonality of purpose, and the strength of the relationship between the United Kingdom and the European Union. This is a bond that will always remain especially strong and of fundamental importance to both sides".

In each of these crises, the EIB Group took up the challenge by adapting, upscaling, and diversifying its instruments while cooperating with its many partners. This is no different with today's crises.

3.3 COVID-19

The EIB has been on the frontline of the European Union's global response to the COVID-19 pandemic and has rallied with international organisations such as the World Health Organization and the United Nations Children's Fund to take immediate action.

Emergency support from the EIB Group has enabled small and medium enterprises and innovative start-ups to invest despite extreme uncertainty. The EIB backed the creation of a €25 billion European COVID-19 guarantee fund in partnership with local lenders and national promotional institutions. This has enabled the EIB Group to scale up its support for European companies that were struggling because of the pandemic by up to an additional €200 billion—with a focus on small and medium-sized enterprises. As of August 2022, the EGF had already approved €23.8 billion, almost half of the fund's target for 2021, in support of European businesses struggling with the economic fallout of the COVID-19 pandemic. The initiatives financed so far are expected to generate €187.4 billion in funding for the EU economy.

Here, the experience gained with EFSI (described above) was crucial. The fund's guarantees proved to be instrumental in helping the EIB Group quickly provide support to businesses and markets, according to the latest evaluation, which focuses on 2018–2020. The lessons learned from the flexibility of EFSI were also particularly useful. Money could flow where it was most needed. For example, some funds earmarked for infrastructure projects were redirected to small businesses. That flexibility enabled the EIB and EIF to meet market needs as they arose, which was particularly relevant during the COVID-19 crisis.

The EIB has also helped finance the development and purchase of COVID-19 vaccines, solutions to limit the spread of the virus, and other public health projects related to the COVID-19 crisis. The German company BioNTech benefited from €100 million to develop the first COVID-19 vaccine (European Investment Bank 2021e) and the EIB-financed vaccine production capacities in Dakar (Senegal) and in South Africa.

3.4 Support for Ukraine

The EIB has worked with Ukraine since 2007, in line with the European Neighbourhood Policy (ENP), the Eastern Partnership (EaP), and other EU bilateral agreements, financing 54 projects (investing in grain storage and equipment, improving urban transport or public buildings energy efficiency, etc.) for some €8 bn with 15 local partners.

As part of a coordinated EU and international response to the first war on European soil since the Second World War, the EIB has mobilised and deployed rapidly almost 700 billion euros of financial support through the EIB Solidarity Package for Ukraine to help the Government meet its urgent need for liquidity. This first part of the Ukraine Solidarity Urgent Response was followed by a second part of €1.59 billion announced in July to help Ukraine fix damaged infrastructure, restart municipal services, and support urgent energy efficiency measures in preparation for the cold season. As of October, €1.05 billion in immediate assistance to Ukraine had been disbursed. The remaining €540 million will be used to resume implementation of existing EIB-financed projects in Ukraine as they progress, excluding areas of active hostilities and territories not controlled by the Ukrainian government.

In addition, in cooperation with the European Commission, the EIB is providing further financing to enable the Government of Ukraine to continue providing critical public services for citizens that stayed in the country, ensuring that food, medical supplies, and fuel remain available, while also backing transport, energy, urban development, and digital projects.

The EIB has also announced a €4 billion support package for 2022 and 2023 to help cities and regions in EU Member States address urgent investment needs and meet the challenges of welcoming and integrating war refugees from Ukraine. The new EIB programme aims to finance the development of key social infrastructure for the provision of public services to refugees, including housing, schools, hospitals, and kindergartens.

The EIB is continuing to work with European partners to explore further possibilities for supporting Ukraine and Ukrainian refugees. It stands ready to provide its experience, capacity, and know how to help Ukraine develop a comprehensive strategy for the reconstruction of the country ready to be implemented once the war is over.

Here in Europe, the war has made the need to protect our sovereignty and autonomy more urgent than ever.

But, amid the tragedy of war, there is a great opportunity: that the bold investments needed to become independent from Russian fossil fuels will also help us solve the biggest global challenge of ours.

3.5 The EU's Climate Bank

Looking at the world today, at the many urgent challenges, from the pandemic to the energy and food crises triggered by Russia's attack on Ukraine, one might would be tempted to think that choosing between tackling these crises and the preservation of nature is a dilemma.

In fact, there should be no trade-offs. According to the World Economic Forum, $44 trillion of economic value generation—over half the world's total GDP—is dependent on nature and the nature-based economy: forestry, water, oceans, and agriculture. Preserving and increasing the value of these assets, by conserving and restoring nature, is just smart economics.

To achieve this, trillions of investment are required. According to McKinsey research, the transformation of the global economy needed to achieve net-zero emissions by 2050 would require $9.2 trillion in annual average spending on physical assets. The global shortfall is estimated at $700 billion annually between now and 2030. Public funding and the support of philanthropies is essential. But, you cannot be successful without the private sector.

Being one of the world's main financiers of climate action and environmental sustainability, the EIB, the EU's climate bank, will play its part. The European Union is at the forefront of the global fight against climate change and environmental degradation. With the European Green Deal, the EU aims to make the European economy sustainable and inclusive. The EIB is an important partner in this new growth strategy, while playing a leading role in the implementation of the Paris Agreement and the Sustainable Development Goals.

In 2019, the EIB Board of Directors approved a new set of ambitious targets for climate action and environmental sustainability. The three key elements are as follows:

(a) The EIB Group will support €1 trillion in investments in climate action and environmental sustainability in the critical decade from 2021 to 2030;
(b) The EIB will gradually increase the share of its financing dedicated to climate action and environmental sustainability to exceed 50% of its operations in 2025;
(c) The EIB Group will align all its financing activities with the principles and goals of the Paris agreement by the end of 2020.

(a) The EIB Group supports climate projects in three main areas: (1) climate mitigation projects, i.e. projects that reduce or prevent the emission of greenhouse gases. For example, this can be done by investing in research and development of low-carbon technologies, renewable energy, low-carbon transport solutions, and industrial decarbonisation. It also invests in (2) climate adaptation projects that anticipate the adverse effects of climate change and take appropriate action to prevent or minimise the resulting damage. Early and well-planned adaptation can save lives and money. Such investments include projects that reduce the risk of floods, develop resilient cities, and increase afforestation. The EIB Adaptation Plan supports the objectives of the European Union Adaptation Strategy inside and outside the EU. The EIB pledges to increase the share of adaptation support to 15% of the Bank's overall finance for climate action by 2025. This represents an almost three-fold increase, compared to adaptation finance over the past five years. The EIB will screen all projects it finances for the risks of climate change and ensure that they are adapted to future changes. A new advisory service called ADAPT will help public and private sector clients understand how climate change affects their operations. And (3) the EIB backs activities that promote sustainable management of natural resources, biodiversity, and the environment. EIB investments tackle the effects of climate change on vulnerable communities, protecting biodiversity, and promoting sustainable farming, thus preserving natural resources and making the environment safe for future generations.
(b) In fact, last year, we had already dedicated 51% of our financing, €27.6 billion, to climate action and sustainability projects. The EIB's operations accelerate green growth and the decarbonisation of economies. We focus on energy efficiency: the cheapest energy is the energy we do not use and the renewable energy. The Bank is the first financier of offshore wind farms in the EU, which help both reduce CO_2 emissions and strengthen our energy security. All of our actions contribute to sustainable social and economic growth.
(c) Beyond the existing 11 Environmental and Social Standards, applicable to all new operations, the bank has put in place a framework—The Climate Bank Roadmap—to ensure that the projects it supports—whether they be in energy, transport, industry or agricultural sectors—are aligned with the goals of the Paris Agreement (European Investment Bank 2021f). We have introduced a new approach for the alignment of counterparties. This applies to large companies active in high-emitting sectors and large financial institutions. Building on the European Union regulations, this requires large companies to disclose their alignment plans, including a mid-term carbon target. Such plans should also

> address building resilience to future climate change. The EIB will work with clients to develop and publish these plans. This general approach, based on disclosure, is powerful. But, it also needs a bottom line for companies that intend to invest in very high carbon activities incompatible with the Paris Agreement. In general, the EIB will not support projects, including low-carbon ones, with companies that invest in activities such as the building of new coal-fired power plants or coal mines, or the destruction of carbon sinks. For the oil-production sector, if companies cannot commit to reducing oil production over time or if they continue to engage in incompatible activities, the Bank will only work with them on highly innovative low-carbon projects, such as carbon capture and sequestration, renewable hydrogen, advanced biofuels, or floating offshore wind.

Furthermore, the EIB has created a Climate and Environment Advisory Council, consisting of leaders from academia, business, civil society, and international organisations, to provide independent advice and expertise on the activities that the EIB Group is carrying out to reach its climate action and environmental sustainability ambitions. Among the topics covered, the focus will be on the Climate Bank Roadmap and on our activities to support adaptation to the impacts of climate change, as well as the EIB Group Paris Alignment for Counterparties framework.

As President Hoyer recently said: "We have still a long way to go when it comes to climate. But, the result shows that the Bank is transforming faster than anyone could have expected into the EU's climate bank."

Financing

And this is also valid for the way we finance ourselves. Every year, the EIB raises money by issuing bonds on international capital markets. Our global borrowing authorisation for 2022 is up to €50 billion reflecting our borrowing needs to achieve our operational targets and making the EIB a large issuer, larger than many EU Member States alone. The euro and the dollar are the main funding currencies, and the size of issuance is typically large (3 billion to 5 billion) with benchmark maturities ranging from 2 to 30 years and issued on a regular basis.

Our AAA credit rating allows us to raise funds at good rates, and these benefits are passed on to clients. For investors, EIB's bonds are considered Level 1 High Quality Liquid Assets (HQLA) for Liquidity Coverage Ratio calculation under the Basel framework. In 2007, we pioneered the green bonds market by issuing the world's first Climate Awareness Bond (CAB), allocated exclusively to climate change mitigating activities in line with the EU's sustainability objectives. This has proven very successful, and the EIB has played a major role in developing the green bond market, which exceeded 600 billion euros of new issuance in 2021. We are the largest supranational issuer of green bonds, which support renewable energy, energy efficiency, clean water, and sanitation. In 2018, our first Sustainability Awareness Bond (SAB) extended this approach to other environmental and social policy objectives. At the end of July 2020, the EIB remains the world's leading supranational green and sustainability bond fund, with more than € 38 billion raised in 17 currencies. In total, CAB and SAB proceeds have helped finance 312 projects in 71 countries around the world.

Together with other experts, the EIB contributed to the EU Sustainability Taxonomy and the EU Green Bond Standard. The EU Taxonomy is a tool to help investors, companies, issuers, and project promoters navigate the transition to a low-carbon, resilient, and resource-efficient economy. The EU Green Bond Standard, based on best market practice and the EU Sustainability Taxonomy classifications, aims to safeguard the robustness of the green capital markets. The EIB is committed to aligning its tracking methodology for climate action and environmental sustainability ("green") finance with the framework defined by the EU Taxonomy Regulation and the EU Green Bond Standard. It plans to align its CAB/SAB Frameworks with the EU Green Bond Standard (EUGBS), as retained and amended by the European Commission. The EUGBS requires that EU green bonds are allocated to economic activities that meet the requirements of the EU Sustainability Taxonomy (EUST). In sectors that are not yet covered by the EUST, the EIB uses its definitions within the spirit and logic of the EUST. In September 2018, we became the first issuer to retain these principles in our CAB/SAB documentation, thus establishing a direct link between sustainability lending and funding in the spirit of the EU Taxonomy Regulation.

4 Conclusions

Confronted with almost continuous uncertainty in the past 15 years, the EIB Group has stepped up to the plate and provided support to the EU economy, its companies, and its workers. It has diversified its financing instruments, such as EFSI (European Investment Bank 2021g), to improve the EIB Group's firepower in dealing with economic crises. It has extended financing outside Europe. And, as Europe intends to lead by example, it has transformed itself into the EU's climate bank.

Cognitive science tells us that our brains are hardwired to dislike uncertainty. Research shows that we get significantly more anxious and upset when we do not know what is about to happen than when we know for certain that something bad will happen.

The EIB's economists, engineers, and financial officers have had plenty of reasons to be anxious and upset. They have adjusted. And they have delivered. How should we adjust the way we think about the future to allow for the current wave of uncertainties and prepare for the upcoming ones, particularly those related to the climate transition, will be the most difficult question ever tackled by the EIB.

References

Bonatesta, A.: European University Institute (EUI-Florence) "The EIB and the "Mezzogiorno" in the context of regional development (1958–1973)" STAREBEI research (2019a)

Bonatesta, A.: European University Institute (EUI-Florence) "The EIB and the "Mezzogiorno" in the context of regional development (1958–1973)", STAREBEI research. In https://institute.eib.org/2019/06/new-research-published-the-eib-and-the-mezzogiorno/ (2019b)

EIB: Investment Survey 2022. In https://www.eib.org/en/publications/digitalisation-in-europe-2021-2022 (2022)

European Investment Bank: Statutory Bodies, Management Committee, Werner Hoyer. An economist member of the German Bundestag (1987–2011) and former Deputy Foreign Minister at the German Foreign Office (1994–1998, 2009–2011), Werner Hoyer became President on 1 January 2012 and was re-appointed for a second term in office, with effect from 1 January 2018. Dr Hoyer has overseen a significant expansion and transformation of the Bank. In https://www.eib.org/en/readonline-publications/information-werner-hoyer (2019)

European Investment Bank: Statute and other Treaty provisions. In www.eib.org. European Investment Bank. https://www.eib.org/en/publications/statute-2020.htm (2020)

European Investment Bank: Shareholders. Each Member State's share in the Bank's capital is based on its economic weight within the European Union (expressed in GDP) at the time of its accession. Under its Statute, the Bank is authorised to have maximum loans outstanding equivalent to two and a half times its subscribed capital. In https://www.eib.org/en/about/governance-and-structure/shareholders/index.htm (2021a)

European Investment Bank: Statutory Bodies, Board of Directors. In https://www.eib.org/en/about/governance-and-structure/statutory-bodies/board-directors/index.htm (2021b)

European Investment Bank: Statutory Bodies, Management Committee. In https://www.eib.org/en/about/governance-and-structure/statutory-bodies/management-committee/index.htm (2021c)

European Investment Bank: Publications, Evaluation of the EFSI; https://www.eib.org/en/publications/evaluation-of-the-efsi-2021 (2021d)

European Investment Bank: Stories, EU Financing for COVID-19 vaccine. https://www.eib.org/en/stories/eu-financing-for-covid-19-vaccine (2021e)

European Investment Bank: EIB Group Climate Bank Roadmap, First and foremost, this means constructing green energy infrastructure for solar and wind energy, power grids, storage facilities and Liquefied Natural Gas (LNG) terminals that can later also be used for green hydrogen. In https://www.eib.org/en/about/priorities/climate-action/cbr/index.htm (2021f)

European Investment Bank: Evaluation of the European Fund for Strategic Investment. Already in 2018, the regulation governing EFSI had been amended to include a soft target for climate finance −40% of all supported finance provided to larger enterprises. EFSI quickly surpassed that goal. Climate funding reached 41.6% of the relevant EFSI-supported finance by the first half of 2020. In https://www.eib.org/en/publications/evaluation-of-the-efsi-2021 (2021g)

Formentini, P.: The EIB, lecture, 26 November 1950, in the Bank of the EU-the EIB 1958–2008 (Bussière, Dumoulin, Willaert), EIB edition (2008)

Applying Benford's Law to Detect Fraud in the Insurance Industry—A Case Study from the Romanian Market

Mirela Păunescu, Elena-Mirela Nichita, Paula Lazăr, and Alexandra Frățilă (Adam)

Abstract Recently, one of the major Romanian insurers was declared insolvent by the market regulator as it was discovered to have fraudulently reported its financial statements. The impact on the insurance prices on the Romanian market was impressive. Significant funds were made available by the Romanian Government to stabilize the market and prevent linked bankruptcies. Over the years, the company was audited by reputable auditors, and yet nothing transpired about the massive fraud, although visible signs of trouble were not difficult to spot for the insurance company. As distressed businesses have stronger inducements to disguise their financial difficulties, they are more likely to manipulate their financials. After years of doubts, it was finally clear that the company manipulated its provisions and the available reserves. Benford's Law is an easy tool that signalizes possible manipulation of data, and it was used frequently to detect manipulation in financial reports. As such, we used Benford's Law to determine if the financial statements reported by the insurance company appeared to have been artificially manipulated. The results obtained from this investigation can be largely extrapolated to research related to other types of fraud in different industries.

Keywords Benford's Law · Insurance · Financial statements fraud · Manipulation of accounting data · Romania

1 Introduction

Over the last years, many financial scandals have shaken the world. Some of them went internationally; some only affected the local markets. In most cases, the accusations referred to manipulation of financial statements. After the scandals, many voices accused the responsible authorities and parties (may they be market regulators or auditors) of lack of diligence as it should have been easy to spot the misreporting of data in the financial reports prepared by the companies.

M. Păunescu (✉) · E.-M. Nichita · P. Lazăr · A. Frățilă (Adam)
Bucharest University of Economic Studies, Bucharest, Romania
e-mail: mirela.paunescu@cig.ase.ro

A. M. Dima and E. R. Danescu (eds.), *Fostering Recovery Through Metaverse Business Modelling*, Springer Proceedings in Business and Economics,
https://doi.org/10.1007/978-3-031-28255-3_4

From the most recent international scandals to this day, we can refer to the Wirecard's collapse, Wells Fargo, or Luckin Coffee. In the case of the Wirecard scandal, different allegations of accounting malpractices (such as inflating the profits) have accompanied the company over the years (Alderman and Schuetze 2020; Kelly 2020). Founded in 1999, Wirecard was listed on the Frankfurt Stock Exchange (Prime Standard segment) in 2005 and became one of the 30 most valuable German companies listed on the Frankfurt Stock Exchange in 2018 after alleged money laundering offenses committed by its senior executives. Meanwhile, the company entered international markets, such as the US and Asia markets, and expanded its activity in the banking industry. In 2019 and 2020, the scandal was at its peak as it was discovered that 1.9 billion euros, part of the cash accounts, never existed. After Germany's financial watchdog, BaFin, ordered an inquiry into Wirecard's accounting in 2019, in 2020, Wirecard filed for insolvency while the financial world was shocked and searched for those responsible for the loss of money in the case of millions of investors, partners, and employees. Plenty of accusations were made not only against the executives of Wirecard (most of them resigning and being prosecuted), but also against the employees working for BaFin and responsible for supervising the financial markets. Germany's financial regulator chief resigned as his institution failed to spot wrongdoing ahead of the collapse.

Almost a copy–paste example is the case of City Insurance. City Insurance is a Romanian insurance company that is currently declared bankrupt and is placed under special administration because of massive fraud. Founded in 1998, by 2020, the company had succeeded in becoming a leader in the Romanian insurance market. According to Romania's financial watchdog, the Financial Supervisory Authority (ASF), in 2021, 75% of the Motor Third Party Liability Insurance (MTPL) market was split between two insurance companies: City Insurance (approx. 43%) and Euroins (approx. 31%). In 2020, City Insurance had more than 24% of the gross written premiums paid on the general insurance policies. The fulminant rise of the company was possible as the result of its selling strategy: sell as many MTPL policies as possible at the lowest prices on the market (ASF 2021a). In 2021, even if it traded for 9 months as an insurance company, City Insurance occupied the third position on the market, with a share of 13% of the gross written premiums, while Euroins moved on the top of the list (ASF 2022).

The Romanian insurance market, although small, was attractive to the actors. The written premiums for 2021 were approximately 2.4 billion euros, 25% higher than in 2020. The market is highly concentrated, as, of the 27 authorized companies in 2021, ten of them covered 96% of the market (ASF 2022).

In 2021, the bankruptcy procedure started for City Insurance, and criminal investigations began. The bankruptcy led to significant increases in the insurance premiums (the prices even doubled in some cases) and massive amounts paid by Romanian authorities to cover the losses of those affected by the liquidation of the insurance. Everyone blamed everyone for allowing the situation to become as bad as it was and for not being able to detect the wrongdoings or stop them earlier.

Benford's Law, also known as the Newcomb–Benford Law, is an empirical observation, reported by Newcomb in 1881 and then by Benford in 1938. After a stagnation period (Mir and Ausloos 2018), the theory was revived by Hill (1995) and then by Nigrini (1996). He put it into use in the accounting and auditing field by trying to see if it is likely for the data to be manipulated. It did not take long for the theory to be applied in other different areas, as well.

On the one hand, non-compliance with the Benford's distribution is not a warrantee that the data is manipulated. This is a Type I error (Cleary and Thibodeau 2005; Barney and Schulzke 2016). On the other hand, manipulated data does not always fail to comply (Type II error). Nevertheless, the model is applied to accounting data, as previous research has shown that in several cases of accounting frauds, the warnings were present.

2 Problem Statement

2.1 Defining the Problem

As in the Wirecard case, over the years, many financial scandals accompanied the Romanian company. As an example, multiple fines and sanctions were imposed by ASF on the executives and the company itself. Nevertheless, the value of the punishments seemed inadequate, especially when comparing the potential wrongdoing of such a company on third parties. During the years 2014–2019, the fines were around 5,000 euros for the executives and did not exceed 12,000 euros for the company itself. In most cases, the fines and decisions of ASF were contested by City Insurance, and it took years in the Court of Justice for the involved parties to win or lose. That was part of a long-time teasing relationship in which each party accused the other of not acting fair. However, starting with 2021, the fines rocketed up to 200,000 euros for each member of the Board and 700,000 euros for the company itself (ASF 2021b).

In 2016, due to a surprise audit, ASF decided to impose a financial recovery procedure for City Insurance. The claimed reasons were the lack of funds, poor liquidity, belated payments for insured parties, and accounting irregularities with an impact on the overstatement of profit. Simply put, the company had no money to pay the potential damages and, like many other firms close to collapse (Rosner 2003), applied earning management techniques to disguise the truth (Ball 2019). A year later, the financial recovery procedure was completed. The company was free to expand on the market even if multiple notifications to the prosecutor's office were made by ASF and concerned the insurance company's activity. Nothing seemed to bother City Insurance, not even the increased complaints about overdue payments for damages.

In one of its statistical reports (ASF 2021c), ASF acknowledges that the two leaders in the market, City Insurance and Euroins, were also the leaders in terms of how many complaints were filled by their clients. The indicators showing the unique number of petitions and non-compliance information were almost 3 times and 6 times over the average on the market, raising important signals that the two companies were non-conforming with the standards.

Only in 2021 did the matter worsen. In June, the Board of City Insurance was suspended (ASF 2021b), and the company's management was conducted by FGA Romania (the Policyholders Guarantee Fund was settled and financed by the Romanian authorities). In September 2021, City Insurance had its license as an insurance company suspended, and it was decided that the bankruptcy process would begin, despite other international investors who showed their interest in buying the company. In February 2022, the insurance company's bankruptcy procedure was officially open.

According to the official statements (ASF 2021d), City Insurance failed to put into practice the recommendation made by ASF. Mainly, it did not increase the equity (not the share equity, nor the reserves) and funds to have enough resources to pay damages. It also used inappropriate evaluation methods for its provisions and indicators. Regarding the availability of funds, ASF stated that the company recorded and presented loans from its shareholders in its financial statements. However, the money reported in a bank account never existed. The fraud was massive, and it was not spotted over the years by the financial supervisor nor by the company's auditors required to state if the financial statements were free from material misstatements (both errors and frauds included here).

Retrospectively, one could say that the fraud was eased by the regulatory loopholes (Gabbioneta et al. 2013; Soltani 2014). The auditors were reputable 2nd tier audit companies (part of international networks, but not Big4 companies). All of them failed to detect the fraud, even though the audit opinions were qualified, and different emphasis of matters were included. They sent confirmation letters for the (false) bank account and received confirmations answers (from false representatives and not from the bank). As for the accounting irregularities, ASF claims that the methods used to estimate the technical provisions were inadequate and led to the overstatement of the profit. After the fraud was discovered, ASF suspended the right of the two audit firms to audit other insurance companies. All these actions were the response to the wrongdoing (Ball 2009), and were considered by the market a bit too late, and less than needed.

In the Romanian insurance market, the reverberating bankruptcy processes of important companies are not new. Only a few years earlier, in 2015 and 2016, two other insurance companies from the top 7 companies were liquidated.

To make matters worse, currently, another Romanian insurance company is suspected to be in a very similar position to City Insurance. Euroins, the corporation we refer to, is included in the top 5 insurance companies acting on the Romanian market, has inadequate prices, and has alarming financials. Plenty of sanctions have recently been imposed on this company and a financial recovery procedure has been implemented, as well. The history of the company is very similar to that of City Insurance. As such, from very small sanctions applied by ASF, in 2021 a fine of almost 1.2 million euro was imposed, followed shortly by others. Multiple cases were settled by different Courts of Justice, and ASF is currently closely monitoring the activity of Euroins. Some of the sanctions imposed allegedly refer to past errors identified in the financial statements of the company.

For the year 2021, despite the fact that the deadline for the financial statements was overdue, to this day Euroins did not publish its financial reports, nor the auditor's report. Previous audit reports were signed by 2nd tier companies (same as in case of City Insurance), were unqualified, but they had emphasis of a matter paragraphs drawing the attention on some of the financial difficulties the company faced.

Just like in case of City Insurance, the financial statements are published on the website in a format that makes it very difficult, if not impossible, to use them with software applications.

The bankruptcy of City Insurance harmed the Romanian insurance market. As a result, in the first months of 2022, the prices for MTPL increased, on average, from 50% up to 120%. The situation led to serious discussions about the need to change the current legislation. The Government analyzed the need for regulation to keep insurance fees flat and to not allow insurance companies to decide their own prices. Another bankruptcy of one of the leaders in terms of market share could impact even more significantly the Romanian insurance market.

2.2 *Theoretical Background*

The general principle of Benford's Law is that lower values for the first digits occur more often within data sets. The leading digits decrease in frequency from 1 (most often found) to 9 (least often used). Advanced analysis using Benford's Law involves the analysis of the combinations of digits, such as the first 2-digits, the last 2-digits, or the second digit. The probabilities of the occurrence of the digits can be calculated, and then the differences between the expected and actual frequency are computed.

$$P_i^B = log_{10}\left(\frac{i+1}{i}\right) \tag{1}$$

where P_i^B is the probability of finding i as the leading digit in a given number and i varies from 1 to 9 (the possible first digits).

Probabilities for the occurrence of the digits on the second place, considering the first digit can be calculated, and then differences between the expected and actual frequency are computed.

$$Prob(D_2 = d_2 | D_1 = d_1) = \frac{log_{10}(1 + \frac{1}{d_1 d_2})}{log_{10}(1 + \frac{1}{d_1})} \tag{2}$$

where $d_1 \in \{1, 2, \ldots, 9\}$, $d_2 \in \{0, 1, 2, \ldots, 9\}$, D_1 is the first digit, D_2 is the second digit.

Providing that the data is expected to comply with Benford's Law, conformity is tested to verify possible irregularities. A weak fit is a warning that there is a high risk that the data contains anomalies (such as duplications, errors, or other abnormalities).

Previous literature on Benford's Law varies in many domains. As such, the model was applied in the area of accounting data manipulation (Durtschi et al. 2004; Grammatikos and Papanikolau 2021), tax (Nigrini 1996; Demir and Javorcik 2020), insurance fraud (Petucci 2005; Park et al. 2016), financial statements of listed companies (Nguyen et al. 2022; Jianu and Jianu 2021), finding possible irregularities for COVID-19 reports (Kolias 2022; Morrilas-Jurado et al. 2021) or for macro-economic reported data (Rauch et al. 2011), and others. A long list of articles is to be found on Mr. Nigrini's website (Nigrini 2022), dedicated to Benford's Law. Some of the scholars mentioned applied the model also on data about which regulators or other stakeholders reported already errors or anomalies (Rauch et al. 2011; Nigrini 2005).

Though recent research seems abundant on the Benford's Law topic, we contribute to the body of literature by using the financial data of companies from the Romanian insurance market. We used as a pretext a recent bankruptcy case above, where there is enough information on accounting data manipulation. We applied the model to demonstrate that the companies' financials should have been a vital clue that possible irregularities are likely.

3 Research Question

In the remaining part of this article, we investigate if the headlines of the financial reports submitted by City Insurance throughout 2014–2020 comply with Bedford's Law. According to the literature, no compliance with the model could be a sign of data manipulation.

To make our research more meaningful, we analyzed the data from the insurance industry throughout 2016–2020 to see if the financial statement extracts have any particularities and how City Insurance fits into the picture.

Finally, we ran the same model for Euroins, which is said to be in an analogous condition to that of City Insurance. The mentioned corporation has a similar pricing policy; it is one of the top insurance companies in Romania; it had similar sanctions imposed during the years by the market regulator and has some bad financials reported over the past years.

As the data from the financial statements were just extracts and the accusation of accounting data manipulation referred to both the results and the technical information that should have been prepared, we used the solvency reports prepared by the two companies to see if the numbers fit the Bedford Law.

Our hypotheses are as follows:

H1: *The financial data reported by the Romanian insurance companies conform to Benford's Law.*

H2: *The financial data reported by the Romanian Companies City Insurance and Euroins do not conform to Benford's Law.*

H3: *The data reported in the solvency reports of City Insurance and Euroins do not conform to Benford's Law.*

The reason for our expectation is that the data to which we applied the Benford's Law model meet all the requirements needed for conformity, namely the data is not assigned manually (it is random), there is no fixed minimum, and no fixed maximum amount. We collected over 4,600 inputs in case of the insurance industry and over 170 for the financial data reported by City Insurance. The condition that there are more small numbers than large numbers in the population is not valid for the financial statement extracts. However, to this point, applying Bedford Law to the data extracted from the financial statements was not rejected as being unfit by the scholars (see, for example, other studies such as Amiram et al. (2015) or Herteliu et al. (2021). The condition is valid for the solvency reports used.

Amiram et al. (2015) constructed a composite, firm-year measure of financial statement irregularities based on the divergence between the observed first digit's distribution in annual financial statements and the theoretical Benford distribution. They found that, at the aggregate level, the numbers of the financial statements are consistent with Benford's Law in all industries and years analyzed, while approximately 84% of the years of individual firms are consistent with the Law. Herteliu et al. (2021) analyzed the compliance with Benford's Laws of financial statements of Romanian companies in the hospitality industry. They found that, despite the high level of tax evasion doubled by the propensity to use cash in the hospitality industry, all samples analyzed conformed to Benford's Laws, though the chi-square statistic was very close to the critical value.

4 Methodology

We analyzed the financial statements of the Romanian insurance companies for the period 2016–2020. Our data are collected from the official sites of the Romanian tax authorities, and they represent extracts from the financial statements of the Romanian companies authorized as such by the Romanian regulatory body, ASF. The yearly number of authorized insurance companies does not exceed 50 per year.

We curated the data and made some adjustments, mainly consisting of removing duplicates (for example, in the case of totals that were equal to subtotals, removing dormant companies, or adjusting for other cases considered outliers). Next, we used Excel software to apply the model, draw the graphs for the visual analysis, and obtain the statistics.

Although we knew that the financial statements of at least some financial statements were manipulated, we did not exclude the company from the industry to have enough observations. Also, only one company should not significantly impact the industry results.

We also applied Benford's Law in the case of the financial data published by City Insurance from 2014 to 2020. As the data extracted from the company's financials were less complex, we extended the analysis period by two years compared to the analysis we conducted for the industry. We also applied Benford's Law in case of Euroins suspected to be on the edge of bankruptcy for the same period.

Even if the chi-square test was traditionally used to confirm the Benford model, other tests were developed more recently (Nigrini 2012; Kossovsky 2021). Among these tests are the Z-statistic and the Mean Absolute Deviation (MAD), which we used, together with the chi-square test, to decide the conformity of our data with Benford's Law.

The chi-square test was used in the Bedford's Law context to show if the observed frequency is significantly different from the expected frequency. A low value implies that the data conforms to Bedford's Law, while a value higher than the critical one implies that the data does not conform to Bedford's Law.

$$\chi_c^2 = \sum_{i=1}^{k} (\frac{(Oi - Ei)^2}{Ei} \tag{3}$$

where c denotes the degrees of freedom, O denotes the observed values, and E denotes the expected values.

The Z-statistic formula, which considers the absolute magnitude of the difference, the size of the data set, and the expected proportion, is used to determine whether two population means are different when the variances are known and the sample size is large.

$$Z = \frac{(\overline{x} - \mu)}{\frac{\sigma}{\sqrt{n}}} \tag{4}$$

where $\bar{x}$ is the mean of sample, μ is the mean of population, σ is the standard deviation of population, and n is the number of observations.

If Z-stats is higher than the critical value of 1.96 at a 95% confidence level, that could be a sign of data manipulation (or accounting fraud in case the data represents a company's financials). As Nigrini and Miller (2008) highlighted, the Z-statistic test indicates many significant differences for large datasets even if the differences are minor, so it is less recommended for use with real data than, for example, the MAD presented above.

The Mean Absolute Deviation test is considered by Nigrini (2012) one of the best tests to confirm whether the actual proportion of a digit differs significantly from the expectation of Benford's Law. The MAD overcomes some difficulties revealed in the case of the Z-statistic test, among the number of records (expected to be high for the Z-test).

$$MAD = \frac{\sum_{i=1}^{k} |Ai - Ei|)}{k} \tag{5}$$

where k represents the number of digits, A denotes the actual proportion, and E the expected proportion.

As a rule, the higher the MAD, the larger the average difference. However, there are no objective, critical scores for decision-making (Nigrini 2012). On the other

Table 1 Critical scores and ranges for testing conformity against Benford's Law

Range for	Close	Acceptable	Marginally acceptable	Non-conformity
First Digit	0.000 to 0.006	0.006 to 0.012	0.012 to 0.015	Above 0.015
Second Digits	0.000 to 0.008	0.008 to 0.010	0.010 to 0.012	Above 0.012
First Two Digits	0.0000 to 0.0012	0.0012 to 0.0018	0.0018 to 0.0022	Above 0.0022

Source Nigrini (2012)

hand, Drake and Nigrini (2000) published some critical scores and ranges for testing conformity against Benford's Law (Table 1).

5 Results

As we can see in Fig. 1, the financial statement extracts for the insurance industry fit almost perfectly in terms of both the first and second digits. City Insurance, on the other hand, seems to be less compliant with the Benford's Law, especially when the second digit is analyzed.

For the next step we computed the MAD, Z-statistic, and chi-square. The results are summarized in Table 2.

The first Hypothesis is confirmed, as both the MAD and chi-square show close conformity with Benford's Law (which is in line with the visual observation based on the graphs presented in Fig. 1). The conformity is close for the first and second digits, while for the first two digits, the MAD shows good conformity, while the chi-square test shows that the Null Hypothesis (Benford's Law describes the data) is rejected. Based on the Z-statistic, only five combinations of the first two digits present a Z-stat higher than 1.96 (Table 3).

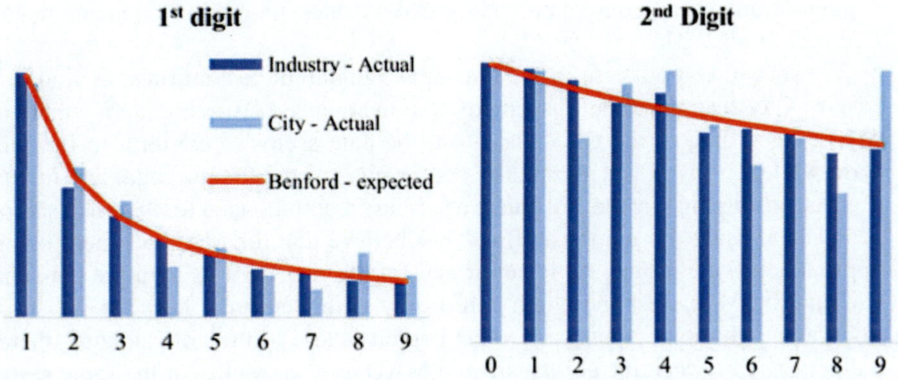

Fig. 1 Fitting analysis among insurance industry and City Insurance. *Source* Authors own projection

Table 2 Results

Indicator	First digit	Second digit	First two digits
Degrees of freedom	8	9	89
Critical value (significance level 0.05)	15.51	16.92	112.02
Result for the insurance industry			
Chi-square	15.191	8.38	114.82
MAD	0.00561	0.00357	0.00129
No. of observations	4,629	4,629	4,595
Result for the financial statements extracts of City Insurance			
Chi-square	8.212	5.068	156.650
MAD	0.01743	0.01349	0.00766
No. of observations	171	171	171
Result for the financial statements extracts of Euroins			
Chi-square	17.161	16.881	120.567
MAD	0.02744	0.02406	0.00696
No. of observations	164	164	164
Result for the solvency report of City Insurance			
Chi-square	8.979	17.424	126.727
MAD	0.00795	0.01369	0.00376
No. of observations	647	647	642
Result for the solvency report of Euroins			
Chi-square	26.391356	25.063422	204.21
MAD	0.01153	0.01747	0.00379
No. of observations	1,123	1,123	1053

Source Authors own calculation

Our findings are consistent with previous ones in other Romanian markets (Herteliu et al. 2021).

The second Hypothesis, for the first and second digit, is confirmed as well in the case of City Insurance, but here there is a divergence between the chi-square and MAD. According to the Chi-square test, the data seems to conform to Benford's Law, while the MAD test shows non-conformity for the first, second, and first two digits. Considering that the chi-square test is less recommended for the small samples of data and using the graphs in Fig. 1, we believe that the MAD test here is more appropriate. For Euroins, H_2 is confirmed for the first digit as both the chi-square test and the MAD test show non-conformity with Benford's law. For the second digit, although the computed chi value is pretty close to the critical value, there is a divergence between the chi-square and MAD tests, as well. For the same reasons presented above, we believe that the MAD test here is more appropriate here. For the first two digits, the second Hypothesis holds true, for both companies (Tables 4 and 5).

Table 3 Results for the insurance industry

Digit	First digit—Actual (%)	First digit—Benford's (%)	Z-stat	Second digit—Actual (%)	Second digit—Benford's (%)	Z-stat
0				12.29	11.97	0.6566
1	31.54	30.10	2.1158	11.75	11.39	0.7543
2	16.22	17.61	2.4550	11.28	10.88	0.8388
3	12.70	12.49	0.4069	10.30	10.43	0.2617
4	9.92	9.69	0.4920	10.74	10.03	1.5737
5	8.01	7.92	0.2164	9.03	9.67	1.4439
6	6.09	6.70	1.6120	9.20	9.34	0.2884
7	6.07	5.80	0.7587	8.99	9.04	0.0887
8	4.58	5.12	1.6194	8.12	8.76	1.5007
9	4.86	4.58	0.8917	8.30	8.50	0.4725
	Chi-square	15.191		Chi-square	8.38	
	MAD	0.00561		MAD	0.00357	

Source Authors own calculation

In the case of the solvency report published by City Insurance, the conformity is proved only for the first digit (acceptable conformity based on MAD). For the second digit and the first two, both the chi-square and the MAD test show the non-conformity of the data with Benford's Law, which enforces the belief that the data is likely to contain irregularities. Euroins, based on both the chi-square and the MAD tests, presents higher risks of abnormalities (Table 2).

6 Conclusions

Manipulation of data, mainly financial fraud, does not happen overnight. Its detection is a long, delicate, and crafty process and involves the concurrence of many agents, some internal—like the internal auditors or the whistle blowers—some external—auditors or market supervisors. Accounting frauds discovery before the wrongdoing becomes too much to handle is an enduring goal for the public (investors, users of information) and market regulators. Over the years, Benford's Law model was used to spot possible irregularities not only in the financial data, but also for other data sets. Although the manipulation of data is not guaranteed, a non-conformity with the model should make stakeholders aware that further investigation may be needed to assess the accuracy of the financial statements.

Our findings, consistent with previous research conducted in other industries or markets (Amiram et al. 2015; Herteliu et al. 2021; Jianu and Jianu 2021; Istrate 2019), show that, for the insurance industry, the financial reports of Romanian insurance

Table 4 Results for the financial statements extracts of City Insurance and Euroins

Digit	First digit—Benford's (%)	City first digit—Actual (%)	Euroins first digit—Actual (%)	Second digit—Benford's (%)	City second digit—Actual (%)	Euroins second digit—Actual (%)
0				0.120	0.129	0.128
1	0.301	0.292	0.274	0.114	0.117	0.183
2	0.176	0.187	0.226	0.109	0.088	0.104
3	0.125	0.146	0.037	0.104	0.111	0.146
4	0.097	0.064	0.104	0.100	0.117	0.079
5	0.079	0.088	0.091	0.097	0.094	0.098
6	0.067	0.053	0.091	0.093	0.076	0.091
7	0.058	0.035	0.085	0.090	0.088	0.067
8	0.051	0.082	0.043	0.088	0.064	0.037
9	0.046	0.053	0.049	0.085	0.117	0.067
	Chi-square	8.212	17.161	Chi-square	5.068	16.881
	MAD	0.01743	0.02744	MAD	0.01349	0.02406

Source Authors own calculation

Table 5 Results for the Solvency report of City Insurance and Euroins

Digit	First digit—Benford's (%)	City first digit—Actual (%)	Euroins first digit—Actual (%)	Second digit—Benford's (%)	City second digit—Actual (%)	Euroins second digit—Actual (%)
0				0.120	0.110	0.179
1	0.301	0.301	0.306	0.114	0.124	0.106
2	0.176	0.187	0.167	0.109	0.125	0.118
3	0.125	0.124	0.111	0.104	0.110	0.117
4	0.097	0.108	0.108	0.100	0.079	0.103
5	0.079	0.053	0.062	0.097	0.076	0.070
6	0.067	0.077	0.067	0.093	0.080	0.066
7	0.058	0.059	0.046	0.090	0.122	0.093
8	0.051	0.043	0.065	0.088	0.093	0.077
9	0.046	0.048	0.068	0.085	0.082	0.069
	Chi-square	9.862	26.391	Chi-square	13.391	25.063
	MAD	0.00795	0.01153	MAD	0.01369	0.01747

Source Authors own calculation

companies are consistent with the Benford's Law. On the other hand, for the two companies subject to our case study (one already declared bankrupt and accused of a massive accounting fraud, the other under scrutiny by the Romanian financial watchdog), our research shows a lack of conformity with Benford's Law, which is a sign that there is a high risk that the data contains anomalies. Previous studies focused on analyzing individual financial statements of different companies, some of them already proven to be involved in frauds (Nigrini 2005; Rauch et al. 2011), others not to that moment.

One possible drawback of our study derives from the data used. As such, previous research shows that subsets of non-manipulated data may deviate significantly from the Benford's distribution (Diekmann and Jann 2010). Another one resides, as scholars previously pointed (Barney and Schultzke 2016; Nigrini 2017; Druică 2018), that conformity or non-conformity with Benford Law may depend on the sample size and on the "usual level of conformity." If, for the industry, we had a large enough set of data, in case of the individual companies analyzed, the information from the financial statements was scarce. Finally, we acknowledge the limitation in respect to the fact that we manually manipulated data from the solvency reports published by the insurance companies on their websites which allows for human errors.

Future research in the field may refer to applying the model to the insurance industry in other countries or even to other industries, such as banking. Also, monitoring the companies analyzed in this research may confirm the robustness of the model used. Not less important, when the data is available, applying the Benford's Law model to specific elements of the financial statements is even more useful, as it can indicate which of the items presented in the financial statements are more prone to irregularities.

As a final conclusion, we contribute to the body of literature by using financial statements extracts from companies in the Romanian insurance market and showing the conformity with the Benford's Law, and by showing non-conformity with the model of one company currently investigated for accounting manipulation. Understanding of Benford's law is essential because it allows forensic investigators to design tests that can effectively detect fraud. Benford's law tests pinpoint nonconformities between actual and expected frequencies that should be investigated for potential fraud.

References

Alderman, L., Schuetze, C.Z.F.: In a German Tech Giant's Fall, Charges of Lies, Spies and Missing Billions. The New York Times, 26 June 2020, Available at: https://www.nytimes.com/2020/06/26/business/wirecard-collapse-markus-braun.html

Amiram, D., Bozanic, Z., Rouen, E.: Financial statement errors: evidence from the distributional properties of financial statement numbers. Rev. Account Stud **20**, 1540–1593 (2015)

Ball, R.: Market and political/regulatory perspectives on the recent accounting scandals. J. Account. Res. **47**(2), 277–323 (2009)

Barney, B., Schulzke, K.: Moderating "'cry wolf'" events with excess MAD on Benford's Law research and practice. J. Forensic Account. Res. **1**(1), A66–A90 (2016). https://doi.org/10.2308/jfar-51622

Cleary, R., Thibodeau, J. C.: Applying digital analysis using Benford's law to detect fraud: the dangers of type I errors. Auditing: J. Pract. Theory **24**(1), 77–81 (2005)

Demir, B., Javorcik, B.: Trade policy changes, tax evasion and Benford's Law. J. Develop. Econ. **144** (2020)

Diekmann, A., Jann, B.: Benford's law and fraud detection: facts and legends. German Econ. Rev. **11**(3), 397–401 (2010)

Drake, P., Nigrini, M.: Computer assisted analytical procedures using Benford's Law. J. Account. Educ. **18**, 127–146 (2000)

Druică, E., Oancea, B., Vâlsan, C.: Benford's law and the limits of digit analysis. Int. J. Account. Inf. Syst. https://doi.org/10.1016/j.accinf.2018.09.004 (2018)

Durtschi, C., Hillison, W., Pacini, C.: The effective use of Benford's Law to assist in detecting fraud in accounting data. J. Forensic Account. **5**(1), 17–34 (2004)

Gabbioneta, C., Greenwood, R., Mazzola, P., Minoja, M.: The influence of the institutional context on corporate illegality. Acc. Organ. Soc. **38**(6–7), 484–504 (2013)

Grammatikos, T., Papanikolaou, N.I.: Applying Benford's Law to detect accounting data manipulation in the banking industry. J. Financial Serv. Res. **59**(1), 115–142 (2021)

Herteliu, C., Jianu, I., Dragan, I.M., Apostu, S., Luchian, I.: Testing Benford's Laws (non) conformity within disclosed companies' financial statements among hospitality industry in Romania. Phys. A Stat. Mech. Its Appl. **582** (2021)

Hill, T.P.: A statistical derivation of significant digit Law. Stat. Sci. **10**, 354–363 (1995)

Istrate, C.: Detecting earnings management using Benford's Law: the case of Romanian listed companies. J. Account. Manag. Inf. Syst. **2019**(18), 198–223 (2019)

Jianu, I., Jianu, I.: Reliability of Financial Information from the Perspective of Benford's Law. Entropy **23**(5), 557 (2021)

Kelly, J.: Fraud Allegations Rock Tech Company Wirecard—Billionaire CEO Earned Millions. 22 June 2020, Forbes, available at https://www.forbes.com/sites/jackkelly/2020/06/22/fraud-allegations-rock-tech-company-wirecard-billionaire-ceo-earned-millions/?sh=442e148413ff

Kolias, P.: Applying Benford's Law to COVID-19 data: the case of the European Union. J. Public Health (2022)

Kossovsky, A.E.: On the mistaken use of the chi-square test in Benford's Law. Stats **4**(2), 419–453 (2021)

Mir, T.A., Ausloos, M.: Benford's Laws: a sleeping beauty sleeping in the dirty pages of logarithmic tables. J. Assoc. Inf. Sci. Technol. **69**(3), 349–358 (2018)

Morillas-Jurado, F.G., Caballer-Tarazona, M., Caballer-Tarazona, V.: Applying Benford's Law to monitor death registration data: a management tool for the COVID-19 Pandemic. Mathematics **10**(1), 46 (2021)

Nigrini, M.: A taxpayer compliance application of Benford's Law. J. Amer. Taxation Assoc. Sarasota **18**(1), 72–90 (1996)

Nigrini, M.J.: An assessment of the change in the incidence of earnings management around the Enron-Andersen episode. Rev. Acc. Financ. **4**(1), 92–110 (2005)

Nigrini, M.: Benford's Law: Applications for Forensic Accounting, Auditing, and Fraud Detection. Wiley, ISBN: 978-1-118-15285-0 (2012)

Nigrini, M. J.: Audit sampling using Benford's Law: a review of the literature with some new perspectives. J. Emerg. Tech. Account. **14**(2), 29–46 (2017)

Nigrini, M.: The Benford Online Bibliography, Available at: https://www.benfordonline.net/list/chronological (2022)

Nguyen, T.T., Duong, C.M., Nguyen, N.T.M.: Is conditional conservatism a source of deviations of financial statements from Benford's Law? J. Appl. Account. Res. (2022)

Park, J.A., Kim, M., Yoon, S.: Evaluation of large-scale data to detect irregularity in payment for medical services. Methods Inf. Med. **55**(03), 284–291 (2016)

Petucci, S.D.: Benford's Law: can it be used to detect irregularities in first party automobile insurance claims? J. Econ. Crime Manag. **3**(1), 1–35 (2005)

Rauch, B., Göttsche, M., Engel, S., Brähler, G.: Fact and fiction in EU-governmental economic data. German Econ. Rev. **12**(3), 243–255 (2011)

Rosner, R.L.: Earnings manipulation in failing firms. Contemp. Account. Res. **20**(2), 361–408 (2003)

Soltani, B.: The anatomy of corporate fraud: a comparative analysis of high profile American and European corporate scandals. J. Bus. Ethics **120**(2), 251–274 (2014)

The Financial Supervisory Authority (ASF): Inform note, Available at: https://asfromania.ro/uploads/articole/attachments/6061d1346b302823938474.pdf (2021a)

The Financial Supervisory Authority (ASF): Inform note, Available at: https://asfromania.ro/ro/a/2191/comunicat-de-pres%C4%83 (2021b)

The Financial Supervisory Authority (ASF): Statistical report, Available at: https://asfromania.ro/uploads/articole/attachments/6076d84132079929466644.pdf (2021c)

The Financial Supervisory Authority (ASF): DECIZIE nr. 1.148 din 17 septembrie 2021, Available at: https://legislatie.just.ro/Public/DetaliiDocument/246668 (2021d)

The Financial Supervisory Authority (ASF): Statistical report, available at: https://asfromania.ro/uploads/articole/attachments/625d3c3d7a4fa967149359.pdf (2022)

Individual Attitudes and Social Norms as Determinants of the Electric Vehicle Purchase

Xose Picatoste, Isabel Novo-Corti, Diana Mihaela Tirca, and Matías Membiela-Pollán

Abstract Within the framework of sustainable development and the reduction of the use of passenger cars as a mechanism for the preservation of the environment and the fulfilment of the Sustainable Development Goals, this paper analyses the purchase intention of electric vehicles according to the postulates of the Theory of Reasoned Action and the advances of other previous research, using structural equation methodology, it is found that purchase intentions are determined by attitudes and perceived control. In contrast, social norms are not found to be significant. This work contributes to research in this field because its results indicate that personal reasons outweigh social norms and can therefore overcome cultural and value differences in different societies so that individual environmental awareness would prevail even in countries less committed to ecological sustainability.

Keywords Sustainable development · Electric cars · Environment · Attitudes · Consumption

1 Introduction

The sustainable development proposed by the 2030 Agenda, according to the postulates of the United Nations (United Nations 2015), sets the path for future development to improve the well-being of people in the present without compromising that of future generations and the maintenance of the planet. Countries have overwhelmingly endorsed these proposals at the global level, and the European Union (EU) has been particularly noteworthy in each of the 17 proposed goals, especially concerning the preservation of the environment. As established in the Paris agreement (United

X. Picatoste (✉) · I. Novo-Corti · M. Membiela-Pollán
University of A Coruna, A Coruña, Spain
e-mail: j.pnovo@udc.es

D. M. Tirca
Constantin Brancusi University, Targu-Jiu, Romania

A. M. Dima and E. R. Danescu (eds.), *Fostering Recovery Through Metaverse Business Modelling*, Springer Proceedings in Business and Economics,
https://doi.org/10.1007/978-3-031-28255-3_5

Nations 2015), the EU's commitment to climate change aims to reduce CO_2 emissions in general. Regarding car emissions, a 37.5% reduction has been proposed for 2030. Still, to achieve this objective, a social commitment is required, beyond political intentions, so that it is citizens who must assume the necessary environmental awareness to change their transport habits, purchase new, less polluting vehicles, etc. (Richardson et al. 2015), hence, the importance of consumer attitudes towards new electric cars, the implementation of which is essential to achieve the proposed goal.

Many studies have been devoted to this issue in different areas of world geography and with different approaches. In terms of economic, cultural, and social levels, each country's characteristics is essential in this aspect and can condition the results. Social norms, personal attitudes, and the ability to understand, control, and engage with the situation are variables that come into play and must be considered. For this reason, in the work proposed here, a study of the situation in Spain is carried out, using the Theory of Reasoned Action as a methodological reference model and a previous study (Afroz et al. 2015) carried out in Malaysia as a starting point. The justification of the theoretical framework of reference proposed by the Theory of Planned Behaviour (Ajzen 1985, 1991; Schifter and Ajzen 1985) is supported by numerous studies in the fields of sociology, economics, and education, among others. Furthermore, in the reference work, the positions of the youngest sector of the population are studied, which is particularly interesting because they are precisely those who will be responsible for committing themselves to sustainability for the longest time and who should continue with the trend of more significant social commitment to sustainable development that has already been observed (Agnisarman et al. 2018).

This article is structured as follows: after this brief introduction, a review of the relevant academic literature is presented, followed by the definition of the theoretical framework and explanation of the objectives and establishment of the working hypotheses, followed by an explanation of the methodology applied. The final part of the paper shows the results obtained and synthesises the main conclusions drawn.

2 Individual Behaviour, Commitment to the Environment, and the Purchase of Electric Vehicles

Consumer behaviour is a crucial point for the adoption of sustainable technologies that are environmentally friendly and substantially influence the decision to purchase an electric vehicle (Wang et al. 2016), since agents make their decisions by assessing the factors that lead them to maximise utility or their satisfaction, through rational behaviour in which resource savings form part of the factors that increase happiness, as well as respect for the environment, and could justify the decision to devote more economic resources to the purchase of these vehicles, although the literature indicates that the lower this cost, the greater the probability of purchasing this type of goods (Diekmann and Preisendörfer 1998).

Considering all of the above, the purchase decision is determined by attitudes (Vermeir and Verbeke 2006), social norms, and perceived control or ability to perform the proposed action. Together, these elements act as explanations of behaviour. The model to be studied would constitute the explanatory variables and the variable to be explained, or the dependent variable would be the purchase intention. Naturally, although individuals are rational and take these aspects into account, automatic mechanisms may decide without linear reasoning (Ajzen and Fishbein 2000).

In this sense, the study by Afroz et al. (2015) on consumer purchase intention towards environmentally friendly vehicles, through empirical research, has been carried out for consumers of Malaysia. The work presented here constitutes an autonomous and independent piece of research, in which a theoretical model is proposed, based on the Theory of Planned Behaviour (Ajzen 1991), and primary data is obtained to contrast it, which allows valuable results to be brought in itself, for the case study, which refers to Spain. However, it has been considered that the value of this work can be increased by relating it to that already referenced by Afroz et al. (2015), given that this presents not only the possibility of extending the results and conclusions to a more extensive global context than to a single country, because the same questionnaire that has been proposed in that work (and which is provided in the annexe) has been followed, but also because, in addition, there is the possibility of comparing behaviours in very different regions: Asia and Europe. The novelty of this work is the extension of an empirical study to a different regional area in a different context and time, with the aim of proving the consistency of the first results over time and territories. It means a significant step forward since it helps generalise attitudes, behaviours, and intentions, considering the social norms at a specific moment, explicitly considering the cultural distance between both countries analysed in the first and second studies.

According to the Theory of Planned Behaviour, the proposed theoretical model is shown in Graph 1, and the causal relationship is shown in Eq. 1.

This model explains that each of the latent variables (represented in circles) is constructed by three explanatory variables, which come from the questionnaire and are directly observable through the results of the survey. The curved arrows assess the possible correlations between the latent variables (constructed), and the straight arrows show the causal relationships which in this model relate the three variables identified by Ajzen (attitude, social norm, and perceived control) as explanatory of purchase intention (PI). The model includes other additional variables such as, on the one hand, planned behaviour (PB), a direct consequence of purchase intention and, on the other hand, the division of attitudes into two sections that determine them (internal and external).

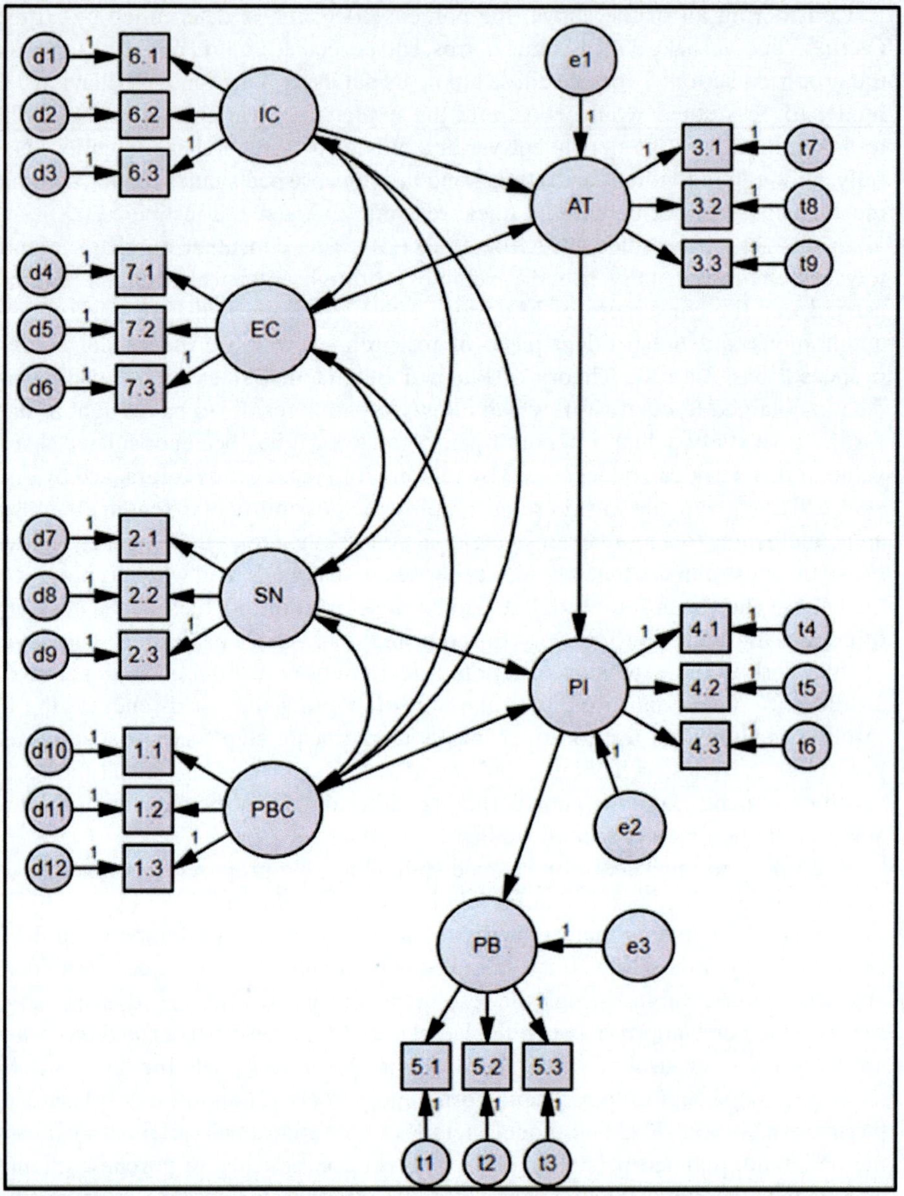

Fig. 1 Model. *Source* own elaboration

The proof hypotheses are represented for arrows from AT, SN, PBC to PI, and PB. The other causal relationships will also be analysed but are not at the core of this research (Fig. 1).

$$y_i = \beta_0 + \beta_1 x_{1i} + \beta_2 x_{2i} + \beta_3 x_{3i} + \varepsilon_i \quad (1)$$

where:

$y_i = Purchase\,intention\,of\,electric\,cars$ (PI)
$x_1 = Attitude$ (AT)
$x_2 = Social\,Norms$ (SN)
$x_3 = Perceived\,Control$ (PBC).

3 Research Questions and Aims of the Research

The research questions which give the line for the hypothesis to contrast are the following:

1. Does personal attitude influence the intention of purchasing an electric car?
2. Do social norms influence the intention of purchasing an electric car?
3. Does perceived control influence the intention of purchasing an electric car?
4. Are there differences in the variables motivating the purchasing decision maintained over time and space?

The hypotheses to test, formulated for Spain young consumers, are:

H1: Personal attitude influences the intention of purchasing an electric car.
H2: Social norms influence the intention of purchasing an electric car.
H3: Perceived control influences the intention of purchasing an electric car.
H4: There are differences in the variables motivating the purchasing decision maintained over time and space.

4 Research Methods

This paper involves working with variables that will be constructed based on a questionnaire carried out to obtain primary data. These variables are not directly observable, so it is necessary to build them, hence the convenience of using the factor analysis methodology. On the other hand, to answer the research questions, causality needs to be demonstrated; therefore, the regression analysis was used.

All this justifies the use of structural equations modelling (SEM) as the best research method, which combines both methodologies and makes it possible to visualise the relationships between the variables and their construction through a path diagram. Considering that this work is based on another previously carried out, the method chosen is confirmatory analysis. The statistical programme used is IBM's SSPS, version 27, combined with the AMOS programme.

The sample was obtained by the snowball procedure among Spanish people during 2019, and 1,496 valid responses were collected. This procedure is commonly accepted in social sciences due to the amplitude of the sample achieved (Goodman 1961; Voicu and Babonea 2011). The questionnaire was based on some affirmations that the respondents should classify according to a 5-point Likert scale ranging from 1 (total disagreement), to 5 (total agreement).

One of the strengths of this work is the use of a questionnaire previously validated by the initial study carried out by Alforz et al. in 2015, which is provided in the annex.

5 Findings

The main findings of this research point to the importance of two of the three variables in explaining purchasing intention: the attitude and the perceived control, but the social norm has not shown statistical significance (p-value = 0.699).

Moreover, the relationships among the attitude and its two components have also been proven as statistically significant. The significance of the influence of purchasing intention and planned behaviour has also been proven.

The adjusted R-squared value to explain the latter variable (planned behaviour regarding the purchase of electric cars) is 0.463, so this model can explain 46.3% of such behaviour. The adjusted R-squared takes the value of 0.260, indicating that this model could anticipate 26% of the purchase intention. The path diagram for results achieved is shown in the path diagram in Graph 2 and in Eq. 2.

$$y_i = 0.406x_{1i} - 0.017x_{2i} + 0.170x_{3i} \tag{2}$$

The results at this point indicate that the social norm is not significant, whilst the other constructs are highly significant for explaining purchasing intention and planed behaviour (Fig. 2 and Table 1).

The contrast of the hypothesis indicates that only H2 (social norms influence the intention of purchasing an electric car) must be rejected. The other hypothesis, H1 (personal attitude influences the intention of purchasing an electric car) and H3 (perceived control influences the intention of purchasing an electric car), should be accepted. Then, the response to the proposed research questions is clear.

Concerning H4 (there are differences in the variables motivating the purchasing decision maintained over time and space), initially it could be accepted, since the behaviour is similar and the only construct not significant is precisely the social norm, strictly related to values and culture of the specific country.

6 Discussion

The practical implications of this research emerge from its results, the topic analysed, and the sample's nature. Regarding the results, which have already been commented on, it has been shown that personal attitude is essential to promote the use of electric vehicles among young people, who are the ones who constitute the most significant part of the potential market of vehicle buyers in the coming years. The path

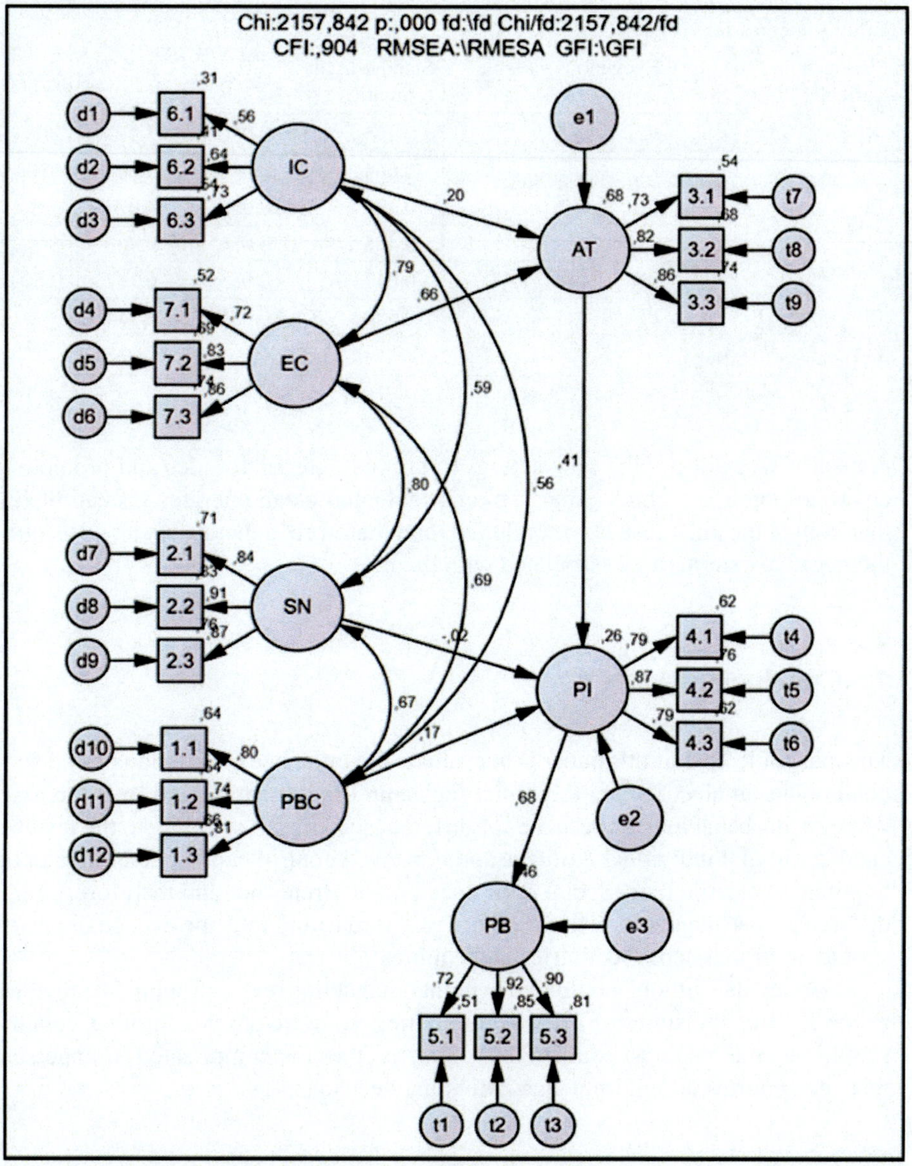

Fig. 2 Results. *Source* own elaboration

to sustainable transport passes through substituting fuel vehicles towards those with cleaner energy, such as electricity. This point has been made clear in the declarations of national and international institutions and in the different efforts to support the population in the transition towards the use of "green energies". In this sense, knowledge of the intentions and attitudes of the people that constitutes the majority of the potential market of car buyers provides valuable information for public policy

Table 1 Regression weights

Endogenous variable		Exogenous variable	Standardised estimates	S.E	C.R	P
AT	<–	IC	0.195	0.050	3.973	***
AT	<–	EC	0.664	0.045	13.607	***
PI	<–	PBC	0.170	0.059	4.074	***
	<–	AT	0.406	0.056	9.968	***
	<–	SN	−0.017	0.055	−0.387	0.699
PB	<–	PI	0.680	0.025	24.144	***

*** p-value < 0.001
Source own elaboration

managers when designing new actions to promote green attitudes and promote the desire to purchase vehicles that use renewable and clean energies instead of fuels that pollute the air, cause noise pollution, and therefore, generate social costs due to the negative externalities associated with them.

7 Conclusions

The main objective of this paper is to evaluate the influence of individuals and social positioning on electric cars to predict their purchase intention and to try to assess whether this behaviour is the same for different societies. According to the results, it can be said that individual attitudes and perceived control can explain the intention to purchase electric cars. Social norms seem to be irrelevant, and therefore, cultural differences between countries would not play a role, and thus the expected outcome should be similar across countries and cultures.

However, the authors would like to point out that this research should be reviewed in the light of the study of other communities, so more studies in other countries should be undertaken to confirm this point, as it seems complicated to understand that social norms do not influence individual decisions.

Annex

Questionnaire and information about unobservable variables:

Items
Perceived behavioural control (PBC) (normed $\chi2 = 1.536$, CFI = 0.995, RMSEA = 0.052)
Respectfulness and politeness is important to me
Self-control such as being restrained and self-disciplined is important to me
A clean and tidy environment is important to me
For the achievement of my life, being hardworking and aspiring is important to me
Subjective norms (SNs) (normed $\chi2 = 1.19$, CFI = 0.999, RMSEA = 0.030)
The conventional car can create air pollution
The conventional car can create smog in large cities
The conventional car produce greenhouse gases such CO_2 and NO_2 that contribute to global warming and climate change
Attitudes towards EVs (ATT) (normed $\chi2 = 2.246$, CFI = 0.991, RMSEA = 0.079)
Environmentally friendly car is a fuel-efficient car. So, it can reduce CO_2 emission
Environmentally friendly car can decrease the use of petroleum
Environmentally friendly car can reduce the greenhouse gas emission
Purchase intention (PI) (normed $\chi2 = 1.335$, CFI = 0.999, RMSEA = 0.041)
I would buy an environmentally friendly car if the quality is lower than a conventional car
I would buy an environmentally friendly car even if the performance is lower than a conventional car
I would buy an environmentally friendly car even if it has a less-appealing design
I would buy an environmentally friendly car even if it is less comfortable
Purchase behaviour (PB) (normed $\chi2 = 1.871$, CFI = 0.923, RMSEA = 0.061)
I often buy environmentally friendly car
I often buy environmentally friendly car to reduce CO_2 emission and air pollution
I often buy environmentally friendly car to protect our natural environment
I often think about environment and human health before purchasing anything
Individual consequences (ICs) (normed $\chi2 = 1.553$, CFI = 0.911, RMSEA = 0.071)
Environmentally friendly car is comfortable to use
Environmentally friendly cars are safe in mode of transportation
Environmentally friendly car can reduce carbon emissions
Environmental consequences (ECs) (normed $\chi2 = 1.442$, CFI = 0.921, RMSEA = 0.081)
Conventional car affects air and water quality because oil and particles get washed into lakes and rivers
Air pollution caused by a conventional car has negative health effects especially for those people who has asthma and other respiratory problems
Conventional car can contribute to environmental degradation

Source own elaboration from Afroz et al. (2015)

References

Afroz, R., Masud, M., Akhtar, R., Islam, M., Duasa, J.: Consumer purchase intention towards environmentally friendly vehicles: an empirical investigation in Kuala Lumpur, Malaysia. Environ. Sci. Pollut. Res., 22. https://doi.org/10.1007/s11356-015-4841-8 (2015)

Agnisarman, S., Madathil, K.C., Stanley, L.: A survey of empirical studies on persuasive technologies to promote sustainable living. Sustain. Comput. Inf. Syst. **19**, 112–122 (2018). https://doi.org/10.1016/j.suscom.2018.08.001

Ajzen, I.: From intentions to actions: A theory of planned behavior. In: Action control, pp. 11–39. Springer (1985)

Ajzen, I.: The theory of planned behavior. Organ. Behav. Hum. Decis. Process. **50**(2), 179–211 (1991). https://doi.org/10.1016/0749-5978(91)90020-T

Ajzen, I., Fishbein, M.: Attitudes and the attitude-behavior relation: reasoned and automatic processes. Eur. Rev. Soc. Psychol. **11**(1), 1–33 (2000). https://doi.org/10.1080/14792779943000116

Diekmann, A., Preisendörfer, P.: Environmental Behavior: Discrepancies between Aspirations and Reality. Ration. Soc. **10**(1), 79–102 (1998). https://doi.org/10.1177/104346398010001004

Goodman, L.A.: Snowball sampling. Ann. Math. Stat., 148–170 (1961)

Richardson, K., Rockström, J., Cornell, S.E., Fetzer, I., Bennett, E.M., Biggs, R., Carpenter, S.R., De Vries, W., De Wit, C.A.: Planetary boundaries: guiding human development on a changing planet [Review of Planetary boundaries: Guiding human development on a changing planet, by W. Steffen]. Science **347**(6223), 1259855 (2015)

Schifter, D.E., Ajzen, I.: Intention, perceived control, and weight loss: an application of the theory of planned behavior. J. Pers. Soc. Psychol. **49**(3), 843 (1985)

United Nations: Convention on Climate Change. Adoption of the Paris Agreement. Draft decision -/CP.21. CCC/CP/2015/L.9/Rev.1 (2015)

Vermeir, I., Verbeke, W.: Sustainable food consumption: exploring the consumer "attitude—behavioral intention" gap. J. Agric. Environ. Ethics **19**(2), 169–194 (2006)

Voicu, M.-C., Babonea, A.: Using the snowball method in marketing research on hidden populations. Chall. Knowl. Soc. **1**, 1341–1351 (2011)

Wang, S., Fan, J., Zhao, D., Yang, S., Fu, Y.: Predicting consumers' intention to adopt hybrid electric vehicles: using an extended version of the theory of planned behavior model. Transportation **43**(1), 123–143 (2016). https://doi.org/10.1007/s11116-014-9567-9

Impact of Governance Indicators on Inclusive Growth and the Achievement of the Sustainable Development Goals in Africa

Aomar Ibourk and Soukaina Raoui

Abstract This study aims to assess the impact of good governance on inclusive growth in Africa. In a sustainable insight, this study explores the widely debated relationship between governance indicators and economic growth rate over time and from a sustainable and inclusive perception. Indeed, from a methodological perspective, the empirical material is compiled from a panel database of 49 African countries. After profiling the state of governance in Africa, a test of the exploratory relationship between governance indicators and the growth rate from 2007 to 2020. We choose the β-convergence test to assess the process of convergence and inclusion of economic growth in African countries. The results of this study indicate the positive effect of governance on economic growth in Africa. Then, the less developed countries of the continent are improving faster than the more developed countries because they have improved their governance rate over time. Therefore, promoting inclusive and sustainable growth in Africa requires a good governance foundation as a perfect stepping stone to achieving the Sustainable Development Goals.

Keywords Africa · Governance · Inclusive growth · SDGs

1 Introduction

The issue of sustainability in Africa remains linked to governance factors. The field of African development is subject to inter-African disparities (Cilliers 2021). Thus, despite the vast reforms undertaken in the fight against corruption in particular and good governance in general. The governance indicators recorded remain low in most African countries. In this context, the question of inclusiveness and sustainability of economic growth in Africa arises. Current research considers governance as a tool for inclusive and sustainable growth, at the international, regional, national, or

A. Ibourk · S. Raoui (✉)
Laboratory of Social and Solidarity Economy Governance and Development (LARESSGD), Department of Economics, Faculty of Law Economics and Social Sciences, Cadi Ayyad University, Marrakech, Morocco
e-mail: soukaina_raoui@hotmail.fr

A. M. Dima and E. R. Danescu (eds.), *Fostering Recovery Through Metaverse Business Modelling*, Springer Proceedings in Business and Economics,
https://doi.org/10.1007/978-3-031-28255-3_6

local level (Ibourk and Raoui 2021, 2022). By definition, the inclusive growth model offers all segments of society and all local territories the opportunity to participate in achieving economic performance.

Research on the importance of governance for sustainable and inclusive growth is growing (Cheeseman 2015; Awan et al. 2018). Inclusive growth as an economic development strategy has received attention due to the growing concern that the benefits of economic growth are not equitably shared (Khaled et al. 2017; Jallab 2012). Good governance facilitates the effective and efficient use of the potential and resources available to each country for its equitable development (UNESCO 2019).

In addition, good governance remains the essential ingredient for sustainable development (Murshed and Mredula 2018). Hence, this may explain from a research perspective why the good economic performance of some African countries in the recent years is slow to be followed by improvements in their SDG performance.

1.1 Governance Issue in Africa

Africa is the least developed and least advanced continent in the world. Although enough of Africa's growth between 2000 and 2020 has improved, less than the rest of the world. The continent ranks second in the world in income inequality, after Latin America. Sub-Saharan Africa's overall gross domestic product (GDP) was $1,743 billion in 2018 or 2.05 percent of global GDP. The GDP study reveals wide regional disparities. For example, in 2015, three countries-Nigeria, South Africa, and Egypt-alone accounted for more than half of Africa's GDP. By 2021, Africa will account for 17% of the world's population but only 3% of global GDP. This fact has raised concerns about the inclusiveness of African growth. The African continent faces several challenges that are most often related to the issue of governance (Sachs 2019; Booth 2012).

Our concern is to test how improving governance in Africa can promote sustainable and inclusive growth and what is the opportunity to achieve the Sustainable Development Goals?

- Countries that have developed their governance indicators over time had the chance to improve their economic status.
- The bad governance and corruption impede the attainment of economic growth and sustainable development in some African countries.

The choice of the panel data sample will allow us to assess the state of the relationship between economic growth and governance indicators that must be explained in its dual spatial and temporal dimensions. Indeed, to verify the nature of the relationship between governance indicators and economic growth, we choose the β-convergence test to assess the process of convergence and inclusion of economic growth in African countries.

2 Literature Review

The study of the consequences of corruption and bad governance on the growth and economic development of countries has not always been unanimous among the authors.

The relationship between governance and growth is presented by two schools: The first believes that corruption promotes economic growth (Goorha et al. 2010; Flatters and MacLeod 1995; Lui 1985; Huntington 1968; Leff 1964;), while contrarians see it as destructive to the economy (Bardhan 1997). However, the originality of this study comes from the extension of the widely debated relationship between governance indicators and economic growth rate in the sustainable and inclusive dimensions.

Existing empirical studies suggest that corruption is favorable for growth in contexts where institutions do not fully fulfill their roles. It can thus have incentive properties to attract investment by allowing firms to avoid burdensome regulations (Méon and Sekkat 2005; Méon and Weill 2010; Egger and Winner 2005; Aidt and Dutta 2008; Houston 2007). For his part, Mendez (2006) suggests that corruption promotes growth in countries with low levels of economic freedom but that this effect fades as the freedom economy improves. However, the studies on the negative impact of corruption. Guetat (2006) and Gyimah-Brempong (2002) confirm the negative impact, respectively, of the case of MENA and African countries. The study by Anoruo and Braha (2005) suggests that corruption hinders the growth of African economies directly through reduced productivity.

3 Methodology

3.1 Database and Source

In order to explain economic growth by governance indicators over time between 2007 and 2020. The empirical materiel uses the 49 African countries, the first indicator we have mobilized in this study is the gross domestic product (GDP) per capita in Africa. GDP per capita is a key indicator of the economic inclusion progress because it reflects economic productivity and relative living standards. It is a relatively crude measure because it does not take into account quality of life or the distribution of economic output across the population. It is calculated by simply dividing a country's total economic output (GDP) in a year by the total population. Because of this simplicity, it remains the most popular measure of national economic productivity and allows for easy comparison of different countries. This first indicator was collected from the World Bank database (2007/2020). We mobilized six indicators of governance: "Voice and accountability", "Political instability and violence", "Government effectiveness", "Regulatory burden", "Rule of law" collected from The Economist Intelligence Unit's (2007/2020), and the "Corruption" represented by the

Table 1 Specification of variables

Nature of the variable	Variable	Symbol	Source
Exogenous variable (Economic growth)	GDP per capita	Y1it	World bank database (2007/2020)
Endogenous variable (Governance)	Corruption perception index	X1it	Transparency International (2007/2020)
	Electoral process and pluralism Government functioning Political participation Political culture Civil liberty	X2it X3it X4it X5it X6it	The Economist Intelligence Unit's (2007/2020)

Source Author's own elaboration

perception of corruption indicator. The data on the perception of corruption was collected from the Transparency International database (2007/2020) (Table 1).

3.2 Estimation Method

This study mobilizes a panel data model, which can be divided into three types: Ordinary Least Squares model, fixed effect model (FE), and random effect model (RE). Indeed, the null hypothesis is that the preferred model is random effects; the alternate hypothesis is that the model is fixed effects. Essentially, the tests are used to see if there is a correlation between the unique errors and the regressors in the model. The null hypothesis is that there is no correlation between the two.

Therefore, the model selection path can be divided into at most two steps. First, the F-test is used to determine whether an individual effect exists. If the p-value of the F-test is significantly greater than 10%, this indicates that there is no significant individual effect, and that a mixed-effects model is therefore appropriate. However, if the p-value of the F-test is significantly less than 10%, this indicates that there is a significant individual effect and that the mixed-effect model will not be appropriate. Then, in the second step, the Hausman test is used to choose between the fixed effect model and the random effect model. If the p-value of the Hausman test is significantly less than 10%, it indicates that the null hypothesis should be strongly rejected, as well as the random error term; therefore, the fixed effect model will be appropriate.

However, if the p-value of the Hausman test is significantly greater than 10%, the random effect model will be appropriate.

Where:

$$\text{yit} = \beta 0 + \beta 1 \times 1\text{it} + \beta 2 \times 2\text{it} + \beta 3 \times 3\text{it} + \beta 4 \times 4\text{it} + \beta 5 \times 5\text{it} + \beta 6 \times 6\text{it} + + \text{uit} \quad (1)$$

$$\text{yit} = \beta 0 + \beta 1 \times 1\text{it} + \beta 2 \times 2\text{it} + \beta 3 \times 3\text{it} + \beta 4 \times 4\text{it} + \beta 5 \times 5\text{it} + \beta 6 \times 6\text{it} + \text{uit} \quad (2)$$

$$\text{yit} = \beta 0 + \beta 1 \times 1\text{it} + \beta 2 \times 2\text{it} + \beta 3 \times 3\text{it} + \beta 4 \times 4\text{it} + \beta 5 \times 5\text{it} + \beta 6 \times 6\text{it} + \text{uit} + \varepsilon\text{i} \quad (3)$$

3.3 Convergence Analysis

The concept of convergence was originally used to describe the process by which poorer economies should catch up with those that initially enjoyed a higher level of per capita income. This is because growth rates in developing countries were assumed to be higher than those in economically more advanced countries over a long period of time, thus narrowing the gap between the levels of development of these two groups of countries.

3.4 The β-Convergence

Beta-convergence refers to the process of adjustment over time of economies toward the same growth path or toward a reference value. Indeed, in growth theories, the idea that poor countries will catch up with rich countries if they achieve a higher growth rate leads to the use of the β-convergence test procedure. It consists of regressing the annual growth rate of a country i's gross domestic product per capita (yit) on its initial level (yi0), while controlling for differences in steady state, i.e., differences in preferences, savings rates, technologies, population growth rates, etc. All these variables are contained in the vector yit of the following equation, which can be estimated using panel data:

$$\frac{\Delta y_{it}}{y_{it-1}} = \alpha + \beta * \log_{(yi0)} + yit + \varepsilon_{it} \quad (4)$$

The estimated Eq. (4) would lead to a β-convergence if the coefficient β is negative and statistically different from zero. This β-convergence is said to be conditional if the parameter γ is different from zero (i.e., the zits are different across countries). In contrast, β-convergence is said to be absolute when $\gamma = 0$ (i.e., the zits are identical). The idea of β-convergence can also be based on the presence of a mechanism of adjustment over time of economic variables toward a reference value (y*) considered as an attractor.

If $\gamma = 0$ (statistically insignificant): we speak of absolute real convergence, with $\beta \neq 0$ ($\beta < 0$) *et* $0 < |\beta| < 1$;

If $\gamma \neq 0$ (statistically significant): we talk about conditional real convergence or relative, with $\beta \neq 0$ ($\beta < 0$) *et* $0 < |\beta| < 1$.

In this type of analysis, the null hypothesis sustains that none of the countries considered converge, whereas the alternative hypothesis sustains that all countries converge without taking intermediate situations into consideration.

(ii) Estimating an "attraction relationship" as follows:

$$\Delta y_t = \beta^* \left(y_{t-1} - y^* \right) \tag{5}$$

Equation (5) verifies the presence of an adjustment mechanism over time of the economic variables toward a reference value ($Y*$) considered as an "attractor". Note that if $\beta < 0$ *et* $\beta \neq 0$ (statistically significant), this implies that there is a mechanism for correcting deviations from the reference value, i.e., there is beta-convergence.

3.5 The σ-Convergence

Sigma convergence measures the degree of convergence, over time, between several economies, concerning one or more indicators or criteria. The analysis is based on the study of the evolution of the dispersion of the series considered. Convergence of the whole sample will occur when the dispersion decreases over time. The indicator of dispersion used can be the variance or the standard deviation of the series. If Xi, t represents the value of the variable X for country i, at date t (with i = 1, …, n and t = 1, …, p), the variance is determined from the following relationship:

$$(\operatorname{var} x\, it) = \frac{1}{n} \sum_{i=1}^{n} (x_{it} - u)^2 avec\, u = \frac{1}{n} \sum_{i=1}^{1n} x_{it} \tag{6}$$

The standard deviation is calculated from the following relationship:

$$\sigma x_t = \sqrt{\operatorname{var}(x_t)} \tag{7}$$

It would be possible to speak of "perverse convergence" when, in the case of real convergence, e.g., the decrease in the standard deviation leads to a decrease in the GDP per capita of the initially richer countries relative to the poorest.

4 Analysis/Results Interpretation

The descriptive analysis indicates that the GDP per capita (current US) ranges from \$172.5 for Burundi to a max value of \$22,943 for Equatorial Guinea. The intra-African inequalities in economic growth are presented by a standard deviation of 3.023. Indeed, from 2007 to 2020, the GDP rate has varied from −1.117 to 1.344 (Table 2).

The analysis of governance indicators shows the corruption perception index (×1) indicator ranging from a min value of 00 in Swaziland Eswatini to 65 in Botswana. Then, the electoral process and pluralism indicator (×2) ranges from 00 in Burundi to 9.580 in Swaziland Eswatini. Then, the indicator of government functioning (×3) ranges from 00 in Burundi to 8.210 in Swaziland Eswatini.

The political participation indicator (X4) ranges from 00 for Chad to 8.330 for South Africa. The political culture indicator (X5) ranges from 1.880 for the Central African Republic to 8.750 for Mauritius. The Civil Liberties indicator (X6) ranges from 0.880 for the Democratic Republic of Congo to 9.710 for Mauritius. Moreover, the overall governance indicator ranges from 3.947 for the Democratic Republic of Congo to 16.67 for Botswana. The SDG SCORE index (Africa SDG Index and Dashboards Report 2019) ranges from 29.18 for South Africa to 66.01 for Mauritius and Tunisia. Indeed, intra-African inequalities in progress and achievement of the SDGs in Africa are presented by a standard deviation of 7.425. Since the distribution of the indicators according to four typological groups:

Group 1 includes countries with high governance and high SDGs score:

This group represents a percentage of 44% which includes Uganda, Mali, Kenya, Ethiopia, Algeria, Ivory Coast, Malawi, Gambia, Zambia, Burkina Faso, Tanzania,

Table 2 Descriptive statistics

Variables	N	Mean	Sd	Min	Max
GDP per capita current US	686	2,379	3,023	172.5	22,943
Ln (GDPt/GDP2007)	686	0.233	0.311	−1.117	1.344
Ln (GDP2007)	686	7.028	1.052	5.150	9.675
X1	686	22.11	17.27	0	65
X2	686	4.253	3.016	0	9.580
X3	686	3.508	2.216	0	8.210
X4	686	4.137	1.618	0	8.330
X5	686	5.213	1.235	1.880	8.750
X6	686	4.768	2.097	0.880	9.710
Overall governance indicator	686	9.182	3.104	3.947	16.67
SDGs Index SCORE	686	52.29	7.425	29.18	66.01

Source Authors own elaboration

Morocco, Rwanda, Swaziland Eswatini, Senegal, Ghana, Tunisia, Namibia, Mauritius, Cape Verde, and Botswana.

Group 2: countries with high governance and low SDGs score:

Through a proportion of 10%, this group includes Liberia, Sierra Leone, Benin, South Africa, and Lesotho.

Group 3: Low governance and high SDGs score countries:

By a proportion of 10%, this group includes Libya, Egypt, Cameroon, Zimbabwe, Togo, and Gabon.

Group 4: countries with low governance and low SDGs score:

This group represents a proportion of 36%, this group includes the Democratic Republic of Congo, Equatorial Guinea, Chad, Sudan, Guinea-Bissau, Central African Republic, Republic of Congo, Eritrea, Comoros, Mozambique, Djibouti, Angola, Guinea, Nigeria, Mauritania, Niger, Burundi, and Madagascar.

According to the descriptive results, countries with low economic growth also have low governance indicators and low progress toward the SDGs (Table 2).

The empirical results (Table 3) indicate a positive effect between governance and economic growth, R-squared = 0.34. Countries recording a high perception of corruption, better government functioning, and political culture enjoy high economic growth. Thus, according to the Breusch pagan test, the p-value = 0.000 > $\alpha = 0.05$. This result indicates that the random effects model is better than the fixed effects model. The most suitable model is the random effect model. Indeed, from the beta-convergence test, the question is whether there are patterns in the data that indicate that poorer African countries are growing faster than richer African countries?

The results of our analysis support this conclusion, as we find a negative and statistically significant coefficient of −0.160 (0.0267). These results confirm a true conditional convergence. The poorest countries in the sample with lower initial economic growth grow faster because they have improved their governance over time.

Based on the results of the convergence, clubs appear first for African countries that moved quickly from lagging to leading: Rwanda-0.0510443, Benin-0.1829983, Gambia-0.4013478, Lesotho-0.0713833, Madagascar-0.0489846, and Mozambique-0.1215395 Rwanda's ambition is to become a middle-income economy by 2035 and to join the high-income countries by 2050. Rwanda's reforms have enabled it to implement two economic development and poverty reduction strategies from 2008 to 2018 with excellent socio-economic results. The country's growth has averaged 7.2 percent over the past decade, while GDP per capita has increased by 5% per year. Indeed, the countries that have gone backward in time have been affected by the Arab Spring—the case of Libya and Egypt in North Africa. The situation is also clearly backward for countries generally in civil war: Burkina Faso, Niger, Nigeria, and Burundi. However, it is necessary to emphasize that governance in Africa has improved since 2007, even if it remains lower than in the rest of the world. Peace and security problems translate into governance problems (Williams 2016; Donnenfeld and Akum 2017; Marshall and Elzinga 2017; Stapleton 2018). The correlation

Table 3 β-convergence test

Variables	Ln (GDPt/GDP2007)
Ln (GDP2007)	−0.160*** (0.0267)
X1	0.00474*** (0.000552)
X2	−0.0305*** (0.00849)
X3	0.0688*** (0.0110)
X4	−6.08e-05 (0.0113)
X5	0.00373 (0.0146)
X6	−0.0143 (0.0143)
Constant	1.187*** (0.193)
R-squared	0.34
Breusch-Pagan LM test	0.0000
Hausman test	0.0701
Appropriate model	Random effects model
Observations	684
Countries	49

Standard errors in parentheses
*** $p < 0.01$, ** $p < 0.05$, * $p < 0.1$
Source Authors own elaboration

between economic growth and governance progress provides insight into how to improve sustainable and inclusive growth in Africa.

5 Conclusions

This study examines the impact of good governance in ensuring inclusive and sustainable growth in Africa. The fact that Africa is the most unequal continent worldwide has inspired us to reflect on the test required for growth inclusiveness in Africa. Through the study of the β-convergence test, the results indicate a positive effect of good governance on the growth rate in Africa. The growth inclusiveness test for intra-African countries affirms the existence of β-convergence. Countries with the lowest economic growth have a higher growth rate than the most developed countries because they have improved their governance over time. This reality has a positive effect on the progress of African countries in achieving the Sustainable Development Goals.

We have shown that countries that have improved their local, regional, and international governance have benefited the most from positive economic growth. The most concrete example is Rwanda, which has attempted to improve its state of governance by decreasing the subnational poverty rate for more inclusive growth. Second, political instability in some countries has worked against their economic growth over time. The challenges of peace and security translate into governance issues, such as managing elections, even terrorism issues, managing diversity, and development, all related to governance. The correlation between economic growth and governance progress sheds light on how to improve inclusive growth in Africa.

In fact, the health crisis has had a significant impact on African countries. Progress toward the SDGs and corrective measures are needed to close the growing inequality gap. African countries that are lagging behind need to invest strategically to put in place these key governance actions to ensure inclusive growth for African women and youth, on the one hand, but also to meet the commitments of the 2030 Agenda, while good governance is the 16th sustainable development goal in its own all other SDGs.

Finally, although our study covers the most representative indicator of inclusion of economic growth in African countries (GDP per capita), indeed, it will be interesting as a future study to test the empirical relationship between governance indicators and other socio-economic indicators, especially the Human Development Index (HDI).

References

Aidt, T.S., Dutta, J.: Policy compromises: corruption and regulation in a democracy. Econ. Politics **20**(3), 335–360 (2008)

Anoruo, E., Braha, H.: Corruption and economic growth: the African experience. J. Sustain. Develop. Africa **7**(1), 43–55 (2005)

Awan, R.U., Akhtar, T., Rahim, S., Sher, F., Cheema, A.R.: Governance, corruption and economic growth: a panel data analysis of selected SAARC countries. Pakistan Econ. Soc. Rev. **56**(1), 1–20, https://www.jstor.org/stable/26616730 (2018)

Bardhan, P.: Corruption and development: a review of issues. J. Econ. Literat. **35**(3), 1320–1346 (1997)

Booth, D.: Development as a Collective Action Problem: Addressing the Real Challenges. oruo(2012)

Cilliers, J.: The future of work. In: the future of Africa, pp. 195–2019. Palgrare Macmillan (2021)

Cheeseman, N.: Democracy in Africa: Successes, Failures, and the Struggle for Political Reform. [Online] Available at: http://democracyinafrica.org/the-state-of-democracy-in-africa (2015)

Donnenfeld, Z., Akum, F.: Gathering storm Clouds: Political and Economic Uncertainty in Central Africa. Pretoria: Institute for Security Studies (2017)

Egger, P., Winner, H.: Evidence on corruption as an incentive for foreign direct investment. Eur. J. Polit. Econ. **21**(4), 932–952 (2005)

Flatters, F., Macleod, W.B.: Administrative corruption and taxation. Int. Tax Public Financ. **2**(3), 397–417 (1995)

Goorha, Prateek, Modernization Theory (March 01, 2010). Published in the Oxford Research Encyclopedia, International Relations, 2010, DOI: https://doi.org/10.1093/acrefore/9780190846626.013.266, Available at SSRN: https://ssrn.com/abstract=3412147

Guetat, I.: The effects of corruption on growth performance of the MENA countries. J. Econ. Finance **30**(2), 208–221 (2006)

Gyimah-Brempong, K.: Corruption, economic growth, and income inequality in Africa. Econ. Govern. **3**(3), 183–209 (2002)

Houston, D.: Can corruption ever improve an economy?. Cato J. **27**(3), 325–342 (2007)

Huntington, S.: Political Order in Changing Societies. Yale University Press, London (1968)

Ibourk, A., Raoui, S.: Scale effect on territorial disparities of sustainable human development in Morocco: a spatial analysis. Discov Sustain **2**, 57 (2021). https://doi.org/10.1007/s43621-021-00068-1

Ibourk, A., Raoui, S.: Impact of cooperative entrepreneurship on territorial human development in Morocco—Spatial analysis. Int. J. Soc. Econ. **49**(6), 914–929 (2022). https://doi.org/10.1108/IJSE-03-2021-0145

Khaled, H. et al.: Les moteurs de la croissance inclusive en Afrique. Projet deSection de la prévision, Division des politiques macroéconomiques. Nations Unies (2017)

Leff, N.-H.: Economic development through bureaucratic corruption. Am. Behav. Sci. **8**(3), 8–14 (1964)

Lui, F.: An Equilibrium Queuing Model of Bribers. J. Polit. Econ. **93**(4), 760–781 (1985)

Marshall, M.G., Elzinga-Marshall, G.C.: Global Report 2017 Conflict, Governance, and State Fragility. Vienna: Center for Systemic Peace, p. 30 (2017)

Méon, P.G., Sekkat, K.: Does corruption grease or sand the wheels of growth? Public Choice **122**(1–2), 69–97 (2005)

Méon, P.G., Weill, L.: Is corruption an efficient grease? World Develop. **38**(3), 244–259 (2010)

Mendez, F., Facundo, S.: Corruption, growth and political regimes: cross country evidence. Eur. J. Polit. Econ. **22**(1), 82–98 (2006)

Murshed, M., Mredula, F.: Impacts of corruption on sustainable development: a simultaneous equations model estimation approach. J. Account. Finance Econ. **8**(1), 109–133 (2018). Available at SSRN: https://ssrn.com/abstract=3059968 (2018)

Sadni Jallab, M.: 24 - Croissance inclusive, réduction de la pauvreté et dynamique des inégalités dans les pays en développement: Une Lecture Critique. Dans: Lahsen Abdelmalki éd., Développements récents en économie et finances internationales, pp. 339–354. Paris: Armand Colin. https://doi.org/10.3917/arco.silem.2012.01.0339 (2012)

Stapleton, T.: Africa: War and Conflict in the Twentieth Century. State Fragility. Vienna: Center for Systemic Peace, p. 30 (2018)

UNESCO: Co-Designing Science in Africa: First Steps in Assessing the Sustainability Science Approach on the Ground, ed. C. Aguirre-Bastos. J. Chaves-Chaparro and S. Aricò. Paris: UNESCO (2019)

Williams, P.D.: War and Conflict in Africa. Wiley (2016)

Sachs, J., Schmidt-Traub, G., Kroll, C., Lafortune, G., Fuller, G.: Sustainable Development Report 2019. Bertelsmann Stiftung and Sustainable Development Solutions Network (SDSN), New York (2019)

SDG Center for Africa and Sustainable Development Solutions Network: Africa SDG Index and Dashboards Report 2019. Kigali and New York: SDG Center for Africa and Sustainable Development Solutions Network (2019)

Bioeconomy Sectors in Romania: An Analytical Cluster Approach

Emilia Mary Bălan and Laura Mariana Cismaş

Abstract Bioeconomy is a field that can contribute to Romania's economic development in the context of the European Union's environmental protection policies. This paper analyzes the cluster hierarchy of economic sectors included in the bioeconomy field in Romania. The main objective of this article is to identify the position of agriculture among the ten sectors of bioeconomy in order to reveal the role and contribution of this important economic activity to the development of the Romanian bioeconomy. For this analysis, we used the clustering of activity patterns and analyzed the hierarchy of activities included in the bioeconomy field based on socio-economic indicators of Romanian sectors. The sample consists of ten activities included in the bioeconomy and the indicators for a timespan between 2008 and 2019. The authors have used the database of the Joint Research Center of the European Commission (EC) for bioeconomy-specific indexes. The hierarchical cluster analysis was the method of investigating the grouping of bioeconomy sectors. The research results show that the most important sectors of the Romanian bioeconomy are agriculture, bio-based electricity, fishing and aquaculture, and biofuels.

Keywords Bioeconomy sectors · Romania · Socio-economic indicators · Cluster research

E. M. Bălan (✉) · L. M. Cismaș
West University of Timisoara, Johann Heinrich Pestalozzi 16, 300115 Timisoara, Romania
e-mail: emilia.balan75@e-uvt.ro; emibalan@iem.ro

L. M. Cismaș
e-mail: laura.cismas@e-uvt.ro

E. M. Bălan
Institute for World Economy, Romanian Academy, 13 September 13, 050711 Bucharest, Romania

A. M. Dima and E. R. Danescu (eds.), *Fostering Recovery Through Metaverse Business Modelling*, Springer Proceedings in Business and Economics,
https://doi.org/10.1007/978-3-031-28255-3_7

1 Introduction

In the current context of the global economy and the apparent climate change in Europe, an economic approach to the bioeconomy is necessary for Romania. We consider that Romania needs to focus on those economic sectors that develop directions of durability, sustainability, and circularity, for a more intensive and efficient transition from the polluting technology economy to the bioeconomy. In this sense, it is necessary to emphasize that economic development models need to be reviewed, and there is a need to focus on sustainability and respect for the environment.

There are several visions on the bioeconomy worldwide (Alviar et al. 2021; Callo-Concha et al. 2020), which is why the European Commission (EC) has worked to develop and uniformize bioeconomy goals at the community level. As a result, the EC recommended that the Member States (MS) reorganize national economies based on the bioeconomic concept. Therefore, in 2018, the EC updated the 2012 Bioeconomy Strategy, which complements sectoral policies and includes countries and regions. In the strategy, the EC suggested developing countries' methods of transition from the classical economy to the green economy, according to their specific challenges and opportunities, based on an integrated, systemic but adaptable legislative framework for each country (European Commission [EC] 2018).

The theoretical definition of the bioeconomy given by the EC in the two different 2012 and 2018 strategies is insufficient. Moreover, there is still a lack of clarity in the scientific literature regarding the role, contribution, and implementation of the bioeconomy in the current socio-economic context (Dieken et al. 2021; Maciejczak 2018; Pașnicu et al. 2018; Rodino et al. 2019a).

The bioeconomy involves the contribution of all actors: from the European Union (EU) and MS institutions, investors, farmers, and managers of industrial establishments to the public, who realize that the bioeconomy is a sustainable alternative to the current economy based on environmentally unfriendly raw materials.

According to Ronzon et al. (2020) and the Economic Activities in the European Community codes (EC 2009), the economic sectors covered by the bioeconomy and making full use of only organic products are agriculture (A01), forestry (A02), fishing and aquaculture (A03), manufacture of food, beverages and tobacco products (C10, C11, and C12), manufacture of leather and related products (C15), manufacture of wood and products of wood and cork (C16), manufacture of paper and paper products (C17). Another category of economic sectors that make up the bioeconomy is those where only part of the products produced are considered organic, as follows: manufacture of textiles (C13), manufacture of wearing apparel (C14), manufacture of chemicals and chemical products (C20), liquid biofuels: production of bioethanol (C2014), production of biodiesel (C2059), manufacturing of basic pharmaceuticals and organic pharmaceutical preparations (C21), manufacturing of organic rubber and plastics (C22), manufacture of furniture (C31), production of renewable electricity (D3511). The bio-based products are outputs that contain a minimum of 10% of the renewable resources input and are used in these sectors (M'Barek et al. 2018). The bioeconomy sectors are presented in Fig. 1.

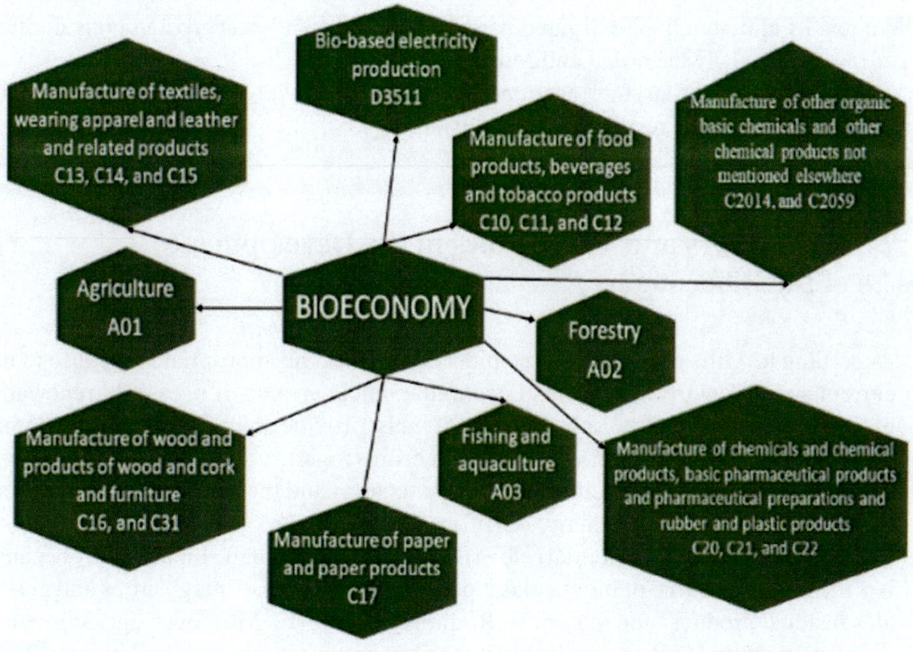

Fig. 1 Bioeconomy sectors. *Source* Adapted from Ronzon and M'Barek (2018)

We selected the relevant indicators for the field of bioeconomy based on established literature for research. According to studies (O'Brien et al. 2017; M'barek 2018; Ronzon and M'Barek 2018; Bracco et al. 2019; Capasso and Klitkou 2020; Kardung et al. 2021), socio-economic indicators that monitor the bioeconomy are the number of people employed, added value, turnover, and apparent labor productivity.

The research aims to determine the sectors of activity in the bioeconomy with potential for development in Romania, based on the principles of sustainability and ecology through the hierarchical method, and the results can contribute to prioritizing economic policies to underpin the current and future approaches to the national economic system. The article's novelty derives from the fact that in the European and Romanian academic research, no hierarchical cluster analysis has been made regarding the grouping of the component sectors of the bioeconomy in terms of specific indicators. In this sense, the study reveals those economic sectors that can adopt models of efficiency and sustainability. Also, we aim to contribute to the development of the literature and facilitate the decision-making of Romanian policymakers by including the bioeconomy in national documents. By extending the analysis to the sectoral level, we continue our previous endeavor that studied the potential of Romania's agriculture at the level of development regions (Cismaș, Bălan 2022). Also, the scope of our study is to extend the concept of bioeconomy to all economic activities that can support the Romanian national authorities in developing a strategy dedicated to this field. Moreover, such a document is necessary for Romania in the context of climate change, limited natural resources, and exacerbated consumption of raw materials (Marinescu and Marinescu 2020).

The article includes four sections: the literature review, methodology, analysis and interpretation of results, and conclusions.

2 The Sectors and Their Roles in the Development of the Bioeconomy

According to Mills et al. (2015), the bioeconomy has the appropriate response to the current social, environmental, and economic challenges, as it uses only renewable biological raw materials to substitute fossil fuels, provide animal feed, or create other organic products. The bioeconomy concept brings together the sectors of agriculture, forestry, fisheries and aquaculture (primary sectors) and the sectors producing food, chemicals, materials, and energy (Griffon 2015).

Agriculture plays an essential role in the overall picture of the bioeconomy because it is the primary source of biomass as it provides the input for energy crops and generates residual products and materials (Rodino et al. 2019b). Moreover, agriculture has excellent potential in Romania due to its various natural resources (Avrămescu 2020).

Also, Pasculea (2015) appreciated that Romania could develop a bioeconomy as it has significant agricultural potential, applies quality standards in the food industry, and can ensure the sustainable consumption needs of the population.

Agriculture contributes to the development of rural areas and the full realization of their growth potential (Volloncs et al. 2005). Moreover, in this area, the bioeconomy can drive new jobs and a circular economy at the regional level (Kardung et al. 2021). At the same time, investment in agriculture is one of the most effective strategies to reduce food scarcity, social disparities, and economic growth, and well-placed investments can lead to sustainable development at the local, regional, and national levels (Panait and Cucu 2020).

In the opinions of Ciutacu et al. (2015), agriculture has been the constituent element of forming social, cultural, moral, linguistic, aesthetic, and artistic structures since ancient times. Subsequently, agriculture helped realize economic concepts through the levers created in trade in raw materials, products, costs, prices, surplus production, efficiency, and profit.

Romania's agriculture "has some structural characteristics similar to those of the agricultural sectors in the other MS but is unique in terms of the size of the gap between the category of large farms and that of small farms, as well as the prevalence of subsistence/semi-subsistence farming" (Ministry of Agriculture and Rural Development-Romania [MARD-R] 2015, p. 18).

Romania's agriculture occupies an important place in the EU (Cismaș, Bălan 2022). Furthermore, according to Ronzon et al. (2022), in 2019, Romania's agriculture generated a turnover of more than EUR 16 million (38% of all sectors of the bioeconomy) and apparent labor productivity of EUR 4,404 per person. Almost two million people were employed in agriculture (81% of the bioeconomy), and the added value obtained was more than EUR 8 thousand million (56% of the bioeconomy).

Romanian agriculture attracted approximately 27% of the national employed population between 2008 and 2019. The trend decreased from 31% in 2008 to only 21% in 2019 but was high compared to other MS (Cismaș and Bălan 2022; Florea et al. 2021). According to statistical data and researchers (Petrescu-Mag et al. 2020), agriculture occupies 1/3 of the employed and approximately 27.3% of the working population.

Agriculture's gross added value accounts for only 6% of the national economy's GVA, and the gross added value per worker is around 50% lower than the EU average (Butu et al. 2020; Celac and Vadineanu 2018).

Therefore, Velten et al. (2021) view that a developed farm enables farmers to work more effectively with authorities and stakeholders, an important element for sustainable agriculture, and is an element of analysis of Romanian farmers. In the opinions of Davidescu et al. (2020), Romania has the necessary conditions to implement, fulfill, guide and establish regional development policies, including regional development strategies and economic and social cohesion plans.

3 Methodology

The research questions to which we set out to find answers through hierarchical analysis of the sectors included in the bioeconomy were the following:

- What are the sectors of the bioeconomy with potential for the development of this field in Romania?
- Is agriculture one of these sectors?
- How can agriculture contribute to the growth of the Romanian bioeconomy?

To identify the most significant potential of the Romanian bioeconomy sectors, we employed the cluster method computed using the SPSS software. Furthermore, the cluster approach allows us to determine the links between the Romanian bioeconomy sectors. Cluster analysis is an instrument used to group information by sectors of activity based on their parallelism or difference from the main components (Babucea and Răbonțu 2020; Balkin and Stephen 2021).

The authors have used the Database of the Joint Research Center of the EC (DataM) for bioeconomy-specific indexes. The sample comprises 10 sectors, covering 12 years, from 2008 to 2019 (Ronzon et al. 2022).

The bioeconomy socio-indicators considered in the analysis are apparent labor productivity (ALP), number of people employed (NPE), turnover (TRNV), and added value at factor cost (VAFC). The NPE measures job creation's impact on a state's economic development (Capasso and Klitkou 2020), and calculates the share of labor in each economic sector to compare the financial dynamics of an area of activity (Jander et al. 2020). In addition, the NPE is a relevant indicator that determines the evolution of economic performance through workers' contribution to turnover and the generation of added value (D'Adamo et al. 2020). VAFC is a component indicator of gross domestic product (GDP) and shows the financial performance of an activity sector (Ronzon and M'Barek 2018; Capasso and Klitkou 2020) due to the specialization of workers (Goschin et al. 2009) and the high-yield technologies used in the production process. Turnover is one of the leading indicators used in quantifying the bioeconomy and its component sectors (Ronzon and M'Barek 2018). Turnover is the total value of sales of goods and services of an economic unit in which input costs are included (Nowak et al. 2021). The ALP shows the workforce's competitiveness relative to the added value, and it produces for an economic good (Ronzon et al. 2020) in a unit of time.

Table 1 presents the average data used to investigate the bioeconomy indicators for each sector for the period 2008–2019.

Testing the null hypothesis and determining the indicator's effect on each subgroup is a standard procedure for quantitative economic research results (Balkin and Stephen 2021; List et al. 2019). Therefore, acceptance of the null hypothesis was acceptance of a value of $p > 0.05$ (95% confidence level). The null hypothesis (H_0) was expressed as the average growth rates of each variable do not differing significantly for each bioeconomy's sector. The alternative hypothesis (H_1) was that at

Table 1 Average of bioeconomy indicators by sector for the 2008–2019 period in Romania

Sector/Index	ALP (Thousand euros/person)	NPE (Thousand persons)	Turnover (Billion euro)	VAFC (Billion euro)
Bioeconomy	193	2,137	36	12
Agriculture	3.01	1,782.33	14.79	6.97
Bio-based chemicals, pharmaceuticals, plastics, and rubber (excl. biofuels)	24.19	10.38	1.10	0.33
Bio-based electricity	51.86	0.12	0.02	0.01
Bio-based textiles	6.93	71.24	1.71	0.64
Fishing and aquaculture	46.04	1.93	0.22	0.11
Food, beverage, and tobacco	11.57	144.13	12.00	2.18
Forestry	11.95	39.27	1.36	0.61
Liquid biofuels	13.15	0.81	0.12	0.01
Paper	15.05	10.23	0.94	0.20
Wood products and furniture	9.3	76.48	3.99	0.93

Source own calculation using the Ronzon et al. (2022) database least one of the selected variable's average growth rates of the bioeconomy's sectors varies considerably from the others.

We used four variables to determine the bioeconomy sectors' hierarchy. The growth rate was calculated for logarithmic values as a difference from the previous year for the period 2008–2019. The variables used are:

Var 1: apparent labor productivity (ALP)
Var 2: the number of people employed (NPE)
Var 3: turnover (TRNV)
Var 4: added value at factor cost (VAFC).

4 Analysis and Interpretation of the Results

The first result obtained in SPSS when running the data entered for the hierarchical case and variable grouping method shall be the values in the distance measurement table between all bioeconomy sectors. This result is obtained using the ward analysis method and the square Euclidean distance. The clustering phase showed the distances, similarities, or inconsistencies between items through a proximity matrix. For example, the values indicate that the highest distance of the square Euclidean distance is between fishing and aquaculture and bio-based electricity (229.440) and the lowest between bio-based textiles and wood products and furniture (10.665). Table 2 concentrates the values of the squared Euclidean distances through the minimum and maximum for each bioeconomy sector.

Table 3 gives the mean of the descriptive statistics of the input variable, which highlights the difference between apparent labor productivity (Var 1) and the number of people employed (Var 2), turnover (Var 3), and added value (Var 4).

A second result of the SPSS grouping procedure is the agglomeration schedule coefficients, which determine the distances between the combined groups at each analysis stage. The coefficients resulting from the groupings in each phase show us the distances between the elements grouped and lead us to determine the optimal level of clusters for the variables introduced in the analysis.

The values of the coefficients indicate an optimal number of three clusters. In iterations lower than 7, agriculture is one of the sectors that constantly forms a cluster of its own, in the formation of more than two clusters. The bio-based electricity sector is another sector that individually includes a group of more than three created.

The steps in the hierarchical grouping solution are also visually expressed in the dendrogram in Fig. 2. We indicated the ward method to stop the ranking process by a red vertical line. The correlation coefficient value has been set at 5 (see Fig. 2). We set the aggregation value level at five based on analyzing the coefficients in each grouping stage and the dendrogram.

The hierarchical cluster analysis indicates a grouping of the bioeconomy sectors in Romania based on the specific indicators examined. Furthermore, the results of the clustering process show that the distance between agriculture and other bioeconomic sectors is significant in the first iterations, as is revealed by both the distance

Table 2 Proximity matrix

Sector	Minimum	Maximum
Agriculture	43,688 (Food, beverage, and tobacco)	521,915 (Bio-based electricity)
Bio-based chemicals, pharmaceuticals, plastics, and rubber (excl. biofuels)	4,563 (Paper)	148,325 (Agriculture)
Bio-based electricity	65,512 (Liquid biofuels)	521,915 (Agriculture)
Bio-based textiles	3,895 (Wood products and furniture)	247,158 (Bio-based electricity)
Fishing and aquaculture	33,031 (Bio-based chemicals)	263,865 (Agriculture)
Food, beverage, and tobacco	6,708 (Wood products and furniture)	319,135 (Bio-based electricity)
Forestry	5,522 (Bio-based textiles)	201,215 (Bio-based electricity)
Liquid biofuels	42,952 (Fishing and aquaculture)	278,684 (Agriculture)
Paper	4,563 (Bio-based chemicals)	137,470 (Bio-based electricity)
Wood products and furniture	3,895 (Bio-based textiles)	261,434 (Bio-based electricity)

Source Authors' calculation based on SPSS output

Table 3 Descriptive statistics of the variables mean

	N	Range	Minimum	Maximum	Mean	Std. deviation
ALP_mean	10	2,86	1,08	3,94	2,5785	0,80,321
NPE_mean	10	10,04	4,63	14,67	9,9023	2,88,447
TRNV_mean	10	7,28	2,31	9,59	6,7702	2,23,245
Valid N (list wise)	10					

Source Authors' calculation based on SPSS output

coefficients and the graphical representation of the classification tree (see Table 2 and Fig. 2).

The solution of the grouping in three clusters of sectors of the Romanian bioeconomy generated the case shown in Fig. 3.

To identify each sector's cluster membership to which it belongs and differentiate it from the other groups, we tested null and alternative hypotheses. We reiterate that to accept the null hypothesis (H_0), the results are statistically significant, with a p-value ≥ 0.05 and a confidence level of 95%.

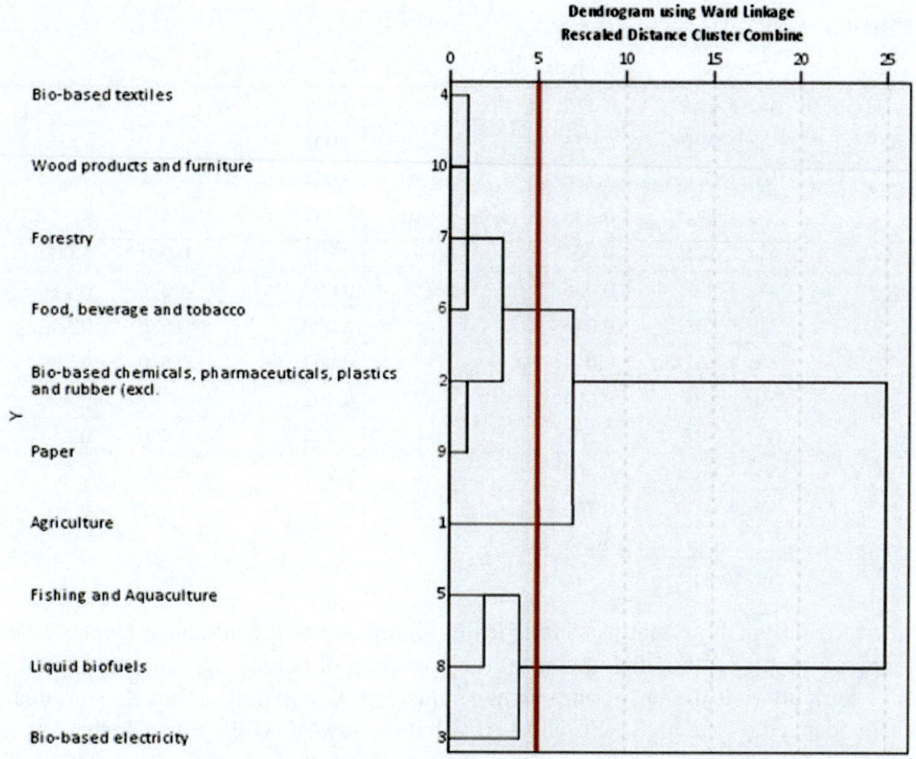

Fig. 2 Dendrogram. *Source* SPSS output

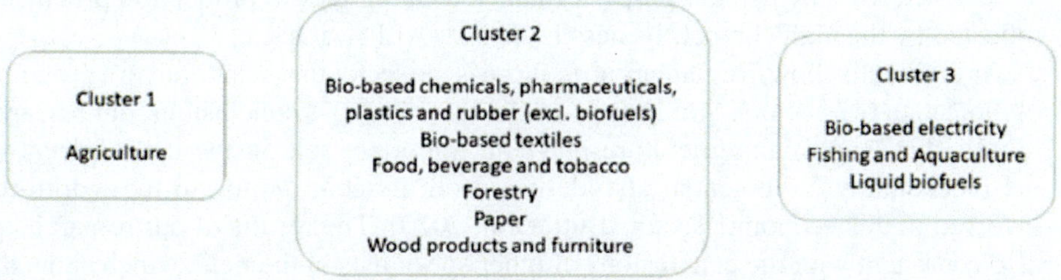

Fig. 3 Structure of the sectors clusters. *Source* Authors' representation based on own calculation

Table 4, one-way ANOVA, gives that the values of the four variables included in the model have a p-value > 0.05. Therefore, the null hypothesis is approved as the differences are at the significance level ($\alpha < 0.05$).

In the variance analysis table, the level of the F values reveals which of the variables included in the ranking best determines the clusters formed (Babucea and Răbonțu 2020). Analysis of F shows that the NPE variable has the highest values ($F = 1.016$ in cluster 2 and $F = 1.430$ in cluster 3), followed by VAFC ($F = 1.018$ in cluster 3) and TRNV ($F = 0.686$ in cluster 2). The p-values ≥ 0.05 for all variables

Table 4 Analysis of variance (ANOVA)

Cluster	Variable	Sum of squares	df	Mean square	F	P-value
C1	Var 1 ALP	0.412	10	0.041	–	–
	Var 2 NPE	0.025	10	0.002	–	–
	Var 3 TRNV	0.236	10	0.024	–	–
	Var 4 VAFC	0.336	10	0.034	–	–
C2	Var 1 ALP	0.007	5	0.001	0.001	1.000
	Var 2 NPE	0.035	5	0.007	1.016	0.416
	Var 3 TRNV	0.046	5	0.009	0.686	0.636
	Var 4 VAFC	0.044	5	0.009	0.510	0.768
C3	Var 1 ALP	0.003	2	0.002	0.001	0.999
	Var 2 NPE	0.669	2	0.335	1.430	0.255
	Var 3 TRNV	0.309	2	0.155	0.542	0.587
	Var 4 VAFC	0.745	2	0.372	1.018	0.373

Source Authors' calculation in SPSS

in each group show that it is statistically significant at a confidence level of 95%. Therefore, the sectors included meet the condition of belonging to that cluster.

Agriculture is the only component of cluster 1. Compared to the other groups, it is evidenced by the high NPE and VAFC but the lowest ALP value. Cluster 2 is the largest, comprising the most economic sectors (6), with the highest ALP values. The food, beverage, and tobacco sectors are marked by the significant turnover and added value it generates. On the other hand, the economic sectors that are part of cluster 3 are characterized by using high-performance technologies in production processes, reflected by the high competitiveness indicator (ALP) values.

As the results show, Romanian agriculture is the sector that stands out in a grouping of more than two sectors. Similarly to Avrămescu (2020)' s conclusions, our research reveals that Romanian agriculture plays an important role in the development of the bioeconomy. Its potential also derives from its contribution to the workforce involved in this economic sector (Butu et al. 2020). The results of our research are also consistent with the conclusions of other specialists in the field, which show the agriculture's contribution to the dynamics of the bioeconomy in the EU (Butu et al. 2020; Cismaş and Bălan 2022; Nowak et al. 2021).

5 Conclusions

Bioeconomy is a new field in Romanian and European academic research. The concept of bioeconomy refers to using natural resources, clean technologies to manufacture finished products, and recycling until the use cycle is entirely exhausted.

The article's authors determined the component sectors of the bioeconomy with the highest potential in Romania using the hierarchical analysis method. Therefore, we answer the research questions raised regarding the importance and role of agriculture in the development of the bioeconomy in Romania. For that purpose, the main socio-economic indicators have been analyzed, highlighting the evolution of the bioeconomy established by European researchers in the field.

At a level of aggregation of 5, three groups of bioeconomic sectors resulted as cluster 1: agriculture; cluster 2: bio-based chemicals, pharmaceuticals, plastics, and rubber (excl. biofuels); bio-based textiles; food, beverage, and tobacco; forestry; paper; wood products and furniture; and cluster three: bio-based electricity; fishing and aquaculture; liquid biofuels.

Agriculture in Romania is an economic sector of significant importance (Nicolae et al. 2021) and contributes to the regional and national development of the Romanian bioeconomy (Cismas and Balan 2022). The authors conclude that agriculture is an important sector with significant potential for the development of the bioeconomy in Romania. However, Romanian agriculture is needed to make the activity more efficient despite a large workforce. The importance of agriculture also comes from its ability to supply bio-based raw materials necessary for manufacturing in other economic areas.

The paper is a scientific endeavor that can contribute to the improvement of the Romanian literature. The results of the research can also be helpful for government decision-makers in developing a bioeconomy strategy. At the same time, the sectoral analysis of the bioeconomy in Romania can play an important role in the allocation of public and private investments at both the regional and national levels.

The research was limited by the lack of detailed information on the roles of agriculture and other bioeconomy sectors in Romania. However, we intend that these future analyses will contribute to the scientific literature on Romania's bioeconomy.

References

Alviar, M., García-Suaza, A., Ramírez-Gómez, L., Villegas-Velásquez, S.: Measuring the contribution of the bioeconomy: the case of Colombia and Antioquia. Sustainability **13**(4), 2353 (2021)

Avrămescu, T.C.: The current state of Bioeconomy in Romania. Ovidius Univ. Ann. Series Econ. Sci. **20**(1) (2020)

Babucea, A.G., Răbonțu, C.I.: The State of Adopting CRM software-solutions as Part of The Enterprises'internal processes integration—a cluster analysis at the level of the EU-Member States just Prior to the Covid-19 Pandemic. Ann. "Constantin Brancusi" Univ. Targu-Jiu. Econ. Series **20**(5) (2020)

Balkin, R.S., Stephen, A.L.: Contemporary issues in reporting statistical, practical, and clinical significance in counseling research. J. Counseling Dev. **99**(2), 227–237(2021)

Bracco, S., Tani, A., Çalıcıoğlu, Ö., Gomez San Juan, M., Bogdanski, A.: Indicators to monitor and evaluate the sustainability of bioeconomy: overview and a proposed way forward. Rome Food Agric. Organization (FAO) (2019)

Butu, A., Rodino, S., Butu, M., Ion, R.: Bioeconomy related perspectives for boosting agriculture development in Romania. Proc. Int. Conf. Bus. Excellence **14**(1), 548–558 (2020)

Callo-Concha, D., Jaenicke, H., Schmitt, C.B., Denich, M.: Food and non-food biomass production, processing and use in sub-Saharan Africa: towards a regional bioeconomy. Sustainability **12**(5) (2020)

Capasso, M., Klitkou, A.: Socio-economic indicators to monitor Norway's bioeconomy in transition. Sustainability **12**(8), 3173 (2020)

Celac, S., Vadineanu, A.: Romania's Sustainable Development Strategy 2030. Bucureşti: Paideia, 2018, ISBN 978-606-748-262-1(2018)

Cismaș, L.M., Bălan, E.M.: Agriculture's contribution to the growth of Romanian Bioeconomy: a regional approach. Eastern Europ. Econ., 1–17 (2022)

Ciutacu, C., Chivu, L., Andrei, J.V.: Similarities and dissimilarities between the EU agricultural and rural development model and Romanian agriculture. Challenges Perspect Land Use Policy **44**, 169–176 (2015)

D'Adamo, I., Falcone, P.M., Morone, P.: A new socio-economic indicator to measure the performance of bioeconomy sectors in Europe. Ecol. Econ. **176**, 106724 (2020)

Davidescu, A.A., Apostu, S.A., Pantilie, A.M., Amzuica, B.F.: Romania's south-muntenia region, towards sustainable regional development. Implications for regional development strategies. Sustainability (Switzerland) **12**(14), 1–46 (2020)

Dieken, S., Dallendörfer, M., Henseleit, M., Siekmann, F., Venghaus, S.: The multitudes of bioeconomies: a systematic review of stakeholders' bioeconomy perceptions. Sustain. Product. Consump. **27**, 1703–1717 (2021)

European Commission: A sustainable Bioeconomy for Europe: strengthening the connection between economy, society and the environment. ISBN: 978-92-79-94144-3 (2018)

European Commission: Commission Regulation (EC), No 250/2009 of March 11, 2009, Implementing Regulation (EC) No 295/2008 of the European Parliament and of the Council as Regards the Definitions of Characteristics, the Technical Format for the Transmission of Data, the Double Reporting Requirements for NACE Rev. 1.1 and NACE Rev. 2 and Derogations to Be Granted for Structural Business Statistics. Off. J. Eur. Comm., 169 (2009)

Florea, N.V., Duică, M.C., Ionescu, C.A., Duică, A., Ibinceanu, M.C.O., Stanescu, S.G.: An analysis of the influencing factors of the romanian agricultural output within the context of green economy. Sustainability **13**(17), 9649 (2021)

Goschin, Z., Constantin, D.L., Roman, M., Ileanu, B.: Regional specialisation and geographic concentration of industries in Romania. South-Eastern Europe J. Econ. **7**(1), 99–113 (2009)

Griffon, M.: Sustainable agriculture, forestry and fisheries in the Bioeconomy. Presentation and reflexions about the SCAR 4th foresight exercise. Euragri Conference 2015, Luxembourg. Available la: http://rb.gy/iqz6yf (2015)

Jander, W., Wydra, S., Wackerbauer, J., Grundmann, P., Piotrowski, S.: Monitoring bioeconomy transitions with economic–environmental and innovation indicators: addressing data gaps in the short term. Sustainability **12**(11), 4683 (2020)

Kardung, M., Cingiz, K., Costenoble, O., Delahaye, R., Heijman, W., Lovrić, M., van Leeuwen, M., M'Barek, R., van Meijl, H., Piotrowski, S., Ronzon, T., Sauer, J., Verhoog, D., Verkerk, P.J., Vrachioli, M., Wesseler, J.H.H., Zhu, B.X.: Development of the circular Bioeconomy: drivers and indicators. Sustainability **13**(1), 413 (2021)

List, J.A., Azeem, M.S., Yang, X.: Multiple hypothesis testing in experimental economics. Exp. Econ. **22**(4), 773–793(2019)

M'Barek, R., Parisi, C., Ronzon, T.: Getting (some) numbers right: Derived economic indicators for the bioeconomy. In: JRC Conference and Workshop Reports, Proceedings of the Side-Event at the EUBCE, Copenhagen, Denmark (Vol. 15) (2018)

Maciejczak, M.: Quality as value-added Bioeconomy: analysis of the EU policies and empirical evidence from polish agriculture. AgBioforum **21**(2), 86–96 (2018)

Marinescu, L.M., Marinescu, E.S.: The Bioeconomic strategy of Romania in the context of a major global crisis. EIRP Proc. **15**(1) (2020)

Mills, E., Franco, J., Feodoroff, T., Kay, S., Vervest, P.: The Bioeconomy. TNI and Hands on the Land, p. 6 (2015)

Ministry of Agriculture and Rural Development-Romania: Strategia de Dezvoltare a Sectorului Agroalimentar pe termen mediu și lung [The Strategy for the Medium- and Long-Term Development of the Agribusiness Sector], pp. 18. Available at: http://rb.gy/hbwvga (2015)

Nicolae, I., Gabriel, P., Diego, B., Raluca, I., Irina-Elena, P., Ionuț-Laurențiu, P.: The impact of COVID-19 crisis on the Romanian agricultural sector. In: Economic Recovery After COVID-19, pp. 17–35. Springer, Cham (2021)

Nowak, A., Kobiałka, A., Krukowski, A.: Significance of agriculture for Bioeconomy in the member states of the European Union. Sustainability **13**(16), 8709 (2021)

O'Brien, M., Wechsler, D., Bringezu, S., Schaldach, R.: Toward a systemic monitoring of the European bioeconomy: Gaps, needs and the integration of sustainability indicators and targets for global land use. Land Use Policy **66**, 162–171 (2017)

Panait, I., Cucu, C. M.: The evolution of Romanian agribusiness in the context of sustainable development of agriculture. In: Proceedings of the International Conference on Business Excellence, **14**(1), pp. 1083–1097(2020)

Pasculea, M.: Perspectives on developing the Bioeconomy Secotor in Romania. Annales Universitatis Apulensis: Series Oeconomica **17**(1), 39 (2015)

Pașnicu, D., Ghența, M., Matei, A.: Transition to Bioeconomy: perceptions and Behaviors in central and Eastern Europe. Amfiteatru Economic **21**(50), 9–23 (2019)

Rodino, S., Butu, A., Butu, M.: Analysis of the perception on Bioeconomy and environmental economics concept. Int. Multidisciplinary Scientific GeoConference: SGEM **19**(5.3), 61–68 (2019a)

Rodino, S., Butu, A., Dragomir, V., Butu, M.: An analysis regarding the biomass production sector in Romania-a bioeconomy point of view. Scientific Papers Series Manag. Econ. Eng. Agric. Rural Dev. **19**(1), 497–502 (2019b)

Ronzon, T., M'Barek, R.: Socio-economic indicators to monitor the EU's bioeconomy in transition. Sustainability **10**(6), 1745 (2018)

Ronzon, T., Piotrowski, S., M'barek, R., Carus, M., Tamošiūnas, S.: Jobs and wealth in the EU bioeconomy/JRC—Bioeconomics. European Commission, Joint Research Centre (JRC) PID: http://data.europa.eu/89h/7d7d5481-2d02-4b36-8e79-697b04fa4278 (2022)

Ronzon, T., Piotrowski, S., Tamosiunas, S., Dammer, L., Carus, M., M'barek, R.: Developments of economic growth and employment in bioeconomy sectors across the EU. Sustainability **12**(11), 4507 (2020)

Vollоncs, E., Sirbulescu, C., Chioreanu, S., Milin, A., Negrut, L., Vlad, S.: Agriculture—the heartbeat of rural areas. Rural Development. 2(1). Proceedings: Globalisation and Integration Challenges to Rural Development in Eastern and Central Europe, pp. 37–39 (2005)

Open Lab—An Innovative Model to Increase Students' Civic Engagement

Magdalena Iordache Platis and Marlen Mouliou

Abstract Higher education institutions have faced several challenges which strengthened their cooperation to share and learn from other institutions' practices; many of the new actions are social responsibility related. The Open Lab is an innovative model of individual and institutional engagement with the major scope of managing local needs-based projects capable of generating positive impact in the local community. Students in general, and student unions, in particular, run several projects in which students get themselves volunteered. Learning from working in projects is considered service learning, a different and innovative approach with multiple benefits for students who become engaged learners, for higher education institutions which run and partner in local projects with different entities, and for communities which are the final beneficiaries. The aim of this paper is to explore the Open Lab as an innovative model to increase students' civic engagement. The study focuses on the students' awareness of the Open Lab opportunities and provides solutions to increase the Open Lab awareness. The research is based on the literature review on Open Lab related concepts, higher education current challenges, and innovative models, and on a survey addressed to students to reveal their understanding of this approach. The main results show that although the students' awareness of the Open Lab's opportunities is low, the students' willingness to get engaged is high and that the students' engagement level is correlated with opportunities communication and motivation effectiveness. The findings demonstrate that communication and motivation mechanisms would be solutions to increase the effectiveness of the Open Lab.

Keywords Higher education · Open Lab · Service learning

M. I. Platis (✉)
University of Bucharest, 050663 Bucharest, Romania
e-mail: magdalena.platis@unibuc.ro

M. Mouliou
National and Kapodistrian University of Athens, 10679 Athens, Greece

A. M. Dima and E. R. Danescu (eds.), *Fostering Recovery Through Metaverse Business Modelling*, Springer Proceedings in Business and Economics,
https://doi.org/10.1007/978-3-031-28255-3_8

1 Introduction: Open Labs in Higher Education

Open Labs in higher education institutions represent functional networks of different stakeholders who decide to work together to develop projects that the local community will benefit from. Many higher education institutions are themselves considered open laboratories when they become active in research clusters and focus on community partnerships (Birks et al. 2020).

Recent studies show the increasing popularity of the Open Labs in the current societies and businesses environment and reveal the characteristics of the functional Open Labs, e.g. allow interaction across institutional boundaries, facilitate innovation, impact the local business ecosystem; Open Labs also make the city innovation real, they stimulate the co-creation-based projects, and they focus on a participatory culture of different stakeholders (Fritzsche et al. 2020). Unfortunately, although Open Labs allow for commercialization and collaboration with the business sector, the implementation process of open innovation practices is still limited, being more favourable for corporative contexts (Moretti 2019).

This paper explores the Open Lab as an innovative model to increase students' civic engagement by focusing on the students' awareness of the Open Lab opportunities. In the end, the findings provide solutions to increase the Open Lab awareness in the academic and local community. The research is based on the literature review in Open Lab related concepts, higher education current challenges, and innovative models and on a survey addressed to students to reveal their understanding of this approach and willingness to get engaged through its projects.

Therefore, although recent studies have been dedicated to Open Lab concepts, little research has covered the students' engagement in Open Lab projects as a group of active citizens of high potential and the student awareness of Open Lab projects and opportunities. As a concrete analysis, a newly established CIVIS alliance is considered, which is a European network consisting of 10 higher education research institutions with the mission of creating a unique European interuniversity campus based on collaboration, joint learning pathways, and development of research facilities (CIVIS mission website). Moreover, the mission of the CIVIS Open Labs is based on a global thinking and a local action; through the Open Lab projects, societal challenges have been addressed and service learning projects proposed where students were encouraged to participate in (CIVIS Open lab mission website, CIVIS Open Lab on UB website, CIVIS Open Lab on NKUA website). The paper addresses the gap between the multiple opportunities provided by Open Labs and the students' level of civic engagement, proving Open Labs as innovative mechanisms for increasing the students' civic engagement. The current paper is dedicated to two CIVIS Open Labs: 1. The CIVIS Open Lab Bucharest at the University of Bucharest (UB) and 2. The CIVIS Open Lab Athens at the National and Kapodistrian University of Athens (NKUA), which are trying to find possible solutions to the gap mentioned above. In other words, the two CIVIS Open Labs will highlight their efforts to support students' engagement in societal or community projects. The main question is: How are the students' engagement level and the students' willingness, together with the effectiveness of the Open Lab communication related?

2 Literature Review on Open Labs and Related Concepts

The Open Labs are important networks for the community, where their projects are implemented. The Open Lab projects generate actions where besides stakeholders, active citizens are involved, and the projects are more or less successful; the Open Lab approach does not have a unique recipe to support sustainable, self-organized, and autonomous communities and can be reconsidered with a community building approach (Tellioglu 2019). Moreover, Open Labs do not only imply the community building, but also a mechanism of testing and evaluating new concepts and tools of effective collaboration; Open Labs enhance innovation in a collaborative work context being a strategy for innovation, change, and also for adoption in other communities, through its successful results (Schaffers et al. 2009; Budweg et al. 2011).

Moreover, Open Labs support the sustainable development of local communities through innovation; experts, civil organizations, consultants, professors, and public administration representatives work together. Therefore, all the multiple parties—society, university, businesses, and government—co-create and innovate for the society benefit and not based on a designed beforehand method (Gomez Zermeño and Aleman de la Garza 2020). In other studies, Open Labs are explained as living labs, where, e.g. volunteer research participants are involved in co-creation approach that integrates research and innovation processes in real life communities and settings; therefore, living labs have an important role in strengthening the territory characteristics by engaging different actors such as citizens, institutions, and organizations in understanding better the territorial needs and dynamics (Battistoni et al. 2022).

In many cases, living labs face development difficulties due to the gap between innovation and market, considering a regulatory mechanism (Shvetsova and Lee 2021). The Open Lab is seen as an important contributor to the knowledge transfer in the ecosystem, where open innovation is a challenge and as an effective initiative of raising awareness with positive impact on the beneficiaries of the projects/activities, where the city itself can be considered a living laboratory of itself (Secundo et al. 2021; Vieu et al. 2007; Veeckman and van der Graaf 2014). In addition to these, civic engagement is a value of the civil society and civic learning, and education is a relevant higher education institutions interest; stimulating the students' civic engagement increases their personal responsibility, self-initiative, preparing them to become accountable citizens, but the potential of young generation is not explored enough in civic engagement actions (Jurs and Samusevica 2018). Other studies show that more experienced students are more engaged in community projects compared to younger colleagues; in other words, the veteran students are more likely to get engaged in voluntary action or volunteerism (Karliani et al. 2019; Albright et al. 2020).

At the same time, several studies show that there is a lot of room to improve the young generation interest in becoming more civic engaged, that there are several factors and barriers to their civic engagement, e.g. cultural and social factors that influence most their motivation, while individual characteristics do not influence much their civic engagement, e.g. personality type or family involvement (Zabolotna and Pidhaietska 2021; Chan 2011; Sam et al. 2019).

3 Methodology

3.1 Research Questions and Hypotheses

The purpose of the current research is to highlight the characteristics of the Open Lab as an innovative model to increase students' civic engagement and to reveal solutions can be adopted in higher education institutions to enhance the Open Lab awareness in the academic community. The research question is: How can Open Lab awareness contribute to increasing students' engagement? As secondary objectives, the research considered the following: to reveal the CIVIS Open Labs characteristics; to understand the students' interest in engaging in civic projects and the students' level of awareness of the CIVIS Open Labs.

Two hypotheses and their alternate hypotheses have been considered:

H1 0. The students' motivation/willingness of engagement has no effect on their effective civic engagement in the Open Lab projects.

H1 a. The students' motivation/willingness of engagement has a positive effect on their effective civic engagement in the Open Lab projects.

H2 0. The Open Lab opportunities communication has no effect on the students' civic engagement.

H2 a. The Open Lab opportunities communication has a positive effect on the students' civic engagement.

3.2 Research Methods

The research methods applied in this study include two methods of data collection—an interview with the two Open Lab coordinators to reveal the higher education challenges in addressing the CIVIS Open Lab mission and two surveys for students to identify their civic engagement interest based on the awareness of the Open Lab opportunities.

A short presentation of the thematic interview guide with the two Open Lab coordinators is described in Table 1.

As for the surveys addressed to students, an online questionnaire on Google Forms was provided in Romania for the students at UB, and in English for the students at

Table 1 Thematic interview guide (authors' own contribution)

Crt. no	Main themes	Support questions
1	Open Lab establishment; short description	When was it established and how (main phases)
2	Open Lab main characteristics	What are the main characteristics of the Open Lab as a new structure within the university?
3	Open Lab capacity of being an innovative model for civic engagement	Do you consider the Open Lab an innovative model for civic engagement?
4	Communication channels of the Open Lab opportunities	How do you communicate the Open Lab and its projects within the academic community, including students? Which channels have been considered?

NKUA. The questionnaires were distributed through emails from the student leaders and the Moodle platform, and responses were collected between January and May 2022 for the students at UB, and during May 2022 for the students at NKUA. The survey is based on a purposive sample, more precisely, on a total population sampling, with two different target groups. At UB, the questionnaire was addressed to students at the undergraduate level at one faculty (Business and Administration), having the most active interaction with the open lab coordinator, while at NKUA, the questionnaire was addressed to all students involved in graduate studies and doctoral studies where the coordinator had the opportunities to explain the Open Lab options during the academic year. The questionnaire included open and closed questions for which the Likert scale with 5 levels was considered (1 being the minimum level and 5 the maximum level of awareness, engagement, etc.). A short description of the survey data collection is reflected in Table 2.

The research methods applied in this study include two methods of data collection—an interview with the two Open Lab coordinators to reveal the higher education challenges in addressing the CIVIS Open Lab mission and two surveys for students to identify their civic engagement interest based on the awareness of the Open Lab opportunities.

Table 2 Survey sections and statistics (authors' own contribution)

<table>
<tr><th>Crt. no</th><th>Main survey questions</th><th>Target groups and valid responses</th></tr>
<tr><td>1</td><td rowspan="2">– Students' level of awareness on Open Lab projects;
– Students' level of engagement in civic projects;
– The effectiveness of the communication of the Open Lab and its projects to students</td><td>Students in undergraduate studies at UB–639 valid responses</td></tr>
<tr><td>2</td><td>Students in graduate and doctoral studies at NKUA–18 valid responses</td></tr>
</table>

4 Analysis/Results Interpretation

The interview with the Open Lab coordinators of the 2 universities revealed the characteristics included in Table 3.

The interview responses of the two Open Lab coordinators are described in connection with the students' responses and centralized in Table 4; therefore, it is important to highlight that at the UB, the coordinator's opinion is similar to the students in relationship to the students' awareness on the Open Lab and the level of engagement in civic projects, but different about the effectiveness of the communication of the Open Lab and its projects, while in case of the NKUA, exactly the opposite case—the coordinator's perception and the students' responses are close about the effectiveness of the communication and different about the students' awareness on the Open Lab projects and the level of engagement, the coordinator considering those variable of higher level (5 versus 2.94 and 4 versus 2.67).

Table 3 Comparative analysis between the 2 CIVIS Open Labs (authors' own contribution)

Aspects	Open Lab at UB	Open Lab at NKUA
Calls for projects	November 2020 July 2021	June 2021
Number of projects	3 + 3 (24 initial project ideas and 14 + 4 effective proposals)	5 (from 45 initial project ideas and 6 effective proposals)
Areas	3	7
Keywords	Innovative Participative Inclusive Flexible structure Community awareness Collaborative environment	Innovative Participative Inclusive Flexible structure Community awareness Collaborative environment
Communication channels	University channels—PR communicate, e-mails, CIVIS coordinators in faculties, some professors during classes, mouth-to-mouth messages	Press releases, special open events focused on Open Labs, online coverage, mouth-to-mouth dissemination of different projects to students online-meetings, email lists, etc

Table 4 Open Lab Students' Awareness: 1–lowest; 5–highest score (authors' own contribution)

Aspects	Open Lab at UB	Open Lab at NKUA
Level of Students' Awareness on the Open Lab	2–coordinator 2.94–students' responses	5–coordinator 2.94–students' responses
Level of engagement in civic projects	3–coordinator 3.22–students' responses	4–coordinator 2.67–students' responses
The effectiveness of the communication of the Open Lab and its projects	5–coordinator 3.94–students' responses	3–coordinator 3.33–students' responses

The two Open Labs were organized based on the same CIVIS methodology, but the discussions with the stakeholders lead to specific topics. At the UB, 3 main areas were considered in the end for the projects to be submitted: Sustainability and urban resilience; Education and culture; Research and digital transformation, while at the NKUA, more topics were considered for debates in a format of seven focus groups, as reflected in Fig. 1.

The students' survey demonstrates that the current motivation of students is high and that they are not much involved in social projects, as seen in Fig. 2.

The Pearson correlation coefficient was calculated to measure the strength of the linear association between the two variables, and the results are observed in Fig. 3.

Therefore, the results show that there is a very small and non-significant positive relationship between the students' willingness to get engaged and their effective engagement in social projects, and that there is a significant positive relationship between how the students see the effectiveness of the Open Lab opportunities communication and the students effective engagement; these results show that all variables move in the same direction. Moreover, as p is close to zero in the case of the non-significant correlation (a).), there is insufficient statistical evidence that the correlation between the two variables is significant; in addition, regarding the second correlation (b).), there is a linear relationship between the effectiveness

Fig. 1 Open Lab focus groups' themes (authors' own contribution)

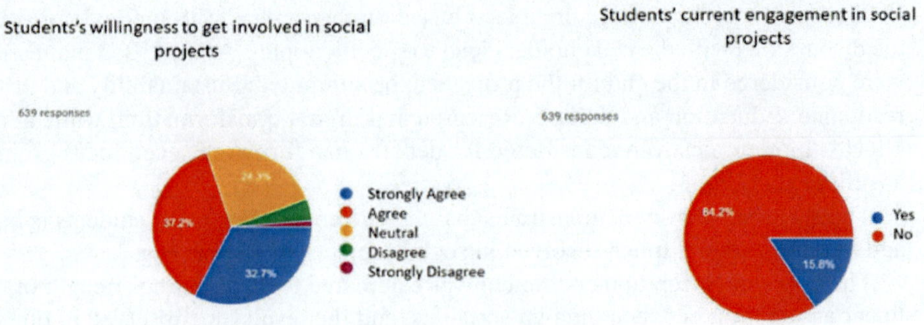

Fig. 2 Current state of students' engagement is social projects (authors' own contribution)

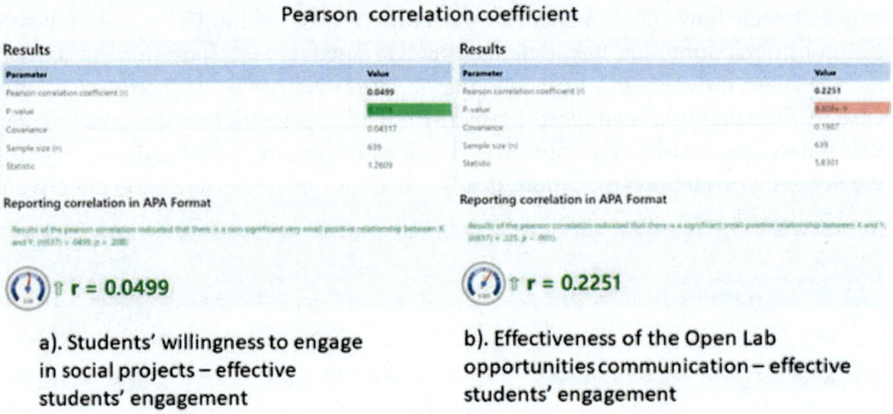

Fig. 3 Students' willingness to get engage and effectiveness of the Open Lab communication correlated with the effective students' engagement in social projects (Statistics calculator) (authors' own contribution)

of the communication of the Open Lab opportunities and the students' effective engagement.

5 Conclusions

The Open Lab is a newly established structure in higher education institutions to address local challenges and involve internal and external stakeholders in writing and implementing social projects. CIVIS students at UB and NKUA have a similar level of awareness (a moderate level) and a close level of engagement in social projects and also a close opinion on the effectiveness of the communication of the Open Lab and its projects. Students' willingness is not significant related to their effective engagement, while the effectiveness of the communication of the Open Lab opportunities is statistically significant and positively related to their engagement. The results show that the communication of the Open Lab opportunities is done in an adequate manner and that students have the potential to increase their civic engagement, although their willingness to get involved is not high. Further research needs to be performed in order to identify the causality between variables, as the Pearson coefficient is limited.

References

Albright, D.L., McDaniel, J.T., Godfrey, K., Thomas, K.H., Fletcher, K.L., Rosen, G.: Civic engagement among student veterans. J. Am. Coll. Health **68**(4), 387–394 (2020)

Battistoni, P., Grimaldi, M., Sebillo, M., Vitiello G.: Living labs and open innovation to support local development policies. In: Borgogno, M.E., Zamperlin, P. (Eds).: Book Series Communications in Computer and Information Science 1507, pp. 339–350 (2022)

Birks, D.L., Ford, R.M., Payne, C.A.: The University as an open laboratory. J. Res. Administ. **2**(44), (2020)

Budweg, S., Schaffers, H., Ruland, R., Kristensen, K., Prinz, W.: Enhancing collaboration in communities of professionals using a Living Lab approach. Production Planning Control **22**, 594–609 (2011)

Chan, W.Y.: An exploration of Asian American college students' civic engagement. Asian Am. J. Psychol. **2**(3), 197–204 (2011)

CIVIS mission, https://civis.eu/en/about-civis/our-mission-and-vision. Accessed 24 August 2022

CIVIS Open Labs: think globally, act locally, https://civis.eu/en/activities/civis-openlab. Accessed 24 August 2022

CIVIS Open Lab Athens, https://civis.eu/el/activities/civis-openlab/civis-open-lab-athens. Accessed 24 August 2022

CIVIS Open Lab Bucharest, https://civis.eu/en/activities/civis-openlab/open-lab-bucharest. Accessed 24 August 2022

Fritzsche, A., Jonas, J.M., Roth, A., Moeslein, K.M.: Innovating in the open lab: preface. In: Innovating in the Open Lab, De Gruyter (2020)

Gomez Zermeño, M.G., Aleman de la Garza, L.Y.: Open laboratories for social innovation: a strategy for research and innovation in education for peace and sustainable development. Int. J. Sustain. Higher Educ. **22**(2), 344–362 (2020)

Jurs, P., Samusevica, A.: Characteristics of youth civic engagement in Liepaja City. In: Lubkina, V., Usca, S., Zvaigzne, A. (Eds.), Society, Integration, Education, Vol. 2, pp. 191–201 (2018)

Karliani, E., Kartadinata, S., Winataputra, U.S., Komalasari, K.: Indonesian civic engagement among college students. J. Hum. Behav. Soc. Environ. **29**(5), 582–592 (2019)

Moretti, F.: "Open" Lab? studying the implementation of open innovation practices in a university laboratory. Int. J. Innov. Technol. Manag. **16**(1) (2019)

Sam, D.L., Wanjohi, R.N., Akotia, C.S.: Civic engagement and participation among Ghanaian and Kenyan students and their correlates. J. Civ. Soc. **15**(1), 42–61 (2019)

Secundo, G., Mele, G., Del Vecchio, P., Degennaro, G.: Knowledge spillover creation in university-based entrepreneurial ecosystem: the role of the Italian "Contamination Labs." Knowl. Manag. Res. Pract. **19**(1), 17–151 (2021)

Schaffers, H., Budweg, S., Ruland, R., Kristensen, K.: Collaborative environments to support professional communities: a living lab approach. In: Camarinha Matos, L.M., Paraskakis, I., Afsarmanesh, H. (Eds.) Leveraging Knowledge for Innovation in Collaborative Networks, Book Series IFIP Advances in Information and Communication Technology, vol. 307, pp. 635+ (2009)

Shvetsova, O.A., Lee, S.K.: Living labs in university-industry cooperation as a part of innovation ecosystem: case study of South Korea. Sustainability **13**(1) (2021)

Statistics calculator, https://www.statskingdom.com/correlation-calculator.html. Accessed 26 August 2022

Tellioglu, H., Wagner, M., Habiger, M., Mikusch, G.: Living labs reconsidered for community building and maintenance. In: Cech, F., Tellioglu, H. (Eds.), 9th International Conference on Communities & Technologies (C&T) Proceedings, pp. 154–159 (2019)

Veeckman, C., van der Graaf, S.: The city as living labortory: a playground for the innovative development of smart city applications. In: Terzi, S., Katzy, B., Cunninghman, S. (eds.), Book Series International ICE Conference on Engineering Technology and Innovation (2014)

Vieu, C., Severac, C., Pons, D., Panissal, N: The "open-lab" initiative or how to raise awareness of nanoscale research in French students before university. In: Baglin, J.E.E. (Ed.). Proceedings of the Symposium and Forum Education in Materials Science, Technology and Engineering, pp. 149–157 (2007)

Zabolotna, O., Pidhaietska, A.: Students' civic engagement in ukraine and canada: a comparative analysis. Multidiscip. J. Educ. Soc. Technol. Sci. **8**(1), 85–101 (2021)

A Dynamic Heterogeneous Panel Model for Predicting Healthcare Expenditure in the Middle East Countries

Shailender Singh and Muhammad Muazu Bala

Abstract This study presents some evidence to the literature concerning the long-run income elasticity of public and private health expenditure and its key determinants in the fifteen countries of the Middle East, for the period of 2005–2016. The findings are consistent with conventional findings of long-run income elasticity of public healthcare expenditure above unity. However, the exact opposite holds true for the elasticity coefficient of private health spending. Therefore, the elasticity estimates suggest that public health care is a luxury while private health care is a necessity in this context. The level of education drives up the growth rate of healthcare expenditure growth. However, though statistically insignificant, the level of real wage and population aging shows signs that are theoretically incongruent. The evidence on panel cointegration remains inconclusive. Therefore, expanding the coverage of chronic diseases services by the public sector is the primary policy implication of these findings. Other implications of the results are also drawn along with possible future research areas.

Keywords Healthcare expenditure · Income elasticity · Dynamic heterogeneous panel · Middle East region

1 Introduction

In the past couple of decades, the level of healthcare expenditure has grown significantly in countries of the world. The nature of rapid growth in public health expenditure has threatened the sustainability of many government budgets and in some instances has led to budget deficits, particularly in developing economies. However,

S. Singh (✉)
Symbiosis Centre for Management Studies (Symbiosis International Deemed University, Pune), Noida, India
e-mail: reshu111us@yahoo.com

M. M. Bala
Department of Economics, SRM University-AP, Amaravati, India

A. M. Dima and E. R. Danescu (eds.), *Fostering Recovery Through Metaverse Business Modelling*, Springer Proceedings in Business and Economics,
https://doi.org/10.1007/978-3-031-28255-3_9

in the USA and other higher-income countries, the share of income spent on healthcare services has increased substantially as the nation's per-capita income increased (Hall and Jones 2007). This led to growing concern among policy practitioners, healthcare stakeholders, and researchers to explore the major causes behind the inexorable rise in healthcare expenditure across the globe and also assess whether it leads to improvement in health outcomes (Murphy and Topel 2006). In the same vein, it has been argued that the expansion of health insurance coverage and a the demographic transition leading to populations aging has contributed to the astronomical rise in gross healthcare expenditure as a share of GDP (Frogner et al. 2012). Perhaps, more importantly, in recent years, the increased prevalence and application of modern technologies such as computer tomography (CT) scanners and medical imaging (MI) have remarkably helped service providers to improve health outcomes (Nocera and Zweifel 1998).

Hitherto, there has been an important debate in the literature regarding the determinants of the cost of health care in general and the magnitude of income elasticity of healthcare spending in particular. The income elasticity of health expenditure is the degree of sensitivity of the change in the total cost of medical care to the change in the total income level. Regardless of the type of data under analysis, if the coefficient of income elasticity is greater than unity, it could be the case that health care is a luxury; below unity, it means that health is a necessity. Generally, obtaining the coefficient of income elasticity of the cost of medical care is of prime importance because it can contribute to policy advice for financing and allocating healthcare expenditures. For instance, it is assumed that if the coefficient of income elasticity of medical expenditure is lower than one, it implies that public sector dominance in running and managing the health system and thus consumption of health services become a necessity in that context. However, this paper extends the literature on Middle East studies by estimating the magnitude of income elasticity of public and private health expenditure and offers some policy advice.

2 Problem Statement

Numerous studies in the past have contributed to the literature on estimating the income elasticity of health expenditure. However, the evidence shows contrasting results. For instance, (Getzen 2000) argued that consumption of health services is both a luxury and necessity because the level of elasticity differs with the level of analysis and the inconsistent results, which are partly due to the variation of data analyzed, the unit of analysis, and the statistical approach to the analysis of the data. (Di Matteo 2003) argued that low-income countries have higher healthcare income elasticities of healthcare spending and higher-income countries have higher income elasticities. (López-Casasnovas and Saez 2007) shows that the income elasticity of health expenditure reduces as income level increases in OECD countries. (Boungnarasy 2011) concluded that rich economies have larger income elasticities of health spending than poor economies. (Hitiris and Posnett 1992) have found the long-run coefficient of health expenditure income elasticity to be roughly one for the OECD countries (Roberts 1999) argues that the long-run coefficient of income elasticity of medical expenditure is above unity for the OECD countries and the long-run income elasticities were responsive to the specification of the two models and the sample structure. Similarly, (Baltagi and Moscone 2010) have argued that the coefficient of income elasticity of medical expenditure is lower than unity. In another study, (Baltagi et al. 2017) have documented that the consumption of health services is a necessity, and the coefficient of income elasticity of healthcare spending depends on the classification of different countries in the global income groups, with higher elasticity associated with poorer countries, across the globe. The recent change in the global burden of disease from infectious to chronic diseases has made private expenditure more crucial in the improvement of health outcomes. (Barkat et al. 2019) observed that the countries of the Middle East are characterized by the growing burden of chronic diseases. (Ventelou and Abu-Zaineh 2016) Middle Eastern countries are among the developing countries with the minimum levels of health expenditure as a share of GDP. However, available evidence shows that the coefficient of income elasticity is mostly computed without accounting for the differences in the types of health expenditure. Thus, understanding the elasticity coefficient of public and private health expenditure will inform policy decisions on how best to improve health outcomes, particularly in countries with a growing burden of chronic diseases.

However, this current study contributes to the literature in this area by estimating and comparing the magnitude of the coefficient of long-run income elasticity between public and private healthcare expenditures, using a dynamic heterogeneous panel model, for the Middle East countries for 2005–2016.

3 Methodology

The study is conducted on the economies of Middle East countries comprised Bahrain, Cyprus, Egypt, Iran, Iraq, Israel, Jordan, Kuwait, Lebanon, Oman, Qatar, Saudi-Arabia, Turkey, United Arab Emirates, and Yemen.

The dynamic heterogeneous model estimates the long-run relationships regarding the cost of medical care and its potential determinants using annual data for 15 countries of the Middle East, between 2005 and 2016 periods. The data for the model are obtained from the (World Development Indicators | DataBank, no date), and all the variables are in logarithmic forms. However, the selection of the variables has been carried out on the basis of long-established literature. For instance, (Grossman 1972) has developed a model of the demand for care where he argued that individual health depends on nominal wage rate, level of education, the relative price of medical care, and aging. Similarly, (Hartwig and Sturm 2018) have provided empirical evidence to the Grossman model using a panel data for the first time. Recently, (Bala et al. 2022) have extended the Grossman model and concluded how health outcomes could be improved for the Middle East countries. Thus, hexp = is the level of total health spending per capita (constant USD prices, PPP adjusted), and gdp = is per capita income level (constant USD prices, PPP adjusted). Similarly, edu = is the level of education which is the average years of formal schooling in a country, which is denoted as edu, and pop is the share of the population above the age of 65 years threshold, which accounts for the vast demand for healthcare services by the elderly cohort of the population. Furthermore, wr = is the level of the wage rate which measures the compensation of employees as a percentage of the expense. Further, the analysis applied GDP deflator series to hexp, y, and wr in order to remove the pure monetary effects they are associated with in the model.

The model of the drivers of medical care expenditure followed in this study emanates from the seminal work of (Grossman 1972). However, unlike many previous studies that relied primarily on using static models, this study argued that better estimates could be obtained by using dynamic panel models. There are numerous reasons to believe that the effect of health expenditure on income, education, employment, demographic transition, excreta does not reflect in the current period, instead, they have lag effects (Roberts 1999). In many democratic countries, public health expenditure is likely to be affected by a periodic change of governments, the political will to improve the health of the population, institutional bottlenecks, the employment of healthcare personnel, the level of technology, and the existing disease burden, among others. There is an equal propensity for the same scenario to happen in most of the countries of the Middle East region with a higher percentage of health workers employed by the public sector. The variables included in this model are used following the (Grossman 1972) model. However, as this model argued, the lagged values could be more sensitive to the contemporary phenomenon. For simplicity, the dynamic panel model can be written as:

$$\begin{aligned} hexp_{it} =& \alpha_{0i} + \alpha_{1i}t + \alpha_{1i}hexp_{it-1} + \beta_{0i}gdp_{it} \\ &+ \beta_{1i}gdp_{it-1} + \beta_{2i}edu_{it} + \beta_{3i}edu_{it-1} + \beta_{4i}emp_{it} \\ &+ \beta_{5}emp_{it-1} + \beta_{6i}pop_{it} + \beta_{7i}pop_{it-1} + c_{it} \end{aligned} \quad (1)$$

i = 1, 2, 3…15, t = 2005…2016,

$hexp_{it}$ denotes both public and private health expenditures, $hexp_{it-1}$ is the lagged value of public and private health expenditures, gdp_{it} is income, gdp_{it-1} is the lagged value of income, edu_{it} is education, edu_{it-1} is the lagged value of education, emp_{it} is employment, emp_{it-1} is the lagged value of employment, pop_{it} is population aging, pop_{it-1} is the lagged value of population aging, and ε_{it} is the error term. All the indicators are measured in natural logarithms, and the coefficients of elasticities can vary across countries. The average value of the long-run elasticities can be computed as:

$$\phi = \sum_{i=1}^{N} \phi / N. \quad (2)$$

Generally, the average impact of the determinants of health spending on medical expenditure growth in a dynamic heterogeneous panel model can be estimated using three different approaches. The mean group estimator consists of obtaining the average estimates for each group in the panel model. In the pooled estimator, a pooled regression equation is obtained by imposing restrictions on the long-run coefficients to be the same for each country but allows for the country-specific short-run coefficients. In the third case, the overall time series regression is estimated across panels. In the last case, cross-section regression is obtained over time.

4 Findings

Prior to the analysis of the dynamic heterogeneous structural model, the level of stationarity of the variables for the model is tested using three alternative criteria for testing panel unit-roots, and the results are shown in Table 1. In the testing equations which exploit the panel structure, all the estimates are responsive to the addition of a timely trend. The null hypothesis is that all the series are stationary. Thus, the result provides absolute evidence to accept the alternative hypothesis for the absence of unit root in all the variables. In order to transform the variables into stationary series to avoid the problem of spurious regression, the analysis takes the first difference for all the series. Overall, the results confirmed that the series are differenced stationary series or integrated of order one I (1), across different panel tests. Further, since all the variables are integrated of order one, the analysis also tests for the possibility of having a long economic relationship among the variables using Padroni and Westerlund panel cointegration tests. Statistical evidence on panel cointegration appears inconclusive because the test statistic shows conflicting results between the two approaches, as shown in Table 2.

Furthermore, the four alternative estimates of the dynamic heterogeneous model for public health expenditure are presented in Table 3. Columns "a" and "c" show the short-run coefficients, while the estimates in columns "b" and "d" are the long-run country-specific means for the mean group and pooled regression models. Clearly, the estimates are consistent, given that the variables are integrated of order one. The short-run coefficients are provided by and large for comparative analysis. However, only income has statistically significant long-run effects among the four regressors. The estimates of the pooled model which are derived from the long-run estimates of the dynamic model are statistically significant indicators. The coefficient of income elasticity is quite lower than the values obtained using the dynamic model; however, it is statistically different from zero. The estimates from the mean group are not similar to those derived from the pooled model on the statistical relevance and the signs of the coefficients. In the last column, the estimates from the cross-section model are given with comparatively higher elasticities for most of the coefficients of the model; they are statistically insignificant, nonetheless. Comparatively, the mean group estimates present better results than the pooled and the cross-section estimates regarding the long-run elasticity coefficients. Perhaps, the presence of the interaction effects between groups may have attributed to this in the model.

Table 1 Panel unit root test of the indicators included in the two models

Indicator	Fisher type		Im-Pesaran-shin type		Hadri type	
	I(0)	I(1)	I(0)	I(1)	I(0)	I(1)
Public health expenditure per capita USD PPP	22.43	221.07***	−1.63	−4.45***	0.72	0.06***
Private health expenditure per capita USD PPP	79.94	229.42***	−2.89	−4.84***	0.79	0.4*
Per capita income USD PPP	75.42	110.30***	−1.62	−3.38***	0.81	0.21***
Years of education	18.27	223.52***	−1.32	−4.51***	0.73	0.23***
Wage rate	118.28	238.59***	−3.08	−5.28***	0.86	0.32**
Population above the age of 65 years (%)	2.89	13.67***	−0.14	−1.23*	1.04	0.88*

***, **, and * significant at 1%, 5%, and 10% levels
Source Data Analysis

Table 2 Panel cointegration tests

Padroni panel cointegration test	Public health expenditure	Private health expenditure
	Statistic	Statistic
Modified Phillips-Perron t	3.4538***	3.7300***
Phillips-Perron t	−7.7303***	−6.4127***
Augmented Dickey-Fuller t	−7.7446***	−5.6079***
Westerlund panel cointegration test	*Statistic*	*Statistic*
Variance ratio	−1.0421	0.2912

***, **, and * significant at 1%, 5%, and 10% levels
Source Data Analysis

Table 3 Results of the long-run elasticity of public health expenditure from alternative estimators

Indicators	Mean group		Pooled		Cross-section
	a	b	c	d	
gdp	0.351 (0.655)	1.979 (0.483)***	1.735 (0.256)***	0.275 (0.080)***	3.256 (4.265)
edu	−1.831 (3.146)	1.021 (2.213)	2.018 (1.983)	−2.246 (0.207)***	−1.032 (3.507)
wr	0.308 (0.340)	−0.508 (0.455)	0.066 (0.203)	0.166 (0.061)***	3.464 (2.530)
pop	4.502 (2.243)	−1.479 (1.420)	−1.303 (1.005)	0.720 (0.220)***	6.407 (2.849)*

***, **, and * significant at 1%, 5%, and 10% levels
Source Data Analysis

Similarly, Table 4 shows the estimates of private health expenditure elasticities from the four alternative estimation techniques. The short-run coefficients are given in columns "a" and "c" along with long-run elasticities in columns "b" and "d" for the mean group and pooled regression. The short-run coefficients differ significantly from the two approaches regarding the statistical significance and the theoretical signs. In the mean group, column, income, education, and population aging are statistically significant, suggesting that they have long-run relationships with private health spending, though the sign of the coefficient of population aging is contrary to apriori expectation. However, the coefficient of real income elasticity associated with private health expenditure is not significantly different from zero. The mean group estimates are almost similar to those of the pooled model. Similar to the estimates of the public health expenditure model, the estimates of the private health spending model also yield statistically insignificant results in the cross-sectional model.

Overall, the current results are reasonably the same across the models regarding the coefficients of long-run income elasticity of the cost of medical care. The coefficient of income elasticity of the cost of medical care is significantly above unity, except in the pooled regression model, and of a sign of the coefficient of the long-run effects is robust across the specification. Apparently, the mean group estimator provides more consistent estimates compared to the cross-sectional estimates, due to the explicit heterogeneity characterized by the model. Moreover, the Hausman specification test provides no statistical difference between the mean group and the pooled model for public and private health spendings. Despite the conflictual evidence of cointegration among the series of the model, there is less evidence to choose between the static and the dynamic models. More importantly, estimates show that medical care has a long-run income elasticity that is significantly different from zero. The positive coefficient associated with edu implies that a unit increase in educational stock would increase health expenditure per capita by roughly 10%. Although statistically insignificant, the coefficients of employment and population aging have signs that are contrary to apriori expectations.

Table 4 Results of the long-run elasticity of private health expenditure from alternative estimators

Indicators	Mean group		Pooled		Cross-section
	a	b	c	d	
gdp	−0.001 (0.000)	0.001 (0.000)***	0.001 (0.000)***	0.002 (0.001)***	0.001 (0.000)
edu	−0.040 (0.041)	0.099 (0.009)***	0.021 (0.015)	−0.089 (0.014)***	−0.087 (0.069)
wr	0.011 (0.005)	−0.002 (0.006)	0.022 (0.005) ***	0.013 (0.003)***	0.004 (0.015)
pop	0.139 (0.047) ***	−0.128 (0.215)***	−0.036 (0.060)	0.149 (0.049)***	0.151 (0.146)

***, **, and * significant at 1%, 5%, and 10% levels
Source Data Analysis

5 Discussion

This study estimates and compares the magnitude of the long-run income elasticity of public and private health spendings per capita in the countries of the Middle East region for the 2005–2016 time periods using a dynamic heterogeneous panel model. However, among the three estimation techniques applied—mean group, pooled regressions, and cross-section regressions, results are comparatively consistent and statistically significant in the first two models. The estimates are not statistically significant in the cross-sectional regressions. The mean group estimates are prepared over the cross-sectional regressions, since heterogeneity is explicit. Unlike the public health expenditure estimates, the private health expenditure estimates show statistically significant long-run effects of the coefficients of income level, education, and aging. Thus, this suggests that consumption of private health is associated with the education among the aged cohort of the population in the long-run. The economic system of these countries and perhaps the demographic composition may have contributed to the statistical insignificance of education, the wage rate, and aging with the public health expenditure. However, this may warrant future investigation.

Furthermore, although the estimate of the long-run elasticity coefficient is quite above unity for public health expenditure, it is below unity for private health spending. This suggests that public health financing is a luxury in contrast to private health expenditure, which is a necessity. A similar result is found regarding public health spending, for instance, by (Ang 2010) that spending on public health services is a luxury and contradicts the findings of (Baltagi et al. 2017) that public health spending is a necessity. The current findings may not be surprising because the public sector exerts a more dominant role in managing the health sector of most of these countries. However, these results must be interpreted with some caution because many studies in both developed and developing economies such as (Atella and Marini 2006; Dreger and Reimers 2005) with few exceptions have for long-established consistent evidence on the necessity of public health care. Essentially, the public health sector is always seen as a preferred destination for most of the vast majority of the poor to visit whenever they demand for a wider range of health services, either freely or at affordable prices.

However, some policy advice can be offered from the present study. Since the income level has an elastic elasticity coefficient with public health expenditure, an increase in the income level by 1 would have a more proportionate increase in the level of public health spending. Therefore, the creation of more gainful opportunities, economic diversification, developing tourism, and openness to trade could stimulate economic growth. As a result, more income would be generated for healthcare financing by both the public and the private sectors, which would eventually lead to improved health outcomes. According to current findings, estimates suggest that an increase in the income level of a particular country or the entire country included in the study alone may not lead to a rise in public health expenditure. However, other factors are also important, especially in the pace of urging the need for the global community to achieve the Sustainable Development Goals (SDGs). The SDGs' target

3.8 aims at achieving universal health insurance coverage for all, at a global level, by the year 2030 (SDG Target 3.8, 2015). The rate of health insurance coverage in these countries may have contributed to the current evidence of the interpretation of public health as a luxury in this context. If that is the case, expanding coverage can improve health outcomes. Therefore, the combined effect of health insurance coverage expansion through the public and the private sector and technology may have greatly contributed to the exponential growth in health care costs. Moreover, since the elasticity coefficient of private health expenditure is less than one, it implies that the poor segment may be deprived from accessing health services if the need arises. Combating the growing burden of chronic diseases across the countries of the Middle East requires urgent expansion in health services by the public sector.

6 Conclusion

The primary objective of this study has been to estimate and compare the coefficients of income elasticity of public and private health expenditure on the determinants of health spending for 15 countries for the span of 11 years. Unlike most of the existing literature that estimates the income elasticity coefficient of public health expenditure in a static model, this study extends the literature by providing some evidence on the elasticity coefficient of private health expenditure in a dynamic way. However, the empirical outcome of this study shows that the coefficients of income elasticity of both public and private health expenditures are greater than unity and less than unity, respectively. Thus, public health expenditure becomes a luxury, whereas private health spending appears a necessity. Therefore, the evidence of higher income elasticity in public health expenditure serves as a reason to regard it as essential in this context. Therefore, this implied that attacking the growing burden of chronic diseases in the Middle Eastern countries requires serious public sector commitment in the provision of health services, particularly to the poor and disadvantaged group.

This study had some limitations. For instance, the heterogeneous model assumes that the variables for the model had lag effects. Although that is justifiable, if no lag effect is present in the dataset, the findings may no longer hold. Additionally, other variables, such as rapid technological application in healthcare services, may significantly contribute to the escalation of healthcare expenditure, nonetheless. Third, variation in health systems across the countries of the study and the nature of the political system and economic development may alter the pattern of health expenditure growth, which is beyond the scope of this study. Therefore, as technology becomes ubiquitous in the rendering of health services, the impact of the application of digital technology on the escalation of healthcare expenditure and improvement in health outcomes in the Middle East region should be of relevant policy consideration.

References

Ang, J.B.: The determinants of health care expenditure in Australia. Appl. Econ. Lett. **17**(7), 639–644 (2010)

Atella, V., Marini, G.: 'Is health care expenditure really a luxury good? Re-assessment and new evidence based on OECD data', Re-Assessment and New Evidence Based on OECD Data (November 2006) (2006)

Baltagi, B.H., et al.: Health care expenditure and income: a global perspective. Health Econ. **26**(7), 863–874 (2017)

Baltagi, B.H., Moscone, F.: Health care expenditure and income in the OECD reconsidered: evidence from panel data. Econ. Model. **27**(4), 804–811 (2010)

Boungnarasy, M.: Health care expenditures in Asia countries: panel data analysis. Econ. Bulletin **31**(4), 3169–3178 (2011)

Di Matteo, L.: The income elasticity of health care spending. Eur. J. Health Econ. **4**(1), 20–29 (2003)

Dreger, C., Reimers, H.-E.: 'Health care expenditures in OECD countries: a panel unit root and cointegration analyses (2005)

Frogner, B.K., Hussey, P.S., Anderson, G.F.: Health systems in industrialized countries. In: The Oxford Handbook of Health Economics. Oxford University Press (2012)

Getzen, T.E.: Health care is an individual necessity and a national luxury: applying multilevel decision models to the analysis of health care expenditures. J. Health Econ. **19**(2), 259–270 (2000)

Grossman, M.: On the concept of health capital and the demand for health. J. Polit. Econ. **80**(2), 223–255 (1972)

Hall, R.E., Jones, C.I.: The value of life and the rise in health spending. Q. J. Econ. **122**(1), 39–72 (2007)

Hartwig, J., Sturm, J.-E.: Testing the Grossman model of medical spending determinants with macroeconomic panel data. Eur. J. Health Econ. **19**(8), 1067–1086 (2018)

Hitiris, T., Posnett, J.: The determinants and effects of health expenditure in developed countries. J. Health Econ. **11**(2), 173–181 (1992)

López-Casasnovas, G., Saez, M.: A multilevel analysis on the determinants of regional health care expenditure: a note. Eur. J. Health Econ. **8**(1), 59–65 (2007)

Murphy, K.M., Topel, R.H.: The value of health and longevity. J. Polit. Econ. **114**(5), 871–904 (2006)

Nocera, S., Zweifel, P.: The demand for health: an empirical test of the Grossman model using panel data. In Health, the Medical Profession, and regulation. Springer, pp. 35–49 (1998)

Roberts, J.: Sensitivity of elasticity estimates for OECD health care spending: analysis of a dynamic heterogeneous data field. Health Econ. **8**(5), 459–472 (1999)

SDG Target 3.8 | Achieve universal health coverage: Available at: https://www.who.int/data/gho/data/themes/topics/indicator-groups/indicator-group-details/GHO/sdg-target-3.8-achieve-universal-health-coverage-(uhc)-including-financial-risk-protection. Accessed 31 May 2021 (2015)

World Development Indicators | DataBank (no date). Available at: https://databank.worldbank.org/source/world-development-indicators. Accessed 17 June 2020

Female Labor Precariousness During the Pandemic Lessons for a Future Better Normal

Simona Ghiță, Cristina Boboc, Valentina Vasile, and Ana-Maria Ciuhu

Abstract Women experienced higher job losses and declining incomes, both during and after the pandemic. The main objective of this paper is to study the level and changes in women's precariousness employment under the COVID conditions, measured with a set of statistical variables characterizing different aspects and complexity of employment quality for European countries. The results indicate a significant reduction in female employment in precarious jobs from the perspective of the duration of employment, during the pandemic. In order to identify the post-pandemic behavioral model, respectively, the simple return to previous jobs or a change in the pattern of employment, we analyzed the gender gap in the quality of employment under the conditions of the COVID-19 pandemic. By applying the principal components analysis and the cluster analysis, three groups of countries were identified, associated with behavioral models to access the opportunity to occupy and/or maintain the job. Based on these results, at the end of the paper, we identified possible ways to restore post-pandemic employment, taking into account the robust recovery, respectively, preserving the benefits of digitalization and changing both the employment model and the life model in households and communities.

Keywords Female labor · Principal component analysis · Cluster analysis · Nonparametric tests

---

S. Ghiță · C. Boboc
Bucharest University of Economic Studies, Institute of National Economy, Bucharest, Romania

V. Vasile
Institute of National Economy—Romanian Academy, Bucharest, Romania

A.-M. Ciuhu (✉)
Institute of National Economy—Romanian Academy, National Institute of Statistics, Bucharest, Romania
e-mail: dobre.anamaria@hotmail.com

A. M. Dima and E. R. Danescu (eds.), *Fostering Recovery Through Metaverse Business Modelling*, Springer Proceedings in Business and Economics,
https://doi.org/10.1007/978-3-031-28255-3_10

1 Introduction

Studies show that favorable developments in the field of gender equality have a positive effect on the entire economic and social life of a country (EIGE 2017). Lately, gender inequality has been on the rise, with a favorable trend, but the COVID-19 pandemic has raised some questions, raising these positive developments to a crossroads.

Some studies show that women's jobs are 1.8 times more vulnerable to this crisis than men's jobs and that, although women account for about 39% of total employment, they are responsible for 54% of total job losses (McKinsey Global Institute 2020). One possible explanation for this disproportionate effect of the pandemic crisis on women's employment is the growing burden of unpaid aid, which is provided/supported to a large extent by women (in the form of childcare or relatives/family members in poor health due to the pandemic). This also meant a reduction in working time and, implicitly, in women's income. As such, it has been observed that female employment has declined during the pandemic period at a faster pace than the average employment, considering gender segregation in employment, with men and women predominantly employed in different sectors and occupations (ibidem).

The "2021 report on gender equality in the EU" published by the European Commission (2021) points out the negative impact of the COVID-19 pandemic on the situation of women, exacerbating the already existing gender inequalities in economic, social, and political life, and hampering progress recorded in recent years in this direction. Therefore, the report shows the presence of large numbers of women in the first lines of the fight against the pandemic: 76% of health and social care workers and 86% of personal care workers in health services are women, making it even more difficult for women, to cope with the high degree of workload (work intensity), risks of infections, and work–life balance. The pandemic has also worsened the situation of women in the labor market. Most sectors of activity that have been severely affected by the pandemic (trade, hospitality, health care)—sectors that do not allow, by the specifics of their work, remote work—are characterized by a predominance of female labor. Women faced a greater difficulty in returning to the labor market in the summer of 2020, as evidenced by the higher increase in the male employment rate (+ 1.4%) than in the female employment rate (+0.8%) (Eurostat database 2022). The 2020 lockdown has had a major impact on both unpaid care services and work–life balance. Thus, while men spent 36 h a week caring for children and 15 h a week for housework, women spent almost twice as much time/time for the same purpose (36 h/week for childcare and 23 h/week, respectively, for household chores) (EIGE 2021). Women were deprived of participation, of active participation in the decision-making process. According to a study in 2021, women were underrepresented in the bodies responsible for overcoming the pandemic (European Parliament 2021).

International Labour Organization (ILO) experts also underlined the deepening of gender imbalance during economic crises, but estimated that the asymmetry will persist in the near future, as the resumption of progress toward gender inequality is a difficult process. During the pandemic crisis, women are expected to feel more job loss and reduced incomes. In the next period, returning to normal with the resumption of activity is expected to be slower and more difficult for women. Thus, the ILO has estimated that the female employed population in 2021 will be 13 million fewer people than in 2019, and that even if the estimated increase in jobs for women in 2021 exceeds that of men, this will not be enough to return to the pre-pandemic level of female employment (ILO 2021).

At world level, female employment-to-population ratio estimation is for slow recovery in 2021–2022, with just 0.4% per year compared to 0.6–0.7% for male. For Europe, the situation is different, and the reduction of the employment rate was below 1% for women and about 1% for men. The decreasing of women's employment rate was higher in Eastern Europe and continued in 2020, so the recovery will be longer (Table 1).

The main objective of this paper is to study the situation and changes in the precariousness of women's employment under COVID-19 conditions. The analysis is based on a set of thirteen statistical variables, characterizing the different facets of precarious employment in 34 European countries, corresponding to 2019 and 2020 for both genders.

Table 1 Recovery estimate of the employment-to-population ratio (age, 15+), percent

	2019 rate (%)	2020 as against 2019 (%)	Estimated recovered (%)		Deficit (%)
			2021	2022	
	Female				
World	45.2	−2.2	0.4	0.4	−1.4
Northern, Southern, and Western Europe	49.1	−0.6	0.2	0.4	0
Eastern Europe	49.8	−0.8	−0.2	0.2	−0.8
	Male				
World	69.4	−2.8	0.7	0.6	−1.5
Northern, Southern, and Western Europe	60	−1.1	0.2	0.3	−0.6
Eastern Europe	64.5	−1	0	0.2	−0.8

Source Authors' calculation based on ILOSTAT, ILO *modeled estimates, November 2021, Appendix C—World Employment and Social Outlook. Trendes 2022, ILO Flagship Report, ISBN 9,789,220,356,975 (print); 9,789,220,356,982 (web PDF)*

The motivation for choosing the EU comparison of the COVID-19 impact analysis on precarious employment in the first year of the pandemic is based on the following assessments:

- In the last decade, employment quality policies associated with reducing inequality measures have been in line with the 2030 Agenda and SDG 8 and have addressed various aspects of job insecurity (ILO 2011; Broughton et al. 2016; Campbell and Price 2016; Gago-Cortés and Alló 2019; UNDP 2016).
- The first year of the pandemic was characterized by similar measures/restrictions—lockdown and remote work, with an emphasis on ensuring the continuity of essential services, which allows a comparative analysis of the effects at the country level; starting with 2021 and depending on the effectiveness of the measures from 2020, the reaction of the states—by relaxing/resuming economic activities and measures on the labor market, although essentially similar, differed by country, depending on a number of characteristics of the pandemic incident and the diversity of the economy, which makes short-term comparative analyses less relevant, respectively, 2021 compared to 2020.
- A short-term analysis of the effects of measures generated by crises outside the business environment (for example, the pandemic as a health crisis) is useful to be able to identify possible directions for intervention to ensure the resilience of the labor market to extreme events.

In addition to this quantitative analysis, in the last part of the paper, we selectively present relevant policy measures initiated after the first pandemic shock, with post-pandemic potential and, thus becoming components of labor market policies for robust, resilient recovery, and promoting the benefits of the digital transition. This border is in line with the European Economic and Social Committee (EESC) 2020 recommendations, which state that we cannot be satisfied with restoring the previous situation, we need to restructure and improve it, respectively, which experts have defined as "better normal," to an external shock symmetrical to EU countries, but with different effects and solutions at the Member State level.

2 Literature Review

The pandemic crisis is associated with Taleb's Black Swan (2007), but our opinion is that the actual crisis has shown that just the recovery is not enough, at least for the labor market. The crisis highlighted not only the need for measures to support employment during the crisis, but also confirmed that labor market mechanisms are not calibrated to future transformations of the business environment; they are based on behaviors and stereotypes, prejudices, and false comparative advantages (reduced wages), through precarious jobs (forms of employment and working conditions), unattractive for young people for multiple reasons. The EESC has stated since mid-2020 that a further combination of policy responses and timing is needed to recover from this crisis, and that measures/actions must reach those targeted to produce real effects (EESC 2020, p. 9). A job-focused strategy is the starting point for responding to multiple labor market challenges, both pre-pandemic and specific pandemic periods, resulting from brutal restrictions and even temporary/total closure of economic, social, or cultural activities.

Precarious work is a multifaceted and complex issue (ILO 2011), respectively, precarious employment is defined by two coordinates: precarious contractual arrangements (fixed-term, short-term, temporary, and seasonal, day labor and casual labor with bogus (self) employment, subcontracting or agency contracts) and precarious working conditions (low wages, poor employment protection, partial or lack to social protection, etc.). Broughton et al. (2016) and Olsthoorn (2014) defined three components of precarious work: less secured work, fewer rights, and vulnerable/less paid work. Campbell and Price (2016) defined as precarious work activities complaining five attributes: precariousness in employment (employees' perspective defined as insecurity, low wages, overtime, and working conditions), precarious work (non-standard jobs), precarious workers (i.e., women), precariat, and precarity. Recently, this approach has been enriched with aspects such as dual labor market for immigrants (Vasile et al. 2019), involuntary temporary work, jobs with high risk of burnout (lack of work task clarity, overworked or/and not being able to disconnect), etc., precariousness forms of occupations have diversified and "work no longer represents a reliable route out of poverty" (Bobek 2018, p. 5). The digital and ecological transformation of the business environment is associated with the reform of the content of work and the requirements of post-pandemic jobs. Redefining work is not limited to the requirements of technology transfer and productivity, but especially to working conditions and quality of work—green and decent jobs.

Recent research on employment has focused on analyses of various forms of insecurity, as well as concerns about the future needs of the business environment, as targets through which to address measures to reduce, manage forms of job insecurity. Previous research on job insecurity has highlighted not only the emerging nature of the concept's content, but also the preference to analyze certain aspects. Thus, a recent research by Kreshpaj et al. (2020) highlighted the interest in the analysis of precarious forms divided into three dimensions: employment insecurity, income inadequacy, and lack of rights and protection. The effects of precarious employment of women are more obvious if we analyze the activities carried out from a broader perspective: domestic and family responsibilities, largely unrecognized as forms of work, part-time, and self-employed work mainly associated with precarious working conditions (EP 2020). According to the OECD database, women spend almost twice the amount of time per week than men in unpaid work (as average OECD countries, 1.93 times in the last year, less time in paid work, as the average 2/3 of time per week worked by men). The effects of the pandemic have been shown to be stronger on the employment of women for multiple reasons, including their predominance in sectors of activity such as health and education (Alon et al. 2020), precarious forms of employment, and various forms of discrimination (Adams-Prassl et al. 2020; Couch et al. 2020; Farré et al. 2020; Forsythe et al. 2020; Yasenov 2020). A query of the WoS database on the topic of precarious employment indicates a number of 124 papers published since 2009, highlighting subtopics such as unemployment, employment,

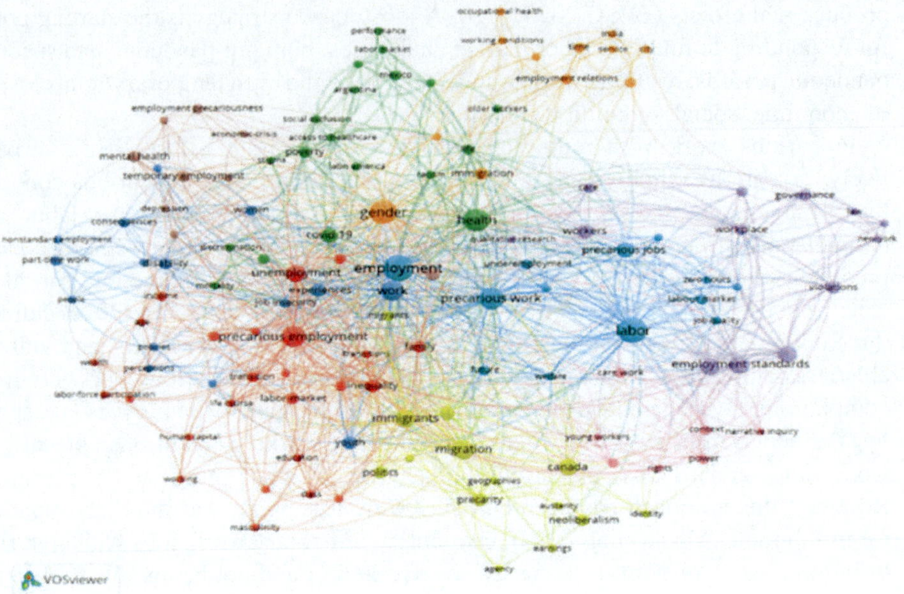

Fig. 1 Bibliometrics on keywords related to job insecurity in WoS, 2009–2022. *Source* Based on the WoS query, April 4, 2022, using VOSviewer

inequality, precarious work, immigrants, youth, work, labor, employment standards, precarious employment, enforcement, precarity, and migration (Figs. 1 and 2).

If we extend the research at the level of gender disparities from the 2009 articles identified for the same period and the same database, three major subdomains of interest for experts stand out, namely the characteristics of gender differences on the labor market (productivity–performance, leadership–authorship, discrimination–stereotypes, participation–access–education–quality), participation and social discrimination (violence, food security, behavior, etc.), and health-related disparities (gender disparities, depression–risk–care–health–quality of life, etc.).

It is interesting to note that, although the perception of experts is that actually the risk of precarious female employment is higher and activation on the labor market in decent and high-quality jobs is discriminatory, women continue to be concerned with education, accessing jobs for independently economic, and more and more they are pursuing a professional career, in the conditions of looking for a balance between work and life. The pandemic highlighted the role of women in the household and in the labor market, but also the risks of precarious post-pandemic employment.

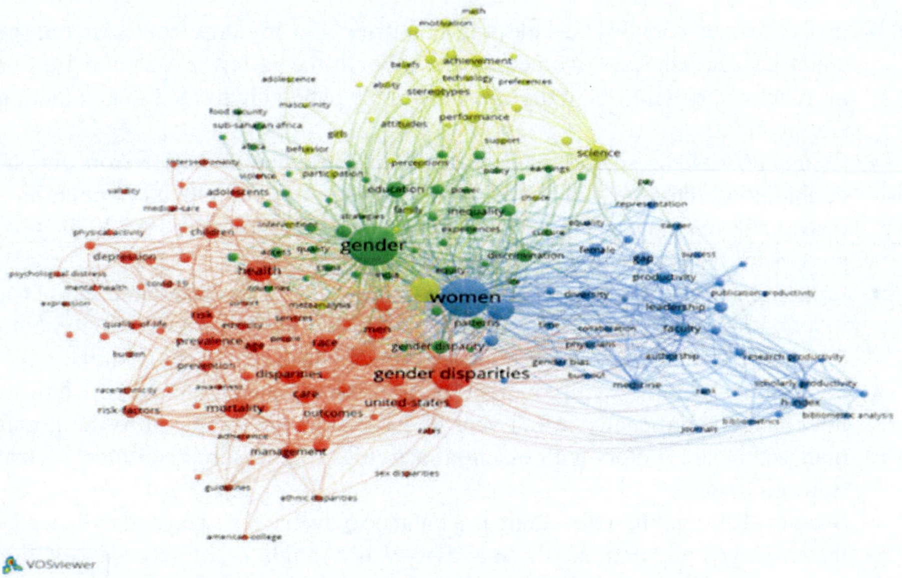

Fig. 2 Bibliometrics on keywords related to gender disparities in WoS, 2009–2022. *Source* Based on the WoS query, April 4, 2022, using VOSviewer

3 Aims of the Research

3.1 Data Description—Female Employment

The dynamics of the employment rate among women, for most European countries, was a negative one, decreasing by 0.5 percentage points (EU average) in 2020 compared to the pre-pandemic year 2019 (Eurostat database 2022).

By age groups, at the EU level, in 2020 there was a sharper decrease in the employment rate among young people, both women and men (by about 2 percentage points), the decrease attenuating with the age increase (Eurostat database 2022). There is a greater stability in the employment rate in the older age groups, so that, in women's case in 2020, it was only 0.4 percentage points lower than in the previous year, and in the case of men it remained constant (ibidem).

If we analyze European countries from two perspectives that of the share of women in the employed population and that of employment changes in the year of the pandemic (2020), compared to the previous one, we can identify two basic patterns of behavior:

- In most European countries (Nordic countries, France, Portugal) the share of women in the employed population is above average, but there has been—under the impact of the pandemic—a reduction in the employed population in 2020 compared to the previous year;

- In the former socialist, developing countries and in some southern European countries, the share of women in the labor force is lower than the European average, given that even in these countries the pandemic has led to a reduction in employment;
- Characterizing the sectors of activity in all European countries from the same double perspective that of the share of women in the employed population and that of the dynamics of total employment in 2020 compared to 2019, several patterns of behavior of these sectors can be identified:
- Predominantly, female employment sectors, in which the pandemic did not lead to a contraction of the employed population, to a restriction of activity, but, on the contrary, to an increase of no more than 8% (Finance, Real-estate);
- Predominantly female employment sectors, whose total employed population did not change significantly in the year of the pandemic compared to the previous one, as they are sectors with essential activities that required continuity (Health, Education);
- Sectors of activity in which there is a balance between the two genders in terms of the employed population, whose activity was strongly negatively affected by the pandemic, suffering a decrease in total employment in 2020 compared to 2019 (Accommodation and Food, Administrative activities, Arts, Trade, Professional activities);
- Sectors of activity in which there is a balance between the two genders in terms of the employed population, but whose activity is essential, as such in the conditions of the pandemic, it was necessary to expand the employed population by about 4% (Public administration, Health);
- Predominantly male sectors of employment that have suffered a restriction of activity and the total employed population, under the rule of the restrictions imposed by the pandemic (Construction, Transport, Agriculture, Manufacturing, Water Supply);
- Sectors of activity with predominantly male employment, but with essential character, whose continuity had to be ensured even during the pandemic, and therefore required an increase of employment (Mining, Electricity, ICT—the last register registering the largest increase of the employed population).

One aspect of the quality of employment is the atypical forms of employment. Regarding employed persons working part-time, 7.8% of the total male employment aged 15–64 worked part-time in 2019, the share of women being over 20% higher in the same year (Eurostat 2022). In the following year, the weights suffered small reductions, both for male and female employees, reaching 7.2% and 27.7%, respectively. The gender gap has remained roughly constant over the past two years. The Netherlands is the country with the highest weights in 2020: 24.3% (male) and 73.8% (female), followed by Switzerland (18.1%—male, 63.4%—female). At the opposite pole, with the lowest share, is Bulgaria, with less than 2% for both genders. The Netherlands is also characterized by the largest gender gap in terms of part-time work (49.5% higher for women than for men). Work on the basis of temporary contracts is more common among women than men, throughout the European Union

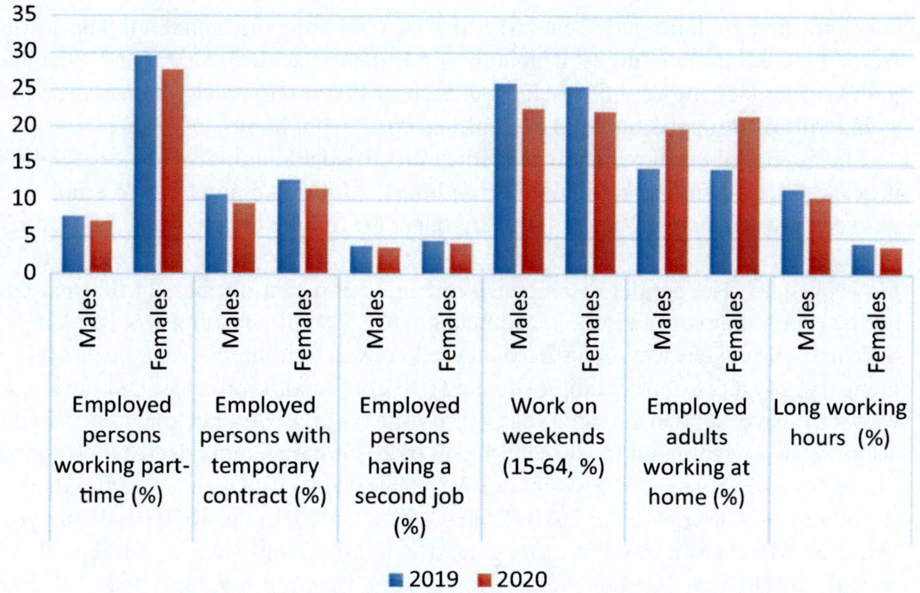

Fig. 3 Share of employees performing atypical forms of work, by gender, 2019 and 2020—EU level. *Source* Eurostat database, online data code lfsa_esegatyp

(with 10.8% for men and 12.8% for women in 2019). In the pandemic year 2020, the weights decreased slightly, the gender gap remaining at 2% in favor of male employees. In 2020, Montenegro recorded the highest shares of employees with a temporary employment contract (24.6%—male, 23.0%—female), while Lithuania and Romania recorded the minimum values of the indicator (around 1% for male and 0.6% for female) (Fig. 3).

In the whole European Union, 3.87% of male and 4.56% of female employees had a secondary job. In the next year, 2020, the weights decreased slightly, the gender discrepancy remaining at a constant level (around 0.5–0.7%). The country with the highest level of the indicator, for both male and female employees, was Germany (with 18.68%—male, 23.89%—female, data for 2020). The minimum level of the indicator was registered, in the same year 2020, in Malta and Cyprus (0.12%—male, 0.08%—female). The COVID-19 pandemic has created, more than ever, the possibility of working from home, regulated by law, favored by the need to comply with restrictions and conditions of physical distance, in order to limit the spread of the virus. Thus, in 2019, in the entire European Union, 14.4% of the male employees and 14.3% of female employees worked at home. The weights increased, predictably in the first year of the pandemic, by 5.4% in the case of male employees and by 7.2% in the case of female employees (reaching 19.8%—male and 21.5%—female). The countries where this type of work was recorded at the highest level in 2020 were Luxembourg (with 44.7%—male and 44.4%—female, practically almost half of the employees), followed by the Netherlands (with approximately 43%—for both genders), and Finland and Denmark (almost 40% for both genders). The lowest weights were found in Turkey, Romania, and Bulgaria (with about 2.0–2.2%—male, 3.9%–4.5%—female), countries that were probably less technically prepared, as well as in terms of infrastructure and educational work from home.

The quality of employment is also illustrated by the length of work, especially if it takes place outside of normal working hours. More than a quarter of employees worked on weekends in 2019 (slightly higher share of men than women), so that next year the level of the indicator was reduced (one in five male/female employees worked on weekends). The gender discrepancy remained constant throughout the analyzed period (0.4% in favor of men). In Montenegro, 61.5% of male employees and 46.8% of female employees worked in 2020 on weekends (maximum percentages), while in Hungary only 8.2% of male employees and 6.8% of female employees had carried out work on the weekend in the same year. Men work in a higher proportion with extended hours (11.6%) compared to women (4.2%) in 2019, the weights decreasing slightly in the following year (10.5%—male, 3.8%—female). The gender gap decreased slightly in 2020 compared to 2019 (from 7.4% to 6.7%). In the 2020 pandemic year, extended work was carried out to a greater extent by employees in Turkey (32.1% of male employees, 20.2% of female employees, maximum values) and to a lesser extent in Lithuania and Bulgaria (1.0%–1.4% for males, 0.6%–0.8% for females).

4 Methodology

The main objective of this paper is to study the precariousness of women's employment, and to identify distinct behavioral patterns of European countries from this point of view, under COVID-19 conditions. The analysis used the variable *Precarious employment* (percentage of employees with a short-term contract of up to 3 months) among women and 12 other variables that characterize the different facets of the quality of employment in 34 European countries (Member and non-EU countries), corresponding to 2019 and 2020, for both genders. For each of these 12 variables, the gender difference was then calculated between the indicator level for the female population and that for the male population (female versus male). In the first stage, the aim was to refine the set of initial variables included in the study, between which there were correlations of different directions and intensities, with obtaining compound variables, new, artificial, uncorrelated with each other, but which keep as much weight as possible from variability of initial data. Following the analysis of the correlation matrix between the gender discrepancies of all these indicators, the variables between which there was a deterministic or insignificant correlation were eliminated, leaving a set of ten variables on which the Principal Component Analysis method was applied.

In the analysis performed, the following hypothesis was tested:

Hypothesis: During the pandemic, there was a significant change in the share of women with precarious work compared to the previous period of time.

To test this hypothesis, two nonparametric tests were applied to related samples (pair): Wilcoxon Signed-Ranks Test and Precarious Employment Variable Sign

(Percentage of employees with a short-term contract of up to 3 months) among women in 2019 and 2020.

Secondly, by applying a Principal Component Analysis and a cluster analysis, it is aimed to identify some patterns of behavior of European countries in terms of gender discrepancy in the quality of employment in the conditions of the COVID-19 pandemic.

5 Results

To test whether the variable as a difference in the share of women with precarious employment in 2020 compared to 2019 is continuous and normally distributed, Kolmogorov–Smirnov and Shapiro–Wilk tests were applied. According to these tests, we cannot confirm that the distribution of the variable is normal (Figs. 4, 5 and Table 2).

Thus, for testing the hypothesis "During the pandemic, there was a significant change in the share of women with precarious work compared to the previous time period." The Wilcoxon and Sign nonparametric tests were applied, and the results are presented in Table 3.

For a probability of 95% it can be stated that indeed, in the first year of the pandemic, 2020, there was a significant change in the share of women whose jobs were characterized by precariousness, compared to the pre-pandemic year 2019. However, this change has a positive, favorable aspect, as the meaning of this change is to mitigate this phenomenon. Although this phenomenon has favorable connotations, it could occur under the impact of a lower return to work of women after the lockdown

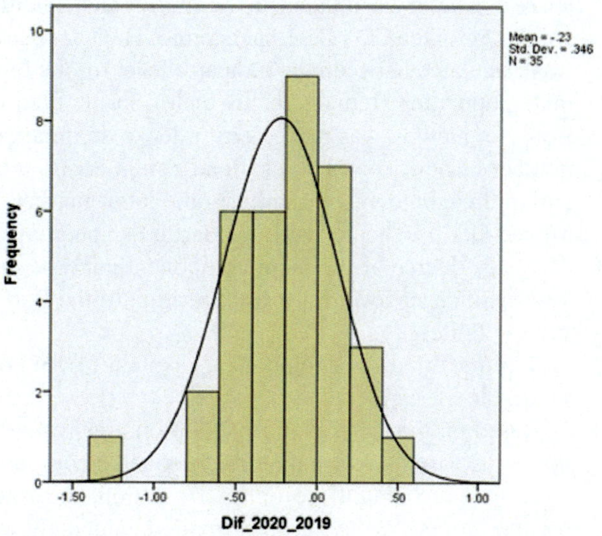

Fig. 4 Histogram of the difference in the share of women with precarious employment in 2020 compared to 2019. *Source* Authors' calculation

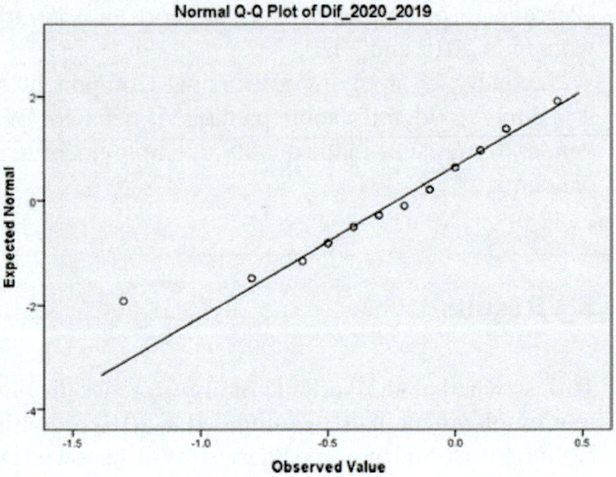

Fig. 5 Normal Q-Q plot of the difference in the share of women with precarious employment in 2020 compared to 2019. *Source* Authors' calculation

Table 2 Tests of normality

	Kolmogorov–Smirnov[a]			Shapiro–Wilk		
	Statistical	df	Sig	Statistical	df	Sig
Dif_2020_2019	0.159	35	0.025	0.949	35	0.104

Source Authors' calculation

period than in the case of men, as evidenced by some studies (Freund and Scott 2022; ILO 2021).

After refining the initial data, ten variables describing the different aspects of the quality of work were used to identify the behavioral patterns of European countries in terms of gender discrepancy in the employment quality on the labor market, under the conditions of the COVID-19 pandemic. Then, for each variable, the gender difference was calculated between the indicator level for the female population and that for the male population (female versus male). In the first stage, the Principal Component Analysis method was applied in order to summarize the initial data set in a small number of new, complex, artificial components, showing the source of the gender gap in the employment quality in the labor market. The calculation of the Kaiser–Meyer–Olkin indicator and the Bartlett's sphericity test resulted in an appropriate adequacy degree of the main component analysis method (KMO > 0.6, and a very low significance level for the application of the Bartlett's test, very close to the null value) (Table 4).

The first three main components explain 71.15% of the variation of the initial data set (Table 5).

Based on the scree plot chart and on eigenvalues, it is recommended to replace the initial variables with the first three main components (Fig. 6).

In order to obtain the optimal solution, the rotation of the main components was performed by the Varimax method, which allows an easier interpretation of the identified factors.

Table 3 Sign and Wilcoxon test results

Wilcoxon signed ranks test					Sign test		
		N	Mean rank	Sum of ranks		Frequencies	
Women_prec_2020-Women_prec_2019	Negative differences [a]	24	17.50	420.00		Negative differences [a]	24
	Positive differences [b]	7	10.86	76.00	Women_prec_2020-Women_prec_2019	Positive differences [b]	7
	Ties [c]	4				Ties [c]	4
	Total	35				Total	35
Z		−3,388			Z	−2,874	
Asymp. Sig. (2-tailed)		0.001			Asymp. Sig. (2-tailed)	0.004	

Notes: a.Women_prec_2020 < Women_prec_2019;
b. Women_prec_2020 > Women_prec_2019;
c. Women_prec_2020 = Women_prec_2019
Note: Based on positive ranks

Source Authors' calculation

Table 4 KMO and Bartlett's test

Kaiser–Meyer–Olkin Measure of Sampling Adequacy		0.638
Bartlett's test of sphericity	Approx. Chi-Square	209,500
	Df	45
	Sig	0.000

Source Authors' calculation

The first component is strongly and directly correlated with the gender discrepancy in terms of employment rate and employed persons having a second job (correlation coefficients between 0.82 and 0.84) and inversely and medium correlated with the gender difference between the share of people working from home (correlation coefficient of −0.67). Indeed, for all 34 European countries, the male employment rate was higher than that of the female. Regarding the share of people who have a second job, the situation is approximately symmetrical from this point of view; in half of the countries included in the study, women have a higher share than men in holding a secondary job, while in the other half the situation is the opposite. Referring to the possibility of working from home, in the first year of the coronavirus pandemic in most countries (23 out of 34) this opportunity was used, exploited more by women, the gender gap of this indicator being positive in all these countries. This component was entitled "Gender-gap in forms of employment" (Tables 6 and 7).

The second component is directly and very strongly correlated with gender discrepancy regarding Average number of usual weekly hours of work (correlation coefficient 0.96), average and directly correlated with the gender difference between women's and men's incomes (correlation coefficient 0.66) and inverse and average correlated with the gender difference regarding employees working part-time (correlation coefficient −0.83). In fact, the average time allocated to work was significantly higher for male employees in all European countries, which is the complete opposite of the gender gap of part-time workers, where women have superiority. This component was named "Gender-gap in income and working time" (Tables 6 and 7).

The third component is strongly and directly correlated with the gender difference in employed persons who work on weekends and employed persons with temporary contract and medium and positive correlated with the share of women working with extended hours. In most countries (22 out of 34), men work more than women on weekends, while women occupy temporary jobs more than men in the first year of the health pandemic. This component was named "Gender gap in job insecurity" (Tables 6 and 7).

By applying the K-means classification method considering as classification criteria the three main components, three models of behavior of European countries whose averages are presented in Table 8.

Greece is included in a separate cluster, a position explained by the fact that this country reported an average annual income of women over EUR 7000 higher than that of men (+28.83%), a unique situation compared to all other European countries, where the gender pay gap is clearly in men's favor.

Table 5 Total variance explained

Component	Initial eigenvalues			Extraction sums of squared loadings			Rotation sums of squared loadings		
	Total	% of Variance	Cumulative%	Total	% of Variance	Cumulative%	Total	% of Variance	Cumulative%
1	3,976	39,762	39,762	3,976	39,762	39,762	2,825	28,250	28,250
2	2,032	20,317	60,079	2,032	20,317	60,079	2,551	25,508	53,758
3	1,107	11,071	71,150	1,107	11,071	71,150	1,739	17,392	71,150

Source Authors' calculation

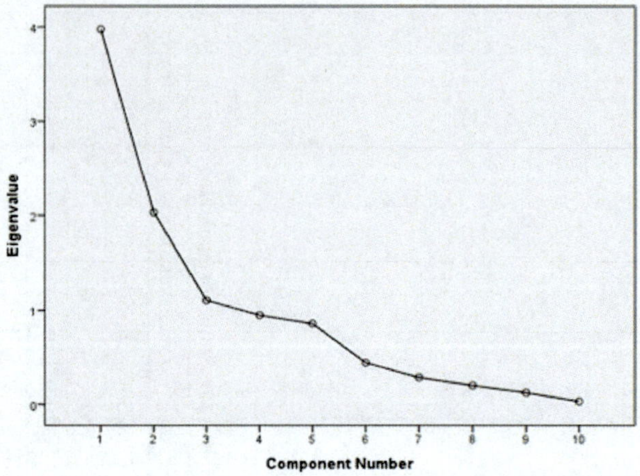

Fig. 6 Scree plot. *Source* Authors' calculation

Table 6 Rotated component matrix

	Component		
	1	2	3
Empl_rate	0.843		0.320
Second_job	0.818		
At_home	−0.676		−0.285
Self_empl	0.615	−0.259	−0.298
Working_time		0.957	
Part_time	0.319	−0.833	
Earnings	−0.431	0.658	−0.410
Long_hours	0.409		0.605
Weekend	0.388		0.775
Temporary			0.752
Extraction Method: Principal Component Analysis Rotation Method: Varimax with Kaiser Normalization			
Rotation converged in five iterations			

Source Authors' calculation

A more complete and detailed characterization of the three behavioral models of European countries in terms of gender differences in the quality of employment, in 2020, is presented in Table 9.

Model 1 is specific to Southern European countries, but also some former socialist countries (BE, CZ, EE, ES, IT, CY, LV, LU, MT, SK, SE—Cluster 1); women are less actively involved in the labor market, normally for religious reasons, but also for pandemic reason evolved in 2020.

Model 2 characterizes countries in the group of former socialist countries (BG, HR, LT, HU, PL, PT, RO, SI, ME, MK, RS, TR—Cluster 2), which are developing,

Table 7 Defining the main components

Component	Name of the main component	Variables included in the main component
Component_1	Gender gap in forms of employment	Employment rate Employed persons having a second job Employed adults working at home Self-employment
Component_2	Gender gap in income and working time	Average number of usual weekly hours of work Employed persons working part-time Mean annual earnings
Component_3	Gender gap in job insecurity	Employed persons with long working hours Employed persons who work on weekends Employed persons with temporary contract

Source Authors' calculation

with a lower level of income; gender gap in job quality is low, in terms of most ranking criteria (in absolute terms).

Model 3 is specific to the group of economically and socially developed countries (DK, DE, IE, FR, NL, AT, FI, IS, NO, CH—Cluster 3); women are actively and largely involved in the labor market, with a gender pay gap and a minimum employment gap; but the level of income for both genders is also high. However, women try to increase their income in relation to men through alternative, atypical forms of employment and work (second job, self-employment, part-time, temporary contracts or work outside working hours, high gap in favor of women).

6 Comments and Labor Market Future Policy Approach

Precarious employment, through its various manifestation forms, has increased in the last three decades, women being among the targeted categories of employees (Oddo et al. 2021). Almost half of women and a fifth of men are in precarious or lower-quality employment trajectories (Eisenberg-Guyot et al. 2020). Women may face employment-related discrimination mainly based on low efficiency of legal rules enforcement and lack of implementation and functioning control mechanisms supported by the state, trade unions, etc. Measuring and monitoring employment precariousness is a concern of experts within the wider European-wide monitoring system using various tools such as Employment Precariousness Scale (Jonsson et al. 2019; Pedrosa et al. 2020; Julia et al. 2017).

The two-year period of the pandemic has reiterated the importance of reducing the gender gap as a driving factor for economic development and the improvement of

Table 8 Cluster means by main components and variables

Cluster mean	COMP_1				COMP_2			COMP_3		
	Employment rate (%)	Second job (%)	Working at home (%)	Self-employed (%)	Weekly hours of work (hours)	Part-time (%)	Mean annual earnings (thous. EUR)	Long working hours (%)	Work on weekends (%)	Temporary contracts (%)
1	−9.94	0.11	1.87	−0.16	−3.85	14.45	−4.76	−5.65	−0.04	2.76
2	−13.01	−1.54	3.00	−0.12	−2.06	3.40	−1.78	−5.53	−4.26	0.48
3	−6.41	1.77	−0.50	0.32	−6.54	27.41	−11.53	−7.36	1.06	2.47
Overall_Mean	−10.21	0	1.63	0	−4.04	14.15	−5.35	−6.24	−1.51	1.88

Source Authors' calculation

Table 9 Description of the behavior patterns of European countries in terms of gender gap in employment precariousness

Model	Component		
	Gender gap in forms of employment	Gender gap in income and working time	Gender gap in job insecurity
MODEL 1	On average, the employment rate of women is almost 10% lower than that of men The share of self-employed men is slightly higher than that of women The lowest gender gap for people with a secondary job (a slight preponderance of women) Higher share of women working from home (an average of almost 2% compared to men)	Average gender pay gap, with women earning more than EUR 4700 less per year than men (on average) Gender discrepancy in average working time for all indicators, with women working less part-time but to a greater extent on a part-time basis	Minimum gender gap in the share of people working on weekends (slightly in favor of men), but maximum in the case of those with temporary employment contracts (with almost 3% more women)
MODEL 2	The largest gender gap in the employment rate (13% higher for male employees), but also the largest gender gap for those working from home (3% more for women) Minimum gender gap for self-employed (slightly higher for men) The share of men with a second job is 1.54% higher	Gender minimum wage gap, with women earning almost EUR 1800 less per year than men (on average) Minimum gender gap in working time for all indicators, with women working less part-time but to a greater extent on a part-time basis	Maximum gender gap in the share of people working on weekends (in favor of men over 4%), but minimum in the case of those with temporary employment contracts (almost 0)
MODEL 3	Gender gap in the average employment rate (over 6% higher male than female rate) The largest gender gap in the share of those with second job and self-employed (higher weights for men, with 1.77% and 0.32%, respectively) Minimum gender gap for domestic workers (almost equal weights for both genders)	Maximum gender discrepancies for all indicators (men earn on average more than 11,000 EU per year more than women, have a work schedule of more than 6 h longer, the share of men working extended hours is more than 7% higher than 27% more women work part-time)	Women work to a greater extent on temporary contracts, but also on weekends. However, in absolute terms, gender disparities are average

Source Authors' calculation

quality of life improvement. Gender gap was reversed during pandemic (UN Women 2020a, b).

The pandemic has shown greater involvement of women in activities related to the management of specific areas (health, care), but also its ability to cope with pressure—burnout, etc., but also women have made significant gains in representation, and especially in senior leadership (McKinsey and Company 2021).

Recovery and resilient closing gender gap in the post-pandemic imply a change in the policy-making model, respectively, starting from the evidence and managing stereotypes. For example, it is clear that women tend to be more educated than men, with the proportion of women in higher education being higher than men. It is equally obvious that women remain underrepresented in higher paid professions, but also that more women than men work in low-paid jobs and sectors, and in lower positions.

Supportive measures to reduce job insecurity in the post-pandemic target at least three levels:

1. Employment recovery in the jobs directly affected by pandemic restrictions by smarter reactivation, with the advantages offered by digitalization;
2. Closing precarious gender gap jobs, with the transformation of employment flexibility into an opportunity for a better work–life balance than the promotion of inequality and inequity in women's employment as an undesirable but necessary solution for maintaining cost competitiveness
3. Jobs' transition toward future labor market framework, based on human-centered economic development and higher efficient employment, based on increasing trend of decent and quality jobs creating, with digital and ecological transformation.

The flexibility of employment and the increase of the forms of temporary or part time employment was considered as a measure to support the entry of women in the labor market, considering that they have greater responsibilities and allocate more time to household activities, childcare, etc. The diminishing importance of the gender gap through the presence of women in activities and jobs specific to men has facilitated discretionary and inequitable behaviors, supported by motivations such as productivity or significantly different quality of work. The pandemic only accentuated these aspects and, moreover, highlighted the need to reconsider policies to reduce the gender gap as a tool to reduce the precariousness of women's employment, both at national and company level (EC 2005; ACCA 2008; UN 2014; OECD 2020; EC 2021).

Labor market regulation to reduce the factors that facilitate the precariousness of women's employment, including, for example, the introduction of paternity leave for childcare or the digital transition and the expansion of remote jobs, even before the pandemic, facilitated not only access to employment, but also attracting talent and senior positions, opening a better woman representation on the labor market and in managerial positions. The pandemic has shown that working remotely and flexible time arrangements could be the future central point of interest for companies' employment policy. A recent study (The Work-life Balance Barometer, conducted in 2021, July), based on the experience of about a year and a half of pandemic, showed that (a) Remote working boosted productivity and work–life balance for the elderly position to a greater degree than employees in less senior roles, and (b) access to remote working equipment, and skill-based training are the main limits for hybrid models work. Almost half prefer to return to work because they feel it is necessary to keep their professional and personal obligations separate.

A review of recommended measures at European level related to future employment (ILO 2011; EU 2019; EIGE 2018; UNDP 2020) but also those associated with post-pandemic recovery (UN Women 2020a, b; McKinsey and Company 2021) highlights aspects such as providing income security and employment opportunities as labor policies measures and instruments that allow for stable and predictable employment, based on multidimensional employment precariousness measurement scale over a simple dichotomy between permanent and temporary workers in empirical research of workers' health and well-being.

It is, in fact, a switch point for reconsidering the employment model both from the perspective of labor market sustainability and resilience, but also for creating a people-centric culture for development, with a long-term perspective on balance between the demands of work, life, and family for men and women.

Policy options are both the responsibility of the business environment (for attracting talent, retaining young people, stimulating the active presence of women in the labor market), but also of public institutions responsible for developing human capital and stimulating its efficient use in economic activities, social, cultural, for the benefit of society as a whole. As directions for interventions, adapted to the fields of activity and to the categories of labor force, with emphasis on the reduction of the gender inequality associated with the precarious employment, we mention.

- Higher level of digitalization and the use of AI to streamline routine operations and optimize current decisions;
- Accepting the digital transition as a facilitator for future decent jobs and better work performance;
- Policy instruments for decreasing risk for precarious involuntary jobs; using employment flexible contracts as an opportunity for women participation in labor market increase and not for a discriminative instrument of employment quality;
- Using work management platform: leveraging a work management platform to align against organizational objectives, teams can move faster and adapt in the face of adversity;
- The flexibility of remote work, improving remote work–life balance;
- Law update, enforcement, and suitable policy initiative for implementation of functioning control mechanisms supported by public authorities, trade unions, etc.;
- Openness to career development opportunities for female and managerial positions; changing stereotypes on gender segregation—career women, equal responsibilities for household activities, equal payment;
- Digital inclusion as a component of long-life training companies' program;
- Reconsider the value of unpaid work and childcare, reduce informal employment, and a wider cover by job retention schemes.

The inventory is far from being exhaustive, but the mentioned directions have been detached following the experience of the current pandemic crisis but also of the previous one (financial). The fragility of the economic recovery after the crisis, whether internal to the business environment or not, not only delays the recovery of employment, but also weakens and postpones policy measures aimed at decent and quality employment, generating adverse effects on microeconomic performance (through lack of interest of young graduates for employment or migration based on criteria of financial advantages and career perspective, low productivity and lack of involvement of employees for overall firms' performance, etc.). Rethinking the post-pandemic employment model and correct implementation of measures (updating labor market regulations and monitoring their correct implementation, increasing training concerns, capitalizing on the benefits of digitization, etc.) will make the difference between voluntary and non-voluntary flexible employment, noting that newer job insecurity policies are needed to target the entire labor force (higher risk for burnout, accentuating the dissipation of the work–life border, career development stress, etc.).

7 Conclusions

The post-COVID-19 recovery is gradual and different in EU member states, with a specific emphasis on the effects on precarious employment. The different impact on precarious forms of employment requires a deep reconsideration of world market policies from the perspective of quality and security of employment, but also of the reduction of the proportion of decent jobs, able to ensure the reduction of the risk of poverty. This means, on the one hand, rethinking employment patterns in terms of adapting jobs to the future demands of the business environment, with efficient and resilient jobs, and, on the other hand, rethinking measures to reduce precarious jobs, labor market vulnerabilities, and active inclusion management of vulnerable groups. The perspective of the robust transformation of the labor market implies the improvement of inequalities on the labor market, starting from accessing the temporary instrument "Next Generation EU," continues with National plans for recovery and resilience, but it is also necessary the orientation toward pre-pandemic vulnerabilities on the labor market.

The first result obtained in the paper is that for a probability of 95% it can be stated that indeed in 2020 there was a significant positive change in the share of women whose jobs were characterized by precariousness, compared to 2019. Although this phenomenon has favorable connotations, it could still occur under the impact of a lower return to work of women after the lockdown period than in the case of men, as evidenced by some studies (Freund and Scott 2022; ILO 2021). In this context, in the second part of the paper, there were identified the behavior patterns of European countries in terms of gender gap in the employment quality, under COVID-19 pandemic conditions. By applying the Principal Component Analysis and the cluster analysis, three patterns were identified. The first pattern consists of countries where women are less actively involved in the labor market, normally for religious reasons, to which was added in 2020 the health pandemic. The second pattern is associated with developing countries, with a lower income level and low gender gap in job quality, despite the fact that the employment levels are more modest than in mostly developed countries for both genders. The third pattern is associated mainly to developed countries where women are actively and largely involved in the labor market, the gender pay gap being maximum and the employment gap being minimal, the level of income for both genders being high. However, the current study can be improved by considering other variables that characterize other aspects of the precariousness of employment among women, by including other non-European countries in the analysis, with the identification of their specific conditions, as well as by analyzing the validity of the trends already outlined on long term, as the pandemic is over.

Labor market pre-pandemic reform starts with the resumption of economic activities and labor performance, but it cannot ignore the need to improve job security, in all its aspects. It is obvious that we will constantly face a risk associated with forms of precarious employment (limited period jobs, involuntary part-time employment, etc.), but it is necessary to consider other forms of precariousness related to labor market policies, respectively, of occupational health—decent employment vs in-work poverty, employment of vulnerable groups, integration of immigrants, equity and non-discrimination, access to education, and a career. Another form of precariousness is associated with the degree of digitalization of jobs, in the sense of optimizing the allocation of work time, digital endowment (jobs' digital infrastructure), and facilitation of education (skills and soft competencies).

We consider that the analysis of the dynamics and gaps regarding the incidence of precarious jobs on the local, national, regional labor market represents the first necessary and mandatory approach for developing the resilience of the labor market through our own tools—reducing inequality of opportunities, discrimination, including labor remuneration. The persisting gender gap in the labor market, employment stereotypes, and career progress are real barriers to the progress of labor market policies, given that the trend in the education system is clear—more women than men complete higher education. The work associated with transformation significantly transforms the relevance of the gender gap in performance, and immigrants have proven to be reference sources in securing employment in essential activities, associated with certain jobs/industries, but also in medium and high-skilled jobs (e.g., in covering the deficit of health personnel, social services, personal services).

Employment security, income sufficiency, and rights and protections in employment relations add other forms of precariousness, either associated with the risk of work (burnout) or vulnerable occupation (temporary, part-time, temporary agency work, or self-employment). Reducing the costs of production factors, respectively, the labor factor, as a valve for maintaining market competitiveness through price has already proved ineffective in the medium and long term, both by the effects on labor quality and by reducing consumer demand, thus slowing economic growth. Moreover, digitization significantly reduces the importance of the comparative advantages of cheap labor on which economic development has largely relied in recent decades in less developed countries. "COVID-19 has finally helped digitalization to make a breakthrough. Big data, artificial intelligence, and connected automation will permanently change the world of work" (Allianz research 2021, p. 4). On the other hand, flexible work arrangements, as voluntary choice, and employment of vulnerable groups (including those with limited levels of formal education) as alternatives for social tax pressure on production cost are possible tools to ensure the resilience of the labor market. An important role is played by the principles of companies' social responsibilities and the extension of the compulsory non-financial reporting of companies, as another barometer for the quality of employment.

The results of this paper represent a first step, strictly necessary in the medium-term analysis of the effects of the pandemic on the labor market. The second one is to highlight the different measures of the member countries after the first year of the pandemic, when, at different times and with different degrees of resilience, the activity resumed, respectively, the analysis of the labor market in 2021 and 2022 (considering that after the first quarter of 2022, the WHO has not yet declared an end to the pandemic, although more and more EU countries have moved to relax, and some have even given up on restrictions altogether). This is our future research interest, because EU countries are differently protected by vaccination rates, the incidence of infections and epidemic waves dissociate, and the degree of voluntary compliance of the population with protection measures is also extremely different in countries and regions.

Acknowledgements This paper received financial support through the project entitled "DECIDE—Development through entrepreneurial education and innovative doctoral and postdoctoral research, project code POCU/380/6/13/125031, project co-financed from the European Social Fund through the Operational Program Human Capital 2014–2020."

References

Alon, T.M., Doepke, M., Olmstead-Rumsey, J., Tertilt, M.: The impact of COVID-19 on gender equality. NBER Working Paper No. 26947. National Bureau of Economic Research, Cambridge, M.A. (2020)

ACCA: Equal Opportunity for Women in the Workplace: A Study of Corporate Disclosure, Research report 102, ISBN: 978-1-85908-442-7 (2008)

Adams-Prassl, A., Boneva, T., Golin, M., Rauh, C.: Inequality in the impact of the coronavirus shock: evidence from real time surveys. J. Public Econ. **189**, ISSN: 0047-2727, https://doi.org/10.1016/j.jpubeco.2020.104245(2020)

Allianz Research: The middle-income trap: inequality across countries after COVID-19, https://www.allianz-trade.com/content/dam/onemarketing/aztrade/allianz-trade_com/en_gl/erd/publications/pdf/2021_11_17_Middle-Income-Trap.pdf. Accessed 15 April 2022

Bobek, A., Pembroke, S., Wickham, J.: Living with uncertainty. Social Implications of Precarious Work, Foundation for European Progressive Studies, https://www.feps-europe.eu/attachments/publications/feps%20tasc%20report_living%20with%20uncertainty_final.pdfBrescoll, VL, Uhlmann, EL, & Newman, GE (2013). The effects of system-justifying motives on endorsement of essentialist explanations for gender differences. J. Personality Soc. Psychol. **105**, 891–908. https://doi.org/10.1037/a0034701 (2018)

Broughton, A., Green, M., Rickard, C., Swift, S., Eichhorst, W., Tobsch, V., Magda, I., Lewandowski, P., Keister, R., Jonaviciene, D., Ramos Martín, N.E., Valsamis, D., Tros, F.: Precarious employment in Europe. Employment and Social Affairs. Brussels: European Parliament. Directorate-General. http://www.europarl.europa.eu/RegData/etudes/STUD/2016/587285/IPOL_STU(2016)587285_EN.pdf. Accessed 15 April 2022 (2016)

Campbell, I., Price, R.: Precarious work and precarious workers: Towards an improved conceptualisation. Econ. Labour Relations Rev. **27**(3), 314–332 (2016). https://doi.org/10.1177/1035304616652074

Couch, K.A., Fairlie, R.W., Xu, H.: Gender and the COVID-19 labor market downturn. stanford institute for economic policy research. Working Paper No. 20–037 Eagly, A.H., Wood, W.: The origins of sex differences in human behavior: edispositions versus social roles. Amer. Psychol. **54**, 408–423 (1999). https://doi.org/10.1037/0003-066X.54.6.408 (2020)

Economist Impact 2022: The Work-life Balance Barometer. The great rebalancing: priorities and work-life balance in a hybrid working environment, WeWork Group, The Economist Group 2022, https://impact.economist.com/projects/nextpectations/barometer/. Accessed 15 April 2022 (2022)

European Economic and Social Committee: RESOLUTION—EESC proposals for post-COVID-19 crisis reconstruction and recovery: "The EU must be guided by the principle of being considered a community of common destiny. "based on the work of the Subcommittee on post-COVID-19 recovery and reconstruction, EESC-2020-02549-00-01-RES-TRA (EN) (2020)

EIGE: Economic Benefits of Gender Equality in the EU–EU and EU Member States overviews, https://doi.org/10.2839/782022, MH-01-16-183-EN-N (2017)

EIGE: Women and men in ICT: a chance for better work–life balance, Research note, https://doi.org/10.2839/310959, MH-04-18-260-EN-N (2018)

EIGE: Gender differences on household chores entrenched from childhood, https://eige.europa.eu/publications/gender-equality-index-2021-report/gender-differences-household-chores (2021)

Eisenberg-Guyot, J., Peckham, T., Andrea, S.B., Oddo, V.M., Seixas, N., Hajat, A.: Life-course trajectories of precarious employment and health in the U.S.: a multichannel sequence analysis. Soc Sci Med. **264**, 113327. https://doi.org/10.1016/j.socscimed.2020.113327 (2020)

European Commission: Discrimination against women in the workforce and the workplace, Report, Committee on Equal Opportunities for Women and Men Doc. 10484, 30 March 2005, https://assembly.coe.int/nw/xml/XRef/X2H-Xref-ViewHTML.asp?FileID=10877&lang=en (2005)

European Commission: 2021 Report on gender equality in the EU, ISSN 2443-5228, doi:https://doi.org/10.2838/57887, https://ec.europa.eu/info/sites/default/files/aid_development_cooperation_fundamental_rights/annual_report_ge_2021_printable_en_0.pdf. Accessed 15 April 2022 (2021)

European Commission: Winter 2022 Economic forecast for Romania, https://ec.europa.eu/economy_finance/forecasts/2021/winter/ecfin_forecast_winter_2021_lu_en.pdf. accessed 15 April 2022 (2022)

European Institute for Gender Equality: Gender, skills and precarious work in the EU, ISBN 978-92-9493-756-8, doi:https://doi.org/10.2839/62350, https://eige.europa.eu/resources/ti_pubpdf_mh0217250enn_pdfweb_20170503163908.pdf. Accessed 15 April 2022 (2017)

European Parliament: Precarious work from a gender and intersectionality perspective, and ways to combat it, Study Requested by the FEMM committee, PE 662.491 https://www.europarl.europa.eu/RegData/etudes/STUD/2020/662491/IPOL_STU(2020)662491_EN.pdf. Accessed 15 April 2022 (2020)

European Parliament: COVID-19 and its economic impact on women and women's poverty. https://www.europarl.europa.eu/RegData/etudes/STUD/2021/693183/IPOL_STU(2021)693183_EN.pdf. Accessed 15 April 2022 (2021)

EU 2019: Directive (EU) 2019/1158 on work-life balance for parents and carers (2019)

Eurostat database, https://ec.europa.eu/eurostat/data/database. Accessed 15 April 2022 (2022)

Farré, L., Fawaz, Y., González, L., Graves, J.: How the COVID-19 lockdown affected gender inequality inpaid and unpaid work in Spain. IZA Discussion Paper No. 13434. Institute of

Labor Economics, Bonn, Germany. Retrieved from http://ftp.iza.org/dp13434.pdf. Accessed 15 April 2022

Freund, R., Scott, D.: Getting back to work after lockdown: Why young women are experiencing slower job recovery than young men, Young Lives, https://www.younglives.org.uk/news/getting-back-work-after-lockdown-why-young-women-are-experiencing-slower-job-recovery-young. Accessed 14 September 2022 (2022)

Forsythe, E., Kahn, L.B., Lange, F., Wiczer, D.: Labor demand in the time of COVID-19: Evidence fromvacancy postings and UI claims. J. Public Econ. **189**, 104238 (2020)

Gago-Cortés, C., Alló, M.: Precarious work and sustainable development. In: Leal Filho, W., Azul, A., Brandli, L., Özuyar, P., Wall, T. (eds.), Decent Work and Economic Growth. Encyclopedia of the UN Sustainable Development Goals. Springer, Cham. https://doi.org/10.1007/978-3-319-71058-7_19-1. Accessed 15 April 2022 (2019)

ILO: World Employment and Social Outlook. Trendes 2022, ILO Flagship Report, ISBN 9789220356975 (print); 9789220356982 (web PDF) (2022)

ILO: Fewer women than men will regain employment during the COVID-19 recovery says ILO, https://www.ilo.org/global/about-the-ilo/newsroom/news/WCMS_813449/lang--en/index.htm. Accessed 15 April 2022 (2021)

ILO: Policies and regulations to combat precarious employment. https://www.ilo.org/wcmsp5/groups/public/@ed_dialogue/@actrav/documents/meetingdocument/wcms_164286.pdf. Accessed 15 April 2022 (2011)

Jonsson, J., Stein, M., Johansson, G., Bodin, T., Stro¨mdahl, S.: A performance assessmentof web-based respondent driven sampling amongworkers with precarious employment in Sweden. PLoS ONE **14**(1), e0210183. (19) (PDF) A performance assessment of web-based respondent driven sampling among workers with precarious employment in Sweden. Available from: https://www.researchgate.net/publication/330298700_A_performance_assessment_of_web-based_respondent_driven_sampling_among_workers_with_precarious_employment_in_Sweden. Accessed 14 September 2022 (2019)

Julià, M., Vanroelen, C., Bosmans, K., Van Aerden, K., Benach, J.: Precarious employment and quality of employment in relation to health and well-being in Europe. Int. J. Health Serv. **47**(978656), 002073141770749 (2017). https://doi.org/10.1177/0020731417707491

Kreshpaj, B, Orellana, C, Burström, B, Davis, L, Hemmingsson, T, Johansson, G, Kjellberg, K, Jonsson, J, Wegman, D.H., Bodin, T.: What is precarious employment? A systematic review of definitions and operationalizations from quantitative and qualitative studies. Scand J. Work Environ. Health. **46**(3):235–247. https://doi.org/10.5271/sjweh.3875. Epub 2020 Jan 5. PMID: 31901944. (2020)

McKinsey Global Institute: COVID-19 and gender equality: Countering the regressive effects, https://www.mckinsey.com/~/media/mckinsey/featured%20insights/future%20of%20organizations/covid%2019%20and%20gender%20equality%20countering%20the%20regressive%20effects/covid-19-and-gender-equality-countering-the-regressive-effects-vf.pdf?shouldIndex=false. Accessed 15 April 2022 (2020)

McKinsey & Company: Women in the Workplace 2021, https://www.mckinsey.com/featured-insights/diversity-and-inclusion/women-in-the-workplace. Accessed 15 April 2022 (2021)

Oddo, V.M., Zhuang, C.C., Andrea, S.B., Eisenberg-Guyot, J., Peckham, T., Jacoby, J., Hajat, A.: Changes in precarious employment in the United States: a longitudinal analysis. Scand. J. Work Environ. Health **47**(3), 171–180 (2021)

OECD: Advancing Gender Balance in the Workforce: A Collective Responsibility: Gender Balance Network, Forum on Tax Administration, OECD, Paris. www.oecd.org/tax/forum-on-tax-administration/publications-and-products/advancing-gender-balance-in-theworkforce-a-collective-responsibility.htm. Accessed 15 April 2022 (2020)

OECD database: Data extracted on 03 Apr 2022, https://stats.oecd.org/index.aspx?queryid=54757

Olsthoorn, M.: Measuring precarious employment: a proposal for two indicators of precarious employment based on set-theory and tested with Dutch labor market-data. Soc. Indic. Res. **119**(1), 421–441 (2014)

Pedrosa, A.L., Bitencourt, L., Fróes, A.C.F., Cazumbá, M.L.B., Campos, R.G.B., de Brito SBCS & Simões e Silva, A.C.: Emotional, Behavioral, and Psychological Impactof the COVID-19 Pandemic. Front. Psychol. **11**, 566212. (19) (PDF) Emotional, Behavioral, and Psychological Impact of the COVID-19 Pandemic. Available from: https://www.researchgate.net/publication/344905615_Emotional_Behavioral_and_Psychological_Impact_of_the_COVID-19_Pandemic. Accessed 14 September 2022 (2020)

Taleb, N.N: The Black Swan: The Impact of the Highly Improbable, Random House, ISBN 978-1400063512 (2007)

United Nations: Report of the Working Group on the issue of discrimination against women in law and in practice, Thematic report, UN – General Assembly, Human Rights Council, Twenty-sixth session, A/HRC/26/39 (2014)

United Nations: Policy brief: The impact of COVID-19 on women. https://www.unwomen.org/-/media/headquarters/attachments/sections/library/publications/2020/policybrief-the-impact-of-covid-19-on-women-en.pdf?la=en&vs=1406. Accessed 15 April (2020)

UNDP: Annual Report 2019, UNDP Gender Equality Strategy, https://www.undp.org/publications/2019-gender-equality-strategy-annual-report. Accessed 15 April 2022 (2020)

UN Women: Policy brief no 15 Addressing the economic fallout of COVID-19: Pathways and policy options for a gender-responsive recovery, Jade Cochran, Bobo Diallo, Seemin Qayum, Anuradha Seth, and Silke Staab, https://www.unwomen.org/en/digital-library/publications/2020/06/policy-brief-addressing-the-economic-fallout-of-covid-19. Accessed 15 April 2022 (2020a)

UN Women: ONE YEAR OF COVID-19: A Gender Analysis of Emergency COVID-19 Socio-Economic Policy Responses Adopted in Europe and Central Asia, Authors: Faria Salman Asif and Sara Cantillon; Jeffrey Stern (editor) https://eca.unwomen.org/sites/default/files/Field%20Office%20ECA/Attachments/Publications/2021/11/1%20STUDY%20%20One%20Year%20of%20COVID19min.pdf. Accessed 15 April 2022 (2020b)

Vasile, V., Bunduchi, E., Ciuhu, A. M.: Immigrants' Economic and Social Integration in Host Country—from Preconceived Ideas to Real Life. Case Study On The Romanians', Challenges of the Knowledge Society 2019 Conference, pp. 1143–1150, ISSN 2359-9227, ISSN-L 2068-7796, Indexed by EBSCO, ProQuest, DOAJ, Index Copernicus, Ulrich's Databases, http://cks.univnt.ro/download/215_ebook_CKS_2019.pdf. Accessed 15 April 2022 (2019)

Yasenov, V.I.: Who can work from home? IZA Discussion Paper No. 13197. Institute of Labor Economics, Cambridge, MA. Retrieved fromhttp://ftp.iza.org/dp13197.pdf. Accessed 15 April 2022 (2020)

Developing Organizational Resilience Through Decreasing Artificial Intelligence Anxiety in VUCA World

Simona-Andreea Apostu and Bulent Akkaya

Abstract The environment is very complex and constantly changing, and resilience is of great importance. Since organizations play an important role on the market, resilience is applicable in their case and is the ability of a system to maintain functions by organizations. All changes are positively correlated to digitalization, also merging the fear of people losing their job due to artificial intelligence, known as artificial intelligence anxiety. In this context, our article aims to present the relationship between organizational resilience and artificial intelligence anxiety. For this, data was considered from 146 middle level managers working in production/manufacturing department companies that produce white goods markets operating in Turkey. Two survey questionnaires were used. To collect data, the random sampling technique was used. The analysis was performed using SPSS and implied correlations and regression. Using regression analysis, our results concluded that the managers perceived that organizational resilience has an important role in decreasing artificial intelligence anxiety. The research results could be useful for policymakers, employers, research, and academics, being, from our knowledge, the first attempt relating these two terms.

Keywords Organizational resilience · Artificial intelligence anxiety · VUCA world

1 Introduction

Considering the complexity of the environment and the crisis we faced over time, resilience is an important concept today to deal with the impacts these changes bring. Resilience is applicable also in the case of organizations. The development of resilience promotes future success to survive complex environments.

S.-A. Apostu (✉)
Bucharest University of Economic Studies, Bucharest, Romania
e-mail: simona.apostu@csie.ase.ro

B. Akkaya
Manisa Celal Bayar University, Manisa, Turkey

A. M. Dima and E. R. Danescu (eds.), *Fostering Recovery Through Metaverse Business Modelling*, Springer Proceedings in Business and Economics,
https://doi.org/10.1007/978-3-031-28255-3_11

Digitalization and artificial intelligence (AI) have recently registered an increasing trend, with both advantages and disadvantages for the population. One major disadvantage is represented by the anxiety related to digitalization and the AI, such as stress and the threat of job loss.

The fear of being replaced by machines switches on the alarm in some countries (Johnson and Verdicchio 2017a, b, c). Although such threat is a major concern and receives widespread attention, the research on this topic is not comprehensive.

In order to minimize or to eliminate the AI anxiety, the organizations have a vital role through resilience. In this context, the main aim of the paper is to determine if there is a relationship between the anxiety generated by AI and the organizational resilience. Therefore, we created the hypothesis: Organizational resilience significantly decreases employees' artificial intelligence anxiety. To test this, we used data from 146 middle level managers working in production/manufacturing department companies that produce white goods markets operating in Turkey using two survey questionnaires. To collect data, the random sampling technique was used. The analysis was performed using SPSS and implied correlations and regression.

The originality of this paper consists of presenting the relationship between artificial intelligence anxiety and organizational resilience, being, to our knowledge, one of the first study relating these two terms on which limited studies exist in the literature.

The rest of the paper is organized as follows: Sect. 2 explores the organizational resilience, the artificial intelligence anxiety, and the relationship between these two in the existent literature, Sect. 3 introduces the data and explains the methodology used. Section 4 presents the empirical findings and discusses the results. Concluding observations are provided in Sect. 5.

2 Literature Review

2.1 Problem Statement

2.1.1 Organizational Resilience

Significantly rapid changes in the environment generate changes for all the actors in the economy. Lately, the information system, crisis, and smart machines replacing employees have caused both individual and organizational to high levels of stress (Riolli and Savicki 2003). In order to face stress and changes, resilience is necessary.

Resilience is a system's ability to meet difficulties, meaning both the ability to endure disruptions, as well as the capability to adapt changes and transform (Barasa et al. 2018). Thus, it reflects how an organization adapts to its environment (Mallak 1998a, b).

According to Carvalho et al. (2012), resilience is the capability of a system to return to its original state. Today, the business environment is increasingly random, asking for organizations to be more resilient (Kantur and İşeri-Say 2012).

The changes in the marketplace and the technological advances lead to a swift reaction toward organizations. Organizations need to reinvent themselves to face the external pressures (Brown and Eisenhardt 1998; Fulcheri et al. 1995).

Organizational resilience represents the capability of an organization to face disruptions and unexpected events thanks to strategic awareness and linked to operational management (Annarelli and Nonino 2016).

Considering the crises, the society faced over time, resilient organizations can be the solution to aid organizations survive and thrive in difficult or volatile economic times (Horne and Orr 1998; Mallak 1998a, b).

In order to experience surprising, uncertain, adverse, and unstable conditions (Cynthia et al. 2011), organizational resilience presents three principal characteristics: situation awareness, management of keystone vulnerabilities, and adaptive capacity (McManus et al. 2008).

Organizational resilience is developed through the management of human resources so that it creates competencies among core employees, achieving organizations that are resilient respond when faced with severe shocks (Cynthia et al. 2011).

Thus, organizational resilience is the result of proper human resource management and employee creativity (Lengnick-Hall et al. 2011a, b), organizational culture (Coutu 2002), flexibility (Kantur and Iseri-Say 2012), strategies regarding business model innovation (Carraresi and Bröring 2021), and technological capabilities (Afuah 2002).

Organizational resilience implies that people are able to respond quickly and effectively to change while enduring minimal stress (Mallak 1998a, b).

The main factors influencing organizational resilience are reflected by: material resources, preparedness and planning, information management, collateral pathways and redundancy, governance processes, leadership practices, organizational culture, human capital, social networks, and collaboration (Barasa et al. 2018).

2.1.2 Artificial Intelligence Anxiety

Technology conquered the entire world, a representative technology being represented by artificial intelligence (AI). AI presents many positive aspects, enriching human life and creating more comfort (Rhee and Jin 2021), but also disadvantages.

AI represents a system using technology in order to evaluate scenarios regarding services with the aim to provide personalized recommendations, alternatives, and solutions to issues or problems (Xu et al. 2020).

AI has been widely adopted in different domains, from communications (Acikgoz and Vega 2021) to customer service (Cao 2021) or employee satisfaction (Van Esch and Black 2019).

However, in case of specific tasks, such as financial transactions, people are not very comfortable with AI, presenting a lack of trust on this regard (Glikson and Woolley 2020). Thus, AI also has a negative impact, especially due to replacing the job of organizational members' job and the skills associated with it (Rhee and Jin 2021).

Since AI has developed very quickly (Li and Huang 2020), in some cases not being aware of its use (Black and Van Esch 2020), people expressed stress regarding AI (Johnson and Verdicchio 2017a, b, c; Waltz 2006; Van Esch et al. 2017), the result being the emergence of AI anxiety. AI anxiety represents being obsessed with the fear of developing technologies; Johnson and Verdicchio (2017a, b, c) defining AI anxiety as "fear of the stability and the capabilities of AI" (Galloway and Swiatek 2018).

People respond to environment changes, adaptating differently (Roy et al. 2009), the response being more pronounced and clearer in the case of stress and anxiety (Ghazwani et al. 2022).

The Global Institute (2017) estimates that until 2030 AI will replace almost 800 million workers, negatively affecting the humanity (Future of Life Institute 2015; Müller and Bostrom 2014). Thus, AI anxiety represents an universal phenomenon significantly influencing the population study, work, and life paths in the future (Johnson and Verdicchio 2017a, b, c; Scherer 2015).

AI anxiety is positive correlated with the advances in technology (Li and Huang 2020). Besides AI anxiety, AI may generate other anxieties, such as anxiety of job replacement (McKinsey Global Institute 2017), anxiety regarding privacy violation (Chopra and White 2007), and safety and regulation anxiety (Scherer 2015). Considering the technology advances, Lu et al. (2018) and Nyholm and Smids (2016) estimate that new anxieties and issues related to safety will arise in the future.

2.1.3 Organizational Resilience and Artificial Intelligence Anxiety

Being obsessed with the fear of developing technologies, the solution can be in the hands of organizations through organizational resilience.

Organizations must recognize the AI anxiety and provide solutions in order to reduce it or eliminate it (Rhee and Jin 2021). For this, the organizations must be agile, flexible, and constantly learning (Młody and Weinert 2020).

The relationship between these two concepts is not found in the literature, from what we know, there is a gap regarding this connection.

2.2 Research Questions/Aims of the Research

Therefore, we hypothesized that organizational resilience significantly decreases middle level managers' artificial intelligence anxiety. The hypothesis model is presented in Fig. 1.

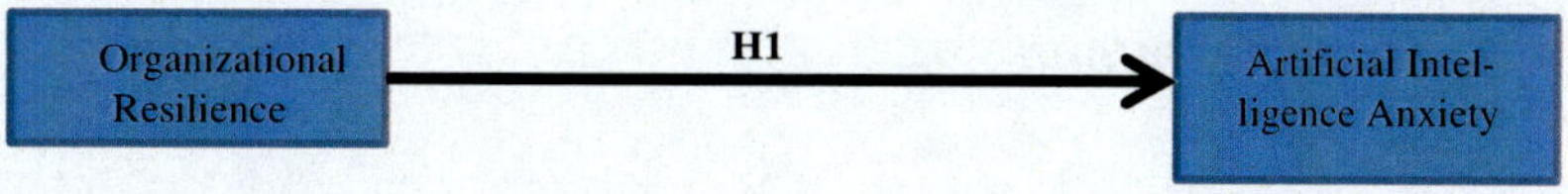

Fig. 1 Research model. *Source* Authors

H$_1$: Organizational resilience significantly decreases employees' artificial intelligence anxiety.

This study was designed to use the quantitative method approach in order to determine the relationship between organizational resilience and artificial intelligence anxiety (Fig. 1).

3 Methodology

3.1 Data Collection, Procedures, and Sampling

The present study used a quantitative approach to test the recommended hypothesis. The data was collected from the 146 middle level managers working in 25 companies that sell and intermediate white goods markets operating in a city called Manisa in Turkey by two survey questionnaires. The companies have about 250 managers, as the participants stated. The simple random sampling technique was used to collect data (Etikan et al. 2016). The simple random sample means that every case of the population has an equal probability of inclusion in sample (Taherdoost 2016).

All middle managers have participated voluntarily in this study. The participants were informed that participation was voluntary and return of the completed questionnaire, considering the informed consent. Of which 58.2% have more than 250 employees, while 41.8% have less than 250 workers. With respect to the gender of the managers, 78.3% were males and 21.7% were females. Regarding managers working years, most participants 52.5% have been working between 1 and 5 years, 14.2% have been working between 6 and 10 years while 33.3% have been working more than 10 years.

3.2 Measures

Three questionnaires were used to obtain data from the participants. The first one measures organizational resilience developed and validated by Campbell-Sills and Stein (2007). The second scale was developed by Wang and Wang (2019) and adapted to Turkish by Akkaya et al. (2021). To measure the items of the corresponding variables, a standardized five-point Likert scale was used to organize the scale ranging from 1 (Strongly Disagree) to 5 (Strongly Agree).

3.3 Analytical Method

SPSS was used to determine demographic characteristics, descriptive statistics, test of normality and regression.

4 Analysis/Results Interpretation

Before analyzing the data, it is necessary to check the values for normal distribution of the data. For conducting parametric tests such as T test, Anova, Regression, and Pearson Correlation, the distribution of data should be normal. Skewness and Kurtosis values must be between +1 and −1 (Gliem and Gliem 2003), and to test the reliability of the scales, Cronbach Alpha (α) was calculated. As seen in Table 1, the Cronbach Alpha (α) value is greater than 0.70 for all scales, indicating the reliability of the scales (Gliem and Gliem 2003).

As presented in Table 1, the Skewness and Kurtosis values are between +1 and −1, therefore, we applied parametric analyses such as regression and correlation.

As the aim of this study was to test the relationship between organizational resilience and artificial intelligence anxiety, we first tested the correlation between those variables. We found that there is a negative relationship between organizational resilience and artificial intelligence anxiety ($r = -0.276$; $p < 0.001$). Statically, it means that the higher organizational resilience, the lower artificial intelligence anxiety (Table 2).

We also applied linear regression to check the relationship between organizational resilience and artificial intelligence anxiety.

The model indicates the significant prediction of organizational resilience in artificial intelligence anxiety ($F = 11.9$, $p = 0.001$ (Table 3), $\beta = -0.28$, $p = 0.001$ (Table 4)). Managers' belief in their organizational resilience predicts decreasing

Table 1 Test of normal distribution

	Mean	Std. deviation	Skewness		Kurtosis		Cronbach alpha (α)
	Statistic	Statistic	Statistic	Std. error	Statistic	Std. error	
Organizational resilience	3.52	1.182	−0.251	0.201	−0.849	0.399	0.838
Artificial intelligence anxiety	1.88	0.742	0.202	0.201	−0.935	0.399	0.784

Source Authors

Table 2 Correlations

		OA	AIA	SE
OA	Pearson correlation	1		
	Sig. (2-tailed)			
	N	146		
AIA	Pearson correlation	−0.177[a]	1	
	Sig. (2-tailed)	0.033		
	N	146	146	
SE	Pearson correlation	0.544[b]	−0.276[b]	1
	Sig. (2-tailed)	0.000	0.001	
	N	146	146	146

[a] Correlation is significant at the 0.05 level (2-tailed)
[b] Correlation is significant at the 0.01 level (2-tailed)
Source Authors

Table 3 ANOVA

Model		Sum of squares	df	Mean square	F	Sig.
1	Regression	17.466	1	17.466	11.907	0.001[b]
	Residual	211.228	144	1.467		
	Total	228.694	145			

[a] Dependent variable: AIA
[b] Predictors: (constant), OR
Source Authors

Table 4 Coefficients

	Unstandardized coefficients		Standardized coefficients			95.0% Confidence interval for B	
	B	Std. error	Beta	t	Sig.	Lower bound	Upper bound
(Constant)	2.116	0.349		6.071	0.000	1.427	2.805
OR	−0.297	0.086	−0.276	−3.451	0.001	−0.467	−0.127

[a] Dependent Variable: AIA
Source Authors

their artificial intelligence anxiety. In other words, organizational resilience negatively and significantly affects artificial intelligence anxiety. Therefore, our hypothesis is supported.

Statistically, when managers' belief in their organizational resilience increased by 1 point, their artificial intelligence anxiety decreased by 0.28 point, and 8% of the decrease in artificial intelligence anxiety can be explained by their organizational resilience improvement (Table 4). The values in the 95% confidence interval obtained as a result of the analysis should not include the zero (0) value in order to support the research hypothesis (Gürbüz 2019), Lower Bound and Upper Bound being −0.47 and −0.13.

It can be concluded that the relationship between organizational resilience and artificial intelligence anxiety is negatively significant. In other words, according to managers' perceptions, organizational resilience has an important role in decreasing artificial intelligence anxiety.

5 Conclusions

Given the uncertainty we are facing and the results of the crises we are going through, it is necessary that all the actors on the market are resilient and resist these shocks. This is also applicable in the case of organizations. Artificial intelligence has developed very rapidly over time, registering both advantages and disadvantages. One disadvantage is related to the population, which presents stress and anxiety considering that it can lead to losing the job.

In this context, this paper examined the link between resilience in organizations and anxiety about artificial intelligence. The data used are provided from 146 middle level managers working in production/manufacturing department companies that produce white goods markets operating in Turkey using two survey questionnaires. The random sampling technique was used to collect data.

The hypothesis we have tested is if organizational resilience leads to decreasing the employee's anxiety related to artificial intelligence. Using regression analysis, our results concluded that the relationship between organizational resilience and artificial intelligence anxiety is significant, being negative. The manager's perception is that organizational resilience has an important role in decreasing artificial intelligence anxiety.

The research results could be useful for policymakers, employers, researchers, and academics. This study is expected to be the base for further studies dedicated to decreasing artificial intelligence anxiety through organizational resilience, promoting the awareness on artificial intelligence, and the relationship between the employer and AI.

As an element of originality, our study demonstrated that organizational resilience significantly influences decreasing the employee's anxiety related to artificial intelligence, being, to our knowledge, the first study on this topic.

As a limitation of the analysis, we mention the lack of available data, the analysis being performed in Turkey, on middle level managers working in production/manufacturing department companies that produce white goods markets operating. As further research, we want to extend the sample to other countries and other domains.

References

Acikgoz, F., Vega, R.P.: The role of privacy cynicism in consumer habits with voice assistants: A technology acceptance model perspective. Int. J. Hum. – Comput. Interact. 1–15 (2021)

Afuah, A.: Mapping technological capabilities into product markets and competitive advantage: the case of cholesterol drugs. Strateg. Manag. J. **23**, 171–179 (2002)

Akkaya, B., Ozakan, A., Ozkan, H.: Yapay Zeka Kaygı (YZK) Ölçeği: Türkçeye Uyarlama, Geçerlik ve Güvenirlik Çalışması. Alanya Akademik Bakış **5**(2), 1125–1146 (2021)

Annarelli, A., Nonino, F.: Strategic and operational management of organizational resilience: current state of research and future directions. Omega **62**, 1–18 (2016)

Barasa, E., Mbau, R., Gilson, L.: What is resilience and how can it be nurtured? A systematic review of empirical literature on organizational resilience. Int. J. Health Policy Manag. **7**(6), 491–503 (2018)

Black, J.S., Van Esch, P.: AI-enabled recruiting: what is it and how should a manager use it? Bus. Horiz. **63**(2), 215–226 (2020)

Brown, S.L., Eisenhardt, K.M.: Competing on the edge: strategy as a structured chaos. Harvard Business School Press, Boston, MA (1998)

Campbell-Sills, L., Stein, M.B.: Psychometric analysis and refinement of the Connor-Davidson resilience scale (CD—RISC): validation of a 10 item measure of resilience. J. Trauma. Stress: Off. Publ. Int. Soc. Trauma. Stress Stud. **20**(6), 1019–1028 (2007)

Cao, L.: Artificial intelligence in retail: applications and value creation logics. Int. J. Retail Distrib. Manag. **49**(7), 958–976 (2021)

Carraresi, L., Bröring, S.: How does business model redesign foster resilience in emerging circular value chains? J. Clean. Prod. **289**, 1–14 (2021)

Carvalho, H., Cruz-Machado, V., Tavares, J.G.: A mapping framework for assessing supply chain resilience. Int. J. Logist. Syst. Manag. **12**(3), 354–373 (2012)

Chopra, S., White, L.: Privacy and artificial agents, or, is Google reading my email? In: IJCAI, pp. 1245–1250 (2007)

Coutu, D.L.: How resilience works. Harv. Bus. Rev. **80**, 46–55 (2002)

Cynthia, P., Timothy, S., Isabelle, E.: What is the impact of diabetes for Australian Aboriginal women when pregnant?. Diab. Res. Clin. Pract. **93**(1), e29-e32 (2011)

Etikan, I., Musa, S.A., Alkassim, R.S.: Comparison of convenience sampling and purposive sampling. Am. J. Theor. Appl. Stat. **5**(1), 1–4 (2016)

Fulcheri, M., Barzega, G., Maina, G., Novara, F., Ravizza, L.: Stress and managerial work: organizational culture and technological changes: a clinical study. J. Manag. Psychol. **10**, 3–9 (1995)

Future of Life Institute (FLI) Homepage: http://futureoflife.org/open-letter-autonomous-weapons (2015). Last accessed 22 May 2022

Galloway, C., Swiatek, L.: Public relations and artificial intelligence: it's not (just) about robots. Public Relat. Rev. **44**(5), 734–740 (2018)

Ghazwani, S., van Esch, P., Cui, Y.G., Gala, P.: Artificial intelligence, financial anxiety and cashier-less checkouts: a Saudi Arabian perspective. Int. J. Bank Mark. (2022)

Gliem, J.A., Gliem, R.R.: Calculating, interpreting, and reporting Cronbach's alpha reliability coefficient for Likert-type scales. Midwest Research-to-Practice Conference in Adult, Continuing, and Community Education, pp. 82–88 (2003)

Glikson, E., Woolley, A.W.: Human trust in artificial intelligence: review of empirical research. Acad. Manag. Ann. **14**(2), 627–660 (2020)

Gürbüz, S.: Sosyal bilimlerde aracı, düzenleyici ve durumsal etki analizleri. Seçkin Yayıncılık [Mediator, regulatory and situational impact analysis in social sciences. Seçkin Publishing], Ankara, Turkey (2019)

Horne, J.F., Orr, J.E.: Assessing behaviors that create resilient organizations. Employ. Relat. Today **24**, 29–39 (1998)

Johnson, D.G., Verdicchio, M.: AI anxiety. J. Assoc. Inf. Sci. Technol. **68**(9), 2267–2270 (2017)

Johnson, D.G., Verdicchio, M.: AI anxiety. J. Am. Soc. Inf. Sci. **68**(9), 2267–2270 (2017b)

Johnson, D.G., Verdicchio, M.: AI anxiety. J. Am. Soc. Inf. Sci. **68**(9), 2267–2270 (2017c)

Kantur, D., Iseri-Say, A.: Organizational resilience: a conceptual integrative framework. J. Manag. Organ. **18**, 762–773 (2012)

Kantur, D., İşeri-Say, A.: Organizational resilience: a conceptual integrative framework. J. Manag. Organ. **18**(6), 762–773 (2012)

Lengnick-Hall, C.A., Beck, T.E., Lengnick-Hall, M.L.: Developing a capacity for organizational resilience through strategic human resource management. Hum. Resour. Manag. Rev. **21**(3), 243–255 (2011a)

Lengnick-Hall, C.A., Beck, T.E., Lengnick-Hall, M.L.: Developing a capacity for organizational resilience through strategic human resource management. Hum. Res. Manag. Rev. **21**, 243–255 (2011b)

Li, J., Huang, J.S.: Dimensions of artificial intelligence anxiety based on the integrated fear acquisition theory. Technol. Soc. **63**, 1–10 (2020)

Lu, H., Li, Y., Chen, M.: Brain intelligence: go beyond artificial intelligence. Mobile Network. Appl. **23**, 368–375 (2018)

Mallak, L.: Putting organizational resilience to work. Ind. Manag. (Chicago Then Atlanta) 8–13 (1998)

Mallak, L.: Putting organizational resilience to work. Ind. Manag. **40**, 8–14 (1998b)

McKinsey Global Institute Homepage: https://www.mckinsey.com/global-themes/future-of-organizations-and-work/what-the-future-of-work-will-mean-for-jobs-skills-and-wages (2017). Last accessed 22 May 2022

McManus, S., Seville, E., Vargo, J., Brunsdon, D.: Facilitated process for improving organizational resilience. Nat. Hazard. Rev. **9**(2), 81–90 (2008)

Młody, M., Weinert, A.: The importance of technological anxiety for the digital transformation of industrial processing companies in Poland. In: Michałkiewicz, A., Mierzejewska, W. (eds.) Contemporary Organization and Management: Challenges and Trends, pp. 15–34 (2020)

Müller, V.C., Bostrom, N.: Future progress in artificial intelligence. AI Matters **1**(1), 9–11 (2014)

Nyholm, S., Smids, J.: The ethics of accident-algorithms for self-driving cars: an applied trolley problem? Ethical Theory Moral Pract. **19**(5), 1275–1289 (2016)

Rhee, T., Jin, X.: The effect of job anxiety of replacement by artificial intelligence on organizational members' job satisfaction in the 4th industrial revolution era: the moderating effect of job uncertainty. J. Digit. Converg. **19**(7), 1–9 (2021)

Riolli, L., Savicki, V.: Information system organizational resilience. Omega **31**(3), 227–233 (2003)

Roy, C., Whetsell, M., Frederickson, K.: The Roy adaptation model and research: global perspective. Nurs. Sci. q. **22**(3), 209–211 (2009)

Scherer, M.U.: Regulating artificial intelligence systems: risks, challenges, competencies, and strategies. Harv. J. Law Technol. **29**(2) (2015)

Scherer, M.U.: Regulating artificial intelligence Systems: risks, challenges, competencies, and strategies. Harv. J. Law Technol. **29**(2)

Taherdoost, H.: Sampling methods in research methodology; how to choose a sampling technique for research. How Choose Sampl. Tech. Res. **5**(4), 37–41 (2016)

Van Esch, P., Black, J.S.: Factors that influence new generation candidates to engage with and complete digital. AI-enabled recruiting. Bus. Horiz. **62**(6), 729–739 (2019)

Van Esch, P., Northey, G., Striluk, M., Wilson, H.: Autonomous weapon systems: is a space warfare manual required? Comput. Law Secur. Rev. **33**(3), 382–389 (2017)

Waltz, D.L.: Evolution, sociobiology, and the future of artificial intelligence. IEEE Intell. Syst. **21**(3), 66–69 (2006)

Wang, Y.Y., Wang, Y.S.: Development and validation of an artificial intelligence anxiety scale: an initial application in predicting motivated learning behavior. Interact. Learn. Environ. 1–16 (2019)

Xu, Y., Shieh, C.H., Van Esch, P., Ling, I.L.: AI customer service: task complexity, problem-solving ability, and usage intention. Australas. Mark. J. **28**(4), 189–199 (2020)

Effects of COVID-19 Pandemic on Higher Education. A Bibliometric Perspective

Cristina Mocanu, Adriana Grigorescu, Anamaria Nastasa, and Ana-Maria Zamfir

Abstract The COVID-19 pandemic has drastically contributed to the change of the educational process. In higher education, teaching and pedagogy, evaluation, as well as experiences of students and teachers have changed profoundly from the beginning of the pandemic to the present. The educational process shifted from face-to-face interactions to online distance learning, changing many aspects of the conventional educational process. This paper presents a comprehensive overview of studies on the COVID-19 impact on higher education. We used bibliometric analysis to unfold how higher education institutions responded and adapted to the pandemic context as well as to the social distancing measures. By analyzing the main occurring terms with the support of the VOS program, we scrutinize the papers written from the beginning of the pandemic and indexed in the Web of Science database. The analysis of the publications from 2020 to 2022 showed, at the beginning, a research focus mainly on the negative effects of the pandemic. But then, diversity of topics increased, shifting to technological acceptance, quality of education and its outcomes, satisfaction with teaching and learning, or quality of life of all actors. The focus on the psychological well-being and mental health issues remained a constant for the entire period. The results are leading to a better understanding of how higher education institutions have adapted to the pandemic context and of the main trends in the field.

Keywords COVID-19 · Distance learning · Online learning · Higher education

C. Mocanu (✉) · A. Nastasa · A.-M. Zamfir
National Scientific Research Institute for Labour and Social Protection, 6-8 Povernei, Bucharest, Romania
e-mail: cristina.mocanu@incsmps.ro

A. Grigorescu
National University of Political Studies and Public Administration, Bucharest, Romania

Academy of Romanian Scientists, Bucharest, Romania

A. M. Dima and E. R. Danescu (eds.), *Fostering Recovery Through Metaverse Business Modelling*, Springer Proceedings in Business and Economics,
https://doi.org/10.1007/978-3-031-28255-3_12

1 Introduction

The outbreak of the COVID-19 pandemic has generated multiple and complex challenges for individuals, organizations, communities, and authorities. It generated significant disruptions, affecting many areas of life in most of the countries and territories. One of the sectors that has been strongly impacted is the higher education sector, where teaching and pedagogy, evaluation, as well as the experiences of students and teachers have changed profoundly from the beginning of the pandemic to the present. In many ways, the COVID-19 pandemic and the closure of universities and then switching to online education had potential negative effects on the students' physical, academic, financial, and psychological well-being (Kecojevic et al. 2020).

While social distancing and preventive measures disrupted the pre-existing educational practices, reopening of schools as part of relaxation brought additional challenges as new approaches have been embraced by teachers, students, and educational institutions as coping strategies (Pokhrel and Chhetri 2021).

2 Literature Review

As many changes and challenges impacted the higher education sector in a very short time span, more and more researchers channeled their work toward these topics of study. Some of them have focused on revealing challenges and impacts for teachers, students, and educational institutions, while others have emphasized future developments of the higher education sector triggered by the COVID-19 pandemic. The impacts have been investigated in various geographical contexts and educational environments, including work-based learning components and tutoring-based systems (Pérez-Jorge et al. 2020), as well as particular fields of study such as medical education (Abbasi et al. 2020). The response of educational institutions to the crisis has also been targeted by many studies (Andrew et al. 2020).

Reviewing the existing evidence on the effects of the COVID-19 pandemic on learning, teaching, and assessment strategies and practices, Khan (2021) identified several key themes in the scientific literature: digital learning, challenges associated with e-learning, emergency virtual assessment, the impact of COVID-19 at a psychological level, and development of collaborative cultures. In this context, new concepts and themes emerged in the research discussion related to the educational crisis during the COVID-19 pandemic, such as "emergency remote teaching" and "emergency virtual assessment" (Khan 2021).

One of the most important topics of research was related to the transition from onsite to online learning. The unprecedented rise of e-learning has been investigated in relation to student satisfaction and academic performance (Nambiar 2020; Keržič et al. 2021), teachers' experiences (Nambiar 2020; Nilsberth et al. 2021), as well as the use and development of various pedagogical approaches (Doucet et al. 2020). The preparedness of educational communities for transiting to digital learning has been one of the most important research topics in this matter (Osman 2020). An important point of view is that digital education will be part of the new normal in education and will become more hybrid as the challenges experienced during the COVID-19 pandemic are overcome and transformed into opportunities (Olasile and Emrah 2020).

Educational inequalities were also addressed, with numerous evidence pointing out that the negative effects are distributed unequally across social groups (Engzell et al. 2020; Maldonado and De Witte 2022). Coping strategies have been unequally available for students, teachers, and schools from various socio-economic backgrounds. Resilience in the face of adverse conditions was higher among those more resourceful. The general view is that the COVID-19 pandemic has widened educational inequalities (Aristovnik et al. 2020; UNESCO 2022).

Another important subject of study for researchers has been related to the mental health of students. Studies have found higher levels of anxiety and depression among students due to restrictions and isolation (Chen and Lucock 2022), with negative effects on their academic performance (Di Malta et al. 2022). Moreover, studies show that universities did play an important role in supporting students' well-being during pandemic times by providing the needed procedures and information (Sarasjärvi et al. 2022). While most of the scholars have been interested in the mental health of students, some studies focused on the mental well-being of teaching staff (Sipeki et al. 2022).

In this paper, we aim to provide a comprehensive overview of studies addressing the effects of the COVID-19 pandemic on higher education. We used bibliometric analysis based on the VOSviewer program to unfold the main occurring terms and subsequently themes through the more than the two years since the pandemic started.

3 Methodology

As stated above, our aims were to identify recurring themes and concepts in the scientific literature on higher education and its adjustments to the conditions imposed by the pandemic. Also, we wanted to observe how the themes and concepts changed and evolved during the three years since the beginning of the pandemic (2020–2022).

To achieve our aims, we conducted a bibliometric analysis of articles published and indexed in the Web of Science Core Collection database from 2020 to 2022. The criteria for selecting publications from the Web of Science Core Collection database were: to contain in the title "higher education" or "universities" or "tertiary education", as well as "covid (-19)" or "corona (virus)"; to be indexed starting with 2020 till present; and to be included in the "articles" category. From the Web of Science, 1963 articles were initially extracted that contained the above-mentioned criteria. We excluded early-access articles, retracted papers, and book chapters. The final database had 1755 articles; the highest number of articles was published in 2021 (1087); 330 papers were published in 2020, while 338 articles were published so far in 2022.

Table 1 Parameters for each map designed

Map	No. of words	Counting method	Min. no of occurrences	Min. no of words per cluster	No. of clusters
2020–2022	383	Full counting	5	15	5
2020	117	Full counting	3	15	4
2021	455	Full counting	3	15	10
2022	162	Full counting	3	15	7
Authorship	–	Full counting	5	8 (countries)	5

Source Web of science core collection. Authors' design through VOSviewer

In order to observe the themes and terms used in publications, we focused our analysis on the keywords of the indexed articles, as well as their evolution over the three years. Also, in order to observe the countries with the highest contribution of publications during the pandemic, we studied the co-authorship according to the country of the authors. To meet the study objective, but also to bring novelty to the bibliometric studies that address the pandemic, we used VOSviewer, a free software program, to create and analyze maps based on network data, bibliographic data, and text data. The software can use bibliographic data to explore co-authorship (by authors, organizations, or countries), co-occurrence (based on keywords), citations, bibliographic coupling, and co-citations (van Eck and Waltman 2021). Thus, the program simplifies the process of analyzing bibliometric analysis of scientific publications by journals, authors, organizations, keywords, titles, abstracts, etc. (van Eck and Waltman 2021). In our keyword analysis, nodes represent keywords, and lines link strongly connected words, namely words with many co-occurrences. Node spacing is based on the relationship between words and color with a particular cluster or group of words. Table 1 presents the parameters used to draw the maps for each step of the analysis. In the analysis on co-authorship by country, a node that was not connected was deleted from the chart, namely Bosnia and Herzegovina. We used the normalization association strength method in the analysis.

4 Results Interpretation

Most of the articles published and indexed yearly during 2020–2022 were under the research area of "Education & Educational Research" (cca. 20% of total number of articles), followed by "Public, Environmental & Occupational Health" (cca. 15%), the following positions fluctuating slightly from year to year (see Table 2). So, only

Table 2 Number of articles by research area and year of publication

2020		2021		2022	
Research area	No. of articles	Research area	No. of articles	Research area	No. of articles
Educ & Educ Res	59	Educ & Educ Res	254	Educ & Educ Res	75
Public, Env & Occ Health	51	Public, Env & Occ Health	167	Public, Env & Occ Health	64
General & Internal Med	28	Env Scien & Ecology	130	Env Scien & Ecology	51
Science & Tech—Other Topics	28	Science & Tech—Other Topics	115	Psychology	37
Env Scien & Ecology	25	Psychology	90	Science & Tech—Other Topics	27
Psychology	19	General & Internal Med	79	General & Internal Med	19

Source Web of science core collection. Authors' selection

by analyzing the top research areas of indexed articles we can observe a slight shift in the topics of research from health issues and how to manage pandemic in 2020 to how to make better use of technology in 2021, and then to psychological effects (probably of both health measures and use of technology) in 2022.

As presented in the methodology section, we started our exploratory analysis by drawing the map of the keywords from all the articles addressing tertiary education and the COVID-19 pandemic published in 2020–2022.

Five thematic clusters were generated, covering areas of research related to challenges that students and teachers faced in integrating and operating technologies and tools that support online education (cluster 1), mental health and psychological well-being (cluster 2), hygiene, infection control, and vaccination attitudes and opinions among medical students and healthcare workers (cluster 3), methodological designs used to assess effects, well-being and mental health (cluster 4), and pandemic measures (especially containment measures) and their potential health effects on students or the general public (cluster 5). Figure 1 also shows the short distance between clusters 3 and 4, as well as between clusters 3 and 5.

Subsequently, we present the thematic clusters generated when analyzing the articles indexed year by year, aiming to better picture the puzzle of themes addressed by research articles addressing higher education issues during the pandemic.

For 2020, only four clusters of research themes were generated; the initial studies being largely focused on how students accepted and were satisfied with the shift to online education (cluster 1), general psychological impact of pandemics (cluster 2), students' mental health (cluster 3) and students' attitudes, challenges, and behaviors toward the trauma of pandemic (cluster 4). In conclusion, at the beginning, the themes

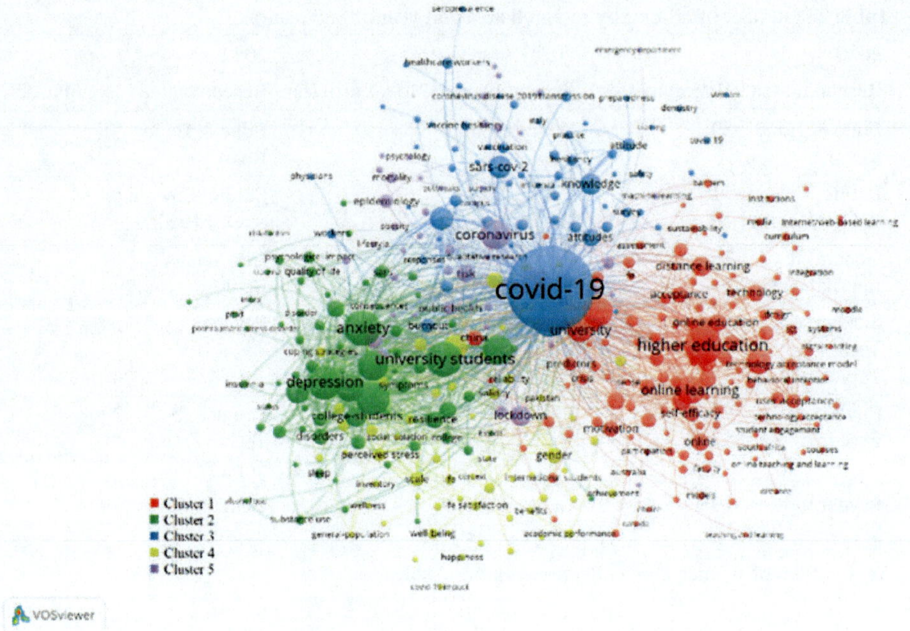

Fig. 1 Co-occurrence of keywords in articles in the period 2020–2022. *Source* Web of science core collection database. Authors' design through VOSviewer

were rather general and aimed at identifying different effects of the pandemic at the level of different organizations and individuals (Fig. 2).

For 2021, the same analysis shows a larger number of themes addressed by studies in the area. Ten clusters of keywords were generated, the focus of papers covering: experiences and risk perceptions of medical students and health care workers during pandemic (cluster 1), integration of digital technology in online teaching and learning and technology acceptance (cluster 2), engagement, motivation, and learning outcomes of online education (cluster 3), lifestyle (eating habits, alcohol use, fitness, etc.), effects of sedentariness and isolation (cluster 4), effects on mental health (cluster 5), safety behaviors and quality of life (cluster 6), digital literacy and public health (cluster 7), effects of mental health on academic performance (cluster 8), effects on internationalization of education (cluster 9), and quality of online education (cluster 10) (Fig. 3).

The diversification of themes is expected to increase in 2022. The map designed only for the first months of the year 2022 evidenced seven clusters covering the following themes: technology acceptance mainly among teachers (cluster 1), students' mental health and academic performances (cluster 2), students' mental health and quality of life (cluster 3), beliefs and attitudes on vaccine among students and particularly among health care workers (cluster 4), institutional developments of universities during pandemic (cluster 5), satisfaction with online teaching (cluster 6), and negative effects of remote learning (cluster 7) (Fig. 4).

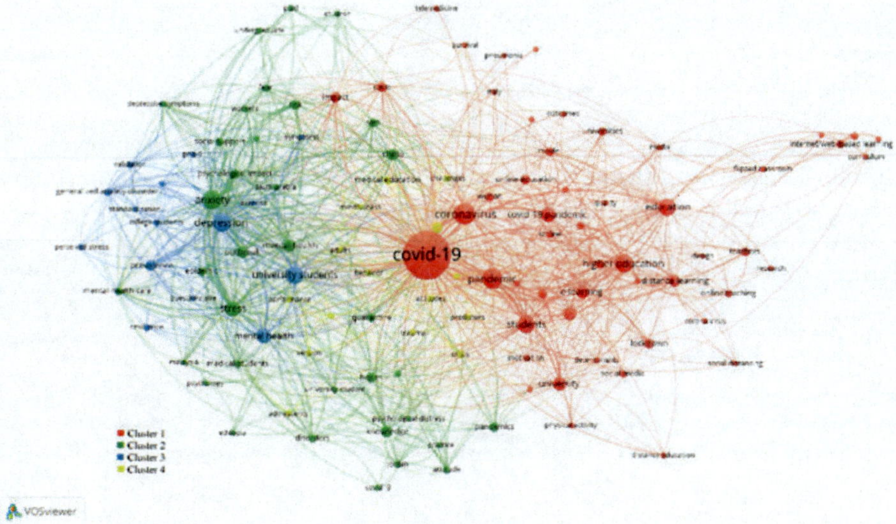

Fig. 2 Co-occurrence of keywords in articles in 2020. *Source* Web of science core collection database. Authors' design through VOSviewer

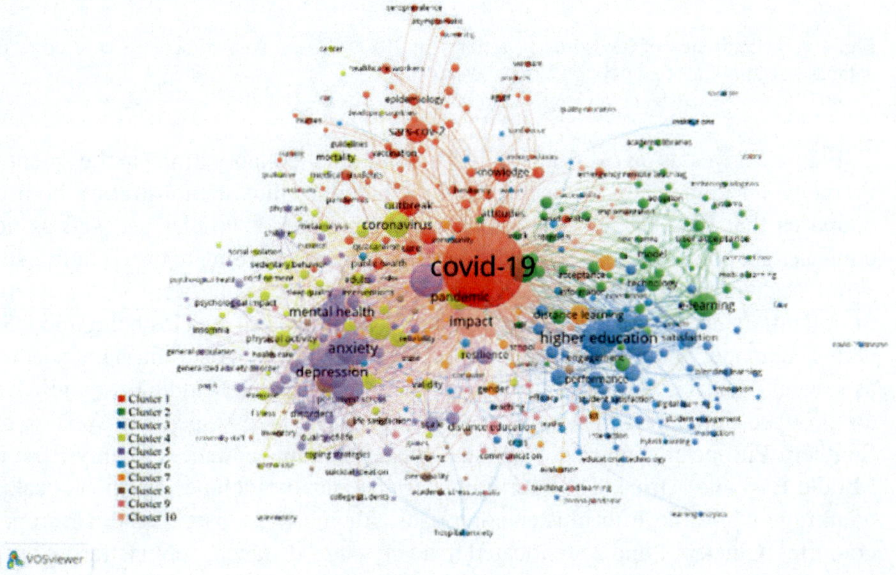

Fig. 3 Co-occurrence of keywords in articles in 2021. *Source* Web of science core collection database. Authors' design through VOSviewer

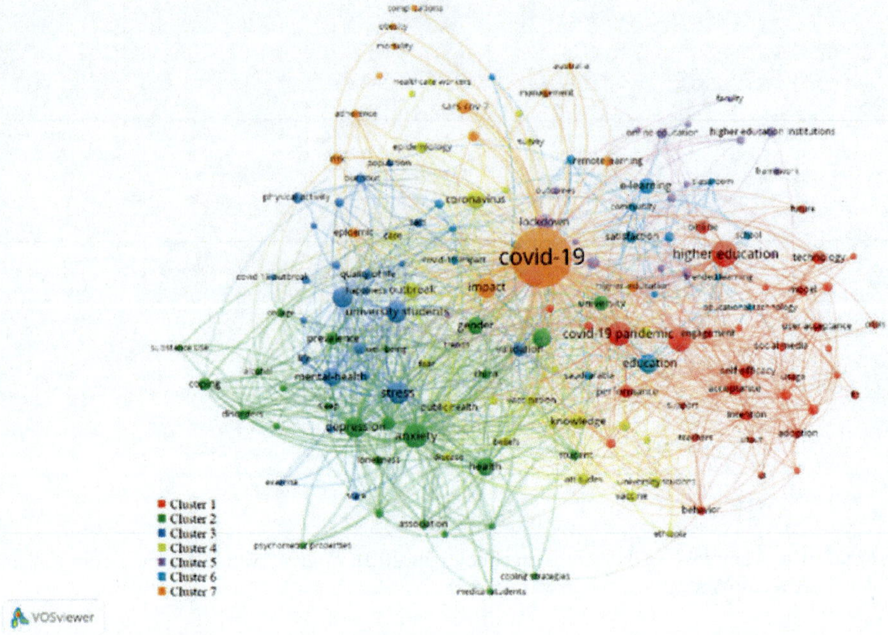

Fig. 4 Co-occurrence of keywords in articles in 2022. *Source* Web of science core collection database. Authors' design through VOSviewer

Figure 5 gives us an overview of the international collaborations in the scientific literature on higher education during the pandemic, thus demonstrating both the countries that have the most significant contributions of articles, as well as how countries are connected. Five clusters were generated according to the co-authorship. From the diagram, we can observe that most countries are strongly connected in terms of co-authorship, the countries with the highest infusion of articles being the USA, China, England, Spain, and Saudi Arabia. China, the USA, Australia, Japan, as well as several countries from Eastern Europe, but also from the Middle East and Africa are grouped in the first cluster. The second cluster includes especially Western and Southern European countries. The third cluster contains countries mainly from the Middle East and Africa. The fourth cluster specifically includes Spanish-speaking countries, while the fifth cluster comprises, for the most part, Eastern European countries. Clusters 1 and 2 are located in a very short distance, demonstrating on the one hand that most of the research on the COVID-19 pandemic was conducted in the countries covered by these two clusters, but also how strong were the research partnerships during the analyzed period of time.

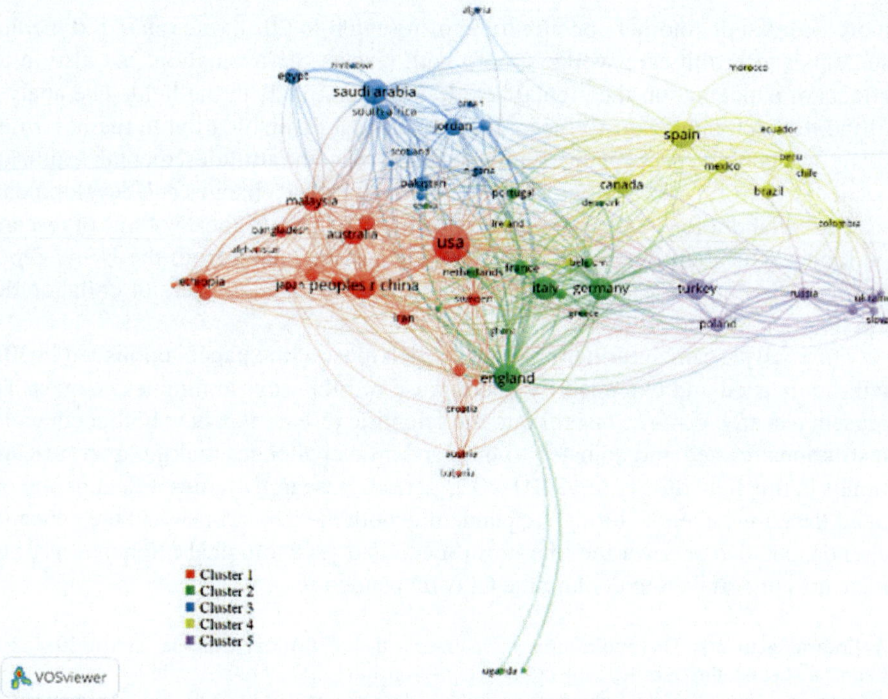

Fig. 5 Co-authorship analysis by countries on articles in the period 2020–2022. *Source* Web of science core collection database. Authors' design through VOSviewer

5 Conclusions

The paper summarizes through the use of bibliometrics how universities were affected and responded to the COVID-19 pandemic, the analysis by year evidencing the increasing focus on psychological well-being and mental health as the time passes. The analysis of the main research areas indicates that scientific interests shifted from focusing on health effects to addressing the use of technology and then on the psychological and social effects of the pandemic. Most of the keywords under the clusters analyzing all the publications from 2020 to 2022, point to the negative and long-term effects of pandemic and social distance measures in higher education sector, such as psychological and physical effects, infection control, or attitudes toward vaccination. Also, the efforts that institutions made to shift to online education, the technological acceptance, and digital literacy were extensively and regularly addressed.

In 2020, the research was rather general, focusing on students' satisfaction with online education, mental health among students and the general population, and students' attitudes, challenges, and behaviors toward the pandemic. In 2021, alongside mental and physical health effects of the pandemic, the quality of education, quality of learning outcomes, and academic performances also started to be more and more addressed. Another specific topic of research in 2021 was related to medical students and health care workers, both with respect to vaccination, but also to the effects of pandemic on the mental health of professionals in the field. The analysis of the research published so far in 2022 revealed a diversification in themes with a focus on technology acceptance among teachers, vaccine attitudes, mental health, and academic performances among students and institutional changes and developments.

The collaboration analysis by country revealed that the highest volume of research on higher education during the COVID-19 pandemic came from the USA, China, England, Spain, and Saudi Arabia. In addition, four main clusters of collaboration of countries were identified.

The analysis can be further replicated when most of the papers published in 2022 will be indexed and extended by making use of other text mining techniques. The present research gives us insight into the scientific research on how higher education institutions reacted and adjusted to the pandemic challenges and the main research trends in this field during the 2020–2022 period. Research themes reflect on the one hand the public agenda during the pandemic, both the general one and the education agenda, but also uncover the long-term social and psychological implications of the measures undertaken to contain the COVID pandemic.

Acknowledgements This publication was realized with the EEA Financial Mechanism 2014–2021 financial support through the Project "Moving toward the new normal in digital learning—new dimension of human capital in higher education", contract number 20-COP-0043. Its content does not reflect the official opinion of the Programme Operator, the National Contact Point, and the Financial Mechanism Office. Responsibility for the information and views expressed therein lies entirely with the authors.

References

Abbasi, M.S., Ahmed, N., Sajjad, B., Alshahrani, A., Saeed, S., Sarfaraz, S., et al.: E-Learning perception and satisfaction among health sciences students amid the COVID-19 pandemic. Work **67**(3), 549–556 (2020)

Andrew, A., Cattan, S.D, Costa-Dias, M. C., Farquharson, C., Kraftman, L., Krutikova, S., Phimister, A., Sevilla, A.: Learning during the lockdown: real-time data on children's experiences during home learning. (IFS Briefing Note BN288). The Institute for Fiscal Studies. https://ifs.org.uk/publications/14848 (2020). Last accessed 15 June 2022

Aristovnik, A., Keržič, D., Ravšelj, D., Tomaževič, N., Umek. L.: Impacts of the COVID-19 pandemic on life of higher education students: a global perspective. Sustainability **12**(20), 8438 (2020)

Chen, T., Lucock, M.: The mental health of university students during the COVID-19 pandemic: an online survey in the UK. PLoS ONE **17**(1), (2022)

Di Malta, G., Bond, J., Conroy, D., Smith, K., Moller, N.: Distance education students' mental health, connectedness and academic performance during COVID-19: a mixed-methods study. Distance Educ. **43**(1), 97–118 (2022)

Doucet, A., Netolicky, D., Timmers, K., Tuscano, F.J.: Thinking about pedagogy in an unfolding pandemic (An Independent Report on Approaches to Distance Learning during COVID-19

School Closure). Work of Education International and UNESCO. https://issuu.com/educationinternational/docs/2020_research_covid-19_eng (2020). Last accessed 15 June 2022

Engzell, P., Frey, A., Verhagen, M.: Learning inequality during the COVID-19 pandemic. SocArXiv (2020)

Kecojevic, A., Basch, C.H., Sullivan, M., Davi, N.K.: The impact of the COVID-19 epidemic on mental health of undergraduate students in New Jersey, cross-sectional study. PLoS ONE **15**(9), e0239696 (2020)

Keržič, D., Alex, J.K., Pamela Balbontín Alvarado, R., Bezerra, D.d.S., Cheraghi, M., Dobrowolska, B., et al.: Academic student satisfaction and perceived performance in the e-learning environment during the COVID-19 pandemic: evidence across ten countries. PLoS ONE **16**(10), (2021)

Khan, M.A.: COVID-19's impact on higher education: a rapid review of early reactive literature. Educ. Sci. **11**(8), 421 (2021)

Maldonado, J.E., De Witte, K.: The effect of school closures on standardised student test outcomes. Br. Educ. Res. J. **48**(1), 49–94 (2022)

Nambiar, D.: The impact of online learning during COVID-19: students' and teachers' perspective. Int. J. Indian Psychol. **8**(2), 783–793 (2020)

Nilsberth, M., Liljekvist, Y., Olin-Scheller, C., Samuelsson, J., Hallquist, C.: Digital teaching as the new normal? Swedish upper secondary teachers' experiences of emergency remote teaching during the COVID-19 crisis. Eur. Educ. Res. J. **20**(4), 442–462 (2021)

Olasile, B.A., Emrah, S.: Covid-19 pandemic and online learning: the challenges and opportunities. Interact. Learn. Environ. (2020)

Osman, M.E.: Global impact of COVID-19 on education systems: the emergency remote teaching at Sultan Qaboos University. J. Educ. Teach. **46**(4), 463–471 (2020)

Pérez-Jorge, D., Rodríguez-Jiménez, M.C., Ariño-Mateo, E., Barragán-Medero, F.: The effect of COVID-19 in university tutoring models. Sustainability **12**, 8631 (2020)

Pokhrel, S., Chhetri, R.: A literature review on impact of COVID-19 pandemic on teaching and learning. High. Educ. Futur. **8**(1), 133–141 (2021)

Sarasjärvi, K.K., Vuolanto, P.H., Solin, P.C.M., et al.: Subjective mental well-being among higher education students in Finland during the first wave of COVID-19. Scand. J. Public Health (2022)

Sipeki, I., Vissi, T., Túri, I.: The effect of the Covid-19 pandemic on the mental health of students and teaching staff. Heliyon **8**(4), (2022)

UNESCO: The impact of the COVID-19 pandemic on education: international evidence from the Responses to Educational Disruption Survey (REDS). https://unesdoc.unesco.org/ark:/48223/pf0000380398 (2022). Last accessed 15 June 2022

van Eck, N.J., Waltman, L.: Manual for VOSviewer version 1.6.17. Leiden University. https://www.vosviewer.com/documentation/Manual_VOSviewer_1.6.17.pdf (2021). Last accessed 15 June 2022

Skills in Demand for Blockchain Related Jobs

Monica Mihaela Maer Matei and Anamaria Năstasă

Abstract Technology development has a major impact on the economic systems, transforming all its components. For instance, the emergence of the blockchain technology changes the means of collaboration and transactions in society and economy, generating opportunities for financial markets, software companies, public and social services, to mention just a few. Furthermore, the challenges related to privacy, storage space, and networking are arising, creating new jobs. All over, different industries are looking for blockchain skills. This study aims to investigate the current requirements associated with blockchain-related jobs in the Romanian labor market, also examining the similarity to the worldwide situation. The importance of this topic lies in the fact that understanding employers' requirements it is a major step for signaling current trends related to labor demand and skills mismatching. The findings are extracted using unsupervised text mining techniques on textual data sourced from the LinkedIn platform. The results present a snapshot of the current situation in Romania, revealing two main subsets of characteristics required for blockchain-related jobs. These define the two broad categories of actual vacancies: software engineers, which are expected to have a computer science background, programming skills, and product designers where marketing, communication, and design skills are essential.

Keywords Blockchain · Jobs · Skills · Text mining · Topic models

M. M. M. Matei (✉)
National Scientific Research Institute for Labour and Social Protection, Bucharest University of Economic Studies, Bucharest, Romania
e-mail: monica.matei@csie.ase.ro

A. Năstasă
National Scientific Research Institute for Labour and Social Protection, Doctoral School of Sociology, University of Bucharest, Bucharest, Romania

A. M. Dima and E. R. Danescu (eds.), *Fostering Recovery Through Metaverse Business Modelling*, Springer Proceedings in Business and Economics,
https://doi.org/10.1007/978-3-031-28255-3_13

1 Introduction

Technological progress has a major impact on our lives, transforming working, learning, and living conditions. Recent years have witnessed the expansion of innovative technology which arises as a solution for sharing and storing big data. This distributed ledger technology known as blockchain (BC) technology has grown rapidly since 2008 (Nakamoto 2008). It was implemented for the first time in 2009, representing the core mechanism for Bitcoin. Besides that, the emergence of the (BC) technology changes the means of collaboration and the nature of transactions in society and economy, generating new possibilities for financial markets, software companies, public and social services, to mention just a few. Furthermore, the challenges related to privacy, storage space, and networking are arising, creating new jobs. All over, different industries are looking for BC skills. In the past two years, in the technology sector, this is one of the fastest-growing working domains. Moreover, to benefit from the opportunities offered by recent technology, the workforce's knowledge and skills must be updated. Within this context, understanding employers' requirements is a major step for signaling latest trends related to labor demand and skills mismatching.

Therefore, we are witnessing a boost in actions and projects aiming to raise awareness, to find solutions and opportunities opened up by BC technologies. The broad topics connected to this complex issue are: digital transformation, skills mismatch, intelligence from unstructured big data, and text mining methods. The European Commission's Initiative *Digital Skills and Job Platform* is one valuable tool developed to address the gap that exists between employers' needs in the digital sector and job seekers' capabilities. Furthermore, The European Centre for the Development of Vocational Training, CEDEFOP, one of the main EU actors in the policy development related to skills and qualifications, concentrates on anticipating skill demand and supply. An important source of information used within these projects comes from online job advertisements. Therefore, text mining methods are emerging tools to extract up-to-date labor market intelligence.

In this paper, we focus on a small part of this complex issue by investigating one of the most recent technologies, namely, blockchain, and its impact on skills demand for the job market in Romania.

2 Literature Review

Currently, BC technology is widely used in economic transactions and business services improving aspects related to time, security, costs, and risk management. Furthermore, in the literature, potential BC applications are described in sectors like energy, healthcare, or education (Gad et al. 2022; Zheng et al. 2018). Within this framework, businesses could innovate, and society could improve quality of life depending on the availability of a skilled workforce.

Considerable efforts are undertaken by the European Commission through the Digital Skills and Job Platform Initiative to understand the characteristics of BC posts in the European labor market. One of the projects belonging to this initiative is CHAISE: Blockchain Skills for Europe, which brings together 15 European countries, including Romania. This project's goal is to develop a mechanism to reduce BC and distributed ledger technologies skill shortages in Europe. The largest research of skills needs and demands for BC in Europe is available as a result of this project. The findings presented within this report emphasize a lack of talents in this field, companies facing recruiting problems.

The relevance of this topic in the context of skills required is reflected in the evolution represented in Fig. 1, showing the intensity of the global search intensity for the term 'blockchain' for the search category "Jobs and Education". This validates the conclusion presented in the CHAISE report (2021) that in the last two years, the BC labor market has grown exponentially.

Another important actor promoting the importance of the correlation between labor market needs and job seekers in terms of skills, CEDEFOP, shows that technology development is one of the main factors of skills mismatching (CEDEFOP 2019).

Even if a substantial part of BC applications belongs to the ICT or finance sector, a growing interest is also encountered in the retail, energy, research, education, or healthcare sectors. Given that BC technology expands to a variety of sectors, the research showed that industry and specific knowledge become an important requirement for jobs tackling with development of BC applications. Previous studies have underlined that there are significant differences between countries with respect to

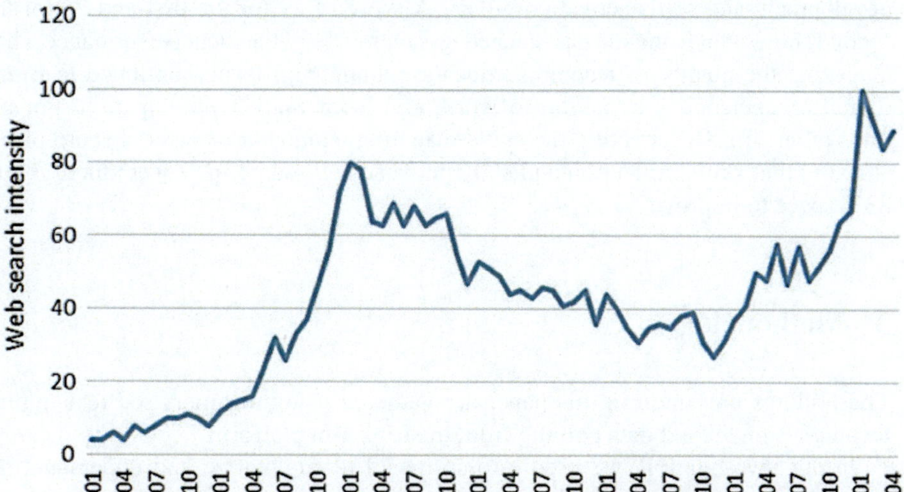

Fig. 1 Blockchain web search. *Source* Google trends

the size of the BC market or BC ecosystem maturity. Country disparities were also observed when investigating the types of jobs being created by BC technology (Cimiterra et al. 2021).

In addition to the research developed by these organisms, there are also scientific articles addressing the BC topic in terms of jobs and skills. Textual data extracted from online job posts represents the most relevant data source. The studies undertaken in the last years in the BC field use this intelligence to understand the needs of the labor market. Results are available for the USA (Kassab et al. 2021), China (Chunmian et al. 2021), and Australia (Atherton et al. 2020).

Background in programming or mathematics, technical skills such as big data, artificial intelligence, machine learning, and database are common requirements independent of the investigated labor market. Java, Python, and C++ are the most required programming languages. Nontechnical skill sets such as finance, operation, and marketing are also important.

According to CHAISE report (2021), in Europe, the blockchain employee is defined by the following attributes: has a bachelor's degree (ICT), is a 30 years old male, full-time employed, proficient in web development, mathematics and statistics, tokens, smart contracts, finance, data, legal, and agile development.

This study aims to investigate the current requirements associated with BC-related employment positions on the Romanian labor market, also examining the similarity with the worldwide situation. With respect to BC ecosystem maturity, Romania is included in Stage 1, meaning that there is no legal framework developed for blockchain or crypto assets (CHAISE report 2021). Moreover, a broad profile of the Romanian labor market is offered by the 2022 European Skills Index (ESI) developed by CEDEFOP. Romania scores extremely low with respect to the skills development and skills activation pillars. A score of 29 for the first and 25 for the second shows that Romania has reached less than 30% of the ideal performance when analyzing the quality of teaching, education attainment level, continued learning, digital competencies, transition to work, and labor market participation. For the third pillar of ESI, reflecting the skills matching, Romania received a score of 67, showing that skills utilization and skills mismatch could be improved; there is still 33% space to improve.

3 Methodology

The findings presented in this paper are gathered using unsupervised text mining techniques on textual data coming from the LinkedIn platform.

In our investigation, we used a topic model to summarize and understand the patterns of the information in the corpus we have built from job requirements. Fundamentally, this is a probabilistic model based on the word frequency occurrences in the corpus documents. The topics could be considered as latent variables that explain the correlation between terms. Concisely, a topic is a mixture of words; meanwhile, a document is a mixture of topics. In this study, the topic model was fitted with

Latent Dirichlet allocation (LDA) method (Blei et al. 2003). This is a probabilistic model, defined as mixture model or hierarchical model. The input of a LDA model is the number of topics (K) to be extracted and a document-term matrix. Each line of this matrix corresponds to a document and represents the frequencies encountered by each word in that specific document. Dimensionality reduction techniques were proposed within this framework (Deerwester et al. 1990), extended with probabilistic approaches (Hofmann 1999). The main assumption used within these models states that the order of words in a document is not relevant (bag-of-words assumption). Also, the ordering of documents in the corpus is neglected. The implications of these assumptions are connected to computational issues.

The generative process behind LDA (Blei 2003) must consider the following distributions:

For each topic k, $k = \overline{1, K}$, a multinomial distribution over all words

$$j,\ j = \overline{1, V}:\ p_k \sim \text{Dirichlet}(\beta). \tag{1}$$

For each document d:

(1) a multinomial distribution that encodes the probability of each topic in the document:

$$\theta_d \sim \text{Dirichlet}(\alpha) \tag{2}$$

(2) for the nth token of d:

– the probability of being generated from a topic

$$z_{d,n} \sim \text{Mult}(\theta_d) \tag{3}$$

– the conditional probability of a token on the topic:

$$w_{d,n} \middle| z_{d,n} \sim \text{Mult}(p_k). \tag{4}$$

Therefore, the distribution of topics in a document and the term distribution for each topic are Dirichlet distributions. These represent prior beliefs regarding: (i) how topics are chosen and (ii) which words describe each topic. The Dirichlet distribution belongs to the exponential family and exhibits properties that reduce the burden for the parameter estimation. A Dirichlet distribution (Dirchlet(α)) is a multivariate probability distribution often used as prior distribution in Bayesian models. The parameter α is a vector of dimension K. The probability density function for the Dirichlet distribution defined over a K-dimensional vector has the following form:

$$p(\theta, \alpha) = \frac{\Gamma(\sum_{i=1}^{K} \alpha_i)}{\prod_{i=1}^{K} \Gamma(\alpha_i)} \prod_{i=1}^{K} \theta_i^{\alpha_i - 1} \tag{5}$$

where: $\theta \in R^K$, $\sum_{i=1}^{K} \theta_i = 1, \theta_i \in [0, 1]$ and $\alpha_i > 0$. The gamma (Γ) function is:

$$\Gamma(z) = \int_0^{\infty} x^{z-1} e^{-x} \mathrm{d}x \tag{6}$$

After that, in the generative process of a document, for each word in the document, we draw a topic and then a word from multinomial distributions. The multinomial distribution is a generalization of the binomial distribution with the probability mass function given by:

$$\frac{\Gamma(\sum_i x_i + 1)}{\prod_i \Gamma(x_i + 1)} \prod_{i=1}^{K} \theta_i^{x_i} \tag{7}$$

where x_i are the counts and Γ is the standard gamma function.

The posterior probability $p(\theta, z|w, \alpha, \beta)$ will be derived using two main inputs: prior probabilities and the likelihood functions built on observed data. The likelihood is multinomial.

In the estimation stage, we want to find the parameters α and β that maximize the log likelihood of the data. Estimating those vectors is equivalent to revealing which words are relevant for which topic and which topics are important for a specific document.

Usually, inference and learning in LDA are carried out with two algorithms, namely: variational expectation–maximization (VEM) algorithm or a Markov Chain Monte Carlo algorithm (Gibbs sampling) (Hornik and Grün 2011). The results presented in this paper were obtained with the second one. Markov chain Monte Carlo (MCMC) is a method used to estimate posterior distributions in Bayesian inference. It is a powerful method showing good performance. Within this approach, a large number of samples are drawn from the posterior and their properties are examined. The generation is undertaken sequentially, each new sample depending on the previous one—a Markov chain. Each state of a chain is an assignment of values to the z variables being sampled. The algorithm computes the probability of a topic z being assigned to a word w, given all the other topic assignments to all the other words (Darling 2011).

The results of LDA will reveal not only the topics defined by subsets of words encountering high probabilities, but also the distribution of these topics within each document. Even if all the documents are explained by the same topics, some of them could be better represented by specific topics. To understand what a topic is about, we extract the words with the highest probabilities. In addition, to see what a document is about, we look at the topic distribution inside it.

4 Analysis / Results Interpretation

The results presented in this section are obtained from a corpus containing 43 documents. Each document represents the requirements associated with a specific job. The job posts were extracted using the following filters: vacancies related to blockchain, in Romania, advertising full-time jobs, for entry-level candidates, in the Software Development or IT services/IT consulting industries, published in the previous month (April 2022). Using this selection, 41 documents containing skills requirements were extracted. Hence, the findings will present a snapshot of the current situation in Romania.

The pre-processing stage involved tokenizing the document, transforming words to their singular form, removing numbers, converting to lower case, and removing stop words and punctuation. We have also defined a list of words that were eliminated from the vocabulary: "experience", "understanding", "development", "skills", "ability", "knowledge", "strong", "e.g.", "role", "hands", "familiarity", "effectively", "based", "excellent", "related", "blockchain", and "technology" which are not relevant to our analysis.

Analyzing the terms in the corpus encountering the highest frequencies (Fig. 2), we detect the main skills required by the employers. First, teamwork and communication skills are frequently required in the vacancies that we have extracted. Next, some technical skills related to software development are identified. These are associated with the terms: "solidity", "agile", and "ci". Solidity is a programming language used to implement smart contracts on BC platforms like Ethereum. The word "agile" stands for a new set of software development methodologies, meanwhile "ci" comes from CI/CD method which means Continuous Integration/Continuous Delivery and represents an approach employed by teams in the applications development process.

Other technical skills are unveiled by the following words: "web", "data", "cloud". The deployment of cloud infrastructure, using cloud environments, and experience with web development or web. 3js libraries are often included in the job requirements.

Fig. 2 Highest frequency Terms. *Source* Authors computation using "wordcloud" R library

Moreover, experience with BC technology such as Ethereum platforms or smart contracts is expected. Finally, the wordcloud reveals another category of skills related to "marketing", "product", and "content". Besides software engineers, companies are also looking for employees able to perform marketing or customer support activities.

In the next phase, LDA models were fitted with different numbers of topics using Gibbs sampling algorithm (Hornik and Grün 2011; Silge and Robinson 2016). Given that the corpus we have used is exceedingly small, the number of topics selected was based on judging the interpretation quality.

When setting $k = 2$, the estimation yielded semantic coherent topics that make sense for our analysis. In order to understand the meaning of the topics, the estimated per-topic-per-word probabilities (denoted beta) are investigated.

The first topic has higher probability for words such as "team", "product", or "design". This topic is a latent factor representing the employers' needs for content creation related to marketing activities. Social media content creation and teamwork are the main specificities of these jobs.

The second topic is associated with the software development requirements, showing the demand for software engineers. The words that have a higher probability of being generated from this topic are represented in the second column of Fig. 3. The candidates applying for software engineering jobs should be proficient in tools defining BC technology like Ethereum platform and smart contracts.

The model also computes topic probabilities for each document as a proportion of words from that document generated from that topic. These are called the gamma probabilities. The job advertisements are drawn from a mix of the two topics. In the corpus analyzed here, the model estimates that the words in documents advertising software engineer jobs are generated with a higher probability from topic 2. The mean estimated probability is about 0.56, meanwhile, the jobs related to product design have a mean probability of being generated from topic 1 of 0.6. Per-document-per-topic probabilities distributions for each category of job advertisements, represented in Fig. 4, point out the relevance of each topic within the employers' requirements for software engineers in comparison to product designers.

In the following tables are presented pairs of two consecutive words, often called "bigrams", that appear with the highest frequency for each job category previously identified.

The bigrams encapsulate the main characteristics in demand for each group. Software engineers are expected to have a computer science background, programming skills, and experience with BC technology tools. Product designers need marketing, communication skills, and the ability to perform in a fast-paced environment (Tables 1 and 2).

Our findings are similar to the previous results obtained in other markets, especially those related to technical skills. Furthermore, the main skills in demand extracted by this study are also revealed by the Skills Online Vacancy Analysis Tool for Europe (Skills OVATE). This is a tool developed by Cedefop and Eurostat to provide information on skills and occupations. According to the data gathered during Q2 2021–Q1 2022, for Romania for the Software and applications developers and analysts occupation, the most requested skills, using ESCO classification

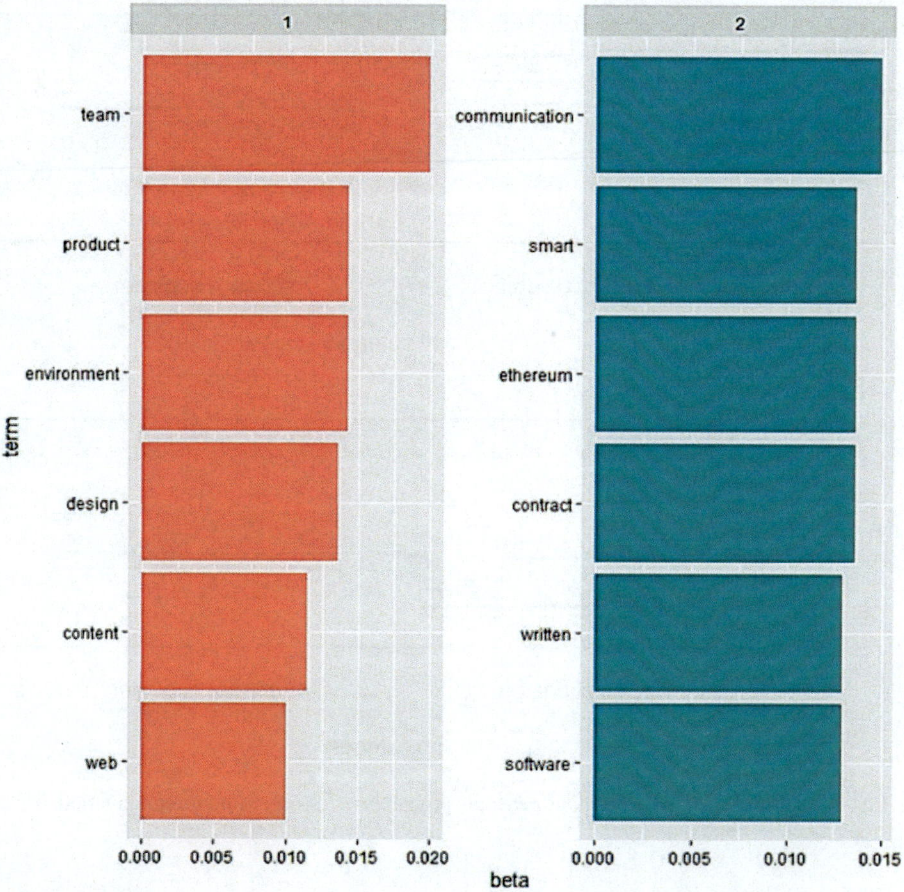

Fig. 3 Top probabilities per-topic-per-word (beta). *Source* Authors computation, using R "topic-models" library

are: accessing and analysing digital data, programming computer systems, working in teams, developing solutions, using digital tools for collaboration and adapt to change. Most of the job posts extracted when performing the text analysis presented in this paper are connected to this occupation, and the skills described in the previous paragraphs belong to these more exhaustive ESCO categories.

However, for a better representation, the analysis should be extended to a wider period. Also, other platforms should be considered in order to increase the corpus size, paying attention to the characteristics of the companies looking for employees. On a larger data set, it would also be feasible to validate the results using different coherence metrics.

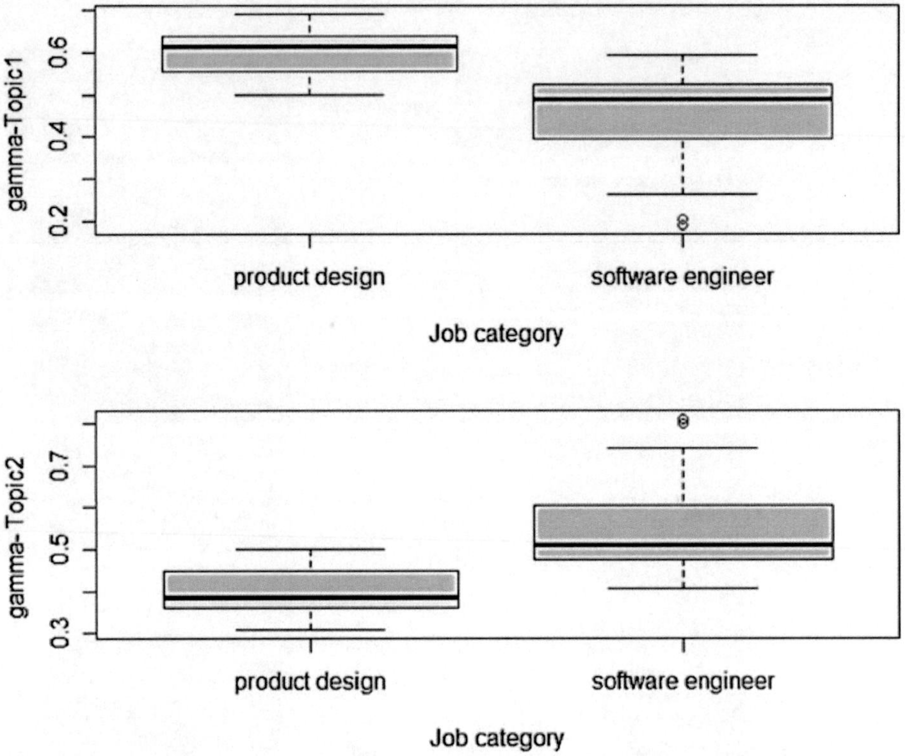

Fig. 4 Distribution of per-document-per-topic probabilities. *Source* Authors computation, using R "topicmodels" library

Table 1 Bigrams with highest frequency-development jobs

Word1	Word2	Freq.
Smart	Contract	16
Computer	Science	11
Written	Communication	11
ci	cd	10

Source Authors computation, using "tidytext" R library

Table 2 Bigrams with highest frequency-product design jobs

Word1	Word2	Freq.
Product	Marketing	5
Communication	Skills	4
Fast	Paced	4
Social	Media	4

Source Authors computation, using "tidytext" R library

5 Conclusions

The topic of this paper is associated with the following problems: blockchain technology and digital transformation, skills mismatch, intelligence from unstructured big data, and text mining methods. Using textual data extracted from an online recruiting platform and specific text mining methods, this study presents a snapshot of the current situation in Romania regarding the new jobs created by BC technology. The findings reveal two main subsets of characteristics required for blockchain-related jobs. These define the two broad categories of actual vacancies: software engineers, which are expected to have a computer science background, programming skills, and product designers where marketing, communication, and design skills are essential. Understanding what employers need is the first step to be taken to address the skill shortage. Besides the benefits brought by reducing skill mismatch, a workforce possessing the skills required by the recent technology, will attract international investors in the Romanian economy, will encourage innovation based on blockchain technology. The limitations of this study are induced by the reduced size of the corpus. Increasing the number of the investigated documents by expanding the time period, removing the country filter, or considering other recruitment platforms will enable a more complex exploration of the skills needed for BC jobs. It would allow us to include findings from document classification techniques with performance evaluation and to select the optimal number of topics. Moreover, relevant insights concerning the labor market needs in terms of skills for BC jobs will be extracted by introducing new variables in the study such as: firm characteristics, industry, and BC ecosystem maturity.

Acknowledgements This paper has been elaborated in the NUCLEU Program 19N/2019, funded by Romanian Research and Innovation Ministry, project PN 19130303.

References

Atherton, J.O., Bratanova, A., Markey-Towler, B.: Who is the blockchain employee? Exploring skills in demand using observations from the Australian labour market and behavioural institutional cryptoeconomics. J. Br. Blockchain Assoc. 13390 (2020)

Blei, D.M., Ng, A.Y., Jordan, M.I.: Latent Dirichlet allocation. J. Mach. Learn. Res. **3**(Jan), 993–1022 (2003)

CEDEFOP: online job vacancies and skills analysis. A Cedefop pan-European Approach (2019). ISBN: 978-92-896-2850-1. https://doi.org/10.2801/097022

CEDEFOP: skills-OVATE. https://www.cedefop.europa.eu/en/tools/skills-online-vacancies. Last accessed 12 Aug 2022

CHAISE report: D2.5.1—study on skills mismatches in European Blockchain sector. https://chaise-blockchainskills.eu/wp-content/uploads/2021/11/CHAISE_WP2_D2.5.1_Study-on-Skills-Mismatches-in-the-blockchain-sector.pdf (2021). Last accessed 12 Aug 2022

Chunmian, G.E., Haoyue, S.H.I., JIANG, J., Xiaoying, X.U: Investigating the demand for blockchain talents in the recruitment market: evidence from topic modeling analysis on job postings. Inf. Manag. 103513 (2021)

Cimiterra, M., Krafft, J., Nesta, L.: Blockchain as Schumpeter Mark 1 Or Mark 2? An empirical analysis of blockchain job offers in France and Germany. Ind. Corp. Chang. **30**(6), 1388–1402 (2021)

Darling, W.M.: A theoretical and practical implementation tutorial on topic modeling and Gibbs sampling. In: Proceedings of the 49th Annual Meeting of the Association for Computational Linguistics: Human Language Technologies, pp. 642–647 (2011)

Deerwester, S., Dumais, S.T., Furnas, G.W., Landauer, T.K., Harshman, R.: Indexing by latent semantic analysis. J. Am. Soc. Inf. Sci. **41**(6), 391–407 (1990)

Gad, A.G., Mosa, D.T., Abualigah, L., Abohany, A.A.: Emerging trends in blockchain technology and applications: a review and outlook. J. King Saud Univ.-Comput. Inf. Sci. (2022)

Hofmann, T.: Probabilistic latent semantic indexing. In: Proceedings of the 22nd Annual International ACM SIGIR Conference on Research and Development in Information Retrieval, pp. 50–57 (1999)

Hornik, K., Grün, B.: Topicmodels: an R package for fitting topic models. J. Stat. Softw. **40**(13), 1–30 (2011)

Kassab, M., Destefanis, G., DeFranco, J., Pranav, P.: Blockchain-engineers wanted: an empirical analysis on required skills, education and experience. In: 2021 IEEE/ACM 4th International Workshop on Emerging Trends in Software Engineering for Blockchain (WETSEB), pp. 49–55. IEEE (2021)

Nakamoto, S.: Bitcoin: a peer-to-peer electronic cash system. Decentralized Bus. Rev. 21260 (2008)

Silge, J., Robinson, D.: tidytext: text mining and analysis using tidy data principles in R. J. Open Source Softw. **1**(3), 37 (2016)

Zheng, Z., Xie, S., Dai, H.N., Chen, X., Wang, H.: Blockchain challenges and opportunities: a survey. Int. J. Web Grid Serv. **14**(4), 352–375 (2018)

From the Beginning to the Present. Exploring the Undeclared Work Patterns in Research Publications Using the Bibliometric Analysis

Adriana AnaMaria Davidescu, Eduard Mihai Manta, Margareta-Stela Florescu, Cristina Maria Geambasu, and Marian Oancea

Abstract The purpose of this study is to explore the research field of undeclared work patterns, highlighting the evolution of the literature and the directions and ramifications of possible future research. A mapping process is used as a tool in investigating scientific knowledge. To establish the temporal evolution of the undeclared work patterns research domain in terms of publications, we extracted articles from Scopus published between 1971 and 2022. The keywords used in the search query were undeclared employment, undeclared wages, envelope wages, undeclared work, and informal employment. We investigated 916 documents, with the focus point being on the author, paper, keyword, and journal. The subject areas of the investigated journals were social sciences, economics, econometrics and finance, business, management, and accounting. The empirical findings emphasize that C. Williams, I. Horodnic, J. Windebank, S. Nadin, F. Schneider, J. Franic, P. Adair, and H. Lehmann are the reference authors for the whole spectrum of undeclared work. Finally, the Indian Journal of Labour Economics, World Development, International Labour Review, International Journal of Sociology and Social Politics, Journal of Development Economics, and Review of Development Economics are the most prolific journals in the field.

Keywords Undeclared employment · Undeclared wages · Envelope wages · Undeclared work · Informal employment determinants · Bibliometric analysis

---

A. A. Davidescu · E. M. Manta (✉) · M.-S. Florescu · C. M. Geambasu
Bucharest University of Economic Studies, Bucharest, Romania
e-mail: eduard.manta@csie.ase.ro

A. A. Davidescu
Institute for Labour and Social Protection, National Scientific Research, Bucharest, Romania

M. Oancea
University of Bucharest, Bucharest, Romania

A. M. Dima and E. R. Danescu (eds.), *Fostering Recovery Through Metaverse Business Modelling*, Springer Proceedings in Business and Economics,
https://doi.org/10.1007/978-3-031-28255-3_14

1 Introduction

Recent literary works have begun to challenge the concept that the informal and formal economies are distinct. All economic activities that are not covered, or are inadequately covered, by legal arrangements are included in the informal economy, according to the International Labour Organization Conference (ILO 2014, 2015). The informal aggregate in today's global economy has been described in a variety of ways, and various aspects of both the informal and formal situations have been taken into consideration (Williams and Windebank 2005; Gialis and Leontidou 2014). Undeclared work is a significant and growing feature of the contemporary global economy (Feige and Urban 2008; Schneider 2008; Charmes 2009).

Undeclared work or what has been referred to as the 'informal sector, the shadow economy, or the hidden economy' must be defined to understand what is being discussed here. This, according to the definition, refers to the compensated manufacturing and sale of goods and services which are not registered or hidden from the government for taxes or advantage reasons, but are otherwise lawful. Although not declaring income or social security benefits usually breaches tax or social security laws, this rule exempts both unpaid employment and work (such as drug trafficking) where the service or product provided is unlawful in and of itself. There are no hard and fast boundaries in this field like there are in many others. As an example, prostitution and other services that are illegal in some countries but not others are included in some definitions.

For more than half a century, the leading theory to explain why people engage in illegal work has been that those who do so are rational economic actors who do so when the anticipated payments outweigh the anticipated costs of being discovered and penalized (Allingham and Sandmo 1972). But the acceptance of the fact that many people avoid doing illegal work even if the benefits outweigh the costs has sparked an alternative approach from social actors (Alm et al. 2012). This helps explain why people engage in illegal work when they lack confidence in government and, more recently, when they lack trust in each other (horizontal trust) (Hallsworth et al. 2017).

"Undeclared work" is work that is not reported for taxes, social security, and/or labour legislation reasons when it should have been. Academics and practitioners agree that this is the case. Illegality in other ways, such as the items or services that are given (e.g., counterfeit goods, illicit narcotics), does not make paid activities undeclared labour, but rather part of the greater criminal economy.

The purpose of this study is to examine the academic area of undeclared labour patterns, focusing on the variety of the literature and future research routes, using science mapping, which allows for the examination of scientific information.

This study is also providing answers to the following questions: (RQ1) Which researchers and publications, institutes, and countries are at the forefront of the study of illegal work practices? (RQ2) What are the most popular search terms and important research evolution themes linked with them? (RQ3) Who are some of the most often mentioned writers in the undeclared work patterns field? (RQ4) Which authors and institutions are involved in collaborative networks?

There are a total of five sections in this document. The purpose of the introduction is to quickly explain the significance of the subject matter. There is a theoretical component in the next section that includes the most important works on the topic. The third section presents data and technique, while the next section demonstrates empirical outcomes. The paper's key conclusions are presented at the end.

2 Literature Review

For several decades, the study of undeclared labour was dominated by a "size matters" approach. Scholars worked on quantifying the scope of this area using methods of indirect measuring (Friedman et al. 2000; Schneider et al. 2011). Insufficient thought was given to analysing the type of undeclared work.

Undeclared labour has traditionally been seen unfavourably in advanced capitalist nations, as it contributes little or no to economic and social growth (Gallin 2001; Grabiner 2000); as a result, the standard public policy response has been to prohibit it (Hasseldine and Zhuhong 1999; Sandford 1999). Most European governments have tried to deter such activity by increasing fines and coordinating strategies and actions to improve detection rates. Many scholarly critics and supranational bodies (European Commission 1998; ILO 2002) have approved such an approach (Castells and Portes 1989).

Self-employment (like in the "worker-entrepreneur" idea) or interdependent employment (as in the "employee" concept) are two examples of undeclared labour. It can also refer to work done in exchange for payment in kind, as additional to labour done for cash (Mingione 1991; Pedersen 1998; European Commission 2007).

In recent decades, a stream of social democratic ideology in Europe has taken up the portrayal of unregistered employment as a site of entrepreneurship, regarding unregistered business as a resource only if it can be controlled and pushed into the formal economic system (Renooy et al. 2004; Small Business Council 2004).

Other types of illicit compensated work have also been discovered. Not only have well-paid unregistered wage-earning jobs been recognized (Williams and Windebank 2011), but it has also been demonstrated that, in addition to "unregistered" jobs that are completely hidden from the country for levy, social welfare, and labour law reasons, also there are "under-declared" official jobs in which proclaimed employees are paid two salaries from their proclaimed employer, one proclaimed and one unreported "envelope wage" (Karpuskiene 2007; Woolfson 2007; Williams 2007). Many nations have established that substantial undeclared labour is done on its own or self-employed premise (Round et al. 2008; Williams 2005).

Until recently, much of this unregistered self-employment was carried out under business conditions for income reasons. However, in certain communities, such possess undeclared work has been identified as being frequently undertaken for nearer human relationships such as relatives, neighbours, mates, and work colleagues, for the reasons of redistributing wealth and helping, instead of primarily for monetary benefit (Persson and Malmer 2006).

However, research related to institutional asymmetry theory has mostly studied the relationship between undeclared employment and the level of “vertical trust” in the workplace (between government and citizens). The relationship between undeclared work and “horizontal trust” is an important part of the social actor technique that has gotten less attention (between citizens). While previous research has found no link between general trust (trusting in others) and non-compliance behaviour (Chan et al. 2018), horizontal trust (willing to trust others to be tax compliant) is linked to undeclared labour participation. Individuals may be more prone to avoid paying taxes when they live in an area where tax avoidance is widely accepted, not only because they might be less concerned regarding statutory and informal penalties, but because they assume that if others do it, why wouldn’t they do it as well? Furthermore, previous laboratory studies have shown that taxpayers’ propensity to cooperate is influenced by their neighbours’ conduct (Ajzen 1991; Chang and Lai 2004; Traxler 2010), and those individuals cooperate when tax law is the norm in society (Alm et al. 1999, 2012). Furthermore, a link has been shown between corporate taxation and the emotional distress associated with breaking a social convention (Dulleck et al. 2016).

3 Methodology

In order to explore the field of undeclared work patterns, the present research focuses on a bibliometric analysis. For this analysis, there were selected articles from Scopus published from 1971 to 2022. The selection was based on the following keywords: “undeclared employment”, “undeclared wages”, “envelope wages”, “undeclared work”, and “informal employment”.

All the documents that were selected were then imported into Bibliometrix and Biblioshiny using the R environment. Biblioshiny facilitates the way in which the user could conduct a visual and bibliometric analysis, since it is an R-tool with an interactive and user-friendly web interface. As it is shown in Fig. 1, the database used for the analysis contains a total of 916 documents split in: articles (805), books (6), book chapters (45), conference papers (17), notes (2), retracted (1), and reviews (40) (Table 1).

This research consists of three major steps. The first one is creating the needed database; during this step, the most important points are to establish the timespan of the search, the selection criteria, and the tools that will be used further in the research for manipulating and analysing the data. The second step is represented by the data analysis; here, the focus is on obtaining information about the evolution of the scientific production over the years, the most productive sources, and the author’s impact. The third step is an interpretation over the social, conceptual, and intellectual structure; here, the focus is on cluster and network analyses. The thematic evolution of the documents (based on the keywords plus), the authors’ co-citation network,

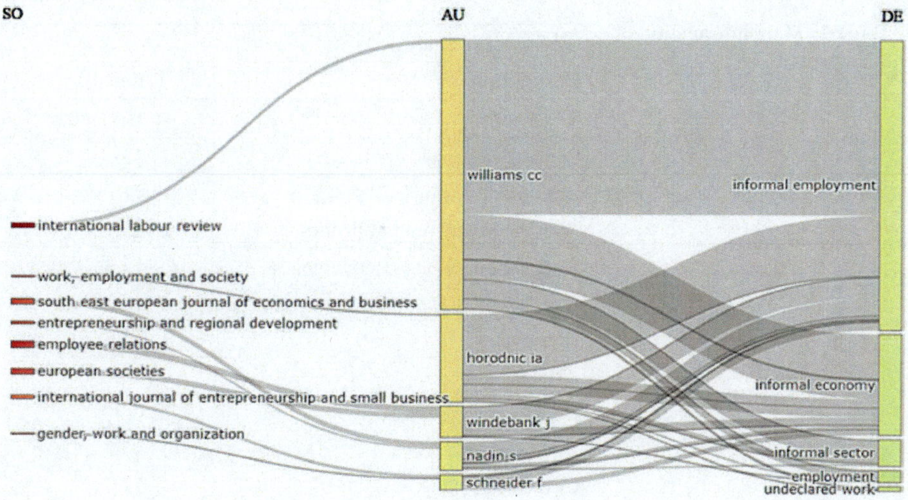

Fig. 1 Three field plots. *Source* Own illustrations

and the institutions and authors' collaboration networks are the main topics of the third step.

The clustering concept implies the separation of the data into understandable, useful, or both groupings (clusters). If meaningful groupings are the aim, the clusters should reflect the data's inherent structure. However, in certain circumstances, cluster analysis is merely a starting point for additional tasks, such as data summarization. Cluster analysis has long been used in a range of domains, including psychology and other social sciences, biology, statistics, pattern recognition, information retrieval, machine learning, and data mining.

4 Analysis/Results Interpretation

This study takes into consideration a total of 916 documents written by a total of 1346 authors, collected from 422 different sources, in a time span of 51 years, from 1971 to 2022. Those documents are split into 805 articles, six books, 45 book chapters, 17 conference papers, two notes, 40 reviews, and 1 retracted. Out of all these documents, 509 are multi-authored documents, and there are 1002 authors of multi-authored documents, this means that the collaboration index is 1.97. Also, looking at the citations, there are a total of 13.3 citations per document, but a 1.23 per year and document. The most cited document, with a total of 681 citations per entire period and a 35.84 total citation per year, is "Informality Revisited" by F. Malony published in 2004 in the "Word Development" journal.

In terms of evolution, the annual scientific production in the field of undeclared work is very low and approximatively on the same level for the period 1971–1986.

Table 1 Main information of documents

Bibliometric analysis	
Description	Results
Timespan	1971:2022
Sources (journals, book, etc.)	422
Documents	916
Average year from publication	9.67
Average citations per documents	13.3
Average citations per year per doc	1.232
References	35,386
Article	805
Book	6
Book chapter	45
Conference paper	17
Note	2
Retracted	1
Review	40
Keywords plus (ID)	1533
Author's keywords (DE)	1852
Authors	1346
Author appearances	1685
Authors of single-authored documents	344
Authors of multi-authored documents	1002
Single-authored documents	407
Documents per author	0.681
Author per document	1.47
Co-authors per documents	1.84
Collaboration index	1.97

Source Own illustrations

Starting with 1987, the interest towards this field has increased, and the number of documents presents an average annual growth rate of 6.75%. Looking at the entire studied period, the top 10 most important countries for the scientific production are: UK (243 documents), USA (233), India (91), South Africa (68), Germany (67), France (58), Italy (42), Australia (38), Canada (31), and Romania (29).

As mentioned earlier, this study covers documents collected from 422 sources. The top 5 sources are: "Indian Journal of Labour Economics" with 33 articles and a h-index of 7, "World Development" with 27 articles but a 18h-index, "International Labour Review" with 24 articles and a h-index of 10, "International Journal of Sociology and Social Policy" with 13 articles and a h-index of 9, "Journal of Development Economics" with 11 articles and a h-index of 9. If the focus is on the number of articles, then the first and most important source is the "Indian Journal of Labour Economics". But the absolute number of articles is not always relevant; in this case, the impact of the source should also need to be taken into consideration, so if the focus moves towards the Hirsch index, then the "World Development" will become the first most relevant source.

Of the 1346 authors present in this study, the most relevant 5, based on the number of written documents in the field of undeclared work, are: C. Williams—with 98 articles published between 1999 and 2022 with the highest point in 2015, I. Horodnic—with 25 articles published between 2015 and 2022 with the highest point in 2015, J. Windebank—with 12 articles published between 1999 and 2017 with the highest point in 2015, S. Nadin—with 10 articles—published between 2010 and 2014 with the highest point in 2012 and F. Schneider—with nine articles published between 2010 and 2022 with the highest point in 2014.

If the top five most relevant authors are based on the impact that the authors had and not on the number of articles, the top will be the same: Williams (h-index 22), Horodnic (h-index 13), Windebank (h-index 9), Nadin (h-index 7), and Schneider (h-index 5). Figure 1 shows each of the five authors and the topics they have written about, and in which sources the articles were published. For Williams, the most common topics ("informal employment", "informal economy", and "undeclared work") are published in the "International labour review" journal. Schneider wrote about "informal economy" and "informal employment" in both "Gender, Work and Organization" and "International Journal of Entrepreneurship and Small Business".

During the studied period, not only the scientific production changed, but also the interest topics that are discussed in connection with the undeclared work changed over time. To analyse this thematic evolution, the time horizon of this study was split into two, before and after 2015. As shown in Fig. 2, in the first period slice of time, 1971–2015, there are three well-defined clusters: "Informal sector"—in the red colour, "Female"—in the green colour, and "Developing country"—in blue colour.

As shown in Fig. 3, in the second period of time, 2015–2022, six clusters are formed: "Employment"—in the red colour, "Women employment"—in blue, "Economic development"—in brown, "Income"—in green colour, "Trade liberalization"—in yellow colour, and "covid"—in colour purple.

Further, this study also analyses the intellectual structure based on the co-citation of the authors. Figure 4 shows the results of the authors' co-citation analysis. There are three main clusters: the green one—the predominant authors are Schneider and Williams, and the main topic is in the informal sector, the red one—the predominant authors are Maloney and De Soto and the main topic is about the developing countries and their macroeconomic factors, the blue one—the main authors are Castells and Davis, and the main topic of the cluster is the gender and age split.

For a better understanding of the clusters structure, it is important to look at the betweenness and closeness measures. For the first cluster (green), the most important author, with the highest influence over the rest authors in the cluster, based on these two measures, is Schneider (85.64—Betweenness; 0.017—Closeness) followed by Williams (48.22—Betweenness; 0.017—Closeness), they both present the highest

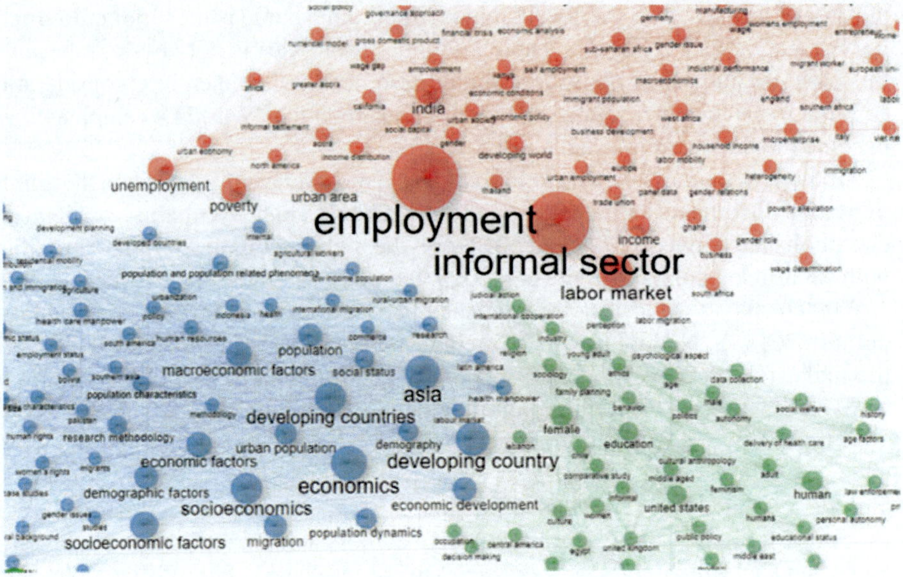

Fig. 2 Thematic evolution network 1971–2015. *Source* Own illustrations

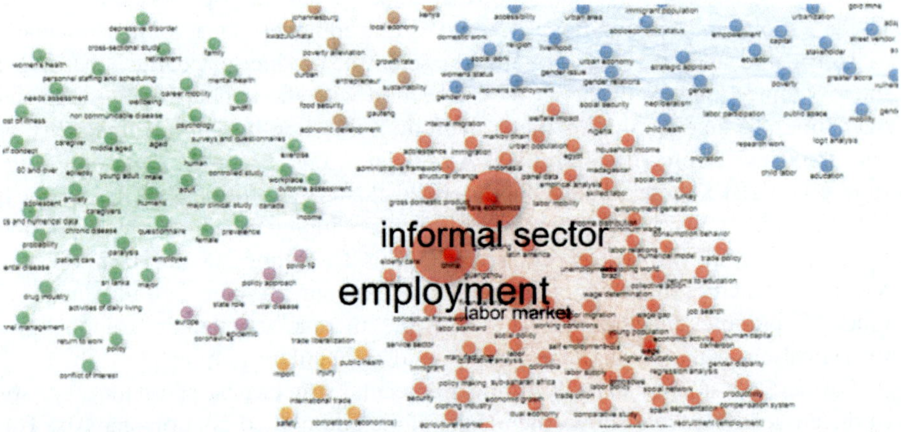

Fig. 3 Thematic evolution network after 2015. *Source* Own illustrations

betweenness and closeness values. In the second cluster, the red one, with a betweenness value of 32.89 and a closeness value of 0.017, the most influent author is De Soto, followed by Maloney (22.74—Betweenness; 0.015—Closeness). In the third cluster, coloured blue, the most influent author is Castells, having a betweenness value of 91.92 and a closeness value of 0.018.

In Fig. 5 are presented two collaboration networks, one between different institutions, and one for the authors. For the authors, there can be distinguished 6 different clusters, but the main one is the red-coloured cluster having Williams and Windebank

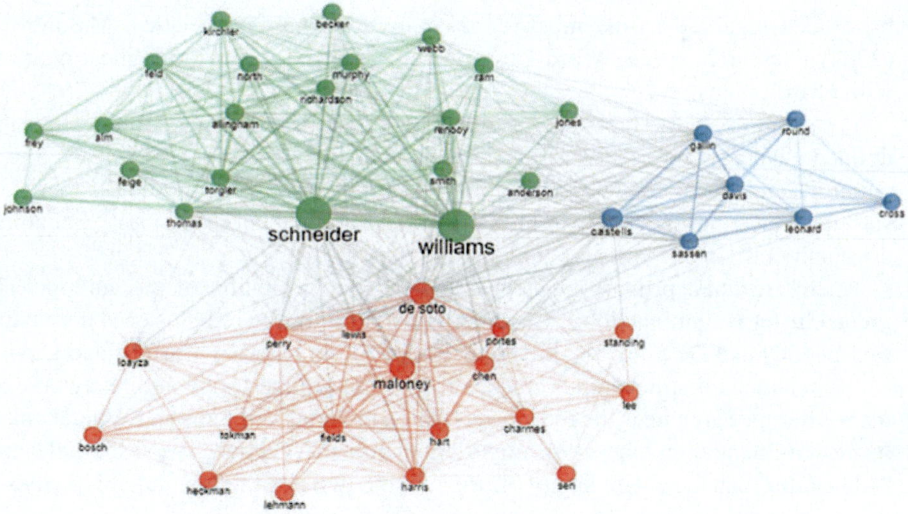

Fig. 4 Authors' co-citation network. *Source* Own illustrations

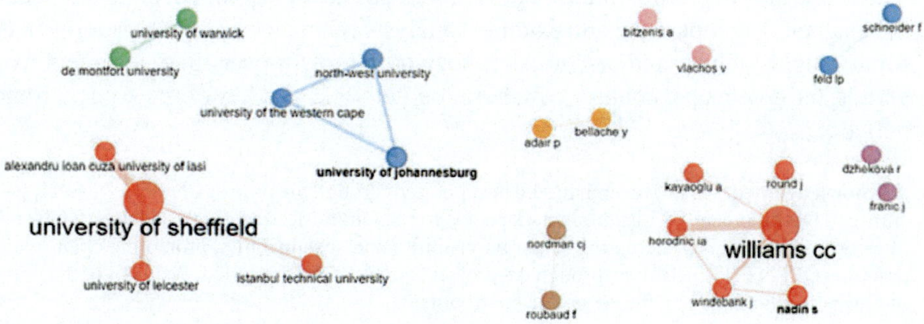

Fig. 5 Institutions and authors collaboration networks. *Source* Own illustrations

as the most influent authors. As for the institutions, there are three main clusters, with the red-coloured cluster as the main one where the "University of Sheffield" and the "Alexandru Ioan Cuza University of Iasi" as the most influent institutions.

5 Conclusions

For the goal of this study, researchers analysed more than 916 scholarly papers published between 1971 and 2022 on the Web of Science platform, concentrating on the dynamics of academic papers and prospective future research subjects.

It began in 1971, with an annual growth rate of about 6.75%, and has continued ever since. The "World Development" and the "Indian Journal of Labour Economics" have been regarded as the most representative journals in the area. Maloney, F. (2004)'s research in the "Word Development" magazine has the highest citations with 681 citations.

For example, in the first slice of time, from 1971 to 2015, there are three clearly defined clusters: "Informal sector" (in red), "Female" (in green), and "Developing country" (in blue). In the second slice of time, from 2015 to 2022, there are six clusters: "Employment" (in red), "Women employment" (in blue), "Economic development" (in brown), and "Income" (in green).

There are three primary clusters based on the co-citation of the authors: The green cluster is dominated by Schneider and Williams, the red cluster is dominated by Maloney and De Soto, and the blue cluster is dominated by Castells and Davis.

There are six distinct author clusters to be found in the cooperation network, but the most important one is the red cluster, which includes Williams and Windebank as its most influential members. It is important to note that "University of Sheffield" and "Alexandru Ioan Cuza University of Iasi" are the two most influential universities in the red-coloured cluster.

In terms of future directions of research and limitations, it can be mentioned that this study does not cover the other main database of scientific papers, namely, Scopus, which is worth exploring in terms of research publications that cover the subject of the chapter. A comparative and extended analysis of undeclared work patterns in the future might include authors' impact, keywords growth over time, abstracts word clouds and tree maps, country collaboration network, and keywords co-occurrence network.

Acknowledgements The research has been supported through the project CNFIS-FDI-2022-0472 entitled "Development of Institutional Capacity for Scientific Research in Bucharest University of Economic Studies by increasing scientific visibility and sustainability, promoting open science practices OPEN FUTURE" and through the project 750/19.05.2022 entitled "Analysis of the impact of current uncertainties on the economic environment".

References

Ajzen, I.: The theory of planned behaviour. Organ. Behav. Hum. Decis. Process. **50**(2), 179–211 (1991)

Allingham, M.G., Sandmo, A.: Income tax evasion: a theoretical analysis. J. Public Econ. **1**(3–4), 323–338 (1972)

Alm, J., McClelland, G.H., Schulze, W.D.: Changing the social norm of tax compliance by voting. Kyklos **52**(2), 141–171 (1999)

Alm, J., Kirchler, E., Muelhbacher, M., Gangl, K., Hofmann, E., Kogler, C., Pollai, M.: Rethinking the research paradigms for analysing tax compliance behaviour. CESifo Forum **10**, 33–40 (2012)

Castells, M., Portes, A.: World underneath: the origins, dynamics and effects of the informal economy. In: Portes, A., Castells, M., Benton, L.A. (eds.) The Informal Economy: Studies in Advanced and Less Developing Countries, pp. 11–37. Johns Hopkins University Press, Baltimore, MD (1989)

Chan, H.F., Supriyadi, M.W., Torgler, B.: Trust and tax morale. In: The Oxford Handbook of Social and Political Trust, pp. 1–71 (2018)

Chang, J.J., Lai, C.C.: Collaborative tax evasion and social norms: why deterrence does not work. Oxf. Econ. Pap. **56**(2), 344–368 (2004)

Charmes, J.: Concepts, measurement and trends. In: Jütting, J.P., Laiglesia, J.R (eds.) Is Informal Normal? Towards More and Better Jobs in Developing Countries, pp. 27–62. OECD, Paris (2009)

European Commission: Communication of the Commission on Undeclared Work. http://europa.eu.int/comm/employment_social/empl_esf/docs/com98-219_en.pdf (1998)

European Commission: Undeclared Work in the European Union. In: Riedmann, A., Fischer, G. (eds.) Report: Special Eurobarometer, p. 284. European Commission, Brussels (2007)

Feige, E.L., Urban, I.: Measuring underground (unobserved, non-observed, unrecorded) economies in transition countries: Can we trust GDP? J. Comp. Econ. **36**, 287–306 (2008)

Friedman, E., Johnson, S., Kaufmann, D., Zoido, P.: Dodging the grabbing hand: the determinants of unofficial activity in 69 countries. J. Public Econ. **76**, 459–493 (2000)

Gallin, D.: Propositions on trade unions and informal employment in time of globalization. Antipode **19**(4), 531–549 (2001)

Gialis, S., Leontidou, L.: Antinomies of flexibilization and atypical employment in Mediterranean Europe: Greek, Italian and Spanish regions during the crisis. Eur. Urban Reg. Stud. **23**(4), 716–733 (2014)

Grabiner, L.: The Informal Economy. HM Treasury, London (2000)

Hallsworth, M., List, J.A., Metcalfe, R.D., Vlaev, I.: The behavioralist as tax collector: using natural field experiments to enhance tax compliance. J. Public Econ. **148**, 14–31 (2017)

Hasseldine, J., Zhuhong, L.: More tax evasion research required in new millennium. Crime Law Soc. Chang. **31**(1), 91–104 (1999)

ILO: Transitioning from the informal to the formal economy. In: International Labour Conference—103rd Session—Report V. International Labour Office, Geneva. www.ilo.org/wcmsp5/groups/public/-ed_norm/-relconf/documents/meetingdocument/wcms_218128.pdf (2014). Last accessed 29 Sept 2017

ILO: Recommendation 204 concerning the transition from the informal to the formal economy. In: Adopted by the Conference at its One Hundred and Fourth Session, Geneva, 12 June. International Labour Office, Geneva. https://www.ilo.org/wcmsp5/groups/public/-ed_norm/-relconf/documents/meetingdocument/wcms_377774.pdf (2015). Last accessed 15 Dec 2018

International Labour Office (ILO): Decent Work and the Informal Economy. International Labour Office, Geneva (2002)

Karpuskiene, V.: Undeclared work, tax evasion and avoidance in Lithuania. Paper presented at Colloquium of the Belgian Federal Service for Social Security on Undeclared Work, Tax Evasion and Avoidance, Brussels (2007)

Mingione, E.: Fragmented Societies. Blackwell, Oxford (1991)

Pedersen, S.: The Shadow Economy in Western Europe—Measurement and Results for Selected Countries. The Rockwood Foundation Research Unit, Copenhagen (1998)

Persson, A., Malmer, H.: Purchasing and Performing Undeclared Work in Sweden: Part 1: Results from Various Studies. Skatteverket, Malmo (2006)

Renooy, P., Ivarsson, S., van der Wusten-Gritsai, O., Meijer, R.: Undeclared Work in an Enlarged Union: An Analysis of Shadow Work—An In-depth Study of Specific Items. European Commission, Brussels (2004)

Round, J., Williams, C.C., Rodgers, P.: Corruption in the post-soviet workplace: the experiences of recent graduates in Contemporary Ukraine. Work Employ Soc. **22**, 149–166 (2008)

Sandford, C.: Policies dealing with tax evasion. In: Feige, E., Ott, K. (eds.) Underground Economies in Transition: Unrecorded Activity, Tax Evasion, Corruption and Organized Crime, pp. 87–100. Ashgate, Aldershot (1999)

Schneider, F.: The Hidden Economy. Edward Elgar, Cheltenham (2008)

Schneider, F., Buehn, A., Monetenegro, C.E.: Shadow economies all over the world: new estimates for 162 countries from 1999 to 2007. In: Schneider, F. (ed.) Handbook on the Shadow Economy, pp. 9–77. Edward Elgar, Cheltenham (2011)

Small Business Council: Small Business in the Informal Economy: Making the Transition to the Formal Economy. Small Business Council, London (2004)

Traxler, C.: Social norms and conditional cooperative taxpayers. Eur. J. Polit. Econ. **26**(1), 89–103 (2010)

Williams, C.C.: The undeclared sector, self-employment and public policy. Int. J. Entrep. Behav. Res. **11**, 244–257 (2005)

Williams, C.C.: Tackling undeclared work in Europe: lessons from a study of Ukraine. Eur. J. Ind. Relat. **13**, 219–237 (2007)

Williams, C.C., Windebank, J.: Eliminating undeclared work: beyond a deterrence approach. Journal of Economic Studies **32**(5), 435–449 (2005)

Williams, C.C., Windebank, J.: Regional variations in the nature of the shadow economy: evidence from a survey of 27 European union member states. In: Schneider, F. (ed.) Handbook on the Shadow Economy, pp. 177–200. Edward Elgar, Cheltenham (2011)

Woolfson, C. (2007). Pushing the envelope: theinformalization'of labour in post-communist new EU member states. *Work, employment and society, 21*(3), 551–564.

Dulleck, U., Fooken, J., Newton, C., Ristl, A., Schaffner, M., & Torgler, B. (2016). Tax compliance and psychic costs: Behavioral experimental evidence using a physiological marker. *Journal of Public Economics, 134*, 9–18.

Factors Affecting Firm Innovation: An Evidence from Vietnam

Khanh Hung Doan

Abstract Firm innovation plays an essential role in the development of enterprises. A firm with innovation can provide products that meet the ever-changing needs of the market and the demands of consumers. From there, it is possible to improve the competitiveness of enterprises in the market, especially in the current, constantly fierce competitive environment. Therefore, building a firm innovation is a significant task for enterprises and policy makers. However, firm innovation is influenced by many internal and external factors of the enterprise. Therefore, it is necessary to identify the factors that affect the firm innovation. From this, they can offer solutions that contribute to the development of firm innovation in a better way. This article focuses on determining the factors affecting firm innovation in the specific case of enterprises operating in Vietnam. Vietnam is a developing country and a young economy with many types of enterprises. The study was carried out based on a sample of 916 enterprises in Vietnam. These research data were provided through the World Bank's Enterprises Survey in 2015. The binary logistic regression method is used. The results show that factors such as the top manager's period work experience, the competition of the firm, the access to finance, corruption, the number of employees of enterprises, and trained workers are factors affecting the firm innovation in Vietnam. Through this article, stakeholders such as businesses, local managers, and policymakers in Vietnam will have solutions to improve the firm innovation. The paper ends with a discussion of the results and implications of the study.

Keywords Innovation · Firm innovation · Binary logistic · Vietnam · Barriers

1 Introduction

Enterprises have long been identified as the driving force and an essential role in the economic development of nations. However, the development of today's businesses is always influenced by many different factors. These factors can be changes in the

K. H. Doan (✉)
Bucharest University of Economic Studies, 010374 Bucharest, Romania
e-mail: doankhanhhung.hat@gmail.com

A. M. Dima and E. R. Danescu (eds.), *Fostering Recovery Through Metaverse Business Modelling*, Springer Proceedings in Business and Economics,
https://doi.org/10.1007/978-3-031-28255-3_15

business environment, advances in science and technology, consumer tastes change, etc. It requires enterprises to innovate to be able to respond to those changes. From there, it is possible to contribute to helping enterprises continue to exist and develop sustainably and improve competitiveness (Abdu and Jibir 2018). From there, it is possible to expand business and profits (Abdu and Jibir 2018). Therefore, it can be said that firm innovation plays a significant role in the development of enterprises (Pelinescu et al. 2019). Firm innovation has always been considered a priority area of enterprise development policies and is a research topic that attracts much attention (Pelinescu et al. 2019).

However, the innovation process of enterprises is influenced by many different factors (Abdu and Jibir 2018). These factors are internal factors of the enterprises or their surrounding environment. Therefore, the problem of determining the factors affecting the innovation of enterprises is always raised. Enterprises need to identify the factors affecting firm innovation. Herein, enterprises and managers can provide policies and solutions to improve the firm's innovation and enterprise development. However, there are still questions regarding how factors influence corporate innovation, including firms in different countries with different environments.

This article attempts to supplement an empirical study on the factors that affect firm innovation in a specific case in Vietnam. Vietnam is a fast-developing country and a young economy with many types of enterprises that operate. Most enterprises in Vietnam face many challenges in terms of infrastructure, finance, human resources, etc., thereby reducing their ability to innovate. Furthermore, along with the change in the business environment, the increasingly fierce competition in the market today requires enterprises to have solutions to innovate their businesses. From there, it is possible to have detailed views on the policy and effectiveness of business innovation solutions in Vietnam today. To achieve the above objectives, the paper used a review of the relevant literature and a quantitative study of enterprise data collected from the World Bank's Enterprises Survey in 2015. Then, it is possible to identify the factors that affect current firm innovation in Vietnam and the results and discussion from the above research results.

The paper is organized into the following sections: the first section provides a brief literature review of the studies. The second part offers the development of hypotheses. In the third part, the research methods used by the authors are provided. The fourth part covers the research results. Then, the last part is the conclusion and discussion of the research results of the paper, establishing future research directions and limitations of the study.

2 Literature Review and Hypothesis

Firm innovation has always been a topic of interest and development for many researchers with the goal of promoting innovation and business development (Pelinescu et al. 2019). Schumpeter (1934) defined innovation as a "new combination" of existing knowledge and resources to create five types of innovation: (i) new product,

(ii) new processes (or new production methods), (iii) new materials (or resources), (iv) new markets, and (v) new organizations of an industry in trade, business, and finance (McGuirk et al. 2015). The OECD (2005) has divided innovation into four categories: (i) product innovation, (ii) process innovation, (iii) marketing innovation, and (iv) organizational innovation. These innovative activities contribute to the survival of businesses, improving competitiveness, expanding business activities, and profits (Abdu and Jibir 2018). In fact, firm innovation activities often focus on the introduction of a new product or process (Crossan and Apaydin 2010; McCann and Oxley 2012). However, the innovation process of enterprises is influenced by many different factors (Abdu and Jibir 2018). These factors can be internal factors of the enterprises as well as factors coming from the surrounding environment of the enterprises. These factors are defined as follows:

Many researchers have identified the role of leadership in firm innovation (Protogerou et al. 2017). In particular, entrepreneurs with higher education will perceive and seize innovation opportunities in the market. Additionally, leadership's work experience also helps businesses identify innovation opportunities more easily (Protogerou et al. 2017). Lund Vinding (2006) also pointed out that the inexperience of management staff is negatively related to firm innovation.

H1: The top manager's period work experience *influences firm innovation.*

In addition, the study by Pezeshkan et al. (2016) determined that governments influence firm innovation through regulations and policies. It includes business and trade policies. These policies affect the business and commercial environment of enterprises. When these policies change, they will change the innovation activities of enterprises.

H2: The commercial and business environment *influences firm innovation.*

Competitive factors, domestic or international, can be the driving force for the enhancement of productivity through innovation (Alder 2010; Abdu and Jibir 2018). Research by Alder (2010) determined that companies with more advanced technology than their competitors have more innovative products.

H3: The competition of the firm influences firm innovation.

Companies' access to finance is considered crucial in influencing a company's innovation performance. Research by Lorenz (2014) shows that financial constraints have a significant negative effect on a firm's innovation activities. In addition, Mahendra et al. (2015) found that the availability of financial resources significantly affects a firm's innovation and other related activities.

H4: Access to the finance of the firm influences firm innovation.

Many studies have identified the political and institutional environment that influences firm innovation (Sartor and Beamish 2014; Krammer and Jimenez 2020). In countries where business constraints are less stringent, firms are more likely to innovate (Back et al. 2014; Boubakri et al. 2008).

H5: The political environment influences firm innovation.

Paunov (2016) and Nguyen et al. (2016) determined that corruption affects firm innovation. Corruption reduces firms' ability to innovate (Nguyen et al. 2016). Additionally, although corruption does not reduce patenting, it does reduce investment in machinery for innovation (Paunov 2016).

H6: Corruption influences firm innovation.

Aloisi and De Stefano (2020) have determined that labor regulations can continue to facilitate firm innovation. It presents the employment relationship as a flexible tool. Additionally, employment standards are considered as a means to achieve efficiency and cost advantages. Labor regulations allow for the full exercise of management privileges and internal flexibility in workforce deployment and constitute an effective device for providing training and skills development. From there, it can drive enterprise innovation (Aloisi and De Stefano 2020).

H7: The working environment of the firm influences firm innovation.

Lundvall and Johnson (1994) argued that more qualified employees can invent and improve new technology. From there, they can also take advantage of technological progress. Additionally, employees with better education and skills are an essential component of innovation (Gallié and Legros 2012). González et al. (2016) determined that the implementation of training for employees will significantly enhance the probability of firm innovation.

H8: Average years of education of a typical employee influence firm innovation.

Both the research results of Abdu and Jibir (2018) and Chang and Nguyen-Van (2021) determined that the firm's total year of operation influences the firm innovation. However, the effect of uptime on corporate innovation is different. In the research by Abdu and Jibir (2018), the result showed a negative impact on firm innovation. But, the study by Chang and Nguyen-Van (2021) shows that it has a positive effect on firm innovation.

H9: Firm's total year of operation influences firm innovation.

Firm's size was also found to be significant in influencing the behavior of firms concerning innovation. In this regard, Zemplinerová and Hromádková (2012) and Sun et al. (2020) found a significant association between firm size and the ability to innovate. Furthermore, in their study, Belsowics and Jakubiak (2009) found that the size, sectors, and structure of the firm also have a significant influence on innovation activities.

H10: The firm's total employees influences firm innovation.

3 Aims of the Research

This study aims to identify the factors that influence corporate innovation at the product level due to the complexity of firm innovation activities. In particular, this article has tried to find out in detail the influence of factors on firm innovation in a specific country, namely Vietnam, through using survey data collected from the World Bank's Enterprises Survey in 2015. However, along with the increasingly fierce competition and globalization process, the role of firm innovation is increasingly important in improving the competitiveness, development, and survival of enterprises. Furthermore, specific assessments of the influence of factors affecting firm innovation help business leaders and policymakers have a more detailed view of enterprise innovation in Vietnam. The two research objectives of interest in this study are as follows:

1. What factors influence firm innovation in Vietnam?
2. What is the extent of the influence of factors that affect firm innovation in Vietnam?

4 Research Methods

4.1 Data Collection

Data on enterprises in Vietnam are collected based on World Bank's Enterprises Survey 2015, with information on different aspects of firms, such as performance, competition, labor, innovation (World Bank 2022). This database has been used in various enterprise studies (Adegboye and Iweriebor 2018; Igwe et al. 2018; Williams and Kedir 2018; Ali et al. 2021; Chang and Nguyen-Van 2021) because these data have comparisons between countries and detailed assessments of the situation and development characteristics of enterprises. There are 996 observations. From the original data, the author conducts a data scan, removing unnecessary data (such as missing data and incomplete data). 916 remaining data were included for analysis.

4.2 Data Analysis

To measure the effect of the factor on firm innovation, we used some questions from the World Bank's Enterprises Survey 2015. The questions and characteristics of the variables (Var) used in the study are shown in Table 1.

The scale used in the study for independent variables is the Likert scale with 5 levels (0: no obstacle; 1: minor obstacle; 2: moderate obstacle; 3 major obstacle; 4 very severe obstacle).

Table 1 Variable description

Variables	Question in the survey	Description
Dependent variable		
Inno	New or significant improved product introduced in last three years?	The level/radicalness of firm innovation, = 0 (no innovation), = 1 (innovation)
Independent variables		
Fina	How much of an obstacle: Access to finance	Access to finance of the firm
Trad	How much of an obstacle: Customs and trade regulations?	The commercial and business environment of the firm
Comp	How much of an obstacle: Practices of competitors in informal sector?	Competitors of the firm
Poli	How much of an obstacle: Political instability	The political environment of the country in which the firm operates
Corr	How much of an obstacle: Corruption	Corruption of the government
Larb	How much of an obstacle: Labor regulations?	Working environment of the firm
Edus	How much of an obstacle: Inadequately educated workforce?	Average years of education of a typical employee
Control variables		
Lead	How many years of experience working in this sector does the top manager have?	Top manager's years of experience in the current sector
LnEm	Number employees at end of last fiscal year	Firm's total employees (log)
Age	Year of operations	Firm's total year in operation

Source Author's own research

To analyze the collected data, the author used binary logistic regression analysis. Binary logistic regression is a popular regression model in research that is used to estimate the probability that an event will occur. The characteristic of the binary regression model is that the dependent variable has only two values (0 and 1). For this study, the dependent variable is the firm innovation variable with two values of 0 (no firm innovation) and 1 (firm innovation). Therefore, the binary logistic regression model used in this study is suitable. The binary regression equation used is the following:

$$\mathrm{Log}(\mathrm{P_i}/(1 - \mathrm{P_i})) = \mathrm{B_0} + \mathrm{B_1X_1} + \mathrm{B_2X_2} + \cdots + \mathrm{B_nX_n}$$

Note: P_i is the probability that the event will occur ($Y = 1$)

$1 - P_i$ is the probability that the event does not occur ($Y = 0$)

B_0 is the regression constant

$B_1, B_2, \ldots, Bn$: regression coefficient

$X_1, X_2, \ldots, Xn$: independent variables.

Furthermore, the steps of data processing, descriptive statistics, and regression analysis are performed using SPSS 23.0 software.

5 Findings

5.1 *Descriptive Statistics*

To better understand the collected data, the author conducted a descriptive statistical analysis of the obtained data. Table 2 shows the statistical results of innovation by enterprise size. Furthermore, the results in Table 2 show that the larger the firm size, the higher the percentage of firm innovation. If in small-scale enterprises with 24.9% of the innovative firm, the rate of innovation in the large-scale firm is 38%. In addition, the rate of firm innovation in Vietnam is quite high, with 31.1% of firms innovating out of the 916 firms surveyed.

Table 3 presents descriptive statistics of the variables used for the analysis. The results in Table 3 show that, on average, the top leaders have almost 18 years of work experience in the current field. The average operating time of an enterprise is approximately 14 years. Furthermore, the average number of employees of enterprises is approximately 211 people. Regarding the obstacles factors of the enterprises, most of the enterprises rated the obstacles as having a small effect on enterprises (the average value from 0.8 to 1.6). Herein, Corruption is assessed to have the biggest influence on enterprises, and the Labor environment has the smallest effect on the surveyed enterprises.

Table 4 shows the pairwise correlation coefficients of the independent and control variables (Pearson correlation coefficient). The results show that all the variables included in the study have a moderate or high significant correlation (the level of significance of P is lower than 0.01 or 0.05). Thus, there is no evidence of a

Table 2 Innovation by firm Size

		Firm innovation				Total	
		No		Yes		Count	%
		Count	%	Count	%		
Sampling size	Micro	3	50.0	3	50.0	6	100
	Small	259	75.1	86	24.9	345	100
	Medium	217	67.8	103	32.2	320	100
	Large	152	62.0	93	38.0	245	100
Total		631	68.9	285	31.1	916	100

Source Author's own research

Table 3 Descriptive statistics

	N	Minimum	Maximum	Mean	Std. Deviation
Inno	916	0	1	0.31	0.463
Lead	916	2	70	17.85	9.495
LnEm	916	0.69	9.74	3.6503	1.50309
Age	916	2.00	114.00	13.8499	9.65243
Trad	916	0	4	0.92	3.514
Comp	916	0	4	0.73	2.260
Fina	916	0	4	0.90	1.082
Poli	916	0	4	0.70	3.381
Corr	916	0	4	1.14	4.010
Larb	916	0	4	0.61	0.999
Edus	916	0	4	0.92	0.989
Valid N (listwise)	916				

Source Author's own research

possible multicollinearity problem (Dormann et al. 2013). Therefore, all variables were entered into the model.

5.2 Research Results

To assess the fit of the model, the study used the Omnibus test. Table 5 shows the results of the Omnibus test through the Chi-square test results. The results show that the Sig value of the Chi-square test in the model row has statistical significance (Sig. value < 0.005). Therefore, it can be said that the given regression model is fit.

In addition, the results in Table 6 are also used to evaluate the fit of the model. The value of −2 Log-Likelihood with the empty model is 1135,851, while the value of −2 Log-Likelihood in the last proposed model is 1059,891. It indicates that the independent variables included in the model reduce the value of −2 Log-Likelihood compared to the empty model. Thus, the regression model is suitable.

The results in Table 7 provide the classification results of the cases observed and predicted. In 631 cases of actual observed no innovation activities, it is estimated that there are 586 enterprises without innovation activities. The prediction rate of success is 92.9%. Similarly, in 285 cases of actual observation of firms with innovative activities, only 41 innovative firms are predicted. Thus, the average correct prediction rate for the entire model is 68.4%.

The results in Table 8 present the results of the Sig value of the Wald test, the regression coefficients, and the Exp(B) values of the independent variables. Furthermore, by the results in Table 6, the variables Trad, Poli, Larb, and Age have no statistical significance in the regression model (Sig. value > 0.05). The other variables are Lead,

Table 4 Correlations

	Lead	Trad	Comp	Fina	Poli	Corr	Larb	Edus	Age	LnEm
Lead	1									
Trad	−0.003	1								
Comp	−0.047	0.077*	1							
Fina	−0.002	−0.150**	0.129**	1						
Poli	0.007	0.029	0.106**	0.023	1					
Corr	−0.048	0.084*	0.119**	0.076*	0.375**	1				
Larb	−0.005	0.028	0.129**	0.199**	0.080*	0.099**	1			
Edus	0.047	−0.013	0.136**	0.282**	0.064	0.152**	0.452**	1		
Age	0.073*	0.021	−0.007	−0.051	0.038	−0.024	0.003	0.001	1	
LnEm	0.234**	0.133**	−0.105**	−0.139**	0.013	−0.026	0.054	0.098**	0.090**	1

* Correlation is significant at the 0.05 level (2-tailed)
** Correlation is significant at the 0.01 level (2-tailed)
Source Author's own research

Table 5 Omnibus tests of model coefficients

		Chi-square	df	Sig.
Step 1	Step	75.960	10	0.000
	Block	75.960	10	0.000
	Model	75.960	10	0.000

Source Author's own research

Comp, Corr, Fina, Edus, and LnEm with statistical significance (Sig. value < 0.05). Also, the regression coefficients B are all positive, so when the independent variables increase, it also increases the possibility of firm innovation. More specifically, the Exp(B) value indicates the degree of impact of the independent variables on firm innovation.

From the results in Table 8, we have the Binary Logistic regression results:

$$\begin{aligned}\text{Log}(\text{P}_\text{i}/(1 - \text{P}_\text{i})) = & -2.483 + 0.02 \times \text{Lead} + 0.089 \times \text{Comp} + 0.192 \times \text{Fina} \\ & + 0.048 \times \text{Corr} + 0.168 \times \text{Edus} + 0.253 \times \text{LnEm}\end{aligned}$$

Based on the regression results of Table 8, among the variables that have an impact on firm innovation in Vietnam, it can be seen that the variable LnEm (Firm's total employees) has the strongest effect (0.253). It is followed by the variables Fina (Access to finance of the firm), Edus (Average years of education of a typical employee), and Comp (Competition of firm). The influences are 0.192, 0.168, and 0.089, respectively. Two variables, Lead (Top manager's years of experience in the current sector) and Corr (Corruption of the government), have the least influence on firm innovation in Vietnam, with a coefficient of 0.048 and 0.02, respectively.

In addition, through the regression results in Table 8, the results of the hypotheses are shown that the hypotheses H1, H3, H4, H6, H8, H10 are accepted (Sig. value < 0.05). However, the hypotheses H2, H5, H7, and H9 are rejected (Sig. value > 0.05).

6 Conclusions

Firm innovation plays an essential role in the existence and development of enterprises (Pelinescu et al. 2019). Firms that regularly innovate will have better competitiveness in the market, as well as higher productivity than other firms (Schumpeter 1934; Ancona and Caldwell 1987; Abdu and Jibir 2018). Therefore, firm innovation always receives the attention of business leaders and policy makers. From there, it can contribute to supporting and promoting the innovation process of enterprises.

This study was conducted with the aim of assessing the factors affecting firm innovation in Vietnam. From there, we can have an overview of the firm innovation process in Vietnam in the current period. The results of the survey show that more than 30% of Vietnamese enterprises are innovative enterprises. It is a relatively modest rate

Table 6 Iteration History[a,b,c,d]

Iteration		−2 Log-likelihood	Coefficients										
			Constant	Lead	Trad	Comp	Fina	Poli	Corr	Larb	Edus	Age	LnEm
Step 1	1	1064.560	−2.080	0.016	0.005	0.067	0.156	0.001	0.035	0.054	0.144	−0.001	0.203
	2	1060.051	−2.458	0.019	0.007	0.087	0.190	0.002	0.047	0.066	0.167	−0.001	0.249
	3	1059.911	−2.484	0.020	0.008	0.089	0.192	0.002	0.048	0.067	0.168	−0.002	0.253
	4	**1059.891**	−2.483	0.020	0.008	0.089	0.192	0.002	0.048	0.067	0.168	−0.002	0.253

[a] Method: Enter
[b] Constant is included in the model
[c] Initial −2 Log-Likelihood: **1135.851**
[d] Estimation terminated at iteration number 4 because parameter estimates changed by less than 0.001
Source Author's own research

Table 7 Classification table[a]

Observed			Predicted		
			Innovation		Percentage correct
			No	Yes	
Step 1	Innovation	No	586	45	92.9
		Yes	244	41	14.4
	Overall percentage				68.4

[a] The cut value is 0.500
Source Author's own research

Table 8 Findings

	B	S.E.	Wald	df	Sig.	Exp(B)	Hypothesis	Findings
Lead	**0.020**	**0.008**	**6.226**	**1**	**0.013**	**1.020**	**H1**	**Supported**
Trad	0.008	0.022	0.120	1	0.729	1.008	H2	Rejected
Comp	**0.089**	**0.037**	**5.814**	**1**	**0.016**	**1.093**	**H3**	**Supported**
Fina	**0.192**	**0.072**	**7.065**	**1**	**0.008**	**1.212**	**H4**	**Supported**
Poli	0.002	0.024	0.009	1	0.925	1.002	H5	Rejected
Corr	**0.048**	**0.022**	**4.899**	**1**	**0.027**	**1.049**	**H6**	**Supported**
Larb	0.067	0.083	0.639	1	0.424	1.069	H7	Rejected
Edus	**0.168**	**0.085**	**3.865**	**1**	**0.049**	**1.183**	**H8**	**Supported**
Age	−0.002	0.002	0.626	1	0.429	0.998	H9	Rejected
LnEm	**0.253**	**0.053**	**23.202**	**1**	**0.000**	**1.288**	**H10**	**Supported**
Constant	−2.483	0.262	89.577	1	0.000	0.083		

Source Author's own research

compared to other countries. In addition, the research results also show that factors such as the top manager's period work experience, competition of the firm, access to finance, corruption, number of employees of enterprises, and trained workers are factors affecting the firm innovation in Vietnam. Factors such as access to finance and the number of employees have the most influence on firm innovation, and the top manager's period work experience has the least influence on firm innovation. Additionally, other factors such as commercial and business environment, political environment, working environment, and Firm's total year in operation do not affect firm innovations. From that, it can be seen that the current policies have not played a significant role in promoting firm innovation because there is no impact on firm innovation. Another factor is that corruption affects firm innovation. It shows the inconsistent impact of policies on enterprise innovation in Vietnam today. Corruption remains an essential barrier that the authorities of Vietnam have not been able to overcome.

Furthermore, the study has certain limitations. First, the observed samples of the research are based on data from a global survey of enterprises conducted by the World

Bank. It is a reliable and scientifically backed survey. However, because it is based on available data, it is not possible to further analyze the specific effects of factors on firm innovation. Secondly, the study has some methodological limitations. Therefore, for further studies, it should be possible to conduct studies in many different countries or to make comparisons between countries. In addition, other research models can be applied. From there, different results and assessments can be compared.

Acknowledgements This paper was co-financed by The Bucharest University of Economic Studies during the Ph.D. program.

References

Abdu, M., Jibir, A.: Determinants of firms innovation in Nigeria. Kasetsart J. Soc. Sci. **39**(3), 448–456 (2018)

Adegboye, A.C., Iweriebor, S.: Does access to finance enhance SME innovation and productivity in Nigeria? Evidence from the World Bank Enterprise Survey. Afr. Dev. Rev. **30**(4), 449–461 (2018)

Alder, S.: Competition and innovation: does the distance to the technology frontier matter? Inst. Empir. Res. Econ. 493 (2010). (Working paper series)

Ali, J., Reed, M.R., Saghaian, S.H.: Determinants of product innovation in food and agribusiness small and medium enterprises: evidence from enterprise survey data of India. Int. Food Agribus. Manag. Rev. 1–20 (2021)

Aloisi, A., De Stefano, V.: Regulation and the future of work: the employment relationship as an innovation facilitator. Int. Labour Rev. **159**(1), 47–69 (2020)

Ancona, D., Caldwell, D.: Management issues facing new product teams in high technology companies. Adv. Ind. Labor Relat. **4**(191), 221 (1987)

Back, Y., Parboteeah, K.P., Nam, D.I.: Innovation in emerging markets: the role of management consulting firms. J. Int. Manag. **20**(4), 390–405 (2014)

Belsowics, E., Jakubiak, A.: Determinants of firms innovation. Konteckscies Posiomo (2009)

Boubakri, N., Cosset, J.C., Saffar, W.: Political connections of newly privatized firms. J. Corp. Finan. **14**(5), 654–673 (2008)

Chang, C.H., Nguyen-Van, D.: Human capital and firm innovation: new evidence from Asean countries. J. Econ. Forecast. **3**, 52–71 (2021)

Crossan, M.M., Apaydin, M.: A multi-dimensional framework of organizational innovation: a systematic review of the literature. J. Manage. Stud. **47**(6), 1154–1191 (2010)

Dormann, C.F., Elith, J., Bacher, S., Buchmann, C., Carl, G., Carré, G., Marquéz, J.R.G., Gruber, B., Lafourcade, B., Leitão, P.J.: Collinearity: a review of methods to deal with it and a simulation study evaluating their performance. Ecography **36**, 27–46 (2013)

Gallié, E.P., Legros, D.: Firms' human capital, R&D and innovation: a study on French firms. Empir. Econ. **43**, 581–596 (2012)

González, X., Miles-Touya, D., Pazó, C.: R&D, worker training and innovation: firm-level evidence. Ind. Innov. **23**, 694–712 (2016)

Igwe, P.A., Amaugo, A.N., Ogundana, O.M., Egere, O.M., Anigbo, J.A.: Factors affecting the investment climate, SMEs productivity and entrepreneurship in Nigeria. Eur. J. Sustain. Dev. **7**(1), 182–200 (2018)

Krammer, S.M., Jimenez, A.: Do political connections matter for firm innovation? Evidence from emerging markets in Central Asia and Eastern Europe. Technol. Forecast. Soc. Chang. **151**, 119669 (2020)

Lorenz, E.: Do credit constrained firms in Africa innovate less? A study based on nine African nations. SSRN Electron. J. (2014). https://doi.org/10.2139/SSRN.2602247

Lund Vinding, A.: Absorptive capacity and innovative performance: a human capital approach. Econ. Innov. New Technol. **15**, 507–517 (2006)

Lundvall, B.Ä., Johnson, B.: The learning economy. J. Ind. Stud. **1**, 23–42 (1994)

Mahendra, E., Zuhdi, U., Muyanto, R.: Determinants of firm innovation in Indonesia: the role of institutions and access to finance. Econ. Financ. Indones. **61**(3), 149–179 (2015)

McCann, P., Oxley, L.: Innovation, entrepreneurship, geography and growth. J. Econ. Surv. **26**(3), 373–376 (2012)

McGuirk, H., Lenihan, H., Hart, M.: Measuring the impact of innovative human capital on small firms' propensity to innovate. Res. Policy **44**(4), 965–976 (2015)

Nguyen, N.A., Doan, Q.H., Nguyen, N.M., Tran-Nam, B.: The impact of petty corruption on firm innovation in Vietnam. Crime Law Soc. Chang. **65**(4), 377–394 (2016)

Organisation for Economic Co-operation and Development (OECD): the measurement of scientific and technological activities Oslo Manual Guidelines for collecting and interpreting innovation data, 3 edn. OECD Eurostat, Paris. https://www.oecd-ilibrary.org/science-andtechnology/oslo-manual_9789264013100-en. Last accessed 11 Jan 2022

Paunov, C.: Corruption's asymmetric impacts on firm innovation. J. Dev. Econ. **118**, 216–231 (2016)

Pelinescu, E., Pauna, C., Saman, C., Diaconescu, T.: Human capital, innovation and economic growth in the EU countries. Rom. J. Econ. Forecast. **22**(4), 160–173 (2019)

Pezeshkan, A., Smith, A., Fainshmidt, S., Sedeh, A.A.: National business systems and firm innovation: a study of developing economies. J. Bus. Res. **69**(11), 5413–5418 (2016)

Protogerou, A., Caloghirou, Y., Vonortas, N.S.: Determinants of young firms' innovative performance: empirical evidence from Europe. Res. Policy **46**, 1312–1326 (2017)

Sartor, M.A., Beamish, P.W.: Offshoring innovation to emerging markets: organizational control and informal institutional distance. J. Int. Bus. Stud. **45**(9), 1072–1095 (2014)

Schumpeter, J.A.: The theory of economic development. Harvard University Press, New York, USA (1934)

Sun, X., Li, H., Ghosal, V.: Firm-levelhuman capital and innovation: evidence from China. China Econ. Rev. **59**, 101388 (2020)

Williams, C.C., Kedir, A.: Evaluating competing theories of informal sector entrepreneurship: a study of the determinants of cross-country variations in enterprises starting-up unregistered. Int. J. Entrep. Innov. **19**(3), 155–165 (2018)

World Bank: survey methodology. https://www.enterprisesurveys.org/methodology. Last accessed 11 Jan 2022

Zemplinerová, A., Hromádková, E.: Determinants of innovations. Prague Econ. Pap. **4**, 487–503 (2012)

Transformation for Supporting Business Resilience in the COVID-19 Pandemic Period: Role of Digitalization

Le Thanh Tung

Abstract The COVID-19 pandemic has caused huge damage to the global economy in the past two years. With some effective vaccines widely used, the most difficult period for enterprises has gradually passed when the world economy has moved forward to the new normal in the post-pandemic era. The paper aims to clarify the role of digitalization in improving business resilience in Vietnam, an emerging Asian economy. The descriptive statistical analysis and the independent-samples t-test were employed for investigating the study issue. The results indicate that digital transformation has brought initial positive outcomes for enterprises during the pandemic and this process is expected to continue to be important in accelerating the recovery of business in the post-COVID-19 pandemic period. However, the study shows enormous challenges for the digitization process to help businesses develop sustainably in the coming time. The study has a critical contribution for the current literature when it is maybe the first evidence of digitalization and business resilience of enterprises in the context of the COVID-19 pandemic. Finally, the paper provides some managerial implications for the digital transformation process in the business community in the near future.

Keywords Digitalization · Digital transformation · Business resilience · Business performance · Pandemic

1 Introduction

After two years of outbreak, the COVID-19 pandemic has been gradually brought under control by some effective vaccines that have helped prevent the spread of infection and the damage to health caused by the virus. However, the business community has gone through difficult times with great economic losses when the isolation and blockade solutions to combat the virus's spread also disrupted transactions in markets

L. T. Tung (✉)
Faculty of Economics and Public Management, Ho Chi Minh City Open University, Ho Chi Minh City, Vietnam
e-mail: tung.lt@ou.edu.vn

A. M. Dima and E. R. Danescu (eds.), *Fostering Recovery Through Metaverse Business Modelling*, Springer Proceedings in Business and Economics,
https://doi.org/10.1007/978-3-031-28255-3_16

and disrupt supply chains worldwide (Amankwah-Amoah et al. 2021). During the period of the pandemic, digitalization in business has been considered as an urgent measure to help the business community maintain and overcome the difficulties (Guo et al. 2020; Rachinger et al. 2019; Veldhoven and Vanthienen 2022).

Located in the Asia-Pacific region, Vietnam is an emerging economy that has had robust economic growth for three recent decades (Tung 2020; Tung and Binh 2021). Because of the high trade openness, the companies have applied digitalization to connect both domestic and foreign markets. The national health strategy changes from the goal of the "zero COVID" policy to the "living together safety with the pandemic" policy have helped companies partly overcome a challenging period during the second year of the COVID-19 pandemic (Thanh and Tung 2022). Although the risks of supply chain disruptions are not new, it is evident that the increased frequency and intensity of numerous social shocks, such as disasters, have increased the frequency of supply chain failures. In particular, the COVID-19 pandemic is a challenging test of the global supply chain's fragility and brings this issue to the forefront not only in two previous years (2020–2021), but also in the future. Along with each country's unique pandemic prevention objectives, the wave of protectionist actions such as tightening border controls or enacting new import-export tax policies exacerbated the complexity of global supply chain recovery in the post-pandemic period. While industries have proven to be better at combating the disease, the current pandemic is still spreading with the emergence of new variants such as Omicron. The business community will continue to have negative effects in 2022. In a business environment with more complexity, enterprises constantly face challenges not only from the pandemic but also from the market demands. These challenges include changing consumer preferences and behavior, increased competition, and the need for resilience to improve supply chains while keeping costs under control and maximizing growth potential.

To identify the role of digitalization in the business of companies in Vietnam during the pandemic and to suggest managerial implications for the leaders of companies forward in the post-pandemic era, we have conducted an online survey through the Google Docs platform to study the digitalization activities of companies during the outbreak period of the pandemic. The study result will deliver the initial evidence of digitalization to support business resilience in Vietnam; hence, it can fill the current empirical research gap in the case of developing countries. Furthermore, the managerial implications are quite good for the decision-making process to support the business resilience in the post-COVID-19 pandemic period.

2 Literature Review

Digitization is the process of converting information into a digital format and is creating a digital version of analog or physical things such as paper documents, microfilm images, photographs, sounds, and others (Ribeiro-Navarrete et al. 2021). Besides, digitalization in the business environment is popularly understood as the application of digital technologies to change the traditional business model and provide new value-producing opportunities; hence, this process is considered a strategy to move organizations to a digital business platform (Rachinger et al. 2019). There are challenges and implications surrounding digitization in the business including time, financial investment, cost production, cultural organization, or human resource change (Linde et al. 2021).

The digitalization of a business organization can give it a competitive advantage by providing better, faster, and lower cost products and services than its competitors. Rachinger et al. (2019) indicate that the increase in digitalization can affect various business activities such as business models and business strategies in companies. Digitalization creates various new kinds of cooperation between organizations and supports the production of new goods and services. On the other hand, it helps to establish new forms of relationships between businesses and customers, and businesses and businesses. However, this process also makes pressure on companies because of the spending of several resources. Guo et al. (2020) revealed that the small and medium enterprises were under huge pressure to survive, hence, requiring these enterprises to respond well to the pandemic. The research results found that digitalization has enabled small and medium enterprises to respond effectively to this global health crisis by increasing their dynamic capabilities in business environments. Furthermore, digitalization can also support the firms' performance to adapt well to the market demand. Veldhoven and Vanthienen (2022) review the digital transformation term in the context of having various changes in business and society because of the increase in the number of applications in digital technologies. The study result notes that enterprises leaders need to understand digital transformation and use it as an efficient factor to improve the competitive advantage in the future.

Linde et al. (2021) argue that the leaders in companies may be faced with difficulties in assessing good digital business models. The managers must then carefully identify the digital business model before applying it in the production process. The three common digitalization traps to avoid are noted and three theoretical frameworks are provided to reference in the decision-making process. Kraus et al. (2021) found that the digitalization of economies has significantly risen; hence, this trend highlighted the important role of digital transformation in increasing the competitive advantage of companies in the market. The study explains the reasons that make the research on digital transformation gain much attention in a variety of topics both theoretical and practical evidence. The policy implications suggest that the government and private sectors need to adapt to the disruptive fluctuations in the business environment and decrease the negative effect of the digitalization process on society and the environment.

Ribeiro-Navarrete et al. (2021) note that digitalization is increasing its positive role in contributing to the value creation between companies. The study result finds that the digitalization of knowledge-intensive business services can support business performance. The empirical analysis confirms that some internal factors can enhance company performance, such as updating social networks, using social networks, high skills in employing the digital tools, and older managers. Amankwah-Amoah et al. (2021) identified that the role of digitalization has increased in recent years.

The COVID-19 pandemic is a huge opportunity to enhance the digitalization in enterprises worldwide. The pandemic is a robust accelerator in employing the new modern technologies and helps to create the transformations in business strategies, business models, and business processes. However, the analysis result indicates that digitalization can have negative effects on employee well-being that harms labor productivity, work-life balance, and working environment.

Reuschl et al. (2022) investigate how enterprises can employ the COVID-19 pandemic-driven digitalization toward a sustainable digital transformation in the post-pandemic era. Obviously, the business organizations urgently established digitalization during the global pandemic as an emergency adaption. The results imply that the high speed of implementation of digitalization makes businesses have little time to change the strategies, structures, production processes, and organizational culture to the new performance platform. Therefore, the leaders need suitable policies to firms back to normal after the pandemic with the high efficiency of digitalization.

Stalmachova et al. (2022) confirm that the enterprises had to renew their strategies to survive in the context of the current pandemic, such as the working from home activities and digital technology applications in business. Then, business activities and business models have been adapted to digital transformation as much as possible due to the COVID-19 pandemic. However, with the applications of digitalization in business, the leaders in companies need to set up new key performance indicators (KPIs) to efficiently examine the productivity of labor or capital. On the other hand, Modgil et al. (2022) note that the pandemic has pressured business organizations to employ digital solutions. Hence, there are huge opportunities for new ideas for start-up projects to enter the digital market. Therefore, the current trend in the global business environment offers both opportunities and challenges for entrepreneurs to join the digital service supply in the future.

3 Methodology

The study applies multiple methods for investigating the current perspective of the digitalization process of the Vietnamese companies in the COVID-19 pandemic. They include: (i) the qualitative analysis by reviewing the literature on digitalization in business. After this process, the online questionnaire is adjusted to prepare for the survey, (ii) the descriptive statistical analysis is employed to investigate the survey of digitalization in business in during the COVID-19 pandemic, (iii) the independent-samples t-test helps to a further analysis of digitalization in business in the companies joining the survey. The business performance efficiency of the companies in the survey is represented by three indicators such as revenue, profit, and labor productivity.

The independent-samples t-test examines the assumption of homogeneity of variance, in detail, both groups have the same variance. This test is done by the Levene method (named the Levene's test), which includes a test for the homogeneity of variance. Levene's test is used to test if 2 samples have equal variances. Equal variances across samples are called homogeneity of variance. The Levene test can be used to verify that assumption by examining two hypotheses below.

$$H0 : \sigma 12 - \sigma 22 = 0 \tag{1}$$

$$H1 : \sigma 12 - \sigma 22 \neq 0 \tag{2}$$

where σ_1 is the population variance of group 1, and σ_2 is the population variance of group 2, respectively. This implies that if the null hypothesis (H_0) of Levene's test is rejected, it suggests that the variances of the two groups are not equal, and the homogeneity of variances assumption is violated.

To investigate the digitalization in the business of enterprises in Vietnam, a primary dataset was collected by the research team of the Vietnam Report Joint Stock company (Vietnam Report company). The questionnaire was delivered by an online survey (the google.doc platform). Finally, there were 82 enterprises that joined this survey run in one month (from November 15 to December 15 2021). This period was selected to conduct the survey to identify whether companies employ digitalization in business during the COVID-19 pandemic. Brief descriptive statistics of the survey are shown below (see Table 1).

Table 1 Measurement of the variables

Variables	Measurement	Mean	S.D.
Performance variables			
Revenue	= 1 if increase; = 0 of decrease	0.35	0.481
Profit	= 1 if increase; = 0 of decrease	0.37	0.485
Productivity	= 1 if increase; = 0 of decrease	0.23	0.425
Digitalization variables			
Digitalization sales activity	= 2 if high-application; = 1 if low-application; = 0 if non-application	1.60	0.541
Digitalization advertising	= 2 if high-application; = 1 if low-application; = 0 if non-application	1.49	0.653
Digitalization after sales service	= 2 if high-application; = 1 if low-application; = 0 if non-application	1.34	0.652
Digitalization office administration	= 2 if high-application; = 1 if low-application; = 0 if non-application	1.72	0.504
Observations		82	

Source own contribution

4 Results

4.1 The Result of the Descriptive Statistical Analysis of the Digitalization in Business

During the two years of the pandemic outbreak in Vietnam, companies suffered huge losses and were forced to change quickly to adapt to survive in the context of applying the social distancing policy. Digitizing the business operation is one of the core strategies to implement not only during the pandemic outbreak, but also during the post-pandemic recovery period. The result of the descriptive statistical analysis shows that businesses have rapidly digitalized to establish an effective channel for supply and demand activities in the market. Digitization has been rapidly implemented in several important areas such as sales, advertising, after-sales service, and office administration at the enterprises in the study sample (see Table 2).

The survey shows that the business activities with the highest adoption of digitization are sales and office administration. 97.6% of the companies confirm that they have implemented digitalization in two areas. The sales area recorded that 35.4% of

Table 2 The descriptive statistical analysis of the digitalization variables

Classification	Frequency	Percent	Cumulative percent
Digitalization in the sales activity			
Non-application	02	2.4	2.4
Low-application	29	35.4	37.8
High-application	51	62.2	100
Total number	82	100	
Digitalization in the advertising activity			
Non-application	07	8.6	8.6
Low-application	28	34.1	42.7
High-application	47	57.3	100
Total number	82	100	
Digitalization in the after-sales service			
Non-application	08	9.8	9.8
Low-application	38	46.3	56.1
High-application	36	43.9	100
Total number	82	100	
Digitalization in the office administration			
Non-application	02	2.4	2.4
Low-application	19	23.2	25.6
High-application	61	74.4	100
Total number	82	100	

Source own contribution

the businesses adapted at a low level and 62.2% applied at a high digitization level. However, the office administration area had up to 74.4% of businesses answering that they applied a lot of digitization tools. The advertising sector has 91.4% of enterprises confirmed to have digitized this activity, with 34.1% applying at a low level and 57.3% applying at a high level. Finally, in the after-sales service field, 90.2% of businesses implemented digitization, with 46.3% at a low application and 43.9% at a high application level.

In summary, the results of the descriptive statistical analysis confirm that companies have strongly digitized their business operations during the outbreak of the COVID-19 pandemic. Hence, this evidence provides the first positive results of digitalization in supporting the business community to overcome difficulties and move toward a new growth phase in the post-COVID-19 era.

4.2 The Independent-Samples t-Test Results

The independent-samples t-test helps to find differences between groups through an analysis of variances. In this study, the Levene's test method is used to perform the examination (see Table 3).

Table 3 The independent-samples t-test results

Method	Indicator	F statistic	Sig.
Digitalization in the sales activity			
Levene' test	Revenue	3.765	0.056*
	Profit	0.113	0.738
	Labor productivity	0.014	0.905
Digitalization in the advertising activity			
Levene's test	Revenue	2.766	0.092*
	Profit	3.269	0.074*
	Labor productivity	0.858	0.357
Digitalization in the after-sales service			
Levene's test	Revenue	0.163	0.687
	Profit	0.009	0.924
	Labor productivity	0.467	0.496
Digitalization in the office administration			
Levene's test	Revenue	0.620	0.433
	Profit	0.319	0.574
	Labor productivity	2.631	0.096*

Note * significance at 10% level
Source own contribution

The quantitative results of performing Levene's test show some interesting findings. First, there is a difference in the revenue indicator of the groups in the study sample. This evidence implies that if the degree level of digitization is different, the revenue will also be different. Second, digitization in the advertising area makes a difference in the revenue and profit of the companies in the survey sample. Third, digitization implemented in the office administration helps create differences in labor productivity between enterprises in the sample. However, Levene's test results did not confirm any differences in revenue, profit, and labor productivity among enterprises implementing digitalization in the after-sales activity.

In summary, the digitization of business activities in Vietnam has accelerated during the outbreak of the COVID-19 pandemic. The results of the descriptive statistical analysis show that more than 90% of companies have digitalized their business activities in areas such as sales, advertising, after-sales service, and office administration. The results of this study have confirmed that digitalization is considered as one of the response strategies to help Vietnamese enterprises survive and overcome the recent difficult period. Besides, the t-test results also confirmed that digitization has had initial impacts on changing revenue, profit, and labor productivity in companies. Some differences in business performance are pointed out and have practical implications for the promotion of business digitization in the next phase of the pandemic in Vietnam. This research result is the first evidence of digitization in business in Vietnam; it highlighted that digitization is considered a key strategy to help companies not only survive during the pandemic outbreak but also play an important role in the recovery process in the post-COVID-19 pandemic era.

5 Conclusions

The purpose of the study is to clarify the role of digitalization in business and analyze the current situation of digitalization, as well as its potential impacts on business in Vietnam during the outbreak of the COVID-19 pandemic. The database of this study was collected by an online survey that included 82 businesses in Vietnam. The research results show that digitization has not only been widely and strongly implemented in business processes but also makes a difference in several indicators such as profits, revenue, and labor productivity in enterprises. However, the study results also imply that digitization in the business process in Vietnam is only in the early stages to deal with the outbreak of the pandemic. Therefore, digitalization is expected and forecast to continue to expand to support businesses in recovering and heading for a strong growth period in the post-COVID-19 era.

There are some managerial implications drawn from the research results. Firstly, leaders of companies must be pioneers in the mindset of digital transformation; obviously, digitalization only succeeds when managers play a critical role as the driving force to motivate employees to overcome difficulties in digitizing business activities. Second, financial resources for digitization are important. Companies need to make huge investments in equipment and software to make a change in business digitization. Investment in digitalization should be seen as an urgent investment for development and can be traded off with a reduction of investment in other areas. Third, human resource is a key point for successful digitization. Leaders of companies need to focus on human resource training because it is an important factor in promoting digitalization. Finally, national policymakers should create financial funds to support the business community in the digitization process. Massive national investments in telecommunications and information technology infrastructure are needed to create the foundation for the digitization of enterprise business.

References

Amankwah-Amoah, J., Khan, Z., Wood, G., Knight, G.: COVID-19 and digitalization: the great acceleration. J. Bus. Res. **136**, 602–611 (2021)

Guo, H., Yang, Z., Huang, R., Guo, A.: The digitalization and public crisis responses of small and medium enterprises: implications from a COVID-19 survey. Front. Bus. Res. China **14**, 19 (2020)

Kraus, S., Jones, P., Kailer, N., Weinmann, A., Chaparro-Banegas, N., Roig-Tierno, N.: Digital transformation: an overview of the current state of the art of research. Sage Open **11**(3), (Forthcoming) (2021)

Linde, L., Sjödin, D., Parida, V., Gebauer, H.: Evaluation of digital business model opportunities. Res. Technol. Manag. **64**(1), 43–53 (2021)

Modgil, S., Dwivedi, Y.K., Rana, N.P., Gupta, S., Kamble, S.: Has COVID-19 accelerated opportunities for digital entrepreneurship? An Indian perspective. Technol. Forecast. Soc. Chang. **175**, 121415 (2022)

Rachinger, M., Rauter, R., Müller, C., Vorraber, W., Schirgi, E.: Digitalization and its influence on business model innovation. J. Manuf. Technol. Manag. **30**(8), 1143–1160 (2019)

Reuschl, A.J., Deist, M.K., Maalaoui, A.: Digital transformation during a pandemic: stretching the organizational elasticity. J. Bus. Res. **144**, 1320–1332 (2022)

Ribeiro-Navarrete, S., Botella-Carrubi, D., Palacios-Marqués, D., Orero-Blat, M.: The effect of digitalization on business performance: an applied study of KIBS. J. Bus. Res. **126**, 319–326 (2021)

Stalmachova, K., Chinoracky, R., Strenitzerova, M.: Changes in business models caused by digital transformation and the COVID-19 pandemic and possibilities of their measurement–case study. Sustainability **14**, 127 (2022)

Thanh, P.T., Tung, L.T.: The role of government risk communication in public health emergencies: evidence from the COVID-19 pandemic. Transform. Gov. People, Process. Policy **16**(3), 277–291 (2022)

Tung, L.T.: Factors affecting labour productivity of employee in an Asian emerging market: evidence in Vietnamese retail sector. Int. J. Bus. Glob. **24**(4), 513–528 (2020)

Tung, L.T., Binh, Q.M.Q.: The impact of R&D expenditure on firm performance in emerging markets: evidence from the Vietnamese listed companies. Asian J. Technol. Innov. **30**(2), 447–465 (2021)

Veldhoven, Z.V., Vanthienen, J.: Digital transformation as an interaction-driven perspective between business, society, and technology. Electron. Mark. **32**, 629–644 (2022)

European Union's Portrayal of Health Expenditure Funding Challenges in Pandemic Crises

Ana-Elena Varadi, Alexandra-Mădălina Ţăran, Sorana Vătavu, and Oana-Ramona Lobonţ

Abstract This study examines the economic repercussions of COVID-19 regarding the funding of health expenditure in the European Union member states over the period 2000–2019. The concern about the future of health expenditure funding at the European level increased even more due to the COVID-19 pandemic stress, evidencing the weaknesses and vulnerabilities of the national health systems. We perform our analysis from two standpoints. Firstly, our scientific approach focussed on bibliometric analysis to determine the novelty and interest in our topic of discussion, which presents a limited number of publications regarding the subject. Secondly, the empirical approach is based on several variables (total COVID-19 cases and deaths per million people, population growth, and health expenditure). The results indicate a direct and statistically significant relationship between the analysed variables. Furthermore, our analysis portrayed the current state of the health sector by examining the hierarchy in the European Union countries. We discover considerable discrepancies among member states regarding health expenditure, between developed and developing countries, which brings the European Union to a relatively low percentage for health expenditure, of 7.14% of GDP.

Keywords COVID-19 · SARS-CoV-2 · Bibliometric analysis · Regression · EU

1 Introduction

Recent years have evidenced the uncertainty and challenges of the recent pandemic crisis. Therefore, the academic research shifted its focus towards the impacts of the Coronavirus pandemic, while looking forward to offering a better understanding of the dynamics surrounding the topic of COVID-19. The virus, which started at the beginning of 2020, sparked a global epidemic and exposed the lack of forethought about the overall healthcare system, especially in terms of funding. The pandemic

A.-E. Varadi · A.-M. Ţăran · S. Vătavu (✉) · O.-R. Lobonţ
West University of Timisoara, Timisoara, Romania
e-mail: sorana.vatavu@e-uvt.ro

A. M. Dima and E. R. Danescu (eds.), *Fostering Recovery Through Metaverse Business Modelling*, Springer Proceedings in Business and Economics,
https://doi.org/10.1007/978-3-031-28255-3_17

spread rapidly throughout Europe, highlighting the vulnerability of the health system together with the realisation of an underfunded health sector.

According to Eurostat (2022), the COVID-19 pandemic meant increasing health expenditure as much as possible, to cover all medical consequences; therefore, health expenditure continued to be the second most funded item after social protection in terms of overall general government expenditure. Despite the nations' prompt mobilisation of obtaining additional public funding for the health system as a response to COVID-19, the burden on healthcare expenditures could intensify as government revenues decline, directing to a financial recession. Garcia-Escribano et al. (2022) predicted that government income in the European Union declined by 1.5% of GDP in 2020 and would not return to its 2019 figures until 2026. Although the consequences and difficulties of increased health spending brought about by the pandemic in the European Union have not been given much attention, this research attempts to assess how the epidemic has affected budgetary allocations for healthcare. Therefore, the goal of our research is to learn more about the financial effects of the current pandemic problem on the healthcare sector. Scientific and empirical methodologies were used to evaluate the impact of the pandemic on the dynamics of health expenditure.

Following the brief introduction of the issue, our objective is further explained in detail. The main findings from the literature are also presented, emphasising the novelty of the subject by concisely presenting the beginning of the COVID-19 virus and the pandemic, while focussing on the repercussions in terms of funding of health expenditure at the level of the European Union. The third and fourth sections enclose the dataset utilised and the time frame of the analysis, as well as the outcomes of the statistical methods considered. The last section concludes with remarks, initiatives, and suggestions for the EU member states.

2 Problem Statement and Literature Review

Our research objective is to offer a clearer view of the health expenditure funding challenges in pandemic crises, focussing on the repercussions brought by the COVID-19 pandemic on health expenditure at the EU level. Our research analysis covers two main perspectives. The first one is the scientific aspect of our study, which was conducted by performing a bibliometric analysis, in order to observe the interest in our research topic, as well as the authors, countries, and other related trends. The second perspective tackled was the empirical analysis, comprised of a statistical investigation (to assess the connection between the two phenomena) and the dataset, visually presented based on a data mapping process, to evidence the hierarchy of the EU countries.

We have observed that the literature does not offer a proper analysis of the challenges brought by the pandemic in terms of health expenditure, but rather a presentation of different health systems in countries that were heavily affected by the COVID-19 pandemic.

The conclusion drawn from the literature was that the overall healthcare system was initially underfunded in most EU countries. Consequently, international healthcare organisations claim that funding in healthcare is crucial when trying to combat an epidemic crisis and have actively demanded to limit as much as possible spending control mechanisms (Yan and Zhao 2020). By comparing our research with the literature presented, it can easily be observed that the novelty of our paper is generated by the methodological approach, the up-to-date data set, and the rather recent COVID-19 topic. In order to properly assess the topic of our study, we concentrated on providing a suitable bibliometric analysis, highlighting in a detailed manner the current state of knowledge in the field, followed by a presentation of the COVID-19 indicators, by further presenting the repercussion and impact that the pandemic had on the healthcare system while focussing on the health expenditure funding.

2.1 Bibliometric Analysis

To understand the complexity of our study, we start by performing a bibliometric analysis, as it is a thorough approach for discovering and evaluating vast volumes of scientific data to determine the level of interest in the scientific topic, the different trends and patterns presented by other authors and their diverse viewpoints while concentrating on possible contradictions on our topic of interest. Doing so allowed us to examine the evolutionary intricacies of this particular discipline, while also offering insight into the field's burgeoning regions. However, we discovered that its use in business research is still very undeveloped and, in many cases, inadequate. Most significantly, bibliometric analysis' appeal in financial research does not represent a novelty, but the consequence of its effectiveness in managing considerable amounts of empirical information, while offering high research value. Researchers use bibliometric analysis for a number of purposes, including identifying developing trends in article and journal performances, cooperation tendencies, and research elements, as well as examining the intellectual structure of a certain area in the existing literature.

As there are numerous ways in which we can compute a bibliometric analysis, for our research paper, the method of choice was the VOSviewer, a software for creating, visualising, and analysing bibliometric systems. As the software uses text mining as a basic function, it allows the creation of network maps of coinciding keywords based on both abstracts and the content of research articles (van Eck et al. 2009). Whilst the programme visualises the data among one database, it is crucial to choose a reliable database, which was Web of Science in this case.

Regarding the usage of both Web of Science and VOSviewer for our research paper, the following keywords were considered: COVID-19, SARS-CoV-2, and health expenditure. As the topic of COVID-19 is recent, the search time span was 2020–2022 and all articles were in English. After the database was selected, by conducting the bibliometric analysis, it seems that there is a global interest in regard to our topic, VOSviewer software identified 13 countries (Fig. 1a) from the 252 papers examined, the most relevant being the United States with 12 documents and with the biggest citations network, followed by England and Republic of China.

As expected, the clusters seem to have a really strong connection to one another, with each one being relevant to our study. The dark blue group is connected to crisis management and public health expenditure, focussing more on the repercussions of SARS-CoV-2, which created some challenges when denoting health expenditure funding. However, the red group is aiming towards the situation in Asian countries, in which the pandemic brought to light the problems of both the healthcare and insurance system.

We discovered other relevant terms for our research, such as crisis management, mortality, and income, which we deem as descriptive in regard to our topic. Therefore, after analysing the 252 papers considered from the Web of Science, the VOSviewer software evidenced 35 keywords. The important keywords and their connections are depicted in Fig. 1b. The main keywords within the list of articles analysed include "covid-19" with 48 occurrences in the forms of "coronavirus", "covid-19 pandemic", and "health spending" (13 appearances).

The most cited authors of scientific articles on the effect of the COVID-19 pandemic on health expenditure are revealed by the citations per author analysis. Based on the parameters used, the VOSviewer system retrieved 32 authors with at least one article per author. The limited number of publications in regard to our topic can be explained by the 2-year minimum indexing time required by the Web of Science; therefore, all articles were written right at the beginning of the pandemic.

2.2 *Background of the COVID-19 Pandemic*

According to Chen et al. (2020) and Zhou et al. (2020), COVID-19 was the seventh human coronavirus, a severe respiratory condition coronavirus 2 (medically known as SARS-CoV-2), that originated in Wuhan, China, in the course of a pneumonia outbreak in January 2020. Scientists have doubted the origins of the new coronavirus SARS-CoV2 since its discovery. It has been implied that SARS-CoV-2 is the result of laboratory experiments. Nevertheless, genomic evidence contradicts this theory, indicating that SARS-CoV-2 did not evolve from a previously identified viral basis.

Andersen et al. (2020) pinpointed that the origin of SARS-CoV-2 began somewhere between late November and early December of 2019, which also corresponds to the first cases ever recorded. As a result, there was an unrecognised and unnoticed human dispersal after the viral event; hence the situation developed into a worldwide pandemic. On the 30th of January 2020, the World Health Organisation (2020) declared a Public Health Emergency of International Concern and a Pandemic on the 11th of March 2020, which marked the official beginning of the lockdown and, moreover, the crisis. Unfortunately, since then, the virus which started in China has spread around the world, infecting 472,114,840 individuals and having caused over 6 million deaths as of March 2021 (Our World in Data 2022).

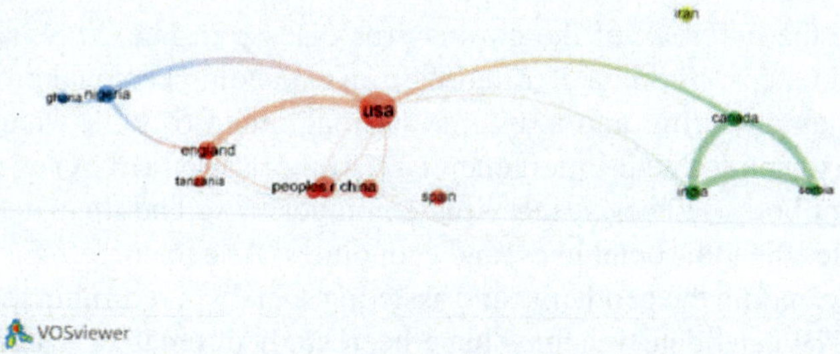

(a) Countries

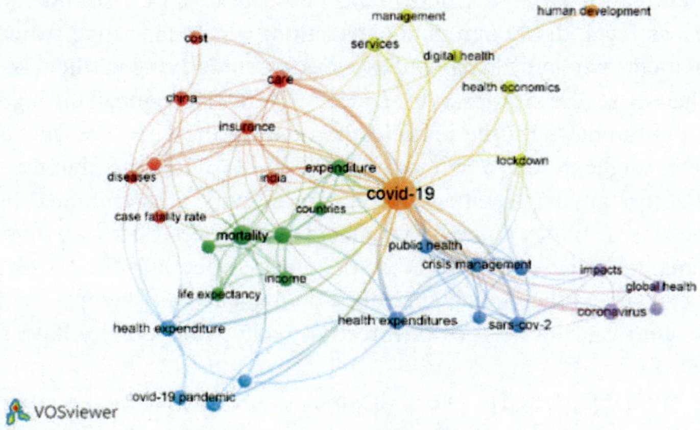

(b) Keywords

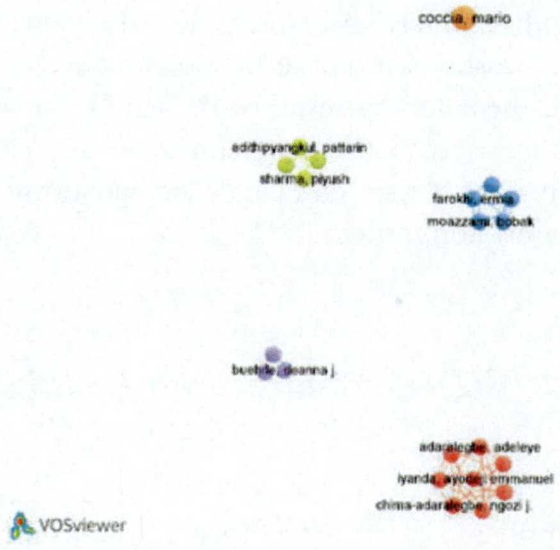

(c) Authors

Fig. 1 Maps resulted from the bibliometric analysis through VOSviewer software

Since the outbreak of the coronavirus disease in late 2019, society has taken a number of steps to combat it, ranging from expanding personal protective equipment (PPE) manufacturing and stressing the magnitude of both wearing the mask and social distancing to the Emergency Use Authorisation (EUA) of therapeutic monoclonal antibody. However, the virus continues to spread unabated, wreaking havoc on people's health, social lives, and economies. As a result, efficient vaccinations are critical to ending the pandemic and assisting society in returning to normalcy. Several COVID-19 candidate vaccines have been studied, created, tested, and reviewed at a frenetic pace. Various vaccines have indeed been provisionally authorised as of the end of February 2021. Several more treatments that are still in clinical trials are anticipated to enter the market in the coming years.

The Centres for Disease Control and Prevention (CDC) summarised the virus' symptoms as fever, dry cough, and exhaustion; which can range from undetectable to fatal. Patients who are elderly or have specific underlying medical issues are more prone to having severe sickness. As an idea, COVID-19 is spread through the air when droplets and minute airborne particles harbouring the virus are inhaled. Breathing them in is most dangerous when individuals are close together, but they may also be breathed across greater distances, especially indoors. Contaminated fluids can also spread the disease if they come into contact with the eyes, nose, or mouth, and, in rare cases, contaminated surfaces. Infected people are infectious for 10 days on average, and they can spread the virus even if they do not show any symptoms. Many strains (variants) with varying degrees of infectivity and pathogenicity have resulted from mutations.

Vaccination is regarded as one of the most significant medical accomplishments of contemporary civilisation. Furthermore, long-term observation is required to determine vaccination effectiveness and rule out unusual adverse concerns. Since the onset of the COVID-19 epidemic, many COVID-19 vaccine candidates have entered clinical trials in less than 6 months and have been provisionally licenced in less than 10 months, demonstrating a record-breaking pace in vaccine development history. Despite the rapid development, the safety criteria for the newly released vaccines' research and licencing procedure were consistent with those for earlier vaccinations, including a careful examination of their clinical data by government regulatory authorities and independent review committees.

2.3 The Impact of the COVID-19 Pandemic on Healthcare Expenditures

Because of a lack of medical supplies, the cost of healthcare benefits increased during COVID-19. As a result, a large amount of government money was obtained in order to implement a stimulus package focussed on the healthcare business. Expenditure has been wisely redirected towards supplying acute care capacity, ventilation systems, and supplies of other vital medical goods, such as protective gear. According to Aon's 2020 Global Medical Trend Rates Report, government investment could enhance the healthcare sector's development by offering public goods that represent a critical portion of aggregate demand. Public investment ineffective compliance, a legal framework for the enforcement of privacy, and conflict resolution, according to Knack and Keefer (1995), are all relevant in improving economic development. Governmental resources dedicated to healthcare and education are driving the healthcare industry expansion, and public policies promoting private-sector investment in health and education should be implemented. Ţăran et al. (2022) also evidenced the need for critical implications in identifying solutions to reduce the gaps between countries in terms of the adoption of e-health, for which new regulations should be developed across EU countries.

The battle against COVID-19, according to the Economic Intelligence Unit (2020), has resulted in a dramatic decline in spending on other ailments, with non-urgent care being delayed and people bypassing clinics and hospitals. Expenditure for non-coronavirus care, on the other hand, was expected to rebound in late 2020. However, healthcare spending was expected to increase by 5.5% in 2021. Unfortunately, it only reached a growth of 3.4% in the overall economy. A factor that was not considered initially in the analysis was the effectiveness of both vaccines and medicines that treat the virus, and as their availability was rather limited in 2020, additional expenditure was needed.

While governments and healthcare administrators have put resources and cash into combating the virus, non-urgent care for other ailments has been cancelled or decreased in many situations. Patients, on the other hand, are hesitant to visit hospitals or clinics, either because they are afraid of catching a coronavirus or because they are concerned about adding to the workload of healthcare professionals. Many hospitals, emergency rooms, and doctor's offices report considerably fewer people than usual, and dental appointments are nearly impossible in countries under lockdown.

The decline in healthcare utilisation has not yet resulted in many job losses in countries where public healthcare financing dominates, but it has resulted in spare capacity, which has been widely welcomed, given prior worries that healthcare systems would be overrun with coronavirus patients. While expenditure on non-coronavirus care has decreased, the pandemic itself, along with the testing and treatment associated with, is expected to be costly. For example, an emergency budget in late March expanded the finances available to the country's Ministry of Health by more than €3 billion, or 20%, in part to help the government in expanding the number of intensive care beds to more than 50,000. Based on the ageing dimension, it is expected for the overall well-being to be affected while life expectancy will be reduced due to the foreseen implications of the pandemic (Cristea et al. 2022). In the light of the above, as the literature did not prove interest in our topic, moreover, it did not assess the same hypothesis, we further focussed on the correlation between the total healthcare expenditure in EU member states (expressed as a percentage of GDP, total national currency, and in euro) and the COVID-19 indicator (comprising in total cases and deaths per million people) at the end of 2020. Through our analysis, we tested two hypotheses, one for the influence of the COVID-19 pandemic on the public health systems, and one for the relationship between health expenditures and population growth. They are the following:

H0a: There is a direct influence of the pandemic on the medical budget allocations in EU member states (observable through data mapping).
H1a: There is no influence of the pandemic on the medical budget allocations in EU member states.
H0b: There is a strong relationship between health expenditure and the population growth.
H1b: There is no relationship between health expenditure and the population growth.

In addition to proving our hypotheses, we also focus on which of the EU member states handled the pandemic best.

3 Research Methods

In this paper, we study the dynamics of health expenditure throughout the years, emphasising the repercussions of the COVID-19 pandemic. Furthermore, we pursued the evolution of the COVID-19 pandemic in both its cases and deaths. In order to portray these estimations, we visually analyse the data, considering the data mapping process to evidence the hierarchy of the EU countries. Then, we employ correlation and regression analysis for indicators available over a longer period of time. The variation in one metric as a result of the change in the other is observed through correlation analysis. A strong correlation indicates a significant association between the two measurements, whereas a weak relationship indicates a poor connection between the two variables. We have chosen the correlation analysis as it can reveal a significant connection between our metrics, more precisely, health expenditure, when taking into consideration the growth of the population.

The simple regression analysis is employed to determine the relative influence of a predictor variable on a certain result, which is not the same as correlation analysis, as it looks further at the intensity of a relation between two stochastic processes (Pfeifer 2010). The model is categorised as "simple" since the independent variable is singular X_i, for i being equal with 1, 2…n (n = 27 in this case) and the period is indicated by t (t = 1…20, from 2000 until 2020). We performed the regression to predict how a dependent variable will vary when the independent variable faces transformation in time. The equation is expressed below:

$$Y_{it} = \alpha + \beta X_{it} + \varepsilon_{it} \tag{1}$$

where Y denotes the dependent variable, X is the independent variable, α represents the intercept, β is the slope or the regression coefficient, and ε is the error term. Therefore, translating this equation to our case study, the regression models proposed would be the following:

Table 1 Description of the indicators employed

Indicator	Definition	Unit of measure	Variable	Source
COVID-19 cases	The total number of COVID-19 cases for 2020 per million people	Total, per million	Independent variables	Our World in Data
COVID-19 deaths	The total number of COVID-19 deaths for 2020 per million people	Total, per million		
Health expenditure	Health expenditure refers to current health spending, which includes both individual and group health care	% of GDP	Dependent variables	Eurostat
		Total, National Currency		
		Total, EUR		
Population growth	The average yearly variation in population size for 2020	Annual, %		World Bank Data

$$\text{COV.c.}_{\text{it}} = \alpha + \beta\text{Health.exp.}_{\text{it}} + \varepsilon_{\text{it}} \quad (2)$$

The study we conducted covered the European Union member countries, taking into consideration all 27 member states at the moment of the study. The research was based on panel data, considering a period of 20 years (2000–2019), employing different statistical approaches: hierarchy based on data mapping, correlation, and regression analysis. The data was collected from the World Bank Data, Our World in Data, and Eurostat, as detailed in the following Table 1.

Even though the data comes from several sectors, information about those links gave us new perceptions, whilst indicating interdependencies between our variables.

4 Findings

As previously described, firstly, we visually analyse the hierarchy of the EU countries, and, secondly, we apply correlation and linear regression, all in the STATA software. Figure 2 depicts the major topics of interest with regard to the COVID-19 pandemic across the European Union at the end of 2020.

The results revealed the greatest number of COVID-19 cases per million (Fig. 2a) arise in smaller countries, such as Lithuania, Croatia, Belgium, and the Czech Republic, which also relates to the COVID-19 deaths (Fig. 2b) in the same countries joining other countries such as Italy, Spain, and Bulgaria. The countries that were

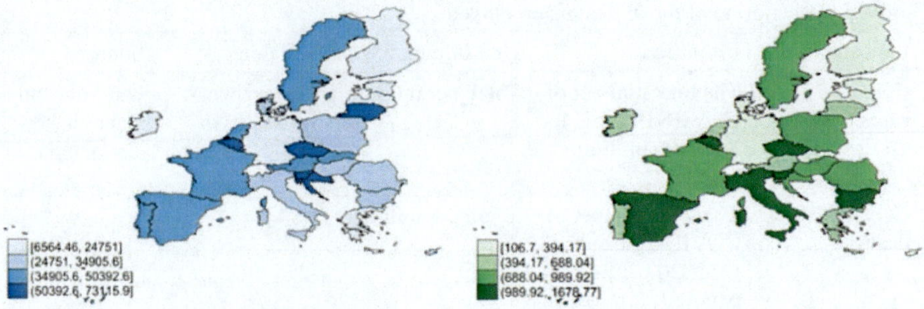

(a) Total cases per million people (b) Total deaths per million people

Fig. 2 Total cases and total deaths from COVID-19 in the EU in 2020

the least affected by the pandemic, in terms of the number of cases and deaths, are Germany, Hungary, Romania, Poland, Finland, Latvia, and Estonia.

Regarding the healthcare expenditure indicators, portrayed in Fig. 3, we can observe that Sweden had the highest population growth in 2020 (Fig. 3a), as well as the highest health expenditure in the national currency (Fig. 3b).

Developed countries which were not heavily affected by the pandemic, meaning Germany, France, Austria, and Denmark, have the highest health expenditure in both

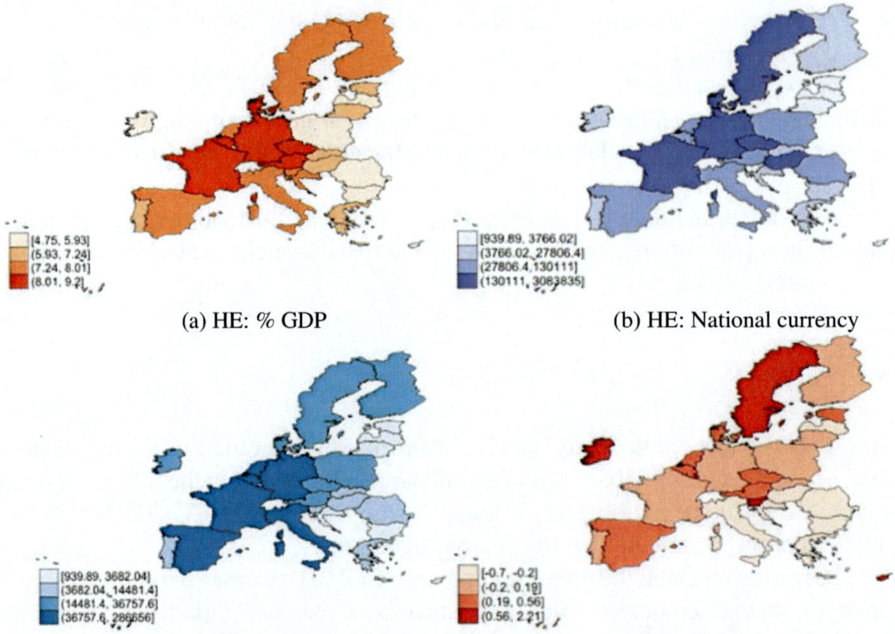

(a) HE: % GDP (b) HE: National currency

(c) HE: Euro (d) HE: Population growth

Fig. 3 The level of health expenditure (HE) in the EU in 2020

Table 2 Results of the simple linear regression model

Indicator	Health expenditure–dependent variable	Growth population–dependent variable
Regression coefficient	1191.39***	0.00025***
Constant	2189.47***	−0.394***
Adjusted R squared	0.2995	0.2995
F statistic	231.06***	231.06***

*** —statistically significant at 1% level

national currency and as a percentage of the GDP. On the other side of the spectrum, most countries that have a lower health expenditure, as well as low population growth, are Eastern European Countries (Romania, Bulgaria, Greece), especially the health expenditure expressed in the euro currency (Fig. 3c and d).

By means of data mapping, we observed a hierarchy of the EU member states, especially based on their level of development, confirming our first hypothesis (Ha), which stated that there is a direct influence of the pandemic on the medical budget allocations in EU.

Going further with our empirical analysis, Pearson's correlation coefficient between health expenditure and population growth was 0.5485, indicating a direct relationship between our chosen variables. Additionally, the correlation coefficient is statistically significant at the 1% level. Based on this significant correlation, we test the simple linear regression model with both variables, considering, in turn, the health and population proxies as the dependent variable. The model was applied to the panel data, considering the 27 EU member states over the 2000–2019 period (Table 2).

We observe a direct and statistically significant relationship in both cases. Accordingly, in the EU, we expect higher health expenditures when the population is growing, but also, to a more limited extent (based on a lower value of the regression coefficient), increasing health expenditures as % of GDP would induce an increase in the population. For both regression models, the F-test and its statistical significance confirm the ability to explain the variance in the dependent variable. In addition, the R squared indicates that approximately 30% of the variance in the dependent variable may be explained through the independent one. Based on these results we confirm the second hypothesis (Hb), as there is a significant relationship between health expenditure and the growth of population in the EU member states.

5 Conclusions

There is an increased concern about the future of health expenditure funding at the European level. The COVID-19 pandemic stresses the weak and vulnerable overall health system; therefore, it has raised awareness that authorities lack the capacity to respond properly to the health crisis and the appeal for additional health expenditure.

We have discovered great discrepancies in the amount EU member states allocate to the healthcare systems, however, the variation in percentage when it comes to the GDP is not as significant as anticipated, with a minimum of 4.75% of the GDP in Latvia and with a high in both Austria and the Czech Republic, of 9.20% from the GDP. The average of the European Union for 2020 in terms of health expenditure expressed as a share of GDP is relatively low, at 7.14% of the GDP, insinuating an underfunding of the overall European health sector, as previously suggested in the literature by Yan and Zhao (2020). However, these inconsistencies among EU member states are also reflected in the pre-COVID health expenditure, denoting that the lack of investment in health is not a novelty for today's society. The necessity for public investment and public policies that support the healthcare industry expansion was also emphasised by previous studies (Knack and Keefer 1995; Ţăran et al. 2022). However, our research goes beyond studying the effects and challenges of health expenditure caused by the pandemic in the EU member states.

Regarding the statistical aspect of our paper, we could not find a significant correlation between the COVID-19 pandemic and health expenditure, due to the absence of current data for 2021. Nevertheless, there is a connection between the deaths caused by the coronavirus and the percentage of population growth, which decreased significantly in 2020, compared to previous years. Once the statistical data is available for more recent years, future research could expand this analysis on a larger dataset, re-evaluating the impact of the pandemic on healthcare expenditures.

Concerning health expenditure, even though initially the budget for health expenditure was boosted in order to mitigate the repercussions produced by the pandemic, it seems that the investment was not enough to cover the extra costs that appeared along the way, meaning the newly-developed medicines and vaccines, and overall, the funding for health expenditure is on a declining trend.

Our study brings novelty to the literature from the interest in our topic of discussion and also from the fact that there are only a few publications regarding the subject in academic journals, as our bibliometric analysis proved. However, the limited available data made us consider the impact of the pandemic only over the year 2020. Further research should focus on a longer period of time, especially in terms of analysing the effect of the pandemic on the development of the national health systems and the increase in health expenditure in all the EU member countries.

Acknowledgements This work was supported by a grant from the Romanian Ministry of Education and Research, CNCS—UEFISCDI, project number PN-III-P1-1.1-TE-2019-2182, within PNCDI III.

References

Andersen, K., Rambaut, A., Lipkin, W., Holmes, E., Garry, R.: The proximal origin of SARS-CoV-2. Nat. Med. **26**(4), 450–452 (2020)

Chen, T., Dai, Z., Mo, P., Li, X., Ma, Z., Song, S., Chen, X., Luo, M., Liang, K., Gao, S., Zhang, Y., Deng, L., Xiong, Y.: Clinical characteristics and outcomes of older patients with coronavirus disease 2019 (COVID-19) in Wuhan, China: a single-centered, retrospective study. J. Gerontol. Ser. A **75**(9), 1788–1795 (2020)

Cristea, M.S., Pirtea, M.G., Suciu, M.C., Noja, G.G.: Workforce participation, ageing, and economic welfare: new empirical evidence on complex patterns across the European Union. Complexity 2022, Article ID 7313452 (2022)

Economist Intelligence Unit. https://www.eiu.com/n/novel-coronavirus-outbreak/?mkt_tok=eyJpIjoiT1dGbU1qSm1aVGswWVdZNSIsInQiOiJ3eG5MSXpMWnpmQkxWR1I1WGtkZkJGb3ZcL0xScUpzVjl5d3B5Qm1tMjA5RVVMS2xUWUZUS3FTcWplN05Dd1UxeDJ4OHhubzBEeDhHcERXVVF6SHg2OVBXeXFBWHRHVlliUVdRb3UrV0wrMXRibmxpUW9tZ29hUFh5ajNyOTd3dVIifQ%3D%3D. Last accessed 05 May 2022

European Commission: Government expenditure on health–statistics explained. https://ec.europa.eu/eurostat/statistics-explained/index.php?title=Government_expenditure_on_health. Last accessed 05 May 2022

Garcia-Escribano, M., Mogues, T., Juarros, P.: Patterns and drivers of health spending efficiency. IMF Work. Pap. **2022**(048), 1 (2022).

Knack, S., Keefer, P.: Institutions and economic performance: cross-country tests using alternative institutional measures. Econ. Polit. **7**(3), 207–227 (1995)

Our World in Data.: COVID-19 Data-Explorer (2022)

Pfeifer, P.: Assumptions behind the linear regression model. SSRN-Darden case no. UVA-QA-0271 (2010)

Ţăran, A., Mustea, L., Vătavu, S., Lobonţ, O., Luca, M.: Challenges and drawbacks of the EU medical system generated by the COVID-19 pandemic in the field of health systems' digitalization. Int. J. Environ. Res. Public Health **19**(9), 4950 (2022)

van Eck, N., Waltman, L.: Software survey: VOSviewer, a computer program for bibliometric mapping. Scientometrics **84**(2), 523–538 (2009)

World Health Organization. https://www.who.int/director-general/speeches/detail/who-director-general-s-opening-remarks-at-the-media-briefing-on-covid-19---11-march-2020. Last accessed 11 Mar 2022

World Health Organization. https://www.who.int/emergencies/diseases/novel-coronavirus-2019/covid-19-vaccines/advice. Last accessed 12 Apr 2022

Yan, J., Zhao, D.: Institutional diversity in response to the COVID-19 emergency. Healthcare **8**(4), 515 (2020)

Zhou, P., Yang, X., Wang, X., Hu, B., Zhang, L., Zhang, W., Si, H., Zhu, Y., Li, B., Huang, C., Chen, H., Chen, J., Luo, Y., Guo, H., Jiang, R., Liu, M., Chen, Y., Shen, X., Wang, X., Zheng, X., Zhao, K., Chen, Q., Deng, F., Liu, L., Yan, B., Zhan, F., Wang, Y., Xiao, G., Shi, Z.: A pneumonia outbreak associated with a new coronavirus of probable bat origin. Nature **579**(7798), 270–273 (2020)

The Moderating Role of Trust in Managers Between Strategic Innovation and Firm Performance

Bulent Akkaya and Simona-Andreea Apostu

Abstract The objective of this research is to emphasize the importance of trust in managers in moderating the relationship between strategic innovation and firm performance in Turkish service firms. The data was gathered at random from 340 employees. Structural Equation Modeling (SEM) was used to examine the data, which was done with the AMOS SPSS program. According to the study findings, there is a considerable association between trust in managers and firm performance, as well as strategic innovation and firm performance. The study also discovered that trust in managers acts as a moderator between strategic innovation and firm performance. This study adds to the advancement of scientific research, notably in terms of testing the model's content, as well as the variables and factors influencing them. Furthermore, this study demonstrated the need for firms to practice trust in management and strategic innovation in order to increase company performance. Strategic innovation and trust in managers are crucial to improving company performance, and high levels of strategic innovation may lead to higher firm performance, since service companies' trust in managers is frequently more directly related to firm success. Additionally, managers should account for manager trust when examining the link between strategic innovation and firm performance.

Keywords Trust in managers · Strategic innovation · Firm performance · Partial least squares structural equation model

B. Akkaya
Manisa Celal Bayar University, Manisa, Turkey

S.-A. Apostu (✉)
Bucharest University of Economic Studies and Institute of National Economy, Bucharest, Romania
e-mail: simona.apostu@csie.ase.ro

A. M. Dima and E. R. Danescu (eds.), *Fostering Recovery Through Metaverse Business Modelling*, Springer Proceedings in Business and Economics,
https://doi.org/10.1007/978-3-031-28255-3_18

1 Introduction

In today's globalized world, the requirement of customers' expectations in a hyper dynamic market is increasingly important. Thus, business organizations are subject to fierce competition (Lee et al. 2015); the solution is to meet these expectations by having a competitive advantage from the organizations (Gallego-Alvarez et al. 2011) that can be achieved through innovation (Serrano-Bedia et al. 2012). Thus, innovation represents a critical issue in business organizations, being one of the most important factors of survival and success (Nonaka and Takeuchi 1995).

Innovation increases the financial performance of organizations (Adams-Price 1994), a crucial role being established by trust in the organization and its management. The organizational trust is strengthened by empowerment (Brunetto and Farr-Wharton 2007), which is an important parameter of innovation (Golipour et al. 2011). In this context, trust can be perceived as a mediator between empowerment and organizational performance (Berraies et al. 2014).

Therefore, strategic innovation and trust in managers are crucial to improve company performance, high levels of strategic innovation leading to higher firm performance. Since service companies' trust in managers is frequently more directly related to firm success, this study aims to investigate if the trust in managers has a crucial role in the relationship between strategic innovation and firm performance, being worthy of consideration by scholars and policy makers. Thus, this study demonstrated the need of firms practicing trust in management and strategic innovation to increase company performance. There is much research on innovation and firm performance in the literature. However, limited investigation was applied on the role of trust in managers, strategic innovation, and firm performance. Therefore, the aim of the current study is to determine the impact of both strategic innovation and trust in manager on firm performance, the scope of the research being to establish the moderating role of trust in managers on the relationship between strategic innovation and firm performance.

The rest of the paper is organized as follows: Sect. 2 presents the problem statement in light of the most important papers in the field, and Sect. 3 introduces the research questions and the aims of the research. Section 4 presents data and research method, and Sect. 5 presents the main findings. Concluding observations and discussions are provided in the last part of the paper.

2 Problem Statement

In order to achieve economic growth, a key factor is represented by innovation, a basis of economic development (Prifti and Alimehmeti 2017). Innovation impacts growth and business development and ensures competitiveness within the marketplace (Bigliardi et al. 2020).

According to the definition provided by the OECD and Eurostat (2005), innovation represents implementing something new, such as an improved organizational product, process, or marketing technique. Hurley and Hult (1998) defined innovation as a characteristic of a firm's culture and openness to new ideas. Innovation originates from developing marketable products through invention, generating business performance targets (Aboulnasr et al. 2008).

According to Kazuyuki (2016), innovation is positively correlated with firm performance, being an ongoing research theme in the literature (Vaccaro et al. 2010). Performance represents the ability of measuring organizational effectiveness, productivity, profitability, quality, continuous improvement, work quality, and social responsibility (Al Naqbia et al. 2020).

Market orientation and organizational performance are linked to innovation (Han et al. 1998). Firm performance is difficult to measure. Two significant determinates of firm performance are market power and industry structure (Dubey et al. 2012).

Managerial strategic innovation is important for firm performance (Zhou et al. 2005). For this, organizations have to adapt (Mahoney 2005) and create value (Zahra et al. 2006). Innovation leadership demonstrates trust in organizational members, a strategic fit that mediates the relationship between innovation and firm performance (Carmeli et al. 2010).

Trust represents the key to manage complexity (Luhmann 1979). It reflects the confidence between two parts without exploiting the other's vulnerability (Sabel 1993), for benefits from interactions with others (Koohang et al. 2017). Trust promotes adaptive organizational forms, building social network relations, and reducing harmful conflict (Salam 2017). Trust significantly impacts the economies, facilitating the transactions between the society members (Pratono 2018). In order to interact and share knowledge, trust in management and among individuals is vital (Renzl 2008).

Trust in management leads to increasing organizational effectiveness (Dirks 2000) and organizational performance (Sharkie 2009). Trust in management was positively related to innovation behavior (Michaelis et al. 2009), trust being necessary in order to make outsourcing relationships work because the role of trust is important in the management of outsourcing relationships in perspective of Information Systems outsourcing (Hoecht and Trott 2006).

There is a gap regarding the connection between all three variables (firm performance, innovation, and trust). In this context, our study filled the gap by indicating the association between trust in managers and firm performance, as well as strategic innovation and firm performance, highlighting the role of trust. Thus, this study adds to the advancement of scientific research, notably in terms of testing the model's content, as well as the variables and factors influencing them. Furthermore, this study demonstrated the need of firms practicing trust in management and strategic innovation in order to increase company performance.

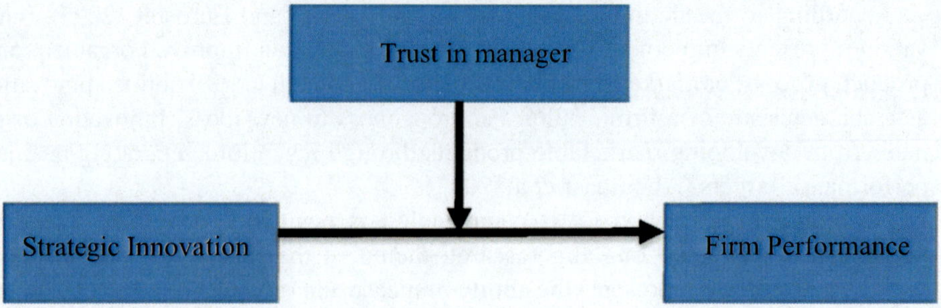

Fig. 1 Research model. *Source* Authors

3 Research Questions

As the above research obviously demonstrates, different researchers have reached different conclusions on the crucial element that influences company success and firm performance. However, there are few studies in the literature that examine the link between trust in managers, strategic innovation, and firm performance. In this context, this study seeks to connect the three variables by attempting to address the problem of whether trust in managers has a moderating role in the relationship between organizational innovativeness and firms perceived success and performance. As a result, we created the research model (Fig. 1) and developed three hypotheses listed below.

In this context, the hypotheses of the model are as follows:

H1: Strategic innovation has a statistical impact on firm performance in service companies.

H2: Trust in manager has a statistical impact on firm performance in service companies.

H3: Strategic innovation has a statistical impact on firm performance with moderating role trust in manager in service companies.

4 Data and Research Methods

4.1 Research Sample Selection and Data Collection

Simple random sampling was used to get data from 340 workers in service companies from January to April 2022. "The simple random sample means that every case of the population has an equal probability of inclusion in sample" (Taherdoost 2016, p. 21). The data was collected using three questionnaires. The first one was Strategic innovation developed by Wang and Ahmed (2004). The second one was Trust in manager developed by Mayer and Davis (1999). The last scale developed by Tseng and Lee (2014) measures a firm's perceived performance. All items are measured on a five-point Likert-type scale (1 = strongly disagree to 5 = strongly agree).

4.2 Descriptive and Frequency

In this study, the frequency analysis revealed that most of the respondents are male (69.4%). Most of the participants have a bachelor's degree (23.5%). A large sample works in marketing department (36.5%), in R&D (23.2%), accounting (14.1%), HRM (12.4%), while (13.8%) work as salesman out of their firms. The mean of participants' age is 35.10 ± 6.78, the youngest age being 22 while the eldest is 52. The mean of participants' working duration (year) is 10.44 ± 7.03, the minimum year being 1 while the maximum is 30.

4.3 Validity and Reliability

The Cronbach's alpha coefficient is used to test the internal consistency for all scales of the research and reliability. (Strategic innovation 0.713; Trust in managers 0.892 and Firm performance 0.973) All scales are in an acceptable range (0.70) (Hair et al. 2013). According to Bougie and Sekaran (2019) criteria, the mean value of strategic innovation (m = 3.582 ± 0,50) is in the category of medium, while trust in managers (m = 4.009 ± 0,98) and firm performance (m = 4.033 ± 0,95) have a high mean score.

4.4 Validity and Reliability

PLS-SEM analysis is imperative to check the severity of the data, but it is not strict to the data normality (Hair et al. 2013). However, we tested the normal distribution of the data. Hair et al. (2013) has recommended applying Skewness and Kurtosis tests to check the normal distribution in the research. Data is normally distributed providing values of skewness and kurtosis in the range of +2 and −2 (George and Mallery (2019). The data is normally distributed. Furthermore, Pearson's correlation was applied to test the correlation between variables. According to Table 1 the three variables present positive and significant correlations.

Table 1 Data distribution and correlation analysis

	N	Skewness		Kurtosis		Correlations		
	Statistic	Statistic	Std. Error	Statistic	Std. Error	1	2	3
Strategic innovation	340	−0.034	0.132	−0.154	0.264	1		
Trust in managers	340	−1.163	0.132	0.744	0.264	0.152**	1	
Firm performance	340	−1.408	0.132	1.576	0.264	0.158**	0.727**	1

** Correlation is significant at the 0.01 level (2-tailed)
Source Authors

5 Results Interpretation

PLS-SEM analysis of the relationship between independent variables and the dependent variables was applied to test and verify the research hypotheses by the AMOS program. The hypotheses tested the impact of both strategic innovation and trust in manager on firm performance and the moderating role of trust in the manager between strategic innovation and firm performance.

According to Table 2, the estimate value from strategic innovation to firm performance is 0.90 and p value is 0.001. This finding had a statistical significance (p value) of 0.001, indicating the acceptance of the H1.

This finding showed a positive and significant relationship between strategic innovation and firm performance. In other words, the probability of getting a critical ratio as large as 37.872 in absolute value is less than 0.001. Thus, the regression weight for Strategic Innovation in the prediction of Firm Performance is significantly different from zero at the 0.001 level (two-tailed).

According to Table 3, the estimate value from trust in manager to firm performance is 0.92 and p value is 0.001, the probability of getting a critical ratio as large as 41.800 in absolute value is less than 0.001. In other words, the regression weight for trust in the manager in the prediction of firm performance is significantly different from zero at the 0.001 level (two-tailed). This finding had a statistical significance (p value = 0.001) showing that H2 is accepted. This finding showed a positive and significant relationship between trust in the manager and firm performance (Table 4).

The probability of getting a critical ratio as large as 9.136 in absolute value is less than 0.001. In other words, the regression weight for Strategic Innovation in

Table 2 H1 hypothesis results

			Estimate	S.E.	C.R.	P	Label
Firm performance	<---	Strategic innovation	0.899	0.024	37.872	***	par_1

Source Authors

Table 3 H2 hypothesis results

			Estimate	S.E.	C.R.	P	Label
Firm performance	<---	Trust in manager	0.915	0.022	41.800	***	par_1

Source Authors

Table 4 Regression weights

			Estimate	S.E.	C.R.	P	Label
Firm performance	<---	Strategic innovation	0.268	0.029	9.136	***	par_2
Firm performance	<---	Trust in manager	0.407	0.026	15.627	***	par_3
Firm performance	<---	Interaction	0.348	0.033	10.602	***	par_4

Source Authors

the prediction of Firm Performance is significantly different from zero at the 0.001 level (two-tailed). The probability of getting a critical ratio as large as 15.627 in absolute value is less than 0.001. In other words, the regression weight for Trust in Manager in the prediction of Firm Performance is significantly different from zero at the 0.001 level (two-tailed). The probability of getting a critical ratio as large as 10.602 in absolute value is less than 0.001. In other words, the regression weight for Interaction in the prediction of Firm Performance is significantly different from zero at the 0.001 level (two-tailed). These results show that this model is statistically significant, which shows that H3 is accepted.

This study has investigated the role of trust in the manager as a moderator between strategic innovation and firm performance. Data analysis has concluded that trust in the manager significantly strengthens the relationship between strategic innovation and firm performance ($\beta = 0.348$, $p < 0.05$). Therefore, the moderating role of trust in the manager is confirmed. The results are shown in Table 5.

When Strategic Innovation goes up by 1 standard deviation, Firm Performance goes up by 0.268 standard deviations. When Trust in Manager goes up by 1 standard deviation, Firm Performance goes up by 0.407 standard deviations. When Interaction goes up by 1 standard deviation, Firm Performance goes up by 0.348 standard deviations.

Based on the data analysis, this study has also presented the graphical results of moderator-trust in manager (Fig. 2).

Table 5 Standardized regression weights: (group number 1—default model)

			Estimate
Firm performance	<---	Strategic innovation	0.268
Firm performance	<---	Trust in manager	0.407
Firm performance	<---	Interaction	0.348

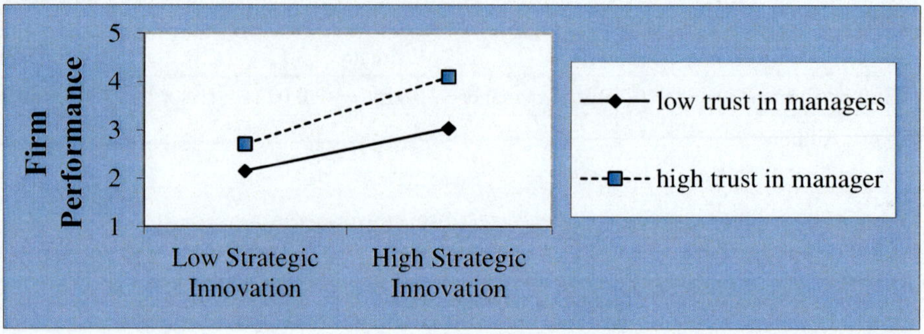

Fig. 2 Moderating role of Trust in manager. *Source* Authors projection

The graphical analysis shows that, in the presence of greater trust in the manager, strategic innovation amplifies its impact on the firm performance of service companies.

6 Discussion and Conclusions

We argue that the link between innovation and firm performance does not happen by accident and that it benefits from removing difficulties to collaboration among different departments of organizations (Garcia et al. 2008), in addition to establishing deep trust in employees and managers in their organization (Lewicki and Bunker 2006). Therefore, this study tested the moderating role of trust in manager between strategic innovation and firm performance of service companies in Turkey.

Our findings contribute to the scholarly discussion of internal relationships between employees and managers about the performance effects of innovation. Firms' innovation endeavors can be more successfully transformed into performance outcomes through a healthy interaction among company members to the extent that functional departments obtain more quality outcomes through management. This relationship is important in transforming new market growth prospects into organizational performance (Alegre and Chiva 2008). Furthermore, trust strengthens the good in managing between innovation and organizations' performance. When business managers have complete trust in one another's honesty and sincerity, they engage more in creative exchanges that will benefit the firm's innovative endeavors (Dayan et al. 2009).

Our results regarding organizational innovation and performance are similar to those of the existing literature, the relationship being positive and significant (Song et al. 2011; Al Naqbia et al. 2020). Regarding the impact of trust in managers, there are studies according to which organizational trust led to performance (Longwei et al. 2011; Cheng et al. 2014) and innovation (Ruppel and Harrington 2020; Wang et al. 2011; Cheng et al. 2014), but to our knowledge, there are no studies concerning the impact of trust on the relationship between organizational performance and innovation. So, our findings are valuable, both for academics, managers, and policy makers, highlighting the importance of confidence in management. There is also a need for managers and policy makers to train the workers on innovation strategies technologies and through trust in supervisors in service companies.

Despite the interest and importance of the research subject, the authors encountered some limitations. One of these limitations is represented by the lack of data; our topic being analyzed based on data availability, restricting the research sample to service companies limits the scope of the findings. Further research directions should include an examination of the relationship between organizational performance and innovation in different countries and departments, an in-depth examination of respondents' perceptions using also qualitative tools.

References

Aboulnasr, K., Narasimhan, O., Blair, E., Chandy, R.: Competitive response to radical product innovations. J. Mark. **72**, 94–110 (2008)

Adams-Price, C.: Can artificial intelligence explain age changes in literary creativity? Behav. Brain Sci. **17**(3), 532–532 (1994)

Al Naqbia, E., Alshuridehb, M., AlHamadc, A., Al, B.: The impact of innovation on firm performance: a systematic review. Int. J. Innov. Creat. Change **14**(5), 31–58 (2020)

Alegre, J., Chiva, R.: Assessing the impact of organizational learning capability on product innovation performance: an empirical test. Technovation **28**, 315–326 (2008)

Berraies, S., Chaher, M., Yahia, K.B.: Employee empowerment and its importance for trust, innovation and organizational performance. Bus. Manag. Strat. **5**(2), 82–103 (2014)

Bigliardi, B., Ferraro, G., Filippelli, S., Galati, F.: The influence of open innovation on firm performance. Int. J. Eng. Bus. Manag. **12**, 1847979020969545 (2020)

Bougie, R., Sekaran, U.: Research methods for business: a skill building approach. Wiley & Sons (2019)

Brunetto, Y., Farr-Wharton, R.: The moderating role of trust in SME owner/managers decision-making about collaboration. J. Small Bus. Manage. **45**(3), 362–387 (2007)

Carmeli, A., Gelbard, R., Gefen, D.: The importance of innovation leadership in cultivating strategic fit and enhancing firm performance. Leadersh. Q. **21**(3), 339–349 (2010)

Cheng, K.C., Chen, T.C., Shih, N.S.: The influence of budgetary participation by R&D managers on product innovation performances: the effect of trust, job satisfaction and information asymmetry. Asia Pac. Manag. Rev. **19**(2) (2014)

Dayan, M., Di Benedetto, C.A., Colak, M.: Managerial trust in new product development projects: its antecedents and consequences. R&D Manage. **39**(1), 21–37 (2009)

Dirks, K.: Trust in leadership and team performance: evidence from N.C.A.A. basketball. J. Appl. Psychol. **85**, 1004–1012 (2000)

Dubey, A.K., Dubey, A.K., Agarwal, V., Khandagre, Y.: Knowledge discovery with a subset-superset approach for Mining Heterogeneous Data with dynamic support. In: 2012 CSI Sixth International Conference on Software Engineering (CONSEG), pp. 1–6. IEEE (2012, September)

Gallego-Alvarez, I., Prado-Lorenzo, J.M., Garcıa-Sanchez, I.M.: Corporate social responsibility and innovation: a resource-based theory. Manag. Decis. **49**(10), 1709–1727 (2011)

Garcia, N., Sanzo, M.J., Trespalacios, J.A.: New product internal performance and market performance: evidence from Spanish firms regarding the role of trust, interfunctional integration, and innovation type. Technovation **28**, 713–725 (2008)

George, D., Mallery, P.: IBM SPSS statistics 26 step by step: a simple guide and reference. Routledge (2019)

Golipour, R., Gholamreza, J., Mirzaei, M.A., Roshandel, A.T.: The impact of organizational trust on innovativeness at the Tehran oil refinery company African. J. Bus. Manag. **5**(7), 2660–2667 (2011)

Hair, J.F., Ringle, C.M., Sarstedt, M.: Partial least squares structural equation modeling: rigorous applications, better results and higher acceptance. Long Range Plan. **46**(1–2), 1–12 (2013)

Han, J.K., Kim, N., Srivastava, R.K.: Market orientation and organizational performance: is innovation a missing link? J. Mark. **62**(4), 30–45 (1998)

Hoecht, A., Trott, P.: Innovation risks of strategic outsourcing. Technovation **26**(5–6), 672–681 (2006)

Hurley, R.F., Hult, G.T.M.: Innovation, market orientation, and organizational learning: an integration and empirical examination. J. Mark. **62**(3), 42–54 (1998)

Kazuyuki, M.: Innovation and entrepreneurship: a first look at the linkage data of Japanese patent and enterprise census. Seoul J. Eco. **29**(1), 69–94 (2016)

Koohang, A., Paliszkiewicz, J., Goluchowski, J.: The impact of leadership on trust, knowledge management, and organizational performance: a research model. Ind. Manag. Data Syst. **117**(3), 521–537 (2017)

Lee, D., Dedahanov, A., Rhee, J.: Moderating role of external networks and mediating effect of innovation performance on the relationship between technology orientation and firm performance. Asian J. Technol. Innov. **23**, 321–334 (2015)

Lewicki, R., Bunker, B.: Developing and maintaining trust in work relationships. Trust in organizations: frontiers of theory and research. In: Tyler, T., Kramer, R. (eds.) Thousand oaks. Sage, CA, pp. 114–139 (1996)

Longwei, W., Jeff, H.Y., Yeung, M.Z.: The impact of trust and contract on innovation performance: the moderating role of environmental uncertainty. Int. J. Prod. Econ. **134**(1), 114–122 (2011)

Luhmann, N.: Trust and power. Wiley, New York, NY (1979)

Mahoney, J.T.: Economic foundations of strategy. Sage, Thousand Oaks, CA (2005)

Mayer, R.C., Davis, J.H.: The effect of the performance appraisal system on trust for management: a field quasi-experiment. J. Appl. Psychol. **84**(1), 123–136 (1999)

Michaelis, B., Stegmaier, R., Sonntag, K.: Affective commitment to change and innovation implementation behavior: the role of charismatic leadership and employees' trust in top management. J. Chang. Manag. **9**(4), 399–417 (2009)

Nonaka, I., Takeuchi, H. (eds.): The knowledge-creating company. Oxford University Press, New York (1995)

OECD, Eurostat: Oslo manual: guidelines for collecting and interpreting innovation data. Paris, SP, p. 46 (2005)

Pratono, A.H.: From social network to firm performance: the mediating effect of trust, selling capability and pricing capability. Manag. Res. Rev. **41**(6), 680–700 (2018)

Prifti, R., Alimehmeti, G.: Market orientation, innovation, and firm performance–an analysis of Albanian firms. J. Innov. Entrep. **6**(1), 1–19 (2017)

Renzl, B.: Trust in management and knowledge sharing: mediating effects of fear and knowledge documentation. Omega **36**(22), 206–231 (2008)

Ruppel, C.P., Harrington, S.J.: The relationship of communication, ethical work climate, and trust to commitment and innovation. J. Bus. Ethics **25**(4), 313–328 (2000)

Sabel, C.F.: Studied trust: building new forms of cooperation in a volatile economy. Hum. Relat. **46**(9), 1133–1170 (1993)

Salam, M.A.: The mediating role of supply chain collaboration on the relationship between technology, trust and operational performance. Benchmarking Int. J. **24**(2), 298–317 (2017)

Serrano-Bedia, A.M., Lopez-Fernandez, M.C., Garcia-Piqueres, G.: Complementarity between innovation activities and innovation performance: evidence from Spanish innovative firms. J. Manuf. Technol. Manag. **23**(5), 557–577 (2012)

Sharkie, R.: Trust in leadership is vital for employee performance. Management Research News (2009)

Song, M., Im, S., Bij, H., Song, L.Z.: Does strategic planning enhance or impede innovation and firm performance? J. Prod. Innov. Manag. **28**, 503–520 (2011)

Taherdoost, H.: Sampling methods in research methodology; how to choose a sampling technique for research. How to choose a sampling technique for research (April 10, 2016)

Tseng, S.M., Lee, P.S.: The effect of knowledge management capability and dynamic capability on organizational performance. J. Enterp. Inf. Manag. **27**(2), 158–179 (2014)

Vaccaro, A., Parente, R., Veloso, F.M.: Knowledge management tools, inter-organizational relationships, innovation and firm performance. Technol. Forecast. Soc. Change **77**(7), 1076–1089 (2010)

Wang, C.L., Ahmed, P.K.: The development and validation of the organizational innovativeness construct using confirmatory factor analysis. Eur. J. Innov. Manag. **7**(4), 303–313 (2004)

Wang, L., Yeung, J.H.Y., Zhang, M.: The impact of trust and contract on innovation performance: the moderating role of environmental uncertainty. Int. J. Prod. Econ. **134**(1), 114–122 (2011)

Zahra, S.A., Sapienza, H.J., Davidsson, P.: Entrepreneurship and dynamic capabilities: a review, model and research agenda. J. Manage. Stud. **43**, 917–955 (2006)

Zhou, K.Z., Yim, C.K., Tse, D.K.: The effects of strategic orientations on technology- and market-based breakthrough innovations. J. Mark. **69**(2), 42–60 (2005)

Archival Perspectives

Pierre Werner (1913–2002)—A life dedicated to Luxembourg and Europe

Elena Rodica Danescu and Henri Werner

1 Pierre Werner (1913–2002)—A life dedicated to Luxembourg and Europe

Exhibition at a Glance

As a long-standing senior civil servant, minister and Prime Minister from the end of the Second World War until the mid-1980s, Pierre Werner gave his country, the Grand Duchy of Luxembourg, a voice that would be heard beyond its borders. He was closely involved in integration and policy-making efforts at the national, regional and European levels. He was an excellent listener and known for his skills of understanding and reconciling apparently incompatible positions. He was committed to defending the vital interests of Luxembourg and Europe over the long term. Pierre Werner is unanimously recognised as one of the main architects of Economic and Monetary Union: the 1970 Werner Report sketched out the fundamental features of what would later become the euro.

Based essentially on Pierre Werner's private collections and other relevant Luxembourg and European archives, the exhibition aims to paint a picture of Pierre Werner from various angles—his personality, his role as a father and family man, his social ties and intellectual interests—while also outlining his thinking and his achievements as a politician and committed European.

Pierre Werner was the first Luxembourger to be elected as an honorary member of the Romanian Academy (in 1993), to be awarded a honorary doctorate from the Lucian Blaga University of Sibiu and to be named as an honorary citizen of the city of Sibiu (in 1998).

Organisers: Europe Direct at the University of Luxembourg (ED-UNILU), University of Luxembourg and Luxembourg Centre for Contemporary and Digital History (C^{2}DH).

Design, texts, documentation and layout: Henri Werner

E. R. Danescu (✉) · H. Werner
Belval Campus, University of Luxembourg, Esch-Sur-Alzette, Luxembourg
e-mail: elena.danescu@uni.lu

A. M. Dima and E. R. Danescu (eds.), *Fostering Recovery Through Metaverse Business Modelling*, Springer Proceedings in Business and Economics,
https://doi.org/10.1007/978-3-031-28255-3_19

2 Pierre Werner (1913–2002)—Key Facts

1913	I Born in Lille (France).
1914	I Returned to Luxembourg with his parents.
1926	I Secondary studies at the École Industrielle (Lycée de Garçons de Luxembourg).
1933	I University course in law in Luxembourg.
1934–1937	I Studies at the Faculty of Law and at the École Libre des Sciences Politiques (Sciences Po) in Paris.
1935–1937	I President of the Akademiker-Veräin, the Luxembourg association of university students (AV-ALUC).
1936	I Vice-President of Pax Romana, the international community of Catholic students.
1938	I Doctorate in Law in Luxembourg; sworn in as a lawyer; trainee lawyer.
1939	I Married Henriette Pescatore.
1938–1940	I Banking apprenticeship at the Banque Générale du Luxembourg.
1940–1944	I Secretary General at the Banque Générale du Luxembourg.
1945–1949	I Registered lawyer in Luxembourg.
1945	I Attaché to the Ministry of Finance.
1946–1949	I Commissioner for Banking Supervision in Luxembourg.
1949–1953	I Government Advisor and ad interim Secretary of the Council of Ministers.
1953–1959	I Finance Minister, Defence Minister.
1959–1964	I Prime Minister, Finance Minister.
1964–1967	I Prime Minister, Foreign Minister, Treasury Minister and Justice Minister.
1965	I Merger Treaty of the EC executives, Pierre Werner secures the seat of the European institutions in Luxembourg.
1966	I Luxembourg Compromise while Pierre Werner is President-in-Office of the Council.
1967–1969	I Prime Minister, Treasury Minister and Minister for the Civil Service.
1969–1974	I Prime Minister, Finance Minister.
1970	I Report on the establishment in stages of Economic and Monetary Union (Werner Report).
1974–1979	I Member of Parliament, leader of the CSV parliamentary group.
1979–1984	I Prime Minister, Minister of Cultural Affairs.
1984	I Withdrawal from political life.
1985–1987	I Chairman of the Board of Directors of the Compagnie Luxembourgeoise de Télédiffusion (CLT).
1989–1996	I Chairman of the Board of Directors of the Société européenne des satellites (SES).
1998	I Member of the Council of the Banque Centrale du Luxembourg (BCL).
2002	I Died in Luxembourg.

Pierre Werner, seen here with Robert Schuman in 1955. His first meeting with the French statesman dates back to 1936, when Schuman, then a member of the National Assembly and Chairman of the Finance Commission, granted the young student an appointment at the Foyer of the Chamber of Deputies. The two men shared the values of the international community of Catholic academics.

© Unknown photographer

15 May 1970—Pierre Werner in conversation with Jean Monnet during an official visit to Paris. Pierre Werner had first met Jean Monnet in 1952 and was involved alongside him in the Action Committee for the United States of Europe.

1951—Pierre Werner, then Government Advisor, during a NATO working group meeting in London.

September 1956—Assembly of the International Monetary Fund. Pierre Werner, Finance Minister, in conversation with Robert B. Anderson, who in 1957 was appointed United States Secretary of the Treasury.

23 October 1963—Pierre Werner, Prime Minister and Finance Minister, fixing the last outer wall of the DuPont de Nemours plant. The diversification of the Luxembourg economy was among his government's priorities.

30 April 1963—State visit by Grand Duchess Charlotte to the United States. Pierre Werner liked to quote John F. Kennedy's statement: "My country favours a world of free and equal states."

29 January 1966 at 1:45 a.m.—Pierre Werner chairs the press conference at Luxembourg City Hall to announce the "Luxembourg Compromise" which put an end to the empty chair crisis in the European Communities. To his right: Albert Borschette; to his left: Christian Calmes.

September 1970—The ad hoc working group discusses the Werner Report on the realisation by stages of Economic and Monetary Union, shortly before its publication (see picture below).

Report to the Council and the Commission
on the realisation by stages of
ECONOMIC AND MONETARY UNION
in the Community
WIRTSCHAFTS-
CONSEIL – COMMISSION
DES COMMUNAUTÉS EUROPÉENNES
Rapport au Conseil et à la Commission
concernant la réalisation par étapes de
L'UNION ÉCONOMIQUE ET MONÉTAIRE
dans la Communauté
«Rapport Werner»
(texte final)
Supplément au Bulletin 11 – 1970
des Communautés européennes

16 October 1971, in Montigny-lès-Metz—Alain Poher presents Pierre Werner with the Robert Schuman gold medal in recognition of his contribution to the European integration process.

The Christian Social People's Party was the big loser in the general election held on 26 May 1974. Determined to respect the voters' verdict, Pierre Werner decided to stand down as Prime Minister and joined the opposition benches in Parliament. The election of 11 June 1979 marked a reversal of the situation and brought Werner back to power.

1979—Pierre Werner and Jacques Santer at the inauguration of Blast Furnace C in Belval. The steel crisis, a major cause for concern, was managed by years of intense dialogue and cooperation between the government, industry and the "social partners".

With the first medium-power satellite for civil applications, Pierre Werner placed Luxembourg on the map in the field of global communications.

31 December 1998, the eve of the launch of the euro—Pierre Werner standing between Jean-Claude Juncker and Jacques Santer.

June 1999—During a conference for the promotion of the European currency, Pierre Werner asks for the microphone to give a personal testimony.